THE ARCHITECTS' LIBRARY

EDITOR: F. M. SIMPSON, F.R.I.B.A.

THE ARCHITECTS' LIBRARY
Edited by F. M. SIMPSON, F.R.I.B.A.
Professor of Architecture in the University of London
Medium 8vo.

A History of Architectural Development.
By F. M. SIMPSON, F.R.I.B.A. Three Volumes.

Vol. I. ANCIENT, EARLY CHRISTIAN, AND BYZANTINE. With 180 Illustrations. 10s. 6d. net.

II. MEDIÆVAL. With 257 Illustrations. 10s. 6d. net.

III. RENAISSANCE IN ITALY, FRANCE, AND ENGLAND. With 268 Illustrations. 10s. 6d. net.

Building Construction.
Vol. I. By BERESFORD PITE, F.R.I.B.A., F. T. BAGGALLAY, F.R.I.B.A., H. D. SEARLES-WOOD, F.R.I.B.A., E. SPRAGUE, Assoc.M.Inst.C.E., etc. With 249 Illustrations. 10s. 6d. net.

II. By J. H. MARKHAM, A.R.I.B.A., HERBERT A. SATCHELL, F.R.I.B.A., Professor F. M. SIMPSON, F.R.I.B.A., and others. [*In preparation.*

THE ARCHITECTS' LIBRARY

A HISTORY OF ARCHITECTURAL DEVELOPMENT

IN THREE VOLUMES

VOL. II

MEDIÆVAL

BY

F. M. SIMPSON

ARCHITECT

PROFESSOR OF ARCHITECTURE IN THE UNIVERSITY OF LONDON; FELLOW OF THE ROYAL
INSTITUTE OF BRITISH ARCHITECTS; SOMETIME PROFESSOR OF ARCHITECTURE
IN THE UNIVERSITY OF LIVERPOOL; ROYAL ACADEMY
TRAVELLING STUDENT, 1884

WITH 257 ILLUSTRATIONS

REISSUE

WILDSIDE PRESS

PREFACE TO VOL. II.

THE aim of this volume, like that of the first, is to trace the development of architecture through the planning, construction, materials, and principles of design of the buildings described; reference being made to the influences which helped to shape that development. The volume deals only with mediæval ecclesiastical architecture. Secular buildings are not included, barely mentioned. The first half treats in detail of the parts of churches, walls, piers, arches, buttresses, windows, vaults, etc.; the second, of the churches themselves. In both, development is traced through all the centuries when Romanesque and Gothic art flourished.

My endeavour has been, whilst describing the examples in different countries, to hold the scales impartially between them all; pointing out, so far as lay in my power, the beauties and defects of each. For French Gothic art I have the greatest admiration—for the Southern even more than the Northern; and I am the more ready to admit its superiority, in some respects, to our own, because the feeling formerly prevalent amongst French architects that Gothic was born and bred, lived and died, in France, and that English art was but the crumbs which fell from the Frenchman's table is rapidly undergoing a change. Amongst the most distinguished of recent French writers there is an increasing readiness to acknowledge the beauty of the art of this country and wherein it excels, which a quarter of a century ago was non-existent.

For over thirty years I have been interested in mediæval architecture. I have visited all the cathedrals in England, the more important ones two or three times, and most of the principal churches. My first visit to France was in 1879, and I cannot remember a year since when I have not been abroad at least once, sometimes more often. Spain I do not know; but there are very few churches of importance in France, Germany, or Italy mentioned in this volume which I have not studied. I have, therefore, relied more on my notes and on my recollections of buildings, than on books; turning to the latter mainly for dates.

As regards the illustrations in the volume, several are from my own sketches, made at different times, which I have included, although conscious that they possess little merit, because in each case I knew of nothing else which could take its place. About a dozen have been redrawn in ink for me by Mr. C. E. Power. Most of the plans, sections, etc., are necessarily from books, only one or two are from my own measurements, and some are from drawings belonging to University College. I am indebted to Messrs. J. Bilson, Talbot Brown, A. H. Kersey, and H. A. Paley, for kind permission to copy drawings made by them. All the diagrams, illustrations, etc., have been prepared specially for this volume, with the exception of half a dozen taken from Gwilt's Encyclopædia.

About one-half of the photographs reproduced are by myself, each being taken with special reference to some point which I wished to illustrate.

F. M. SIMPSON.

UNIVERSITY COLLEGE,
   GOWER STREET, W.C.,
      September, 1908.

CONTENTS

	PAGE
PREFACE	v
LIST OF ILLUSTRATIONS	ix

PART I

CHAPTER		PAGE
I.	MEDIÆVAL ARCHITECTURE: INTRODUCTION	1
II.	ARCH DEVELOPMENT	9
III.	COLUMNS, PIERS, CAPITALS, AND BASES	23
IV.	WALLS, BUTTRESSES, PLINTHS, ETC.	43
V.	DEVELOPMENT OF WINDOWS	55
VI.	VAULTING	70
VII.	TOWERS AND SPIRES	103
VIII.	MURAL DECORATION, SCULPTURE, CARVING, STAINED GLASS	116

PART II

IX.	EARLY CHURCHES IN FRANCE AND GERMANY, PLANS, ETC.	135
X.	THE DEVELOPMENT OF CHURCH PLANNING	143
XI.	ROMANESQUE IN ITALY	165
XII.	ROMANESQUE IN GERMANY	190
XIII.	ROMANESQUE IN SOUTHERN FRANCE	203
XIV.	EARLY ROMANESQUE IN ENGLAND	232
XV.	ROMANESQUE IN ENGLAND AND NORMANDY	242
XVI.	THE CATHEDRALS OF NORTHERN FRANCE	254
XVII.	GOTHIC ARCHITECTURE IN SOUTHERN FRANCE	286

CONTENTS

CHAPTER		PAGE
XVIII.	Gothic Architecture in England and Scotland	294
XIX.	Gothic Architecture in Germany, Belgium, and Holland	324
XX.	Gothic Architecture in Italy	338
XXI.	Gothic Architecture in Spain	349
XXII.	English Parish Churches: Timber Roofs	358
	Appendix.—Table of Dimensions of Typical Churches	373
	Index	379

LIST OF ILLUSTRATIONS

INTRODUCTION.

FIG.		PAGE
1.	Capital, S. Zeno, Verona	1
2.	Sections through Romanesque Cathedrals	6

ARCH DEVELOPMENT.

3.	Sections through Barrel-vaulted Roofs	10
4.	Intersecting Arches	11
5.	Principal Forms of Arches	12
6.	Trefoil and Foliated Arches	13
7.	Pointed Horseshoe Arch, Coire Cathedral	14
8.	Roman Methods, with Archivolts; Romanesque Method, with Label	15
9.	Arches of One and Two Orders	16
10.	English Arch Mouldings, 1050–1170	17
11.	English Arch Mouldings, 1150–1250	18
12.	English Arch Mouldings, 1250–1500	19
13.	French Arch Mouldings, 1050–1500	21
14.	English Arch Labels, 1050–1500	22

COLUMNS, PIERS, CAPITALS, AND BASES.

15.	Pier and Arch Development	24
16.	Peterboro' Cathedral: Capital of Choir Aisle	25
17.	English Columns and Piers, 1060–1500	27
18.	Capital of Column surrounded by Detached Shafts, c. 1220	28
19.	French Piers and Columns, 1050–1500	31
20.	Evolution of Typical Norman Capitals	35
21.	Romanesque Capitals from Bologna, S. Zeno, Verona, Issoire Cathedral (Crypt), and S. Remi, Reims	36
22.	Capital of Pier from Choir of Tours Cathedral	38
23.	English Moulded Capitals and Bases, 1150–1500	39
24.	Spurs	40
25.	Much Wenlock Abbey Church, Shropshire	41
26.	Doorways, c. 1100–c. 1400	42

x   LIST OF ILLUSTRATIONS.

OUTSIDE OF CHURCHES, WALLS, BUTTRESSES, PLINTHS, ETC.

FIG.   PAGE
27. The Pilgrims Chapel, Houghton-le-Dale, Norfolk, Erected 1350 44
28. Thrusts and Abutments 47
29. Buttresses, 1060–1400 48
30. Vitré: Lead Gurgoyle 54

DEVELOPMENT OF WINDOWS.

31. Romanesque 2-Light Window; Plan, Elevations, and Section . 56
32. 3-Light Lancet Window, c. 1200: Plan, Elevations, and Detail. 57
33. Plate Tracery Window, Chartres Cathedral, and Window with Stilted Head, Reims Cathedral 58
34. Head of Bar Tracery Window, showing Jointing of Tracery . 59
35. Window in Aisle, Stone Church, Kent: Plan, Elevation, and Section 61
36. Romanesque Wheel Window, Patrixbourne Church, Kent: Elevation and Section 62
37. Development of Window Tracery 63
38. Brede Church, East Window of South Aisle of Chancel . . 64
39. Development of Mullions 66
40. Cusps and Cusp Endings 67
41. Head of Traceried Window, showing Window Arch, Rear Arch, and Scoinson Arch 68

VAULTING.

42. Plans of Romanesque Vaulting, Continuous and in Bays . . . 72
43. Ribbed Vaults, Three Different Methods, with Main Arches Semicircular 73
44. Winchester Cathedral: Springing of Groined Vaults 76
45. Oblong Vaults with Pointed Arches, etc. 78
46. S. Georges de Boscherville: One Bay of Choir Vault . . *facing* 78
47. Angers Cathedral: Nave Vault . . . . *facing* 78
48. Sexpartite Vaulting, Abbaye-aux-Dames, Caen 80
49. S. Pierre, Lisieux: Quadripartite Vault of Choir . . *facing* 80
50. Laon Cathedral: Sexpartite Vault of Nave . . . . *facing* 80
51. Square and Oblong Vaulting 81
52. Plans of Ribbed Vaults: Durham Cathedral Nave and Lincoln Cathedral Choir 82
53. Methods of Laying Web 83
54. Hand-Center for Web 85
55. Exeter Cathedral: Tierceron Vault of S. John's Chapel. *facing* 86
56. Exeter Cathedral: Tierceron Vaulting of Nave . . . *facing* 86

LIST OF ILLUSTRATIONS.   xi

FIG.		PAGE
57.	DIAGRAMS OF RIB DEVELOPMENT	87
58.	FAN VAULTING FROM HENRY VII.'S CHAPEL, WESTMINSTER. . . .	89
59.	RIBS DETACHED AT SPRINGING	92
60.	PLAN, LONGITUDINAL AND TRANSVERSE SECTIONS OF BAY OF VAULTING, WITH TAS-DE-CHARGE, ETC.	94
61.	LAON CATHEDRAL: LONGITUDINAL SECTION; TRANSVERSE SECTION .	96
62.	REIMS CATHEDRAL: CROSS SECTION	99
63.	MALMESBURY ABBEY CHURCH: FLYING BUTTRESS AND PINNACLE . .	100
64.	LAON CATHEDRAL: INTERIOR . . . . *facing*	102
65.	SÉES CATHEDRAL: INTERIOR . . . . *facing*	102

TOWERS AND SPIRES.

66.	COUTANCES CATHEDRAL: INTERIOR OF LANTERN . . . . . *facing*	104
67.	EVREUX CATHEDRAL: INTERIOR OF LANTERN . . . . . *facing*	104
68.	BRAISNE CHURCH: INTERIOR OF LANTERN . . . . . . *facing*	104
69.	S. MACLOU, ROUEN: INTERIOR OF LANTERN . . . . . *facing*	104
70.	TOWERS OF TRÉGUIER CATHEDRAL	105
71.	S. ZENO, VERONA: WEST FRONT AND DETACHED TOWER . *facing*	108
72.	TOWER OF SS. GIOVANNI E PAOLO, ROME . . . . . . *facing*	108
73.	TOWER OF S. SATIRO, MILAN	109
74.	CIRCULAR TOWER, PISA	110
75.	JUMIÈGES ABBEY CHURCH, FROM THE NORTH-WEST . . . *facing*	111
76.	COUTANCES CATHEDRAL: CENTRAL LANTERN TOWER . . . *facing*	111
77.	TIMBER SPIRES AND TYPICAL GERMAN SPIRE	112
78.	STONE SPIRES	113

MURAL DECORATION.

79.	CHICHESTER CATHEDRAL: TRIFORIUM, AND CLERESTORY PASSAGE ABOVE . . . . *facing*	118
80.	POLEBROOK CHURCH, NORTHANTS: PAINTINGS ON SCREEN . . .	120
81.	S. VULFRAN, ABBEVILLE: VAULT . . . . *facing*	121
82.	S. JACQUES, LISIEUX: PAINTINGS, VAULT . . . . . *facing*	121
83.	AUTUN CATHEDRAL: OPEN NARTHEX . . . . *facing*	122
84.	S. OUEN, ROUEN: NICHES ON PIERS . . . . *facing*	123
85.	CHARTRES CATHEDRAL: TWO FIGURES FROM JAMBS OF CENTRAL WESTERN DOORWAY (FROM CASTS IN TROCADERO MUSEUM, PARIS) . . . . *facing*	124
86.	CAPITALS: S. EUSÈBE, AUXERRE; S. VITALE, RAVENNA	126
87.	ENGLISH CARVINGS	130

PART II.

PLANS OF EARLY CHURCHES IN FRANCE AND GERMANY.

FIG.		PAGE
88.	CHARLEMAGNE'S CHURCH AT AIX-LA-CHAPELLE: PLANS AND SECTION	138
89.	GERMIGNY-LES-PRÉS: PLAN AND SECTION	139
90.	S. CROIX, MONTMAJOUR: PLAN	140
91.	CHURCH AT CHARROUX: PLAN	140
92.	CHURCH OF THE HOLY SEPULCHRE, JERUSALEM: PLAN	141

THE DEVELOPMENT OF CHURCH PLANNING.

93.	ABBEY CHURCH OF S. GALL: PLAN	144
94.	CANTERBURY CATHEDRAL: PLAN	146
95.	ROMSEY ABBEY CHURCH: PLAN	148
96.	CHURCH AT VIGNORY: PLAN	148
97.	LE MANS CATHEDRAL: EAST END . . . . facing	149
98.	LE MANS CATHEDRAL: PLAN	149
99.	NORWICH CATHEDRAL: PLAN	150
100.	LINCOLN AND SALISBURY CATHEDRALS: PLANS	151
101.	ELY CATHEDRAL: INTERIOR . . . . facing	152
102.	SALISBURY CATHEDRAL: INTERIOR . . . . facing	152
103.	LAON CATHEDRAL: AISLE WALL CUT THROUGH FOR CHAPELS . facing	154
104.	COUTANCES CATHEDRAL: CHAPELS AT SIDES . . . . . facing	154
105.	WINCHESTER CATHEDRAL: CHANTRY CHAPEL OF BISHOP WILLIAM OF WYKEHAM . . . . facing	155
106.	NÔTRE DAME, PARIS: PLAN	156
107.	PLAN FROM V. DE HONNECOURT'S SKETCH-BOOK	158
108.	ABBEY CHURCH OF MAULBRONN: PLAN	159
109.	ABBEY CHURCH OF S. MARY, BUILDWAS, SALOP: PLAN	160
110.	EBRACH ABBEY CHURCH, GERMANY: PLAN	160

ROMANESQUE IN ITALY.

111.	S. AMBROGIO, MILAN: PLAN	168
112.	S. AMBROGIO, MILAN: INTERIOR . . . . facing	168
113.	S. AMBROGIO, MILAN: ATRIUM AND WEST FRONT . . . facing	168
114.	S. VINCENZO-IN-PRATO, MILAN: EASTERN APSES	170
115.	S. MICHELE, PAVIA: PLAN AND ELEVATION OF EAST END	171
116.	S. ZENO, VERONA: INTERIOR . . . . facing	172
117.	S. MINIATO, FLORENCE: INTERIOR . . . . facing	172
118.	S. MINIATO, FLORENCE: PLAN AND SECTION	174
119.	MARBLE MOSAICS ON WALL, PISA CATHEDRAL	175
120.	TROJA CATHEDRAL: LOWER PORTION OF WEST FRONT	176
121.	PISA CATHEDRAL: PLANS	177
122.	BARI CATHEDRAL: PIERCED MARBLE SLAB	181

LIST OF ILLUSTRATIONS. xiii

FIG.		PAGE
123.	S. Nicolo, Bari: Section and Plan	182
124.	Molfetta Cathedral: Longitudinal Section	184
125.	Monreale Cathedral: Cloisters . . . . *facing*	184
126.	Monreale Cathedral: Interior . . . . *facing*	184
127.	Monreale Cathedral: Plan of Arch Mouldings, Abacus of Capital, and Shafts in Cloisters	185
128.	Monreale Cathedral: Plan	187
129.	S. Cataldo, Palermo: Interior	188
130.	Cefalû Cathedral, from the North-East . . . . . *facing*	188
131.	S. Giovanni degli Eremeti, Palermo, from the South-East *facing*	188

ROMANESQUE IN GERMANY.

132.	Laach Abbey Church: Plan	192
133.	Worms Cathedral: Plan	193
134.	Worms Cathedral: View of East End . . . . . . *facing*	194
135.	Speier Cathedral: Transverse and Longitudinal Sections	196
136.	Speier Cathedral: Plan	196
137.	Worms Cathedral: Interior, looking West . . . . *facing*	196
138.	Trier Cathedral: Plan	199
139.	S. Maria in Capitolio, Cologne: Plan	200
140.	Tournai Cathedral from the South	201

ROMANESQUE IN SOUTHERN FRANCE.

141.	S. Front, Périgueux: Plan	206
142.	S. Front, Périgueux: Section across Transepts	206
143.	Church at Souillac: Interior	208
144.	Angoulême Cathedral: Plan	209
145.	Angoulême Cathedral: Section of One Bay of Nave	209
146.	Fontevrault Abbey Church: Plan	210
147.	S. Hilaire, Poitiers: Interior	211
148.	Le Puy Cathedral, Dome over One Bay of Nave . . . *facing*	212
149.	S. Ours, Loches, from the South	213
150.	S. Philibert, Tournus, Plans and Sections	214
151.	S. Nazaire, Carcassonne: Interior	216
152.	Issoire Cathedral: Plans and Sections	217
153.	Issoire Cathedral: East Front . . . . *facing*	218
154.	Issoire Cathedral: Apses at East End . . . . . *facing*	218
155.	Issoire Cathedral: Interior . . . . *facing*	219
156.	Issoire Cathedral: Trefoil Horseshoe Arches in Triforium	219
157.	S. Sernin, Toulouse: Plan	220
158.	Vézelay Abbey Church: Interior . . . . *facing*	220
159.	Vézelay Abbey Church: Plan of Narthex and Nave	221
160.	Autun Cathedral: Plan of Western Porch	222
161.	Autun Cathedral: One Bay of North Side of Nave and Details	224

LIST OF ILLUSTRATIONS.

FIG.		PAGE
162.	Angers Cathedral: Plan	226
163.	La Trinité, Angers: Plan	227
164.	S. Pierre, Saumur: Interior	229
165.	Le Puy Cathedral: West Front	facing 230
166.	S. Michel de l'Aiguille, Le Puy	facing 230

EARLY ROMANESQUE IN ENGLAND.

167.	Bradford-on-Avon Church, Wilts: Plan	234
168.	Bradford-on-Avon Church: East End	facing 234
169.	Tower of Earls Barton Church	235
170.	Wall between Caen and Falaise	facing 236
171.	Worth Church, Sussex: Plan	238
172.	Wyckham Church: Window	239

ROMANESQUE IN ENGLAND AND NORMANDY.

173.	Jumièges Abbey Church, from the South	facing 242
174.	S. Etienne, Caen: Triforium	facing 249
175.	Ouistreham Church: Arcade and Clerestory	facing 249
176.	Durham Cathedral: One Bay of Nave	249
177.	Durham Cathedral: Plan	250
178.	Winchester Cathedral: Transept	facing 250
179.	Durham Cathedral: Interior	facing 250
180.	Tewkesbury Abbey Church: Plan of West End	252
181.	Tewkesbury Abbey Church: West Front	facing 252
182.	Durham Cathedral: West Front	facing 252

THE CATHEDRALS OF NORTHERN FRANCE, 1120-1500.

183.	S. Pierre, Lisieux: Interior	facing 258
184.	Noyon Cathedral: Interior	facing 258
185.	Soissons Cathedral: South Transept	facing 260
186.	Le Mans Cathedral: Two Bays of Nave	facing 260
187.	Reims Cathedral: Plan	266
188.	Amiens Cathedral: Plan	267
189.	Nôtre Dame, Paris: Interior	facing 268
190.	Much Wenlock Abbey Church, Shropshire: One Bay of Triforium	270
191.	S. Pierre, Chartres: Interior, showing Glazed Triforium	facing 271
192.	S. Aignan, Orleans: Interior	273
193.	Bourges Cathedral: Section	274
194.	Chartres Cathedral: Plan	276
195.	Amiens Cathedral, from the South	facing 276
196.	Laon Cathedral: West Front	facing 278
197.	Nôtre Dame, Paris: West Front	facing 278
198.	Nôtre Dame de Bon Secours, Guingamp	283
199.	S. Maclou, Rouen: West Front	facing 284

LIST OF ILLUSTRATIONS.

GOTHIC ARCHITECTURE IN SOUTHERN FRANCE.

FIG.		PAGE
200.	Poitiers Cathedral: Interior	287
201.	Albi Cathedral, from the South . . . . *facing*	289
202.	Albi Cathedral: Plan	289
203.	Albi Cathedral: Cross Section	290
204.	Church of the Jacobins, Toulouse: Plan, Sections, etc. . . .	291
205.	Church of the Cordeliers, Toulouse: Plan	292

GOTHIC ARCHITECTURE IN ENGLAND.

206.	Fountains Abbey Church, showing Aisle Vault restored . .	297
207.	Plans of Wells Cathedral Pier and a Romanesque Pier . .	299
208.	Amiens Cathedral, from the West . . . . *facing*	300
209.	Salisbury Cathedral, from the West . . . . . . *facing*	302
210.	Cross Sections of Salisbury and Amiens Cathedrals	303
211.	Wells Cathedral: West Front . . . . *facing*	304
212.	Salisbury Cathedral, from North-East . . . . . *facing*	304
213.	Ely Cathedral: East End . . . . *facing*	306
214.	Westminster Abbey Choir: One Bay; and Lincoln Cathedral Choir: One Bay	308
215.	Exeter Cathedral: Plan	313
216.	York Cathedral: Choir . . . . *facing*	314
217.	Ely Cathedral: Interior of Lantern . . . . . . *facing*	315
218.	Winchester Cathedral, as originally designed: One Bay . .	316
219.	Winchester Cathedral, as altered: One Bay	316
220.	Bath Abbey Church: Cross Section: and One Bay Longitudinal Section	318
221.	King's College Chapel, Cambridge: Plan	319
222.	King's College Chapel, Cambridge: One Bay Longitudinal Section	320
223.	Jedburgh Abbey Church: Choir . . . . *facing*	322
224.	Jedburgh Abbey Church: Nave . . . . *facing*	322

GOTHIC ARCHITECTURE IN GERMANY, BELGIUM, AND HOLLAND.

225.	S. Yved, Braisne; and Liebfrauenkirche, Trier: Plans . . .	326
226.	Cologne Cathedral: Plan	327
227.	S. Mary, Lübeck: Plan	329
228.	S. Mary, Lübeck: Cross Section	329
229.	S. Elizabeth, Marburg: Cross Section	330
230.	S. Peter, Lübeck: Cross Section	331
231.	Ulm Cathedral: Plan	332
232.	Vienna Cathedral: Plan	334
233.	The Cloth Hall, Ypres, Belgium	336

GOTHIC ARCHITECTURE IN ITALY.

FIG.		PAGE
234.	S. ANASTASIA, VERONA: CROSS SECTION AND ONE BAY LONGITUDINAL SECTION	340
235.	FLORENCE CATHEDRAL: CROSS SECTION AND ONE BAY LONGITUDINAL SECTION	341
236.	S. ANASTASIA, VERONA: INTERIOR . . . . facing	342
237.	FLORENCE CATHEDRAL: PLAN	343
238.	S. ANASTASIA, VERONA: PLAN	344
239.	SIENA CATHEDRAL: WEST FRONT . . . . facing	344
240.	S. CROCE, FLORENCE: PLAN	345
241.	MILAN CATHEDRAL: PLAN	346
242.	MILAN CATHEDRAL: DETAIL OF UPPER PART . . . . . facing	346
243.	MILAN CATHEDRAL: CROSS SECTION AND ONE BAY LONGITUDINAL SECTION	347

GOTHIC ARCHITECTURE IN SPAIN.

244.	SALAMANCA OLD CATHEDRAL: INTERIOR AND EXTERIOR OF LANTERN	351
245.	GERONA CATHEDRAL: PLAN	352
246.	BARCELONA CATHEDRAL AND CLOISTERS: PLAN	354
247.	BARCELONA CATHEDRAL: INTERIOR	356

ENGLISH PARISH CHURCHES. TIMBER ROOFS.

248.	IFFLEY CHURCH, OXON: PLAN	359
249.	WARMINGTON CHURCH, NORTHANTS: PLAN	361
250.	S. PATRICK, PATRINGTON: PLAN	362
251.	S. PATRICK, PATRINGTON: WEST ELEVATION	363
252.	S. PETER'S MANCROFT, NORWICH: CROSS SECTION AND ONE BAY LONGITUDINAL SECTION	365
253.	HECKINGTON CHURCH, LINCOLNSHIRE: ROOF OF SOUTH PORCH; AND WIMBOTSHAM CHURCH: NAVE ROOF	368
254.	CONSTRUCTION OF HAMMER-BEAM	369
255.	BACTON CHURCH, SUFFOLK: NAVE ROOF	369
256.	WESTMINSTER HALL: CROSS SECTION	370
257.	BRAMFORD CHURCH, SUFFOLK: ROOF OF SOUTH AISLE	371

A HISTORY OF ARCHITECTURAL DEVELOPMENT

MEDIÆVAL ARCHITECTURE

CHAPTER I.

INTRODUCTION.

THE beginning of the eleventh century marks a new era of development in architectural history. Christianity had by that time taken deep root throughout the whole of Europe, and a wave of church building was passing over all lands. The great monastic order of the Benedictines was at first mainly responsible for the prodigious activity in ecclesiastical matters, and for many of the earlier phases of architectural development. The monks of the order in the previous century naturally followed in their churches the building methods prevalent in Rome. The basilican plan, with its nave and aisles and roofs of timber, formed their model. But not for long. Before the eleventh century opened, a new movement had commenced which, once fairly under weigh, developed with great rapidity and produced lasting results. Where it originated exactly is difficult to state with any certainty. It can hardly be said to have come from the East, although church building had reached a very high level there five centuries before, and excellent work on traditional lines was still being done. Neither was it of Southern growth; for, throughout Central and Southern Italy, Rome and Constantinople—the former through its basilican plan, the latter through its detail mainly—were still the two

FIG. 1.

paramount influences. It came from farther north; and manifested itself partly in a symbolic treatment of ornament—based, perhaps, on Eastern traditions, but rendered with a robustness foreign to the East—and partly in a return to structural methods which had laid dormant for centuries. The intersecting vault reasserted itself, with the result that the timber roof in time disappeared entirely from large churches. The walls thickened; columns were replaced by piers, bulky in proportion since the workmen feared the thrust of the vault, and complex in section because their functions were multiplied. The semi-barbaric symbolism, conspicuous in many of the carvings, forms a striking contrast to the refined, but, in the main, merely sensuous, beauty of Classic and Byzantine art. The west front of S. Michele, Pavia, to mention now one instance only, is covered with carved representations of figures and animals, the proportions of which, it must be admitted, are often very different from those of real life. But the execution of these and other contemporary carvings, if sometimes rude and unskilled, has a character of its own and is always forcible. Its rudeness may be forgiven, because of what its advent meant. The change indicated an infusion of vigorous new blood, and heralded the overthrow of the long paramount Classic traditions, and the approach of the great Northern art which was to prevail throughout Europe from the eleventh century to the end of the fifteenth.

New movement.

The new movement found full expression first on the plains of Lombardy. Thence it spread through Germany, where the seed was already sown, leaving behind it, on the banks of the Rhine, some of its finest monuments, and westward through Southern France, where it had to contend at first with earlier traditions. Soon it reached Normandy, virgin soil almost, and crossed to England to lay the foundation of our national architecture, and to dot the country with fine cathedrals and abbeys and innumerable parish churches.

Until the middle of the twelfth century the development of the new ideas proceeded slowly and methodically. Men were in no haste to throw over the old traditions; in fact, in the greater part of Italy they never entirely abandoned them. Rome, both through its early churches and its still earlier Imperial monuments, was still the quarry for ideas as much as it was a quarry for building materials. But about that time a less conservative tendency manifested itself; owing, in a great measure, to the increasing interest taken by the people in ecclesiastical matters, and to the growing power of the masonic guilds, which coincided with the gradual weakening of the hitherto overwhelming preeminence of the monastic orders. A new era dawned. The younger generation cared little, and in certain parts of Europe knew nothing, about the models which had influenced the work of their forefathers. New forms, new ideas took the place of the old. It might almost be said that a new construction followed; but this is not strictly true, since, although the methods of building piers, arches, and vaults changed somewhat, all the changes proceeded naturally in a regular unbroken sequence. The connecting links are clearly traceable between the large but simple arch of the Romans and the smaller but more complex one of the mediæval men, and between the early, heavy intersecting vault and the later lighter vaults built with ribs. It is to the tracing of the gradual development in these and other parts of a building that the earlier chapters of this volume are devoted.

Nearly all work in Europe from the beginning of the eleventh century to the middle of the fifteenth in Italy, and to the end of the latter century elsewhere, might fairly be termed mediæval, as it belongs to the most famous period of the Middle Ages. But when dealing with the examples in the different countries, in consequence mainly of the jump in progression mentioned above, it is as well to divide the work into two periods. The earlier, up to about 1150, will be termed Romanesque, thus indicating the chief influence which moulded it, and the later by the title generally applied to it, Gothic.[1] A halfway halting-place has its advantages, but it must be clearly understood that this forms no break. It is not a terminus; it is merely a great junction to which many lines converge, and then, to some extent, branch off again. No greater mistake can possibly be made than to suppose that a hard-and-fast line separates Romanesque and Gothic architecture. They are not two independent and separate styles; they are parts of one great style, the greatest of all the arched styles of the world. The shape of the arch employed in different centuries has been counted as a barrier. But it is

Divisions.

---

[1] The word conveys nothing as to the origin of the style, and is meaningless, but it has been in general use for long, and has become a term of endearment, although first used by the purists of the seventeenth and eighteenth centuries as a reproach. Addison describes the temple consecrated to the god of Dullness as "a monstrous Fabrick built after the Gothick manner, and covered with innumerable Devices in that barbarous kind of Sculpture."

4   A HISTORY OF ARCHITECTURAL DEVELOPMENT.

nothing of the sort. Romanesque and Gothic belong to one and the same great wave of evolution, which advanced slowly at first, then, in the thirteenth century, progressed with great strides, and finally, having spent its force and passed its zenith, crumbled to pieces before the revival of learning in Europe and the consequent resuscitation of classic art. These factors, coupled with the decay of the monastic orders, the spread of individual religious thought which culminated in the Reformation, and the restless desire for something new—a trait as marked in the sixteenth century as now—completed the ruin of mediæval art, and brought about what is known as the Renaissance.

Arrangement.   In the chapters immediately following this (and which with it form Part I. of the volume), which deal with the parts of buildings, their plans, proportions, construction, and detail, no division is made between Romanesque and Gothic, because none exists. In the subsequent chapters (or Part II.), which describe the concrete examples in different countries, the halting-place is utilized; the Romanesque ones are taken first, the Gothic ones follow. Each country, as a rule, has two chapters devoted to it; one dealing with the earlier work, the other with the later. In some cases, however, more are given. The early churches in France, for instance, present such variety that further subdivision is necessary. Some are barrel-vaulted, some groined, others are domed; some have naves and aisles, in others the aisleless plan is followed. The barrel-vaulted churches of Auvergne are in many respects different from the similarly covered churches of Burgundy. The early churches of Normandy and England possess traits of their own. In Gothic work the great cathedrals of Northern France are totally distinct from those of the South, and form a group by themselves, the later German cathedrals following in their wake. The English cathedrals are more varied than their neighbours across the water, and the line between the early and the later work—between Durham and Salisbury, for instance—is easily drawn. The peculiarities of Italian Gothic, if Gothic it can be called since Classic influence is always evident, divide it unmistakably from the more northern work. In the description and illustration of these different examples will be found the application of the principles described in the earlier chapters. In this lies their chief value. A student wants to know two things: how the different parts of a building developed, and the results of that development as expressed in actual examples. In dealing with the parts of a building alone and separately, the effect of that building as a whole does not appear. And it is important that it should. For this reason a consideration of actual examples follows the detailed analysis of their parts. In other words, the Grammar of Mediæval Art precedes the Compositions in it.

Before proceeding to either, however, a few words of introduction may be useful to some regarding the sectional ordinances of churches. Whilst some churches are aisleless, and others have nave and aisles of equal height, the majority of cathedrals and other large churches have more or less lofty naves with lower side aisles. A single aisle each side is the rule, but in some of the great continental cathedrals the aisles are doubled. The customary division of a nave wall is into arcade, triforium, and clerestory; in some churches, however, which come under this heading the clerestories are omitted, in others the triforia. The arcades divide the nave from the aisles; the triforia mask the lean-to roofs which cover the vaults over the aisles; and the windows of the clerestories light the nave, rising above the aisle roofs and reaching to the apex of the vault, or to the underside of the wall plate when the church is not vaulted. The same divisions are found in basilican churches, but with a difference. In mediæval churches the middle storey consists either of a spacious gallery, or else of merely a passage-way in the thickness of the wall, just sufficient in width to allow of free circulation all round the church. In both cases pierced arcading comes in front, and in the latter there is a wall at the back, with a few openings for access to the lean-to roof behind, which otherwise would be cut off entirely from the church. This is the typical French plan after 1180. In some examples, mostly English cathedrals of the thirteenth and fourteenth centuries, the back wall is omitted, although there is often no gallery behind except what the roof space affords. In basilican churches the middle storey, with rare exceptions, is unpierced and unarcaded, and forms a broad band of walling which in most examples was decorated either with mosaics, as in S. Apollinare Nuovo, Ravenna, of the sixth century, and in the later Cathedral of Monreale, Sicily, of the twelfth century (see Fig. 126), or with paintings. In Northern countries, craftsmen capable of carrying out similar methods of decoration were not forthcoming, whilst masons were plentiful, and, moreover, had command of the building operations.

Sections of churches.

6   A HISTORY OF ARCHITECTURAL DEVELOPMENT.

Hence arose the custom of treating this space in masonic fashion, and not with applied decoration.

Triforium galleries.

The majority of Romanesque churches in England and France, and some later churches in our country especially, have galleries as wide as the aisles below, and often quite as lofty. The reasons for these galleries, and why some large churches have them and

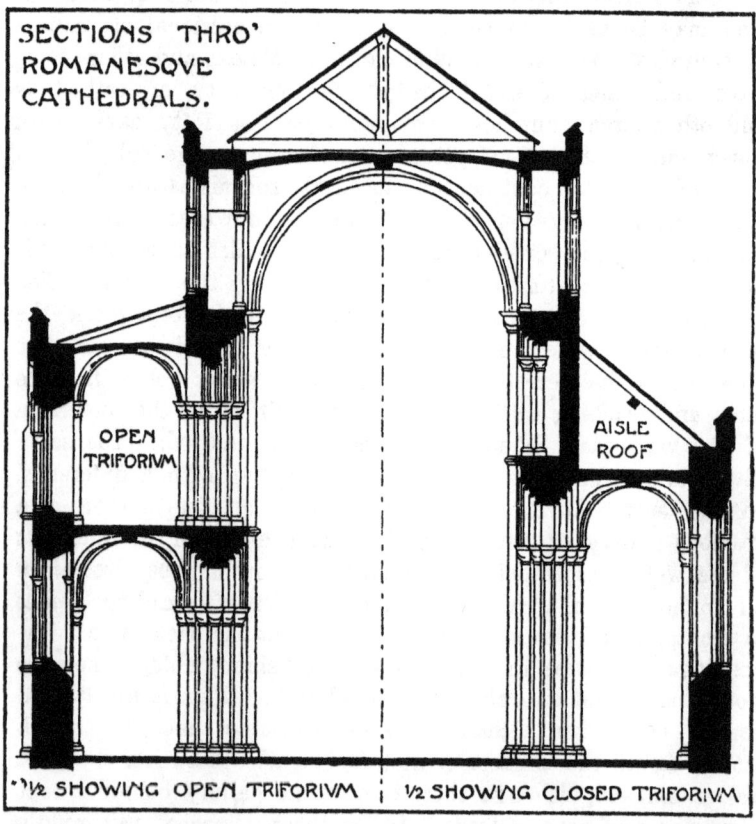

Fig. 2.

others of equal importance are without them, are not quite clear. All large Byzantine churches have galleries, but there are only two basilican ones in Rome with them, S. Lorenzo and S. Agnese, and for centuries they were omitted entirely in Italy. Their reintroduction in the West dates from the outburst of church building which commenced there soon after 1000 A.D. In Byzantine churches the galleries were for the woman; but the separation of the sexes was not insisted upon so strongly in the West, and it is necessary, therefore, to suggest some other reason for them in mediæval examples. In monastic churches galleries were probably provided for the laity, as the monks at first monopolized the whole of the area below, and in cathedral churches they were possibly required to accommodate the crowds which on days of high festival overflowed the nave.[1] Whatever the reason for them was, they were never universal even in Romanesque days, and were omitted in France after the end of the twelfth century, although, in a modified fashion, they continued general in England until the middle of the fourteenth century. In the two largest Romanesque churches at Caen, Normandy, one, S. Etienne, has them, the other, the Nun's Church, has none. In Gloucester Cathedral there are galleries over the aisles of the choir, but in the nave merely a low passage-way with insignificant arcading in front. Amongst other Romanesque churches with spacious galleries are S. Ambrogio, Milan, S. Michele, Pavia, S. Remi, Reims, the Cathedrals of Ely, S. Albans, Peterboro', etc.; and amongst later Gothic ones are Laon, Noyon, and Paris Cathedrals, Westminster Abbey, etc. The Germans seem to have had a rooted objection to triforia in any form, and in both their early and late work the spaces between the windows and the arcades are often left absolutely plain. The galleries in French churches are generally vaulted like the aisles below them; in English churches in most cases they have merely timber roofs, an exception being round the choir at Gloucester, where the gallery is covered by a quadrant vault.

Whether there is a spacious gallery at the triforium level, or merely a passage-way or an aisle roof, does not necessarily affect materially the design of the arcading in front. The effect produced, however, is different, because galleries always have windows on their outside walls, and are consequently light, whereas in the other case the background is dark. Each country possesses its own characteristics in triforium design, and in each these changed considerably from century to century. The developments by which in France the triforia became glazed, and in England disappeared altogether, are traced in subsequent chapters.

In parish churches in England the middle storey is often *Churches without triforia.*

[1] The galleries of Nôtre Dame, Paris, are crowded now on Easter Day during High Mass.

8   *A HISTORY OF ARCHITECTURAL DEVELOPMENT.*

omitted entirely, for the simple reason that the aisles are merely covered by lean-to roofs, which start low down and finish close under the clerestory windows (when there are any) only a few inches above the top of the nave arcades. In some abbey churches, and those not necessarily the smallest, triforia are also omitted, as in Pershore Abbey Church, but the passage-way is often retained below the clerestory, the difference being that the jambs of the windows, and sometimes other portions of them as well, are continued down to the string above the arcade without a middle storey being actually formed. Churches without aisles are also without triforia, because there are no side roofs to mask.

Churches without clerestories. Certain groups of churches abroad with spacious triforium galleries are without clerestories. In Northern Italy there are several, of which S. Ambrogio, Milan, is the most remarkable. This is a rib-vaulted church, but most of the examples of this type are barrel-vaulted. The majority are in Southern France, notably in Auvergne, and the upper windows are omitted because the vault allowed little room for them. Otherwise these churches in their sectional ordinance differ little from those with clerestories.

Churches with neither clerestories nor triforia. The next type of church is totally different. The examples composing it have naves and aisles of equal or approximately equal height. The result is that clerestory windows are impossible, and that the main light comes from the aisles. Many parish churches in England, especially those of the fourteenth century are planned on these lines, but the largest and most remarkable churches of this type are in Germany, and are known as Hallenkirchen. Under this heading may also be included a group of churches which have merely chapels at the sides in lieu of aisles, although these present special traits which are discussed later.

CHAPTER II.

ARCH DEVELOPMENT.

THE keynote of mediæval art is arch construction. The lintel occurs occasionally over small windows and doorways, especially in domestic work, and in most continental churches the large entrance doorways are spanned by lintels, which, however, generally have arches over. Elsewhere the arch reigns alone. Without it the wide openings between columns and piers could not have been bridged, neither could the large floor spaces, necessary for congregational and ritual requirements, have been covered in a sound and satisfactory manner. Timber roofs might, it is true, have been employed, as in the basilican churches—they were to some extent, especially in England, Germany, and Italy—but the mediæval men, as a rule, like the Romans, preferred the greater security from fire, and the more monumental effect which the vault affords. The dome did not travel westward. Except in some Romanesque churches, chiefly in South-Western France, it remained in its native home, the East. Arch construction.

The shape of the arch did not remain unaltered during the five centuries that mediæval art flourished. Until near the middle of the twelfth century the semicircular form was general; but it was not universal. So much has been written about the semicircular arch being the distinctive mark of early mediæval or Romanesque, and about the pointed arch being the exclusive property of Gothic, that it is as well to repeat, what has already been demonstrated in Volume I., that the pointed form was known to, and used by, the Egyptians, Assyrians, pre-Hellenic Greeks and Etruscans hundreds of years before the commencement of our era; and by the Copts of Egypt and their conquerors, the Saracens, some centuries before it appeared in the West. Pointed arch.

It was first employed in Europe in the barrel-vaulted buildings of the South of France, certainly before the end of the eleventh century, and possibly earlier still (Fig. 3). The old Roman Pointed vaults.

traditions were there very strong; and one of these was the solid vault, with its extrados levelled to form two sloping sides, on top of which the outer covering, tiles, slates, or lead, could be laid direct, without the intervening protecting timber roof such as became customary later. In the majority of the eleventh century churches roofed in this manner, such as Conques (c. 1065), S. Sernin, Toulouse (c. 1096), and the group in Auvergne, the vaults are semicircular; but the builders soon perceived the advantages of the pointed form. Not only is it stronger, but it exercises less thrust, and the mass of solid material above the apex is considerably reduced. The nave of S. Nazaire, Carcassonne (c. 1096), is covered by a pointed barrel-vault, the aisles having semicircular vaults.

Fig. 3.

Date of introduction of pointed arch.

Elsewhere in Europe the date when the pointed arch was first introduced varies in different countries. In Northern France it first appeared between 1100 and 1120; in England it was not used constructionally before 1140, the approximate date of Fountains, Malmesbury, and Buildwas abbey churches. It occurs "accidentally," so to speak, in arcading formed by intersecting semicircular arches, both here and abroad, as early as the first half of the eleventh century, and hence arose the idea that the builders obtained the suggestion of the form from these arcades. But this theory has little to recommend it. Even if the pointed arch had not been used long before this interlacing arcading was introduced, the fact remains that the builders would be unlikely to abandon a form which had behind it centuries of tradition merely from a hint conveyed by an accident in decoration. Such might have occasioned a "freak" here and there, but the freak

ARCH DEVELOPMENT. 11

would soon have died a natural death if the pointed form had not elsewhere proved itself to be a most valuable structural asset. In Sicily and in portions of Southern Italy its introduction was early, owing to Saracenic influence;[1] in Germany it was late, as the conservative Teuton clung to his fine round-arched Romanesque until the end of the twelfth century. In the greater part of Italy it did not obtain a footing until later still; in fact, it never entirely superseded the Classic form. In the little Loggia del Bigallo,

FIG. 4.

Florence (c. 1360), and in many contemporary Italian buildings, all arches are semicircular.

The steeper the pointed arch the less its lateral thrust; and many of the early mediæval examples are also the most acute, as though the workmen rejoiced in the new form, and were determined to make the most of its statical advantages. But this is not always the case. Some of the earliest are also amongst the flattest (having a rise only a trifle more than a semicircular arch affords), and suggest that the new form was used reluctantly, and with grave doubts regarding its appearance. It is easy to design a pointed arch so acute that it exercises no side thrust at all, only vertical pressure. Arches of such excessive steepness are not uncommon in blind arcading flanking windows in early thirteenth-century churches in England, but such extremes

Forms of arches.

[1] It is impossible to say how early it appeared in Sicily; but it was certainly in common use there before the Normans appeared in 1061, otherwise they would not have adopted it so universally in their churches in the island.

12　*A HISTORY OF ARCHITECTURAL DEVELOPMENT.*

were rarely resorted to in arches over openings. An arch enclosing a space approximating to or exactly forming an equilateral triangle was the general favourite until the middle of the fourteenth century, and was by no means discarded entirely then. After that date the four-centred form in England, commonly called the Tudor arch, and the three-centred in France, are the most characteristic of the period. But both forms are weak, and are evidence of the decreasing vitality which marks the later work in

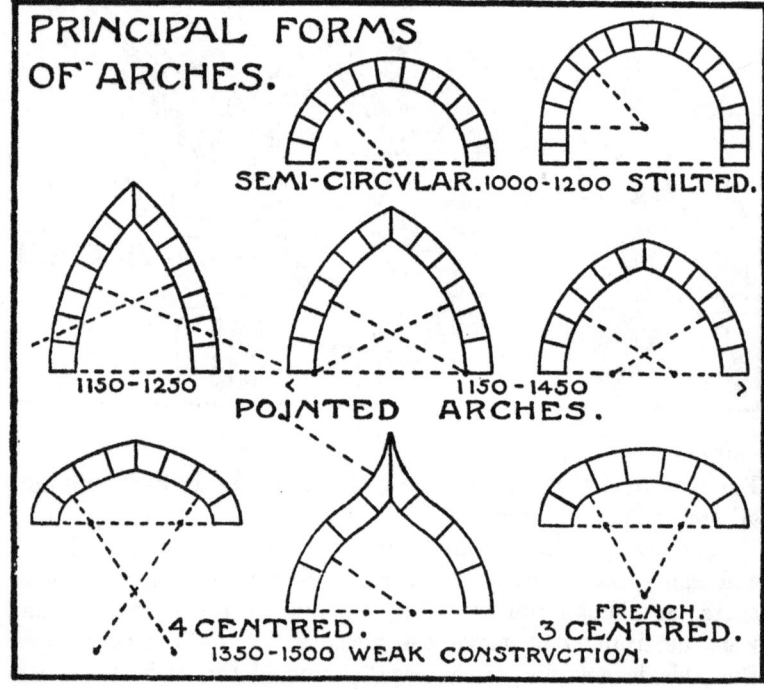

Fig. 5.

both countries. In England this was largely due to the "Black Death," the great plague of 1349, which swept away one half of the artisans of the country; and in France, in great measure, to the hundred years' war, which lasted from 1346 until 1447 and seriously interfered with all building. The other semi-unconstructional arches, the trefoil, cinquefoil, and ogee, are sometimes used alone over small windows and doors, but are more often enclosed by an outer arch. In the latter case, one appertaining chiefly to window lights and to both pierced and sunk wall arcading, they are little more than shaped heads, and the arches are said to be "foliated," or cusped. The west doorway of Byland Abbey Church is trefoil-headed, and all the arch mouldings and the label are worked to this form, but above is a pointed discharging arch, flush with the wall, which carries all the weight.[1]

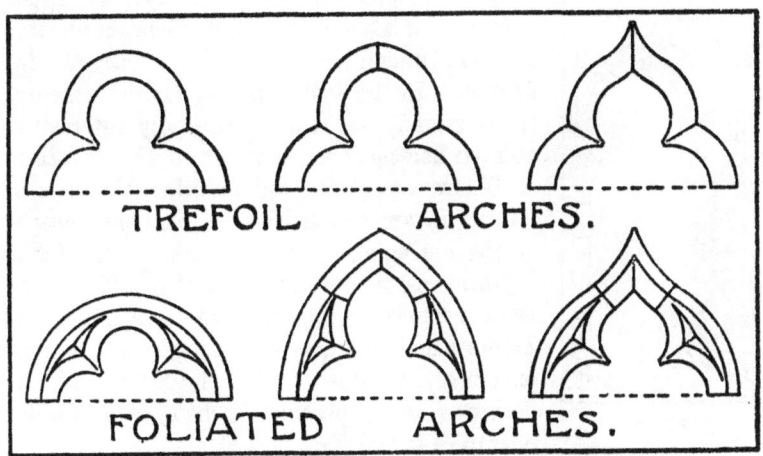

FIG. 6.

Stilted arches are the rare exception in England; on the continent they are the rule in all eleventh and twelfth-century work. They are not so common in Normandy as in Southern France, but in Auvergne, Aquitaine, Burgundy, etc., one seldom sees an arch that is not stilted, no matter what position it occupies or what its form is, semicircular or pointed.

Stilted arches.

A good deal has been written about horseshoe arches in England which is misleading. It is doubtful if one single horseshoe arch was ever built in this country. There are many existing now in different parts, but all were probably semicircular at first. Their present shape is due entirely to faulty construction, fires, settlements, or alterations, which have caused their haunches to bulge and their crowns to drop. The chancel arch of the Church

Horseshoe arches.

---

[1] Whether the pointed arch or the semicircular is the more beautiful is a matter of taste. The former is certainly the stronger; but from the days of Imperial Rome down to the present time (excluding the work of the Gothic revival) it has only been in general use during three centuries, whereas architects, builders, and the public have preferred and employed the other throughout all the remaining ones.

of S. Mary, Eastbourne, may be mentioned as an instance in which one or more of these causes have altered the original shape. Abroad there are many horseshoe arches which were built as such. After excluding the unmistakable examples in Cairo and other Eastern cities, the most numerous of European examples are on

FIG. 7.

the west side of Southern Italy. There they occur over windows and doorways, as in the churches of Caserta Vecchia, Benevento, etc., and are undoubtedly due to Saracenic influence. In the south aisle of Coire Cathedral (Switzerland) are some extremely interesting pointed horseshoe arches, and in the triforium of Issoire Cathedral, and in other churches of Auvergne, are foliated arches curving inwards at the springing. Whence arose these forms in these parts is difficult to say. They may be owing to some lingering tradition left by the Moors when they passed through the country, or simply be due to the playfulness of the designer, who, perchance, had seen similar examples in the East (see Fig. 156).[1]

Construction of arches.

In Roman arches of stone, big material is the rule, and the voussoirs in large blocks reach, in most cases, from the front to the back of the wall. The soffit is flush, or else panelled with moulded and enriched panels sunk below its plane. The mediæval builder preferred smaller stones for two reasons: (1) they were easier to handle; (2) an arch built with a number of small stones, which only bond with one another to a limited extent, is far more elastic than one built of a few large ones. The latter was the more important reason for preference. Elasticity was not necessary in Roman buildings where the mass of material was great, and the thrusts regular; but in a mediæval building, arched and vaulted in the manner which will be described later, it was of the first importance, owing to the multiplicity of thrusts and to the comparative slightness of all supports and abutments. The elasticity of mediæval buildings has proved their salvation; but for this quality many a one would have fallen long ago. The majority of Roman workmen were unskilled, fit only for

---

[1] The original church at Coire is stated to have been destroyed by the Saracens. The cusped arches in S. Isidoro, Leon, Spain, are undoubtedly a reflex of Moorish Art.

rough work; the mediæval workman was an able craftsman who could be trusted to overcome unaided the difficulties resulting

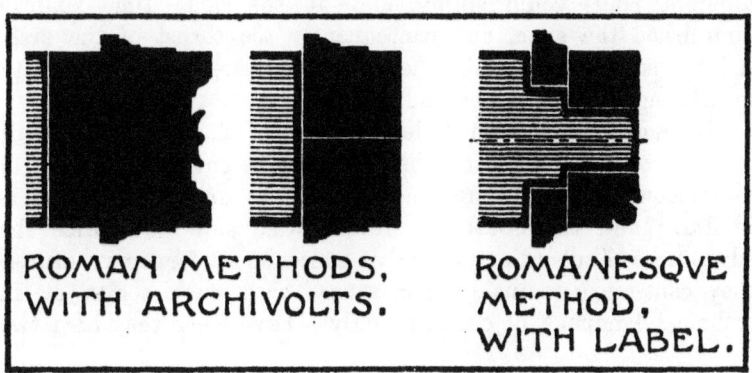

Fig. 8.

from the use of small stones which were also generally of different sizes.

The flat soffit of the Romans was generally retained in countries where Classic influence was strong until the twelfth century was far advanced. It is also found in work of the first half of the eleventh century in England, Normandy, and other countries. The voussoirs, however, are of moderate size, and do not, as a rule, bond more than a few inches into the wall. The intervening space is filled in with rubble. This answered fairly well at first, as the wall above was either merely faced with ashlar, the core being of rubble, or else was rubble throughout; but was soon discarded in favour of a series of voussoirs on different planes, or in what is commonly called in different "orders." {Roman and Romanesque methods.}

In this system of subordination the bottom ring of voussoirs, or inner order, was built first, and formed the central part of the soffit. It was not the full width of the wall above; not more than half its width on an average. It carried the core of the wall, and, in addition, the outer rings, or orders. These partially rested on it, and partially projected in front of it on either side, making the arch the full thickness of the wall above. One advantage of this method of building was that it diminished the amount of centering required, as, when the first order had set, it acted as a centre and support for the rings above it. The "springer," or bottom stone of the arch, was, except in very large churches, in one piece of stone, which reached from side to side and from {Subordination of arches.}

front to back, with two or more orders often worked on it. This stone afforded a solid bed from which the smaller stones of the different rings could spring, and at the same time slightly diminished the span, and consequently the thrust of the arch. A large stone was possible here because there was no difficulty in hoisting it into position and setting it.

In most English cathedrals the arches of the arcades are built in three or four rings, and the Romanesque entrance doorway of Malmesbury Abbey Church has as many as nine. The builders in Italy and the South of France were slow to realize the advantages of subordination, and, in consequence, for some centuries they continued to make their arches with flush soffits, or, in technical language, of one order only. Even when they used two

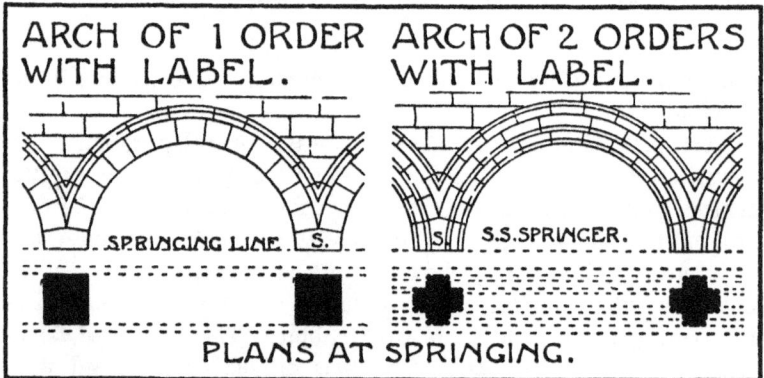

Fig. 9.

orders, the lower one was by far the more important, the upper one projecting merely a few inches in front of it, as at S. Zeno, Verona, S. Ambrogio, Milan, etc. (see Fig. 15). In Central France, that stronghold of fully developed mediæval art, the arches of the arcades of even the largest thirteenth-century cathedrals have seldom more than two orders; the reason being that larger blocks of stone were more easily procurable there than in England.

Mouldings.   An important æsthetic difference between Roman arches and mediæval is that when the former are moulded, which is by no means always the case, the mouldings worked on the voussoirs project in front of the wall and form an archivolt. In mediæval arches mouldings are recessed. It is true that over the arch is often a projecting hood moulding, or label; but this, except in the smallest examples, is never worked on the voussoirs of the arch itself, but on separate stones in long lengths above them. Unmoulded arches are rare in England in churches built after the Norman Conquest, but examples occur on the north side of the nave of S. Albans Cathedral. In Italy and Southern France they were the rule during the eleventh and twelfth centuries, although the label over was moulded when the voussoirs were plain. Mouldings are as sure an index of the advance or retrogression of architectural art as the structural parts of buildings. Moreover, by them the date of any work can often be determined when other evidence is conflicting and unreliable.[1]

The scale and contours of mouldings underwent considerable change as the style developed. When the main structural lines

1050-1170.

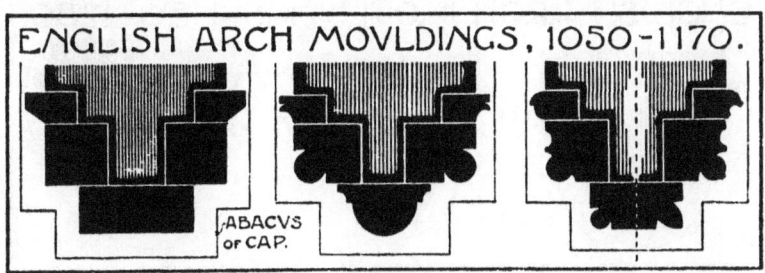

Fig. 10.

were big and strong, the mouldings were few and bold; as the former grew lighter the latter became smaller and also more numerous, until, in the fifteenth century, main lines and mouldings alike were thin and attenuated. Mouldings also followed in section, to a great extent, the shape of the arch in vogue at the time. Thus, when the arch was semicircular, mouldings were segments of circles. The most characteristic of early Romanesque ones is the "torus," or three-quarter round—sometimes called the rounded "bowtell"—which, either with or without a small fillet on its face, was used alone or in combination with a cavetto, or hollow. In many English Romanesque cathedrals the lowest order in the nave arcades often consists of a single semicircular moulding, which, as at Durham, produces a remarkably fine effect.

[1] The sections of mediæval mouldings on paper are very misleading; much more so than those of classic ones. To understand the effect they produce actual examples must be studied and measured.

18   A HISTORY OF ARCHITECTURAL DEVELOPMENT.

1150–1170.   When the pointed arch made its appearance, the pointed "bowtell" took the place of the rounded. For twenty or thirty years new ideas were fighting with old traditions. In the transitional work of this period one finds pointed arches which are moulded like most semicircular ones, and semicircular arches with the more deeply cut mouldings characteristic of somewhat later work. Of the latter type are the arches in S. Mary's Church, Shrewsbury. It was as though the workmen could not make up their minds to a complete change. If they altered the detail of an arch they clung to the old form; if they accepted the new form they quieted their conscience by working the old detail.

1150–1250.   About the middle of the twelfth century the sections of mouldings changed entirely, especially in England, owing largely

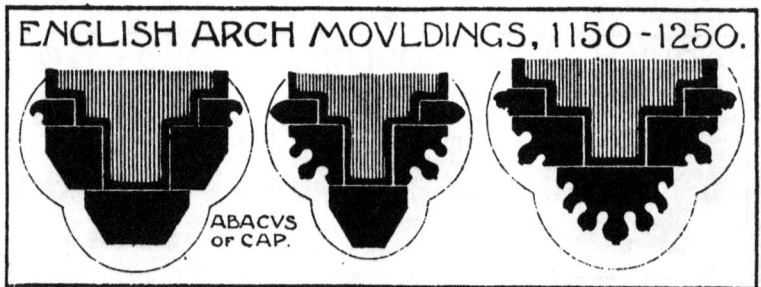

Fig. 11.

to the general employment of soft, easily worked stone, such as Caen (from Normandy), Chilmark, Beer, Ancaster, Bath, etc. They became a series of bold rounds and deep hollows alternating, which produced marked contrasts of dark shadows and strong high lights. These deeply undercut mouldings are, however, by no means universal in English work of this period. In some parts of the country where the stone was hard and not easily worked, as in Yorkshire, simple champers often take their place. Perhaps the most effective method of all is when, as on the west front of the Priory Church of SS. Peter and Paul, Brinkburn, Northumberland, one order is merely champhered, and the other richly moulded. The effect of the moulded order is by this means accentuated, and its richness emphasized.

1250–1350.   The mouldings of the next hundred years are much flatter, and the wave, ogee and double ogee are common forms. These are generally grouped, two or more together, each group being separated from the next by a deep hollow where the stones of two orders meet. The ogee does not appear in English work until about the middle of the thirteenth century, although, owing to the influence of Classic tradition, it occurs much earlier abroad. In twelfth-century churches in the South of France and in Burgundy, most of the mouldings are of this section; and the contours have a delicacy, especially in Burgundy, far greater than is ever met with in more northern examples.

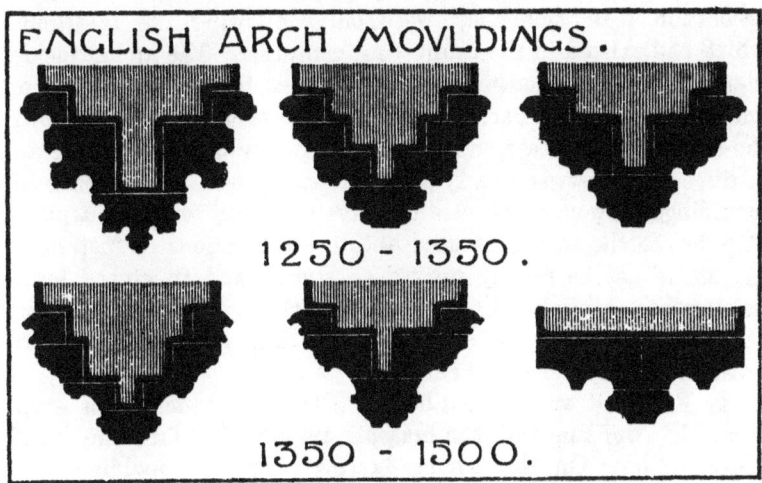

Fig. 12.

When the flat four-centred arch supplanted, to some extent, the more acutely pointed arch, some of the mouldings in sympathy became wide and shallow. Fifteen-century mouldings, as a rule, are distinguishable from earlier ones by a certain angularity and hardness of outline which the others are free from. They are often also smaller in proportion. A small three-quarter round member, which forms an attached shaft and has its own capital and base, is generally met with in window and door jambs of the period. The difference in scale between these and the much larger similarly treated shafts of the late thirteenth and early fourteenth centuries is considerable. *1350–1500.*

Until the middle of the thirteenth century all mouldings were worked only on the face and soffit of a squared stone. Even the most elaborate combinations of deep hollows and bold rounds, such as those on the nave arches of Salisbury Cathedral, come *Mouldings on different planes.*

20   A HISTORY OF ARCHITECTURAL DEVELOPMENT.

under this category. In later work, however, the corners of the stone were champhered off before the mouldings were worked, in order to obtain the series of shallow mouldings which the architects of the fourteenth and fifteenth centuries preferred.

Italian mouldings.

The same attention was not paid to mouldings in Italy as in other countries. The workers there had not the love for the mason's craft which is one of the most distinctive traits in Northern art of the Middle Ages. When they wanted relief from too great a simplicity they preferred to rely on coloured decoration. In this they were only following the traditions which had existed in the country for centuries. The arches inside many a thirteenth-century church, such as S. Anastasia, Verona, and SS. Giovanni e Paolo, Venice, are unmoulded. Even when the contrary is the case, the mouldings are few and little difference is discernible between early and late examples. The absence of mouldings, however, is not due only to traditions of craftsmanship, but to the materials used and to combinations of materials. Marble is not so readily worked as stone; and in arches built in alternate voussoirs of marble and brick, as many in Northern Italy are, mouldings are unnecessary, in fact, would destroy, to a great extent, the colour scheme.

French mouldings.

In France it was quite different. There, as much as or even more than in England, the mason's art was the first and chief consideration. On the whole, however, French mouldings are simpler and fewer than English ones, and they also underwent less change from century to century. The Frenchmen clung to the rounded "bowtell" long after it had been discarded in England. It was eminently suited to the somewhat hard, coarse-grained stone of which many of their churches are built. The deep hollows and bold rounds, so characteristic of English early thirteenth-century work, are rarely found in France, except in Normandy, where Caen stone was easily procurable. But even there the mouldings are generally bigger and fewer, as in S. Pierre, Lisieux, Coutances Cathedral, etc. In one example, however, the ruined church of the Abbaye d'Ardennes, near Caen, the details are practically identical with contemporary ones in England, and in Le Mans Cathedral they are very similar.

After the hundred years' war French mouldings lost all their boldness, and became attenuated and weak. They are also in some cases very numerous, as in S. Maclou, Rouen. Interpenetration, or the carrying of one moulding through another instead of stopping it on top of the other, became general, although it was in Germany that this custom flourished most. Late French arch mouldings have little to recommend them, and contrast

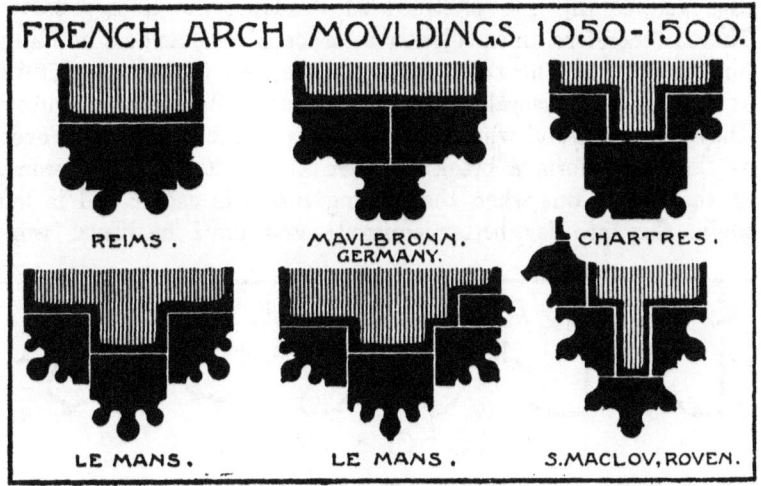

Fig. 18.

unfavourably with the squareness and simple severity of the twelfth and thirteenth-century ones.

Whilst the mouldings of different countries possess their own peculiarities, contemporary ones in each country are strangely like one another. It is true that there are often localisms, distinguishing the work of one district from that of another, but these are, as often as not, the result of the material available. Thus, in Cornwall and also in Brittany, where the old churches are built of granite, the mouldings are naturally simpler and bigger than in those parts where a soft limestone was employed. But, local differences apart, a freemasonry undoubtedly existed. Workmen travelled from building to building, from town to town; and wherever they went they carried with them, if not the actual templates they had used, a keen recollection of the mouldings they had worked. In no other way can the strong likeness pervading contemporary work be accounted for. This is more marked, perhaps, in England than elsewhere, as the country is small, and it was united; whereas France and Italy, besides being larger, were split up into different duchies and kingdoms. In England

Similarity between contemporary mouldings.

22 A HISTORY OF ARCHITECTURAL DEVELOPMENT.

Arch labels.

certainly, when a change in detail was introduced in one locality, time was short, as a rule, before it found its way into another.

Labels, or hood mouldings, over arches, throw the wet to the sides, and prevent it from running down and injuring the mouldings and, in the case of traceried windows, the tracery below. There is, therefore, an excellent reason for labels outside a building, but there is none for them inside, unless they frame in sculpture, as in Lincoln Cathedral, or diaper work, as in Westminster Abbey. They are also useful when the walling is of rubble plastered over, as then they form a break between the plaster and the stones of the arch. But when the walling inside is ashlar and is left plain, they are far better omitted; and until mediæval work

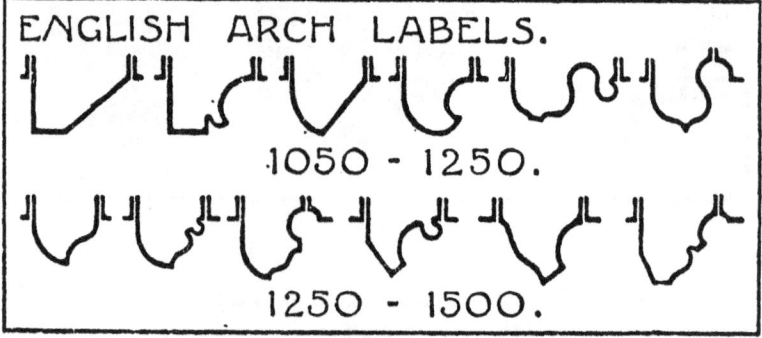

FIG. 14.

became somewhat stereotyped, they often were. There are no labels over the arches inside Nôtre Dame, Paris, Amiens Cathedral, and the majority of large French churches, and the increased amount of plain unbroken wall space obtained by their omission is a great gain. In England, unfortunately, they are seldom absent; but there can be little doubt that the French plan is the more sensible and also æsthetically the better.

The mouldings of labels, string-courses, and other minor details are always characteristic of their several periods. In Romanesque times they were often little more than a fillet and chamfer; later, the forms changed frequently, keeping pace with the developments of other parts, and besides being moulded were frequently enriched by carved ornament.

CHAPTER III.

COLUMNS, PIERS, CAPITALS, AND BASES.

ROMANESQUE columns in most continental work are more slender Columns.
than contemporary ones in England and Normandy. The heavy
bulk of the so-called "Norman" column is unknown outside the
two countries mentioned. In Italy, Southern France, and Germany,
many columns of the eleventh and twelfth centuries retain, to a
considerable extent, Classic proportions, and not only taper, but
have an entasis. These two refinements seem to have been little
practised in early work elsewhere, although there are a few
examples of the eleventh century in England and Northern France
in which they appear. Columns in subsequent work throughout
Christendom are straight-sided, and this in itself differentiates
them from Classic ones. An important exception to the general
rule is in the choir of the great abbey church of Vézelay, in
Burgundy. Although this portion of the church was not built
until about 1180, and is of fully developed Gothic, the columns
round the apse diminish in diameter, and are entasised as well.

English columns of the eleventh century and first half of the English
twelfth are only faced with ashlar, their cores being of rubble. columns.
Hence their excessive bulk, apparent strength, and real weakness;
the result often being disaster. They have no fixed or even
approximate proportions, such as were universally followed in
Classic work. The columns of Tewkesbury Abbey Church and
Gloucester Cathedral, for instance, are about double the height
of those at Hereford; and yet the diameters are practically the
same (6.6 inches) in all three churches. Many English columns
are ornamented by flutings, which are vertical, spiral, zigzag,
or else form lozenges. These were cut in the stones after the
columns were built. All patterns occur in Durham Cathedral and
Waltham Abbey Church, and the only two columns in the nave
of Norwich Cathedral are carved in this way. The treatment was
a relic of Classic times, when columns were generally fluted,

although no doubt the masons in England knew nothing of these. They took the idea from the smaller shafts, ornamented in similar fashion, which surround cloister garths, especially in early continental churches. In Italy and Sicily the flutes or grooves in many of these are filled with an inlay of glass mosaic, a similar treatment apparently having been applied to the grooved shafts round the cloisters of Chester Cathedral.[1] In Italy, cylindrical columns remained the usual support to arches all through the Middle Ages, and in France and Germany they never entirely disappeared. But the exigencies of construction called for their removal, and in all large churches they were finally entirely supplanted by that most characteristic feature of mediæval architecture, the clustered pier.

Piers.   Piers, of course, were no novelty in the eleventh century. They had been used long before, in sixth-century churches in Syria,

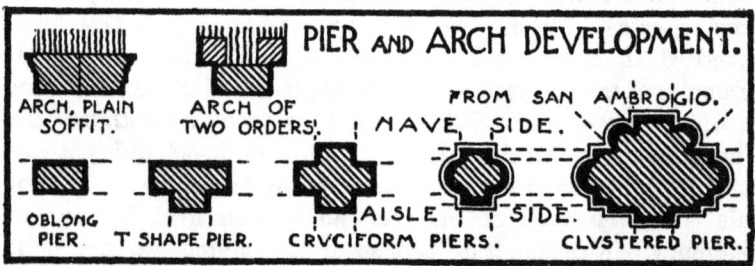

FIG. 15.

and, in conjunction with columns, in S. Clemente and S. Maria in Cosmedin, Rome, and in S. Demetrius, Salonica (see Vol. I., Figs. 112, 114, 130). In other Italian churches they had been employed throughout, partly because the supply of antique marble columns, which for centuries after the fall of the Roman empire had been so plentiful, had begun to fail, and partly because a simple pier can be built with unskilled labour, at much less cost and with cheaper material than a column. These early piers are all rectangular and unmoulded. The first alteration in their form was made in the ninth or tenth century, when aisles began to be divided longitudinally into bays by transverse arches. To carry these arches a "nib," or pilaster, was added to the back of each

---

[1] Round the tomb of Edward the Confessor in Westminster Abbey are twisted shafts, fluted and inlaid, which, however, are later in date than the columns of Durham and shafts of Chester.

pier, a corresponding pilaster projecting from the wall on the other side of the aisle. The pier thus became T-shape.[1] The next step was to make it cruciform in plan, so that arches thrown across the nave as well as the aisles could have something substantial to spring from. In S. Miniato, Florence (c. 1013),[2] the nave is divided longitudinally, into three divisions of three bays each, by piers quatrefoil in section, the front and back projections carrying transverse arches (see Fig. 117). For the changes which followed, the subordination of arches and vaulting considerations are mainly responsible. Neither a cylindrical column nor a cruciform pier is manifestly the best form to support an arch composed of several members lying in different planes; and both forms became still more unsuitable when, in addition to the arch, the ribs of a vault had to be carried as well. The unsuitability of a column to perform the first of these functions in a satisfactory manner is manifest in, for instance, Gloucester Cathedral and Tewkesbury Abbey Church, where no attempt has been made to bring arch and column into harmony. In the choir of Peterboro' Cathedral, where

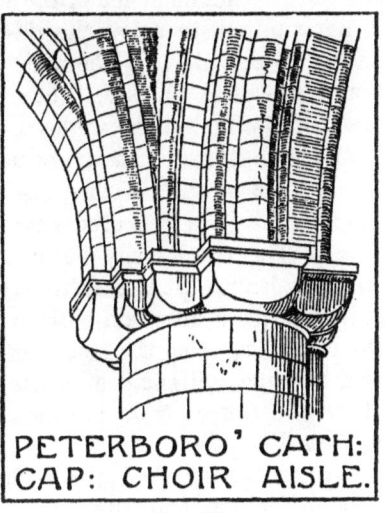

Fig. 16.

some of the supports are columns and others twelve-sided piers, the capitals have been designed to agree with the orders of the arches above and the ribs of the aisle vaulting, but they fit somewhat awkwardly on to the supports below. The difficulties were the same when the pier was octagonal, as in Christ Church Cathedral, Oxford.

To get over these difficulties and to reconcile all parts, the subordinated, or clustered pier was devised. It is so planned that

<small>Clustered piers.</small>

---

[1] T-shaped piers were used in Syria in the sixth century, in the church at Roueiha (see Vol. I., Fig. 134), for much the same reason as they were adopted in later Italian churches.

[2] Some archæologists place S. Miniato at the end and not at the beginning of the eleventh century.

each order of an arch, and, in early vaulted churches, each rib of a vault as well, has its corresponding member in the pier below. Nowhere can its development be better traced than in England and Normandy, as the architects of the Isle de France were by no means unanimous at first in adopting it, neither did they create so many varieties of it as we did. A clustered pier is formed by the addition of shafts to either a column or a rectangular pier. The simplest form, a somewhat incomplete one, is when one or more shafts are attached to the aisle side of a column to support the side vaulting, whilst a like shaft on the nave side is carried up the wall to the underside of the vaulting ribs, or, when the church is not vaulted, to below the tie-beam of the roof. In S. Albans Cathedral the piers on the north side of the nave are amongst the plainest of piers which are not simply rectangular. They have no attached shafts, but the angles are rebated to agree with the orders of the arch above. Lastly, comes the complete clustered pier, in which some of the attached shafts correspond with the orders of the arch above, whilst others support the vaulting ribs of nave and aisles. The result may be a nearly square form, or an oblong with its length from east to west. In Durham Cathedral large clustered piers alternate with cylindrical columns (see Fig. 179), the former carrying the main ribs of the nave vault. This alternation of large and small supports was a common one in Northern Italy and Germany in particular, and the reasons for it will be discussed later.

English piers, 1150–1250.

About the middle of the twelfth century all parts of a building became lighter, and the piers gradually lost their bulky proportions; they also assumed a more clustered form. Typical examples, such as those in the naves of the abbey churches of Jedburgh, N.B., and Much Wenlock (c. 1180) (see Fig. 25), consist of a series of attached shafts, in section alternately round and pointed, each of the rounded shafts having a fillet on its face. A circle drawn round them touches the extreme point of each shaft. Plain columns and octagonal piers continued to be built, especially in parish churches, but the most characteristic form between 1180 to 1250 was the column surrounded by detached shafts. This was employed almost universally in the South of England, and occasionally in other parts of the country, the shafts being generally of Purbeck marble from Dorset, as in Westminster Abbey and Salisbury Cathedral, etc. Elsewhere other marbles were used, notably in the Chapel of the Nine Altars in

Durham Cathedral, where those in the responds are of Frosterley marble. They are always in long lengths, 10 to 12 feet long, and

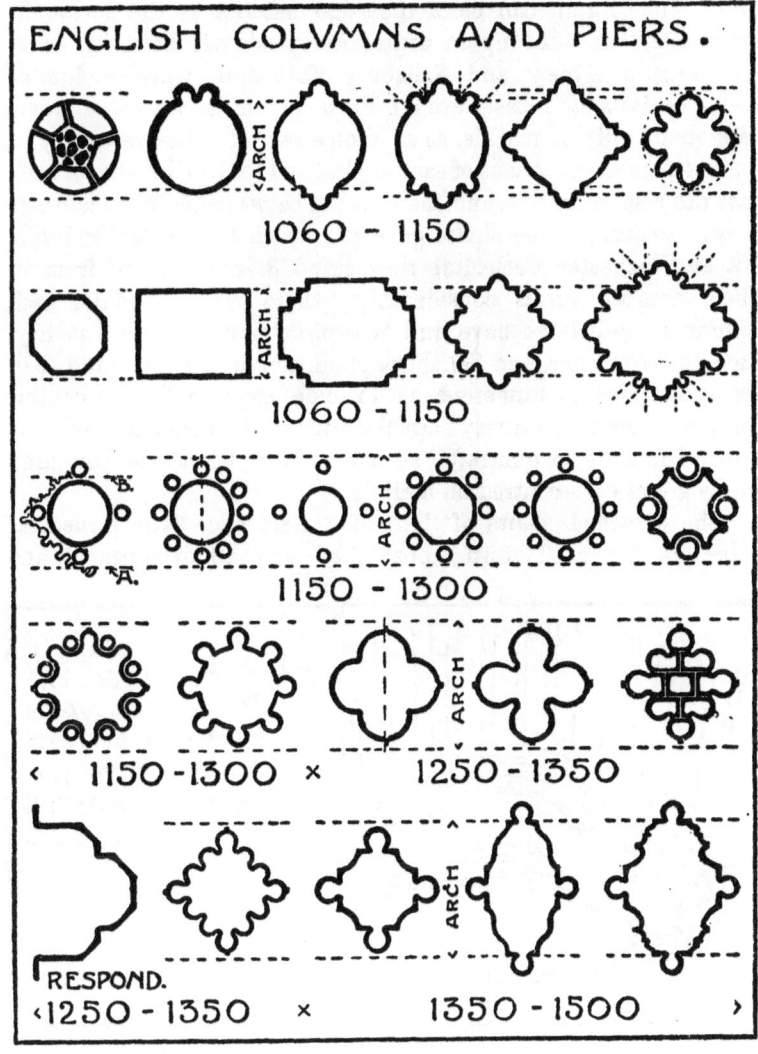

Fig. 17.

where one piece joins another they are connected either by a moulded band of the same material, as in Westminster Abbey, or by a narrow ring of bronze, as at Salisbury. Examples of both

28   A HISTORY OF ARCHITECTURAL DEVELOPMENT.

methods occur in the presbytery of Worcester Cathedral. The moulded band sometimes merely grips the shafts and stops against the central column, sometimes it is carried round the column as well. The column can be of the same material as the surrounding shafts, but built up in drums independently of them, as at Westminster Abbey and Salisbury Cathedral, where columns, shafts, capitals, and bases are all Purbeck; or it can be of stone, with shafts only of marble, as at Worcester. In the presbytery of the last-named the abacus of each capital and the top member of each base are also of marble, and the contrast between the two materials is very striking. The shafts generally touch the central column, but at Chichester Cathedral they stand 8 inches away from it. Their number varies considerably; there are four round each column in Salisbury nave and Westminster choir, eight at Ely, Lincoln, Worcester, and Salisbury choir, ten at Lichfield, and they are sometimes so numerous as to hide completely the central column. This is not always circular; it can be octagonal, as in the choir of Lincoln, or quatrefoil as at Salisbury, but the surrounding shafts are always centred on a circle.

Weight on shafts. The detached shafts of the above piers had little structural value; in fact, at Tintern Abbey they have all disappeared, and

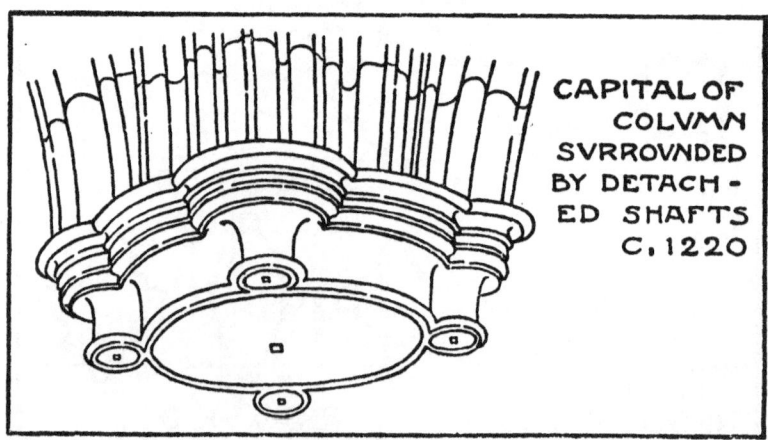

FIG. 18.

yet the piers stand almost as strong as ever. The builders of the thirteenth century were careful that as little weight as possible should fall on them. The upper members, at least, of the capital always followed round both shafts and pier, and, whenever size prevented their being worked on a single stone, the separate stones were thoroughly well bonded together, so that the capital acted as a corbel to some extent, and transmitted all pressure on to the central support. Notwithstanding this, many shafts have split or been thrust out of the perpendicular, and have had to be replaced by others, or refixed; the reason being that columns built in drums with many joints are likely to settle more than long shafts with few joints, and, in consequence, weight has fallen on the shafts which they were never intended to bear. The bands or rings allowed, it is true, a certain amount of "play," as the shafts could be somewhat loosely fitted between them, but the many restorations which have been necessary show that the allowance made was often insufficient.

After 1250, detached shafts were abandoned, possibly because it was found that, notwithstanding the precautions taken, they were structurally faulty, and a return was made to a cluster of attached shafts. For small columns a quatrefoil plan, either with or without a fillet on each face was usual, and this was followed by a somewhat similar form, with shafts slightly ogee in outline and a deep hollow between each. The large piers consist of a series of shafts, eight in number at Lincoln and twelve at Exeter, which are placed diamond-wise, and not enclosed within a circle, as in earlier work. The moulded bands uniting the shafts disappear; there was no longer any reason for them, now that all shafts were attached and the whole pier built in drums. In the naves of Westminster Abbey and Worcester Cathedral, however, which were built a century or more after the choirs, they are retained, in order that the later piers should be in harmony with the earlier ones. *Piers, 1250-1350.*

In the work of the next hundred years a marked change is perceptible in all the details of churches, and nowhere is this more marked than in the piers. The builders had gained the confidence which successful experiments give, the construction was more skilful, and all the parts of churches much more slender. But although their skill was greater, the vigour which characterized the earlier work was lacking. The cry was for spaciousness; for a saving of material wherever it could be saved; for small supports and wide spans. The rubble core was definitely abandoned, and the piers, and in many cases the walls also, became of ashlar throughout. Moreover, many piers were made oblong—the greater dimension being from north to south and the less from east to west—in order to interfere with the floor *Piers, 1350-1500.*

30 A HISTORY OF ARCHITECTURAL DEVELOPMENT.

space as little as possible and yet be sufficiently wide to carry the wall above. Of this character are the piers in Cromer and Lavenham Churches and in many other parish churches throughout England. The most general forms, however, are the octagonal, and a pier consisting of four attached three-quarter shafts with mouldings in between. The shafts alone have capitals, the mouldings continuing above the springing line and round the arch without a break. Many piers are panelled all over with small panels, the panelling generally continuing round the arch as well, as in Sherbourne Abbey Church and in the better known and most elaborate of all examples, Henry VII.'s Chapel, Westminster. It is a joinery treatment, and has little to recommend it. When extended to walls as well as to piers and arches, as in Henry the VII.'s Chapel and the Houses of Parliament, Westminster, it defeats its own object; as buildings are only rich or plain by comparison, and when there is no plain wall space to accentuate the richness of other parts, the elaboration of these is labour lost.[1]

Responds.   In the central columns of an arcade, the lateral thrust of one arch is counteracted by that of another, but at each end additional abutment has to be provided. This, in mediæval work, is partially afforded by external buttresses (see Chap. IV.). These, however, could seldom be made of sufficient projection, and hence the custom arose of building inside a church, at the ends of an arcade, a piece of wall known as the "respond." The respond, unlike the columns or piers, is generally the full width of the wall above, and differs from them in section. In parish churches it is often merely champhered in one or more planes, according to the number of orders in the arch above.

Continental piers.   Priority for English workers is not claimed in the above brief account of pier development, especially for the forms employed before 1200. The clustered pier found its way into England from Normandy, where it occurs, fully developed, in the Church of S. Etienne, Caen, commenced 1066, an earlier example than any we can boast. Elsewhere on the continent there are many examples of it in eleventh-century work. In the nave of S. Ambrogio, Milan, built probably in the latter half of the century, the large piers are clustered, the small ones cruciform. On the other hand, in the fine Romanesque work in Germany the

[1] The Westminster buildings possess one great advantage; in one, the plain mass of Westminster Hall acts as a foil to the Houses of Parliament, and the choir of the abbey church to the chapel in the other.

COLUMNS, PIERS, CAPITALS, AND BASES.

piers are extremely simple, and whilst columns are general, clustered piers are rare. In S. Michael's, Hildesheim, a church of the early eleventh century, every third support is a plain rectangular pier, the intermediate ones being columns. In S. Maria in Capitolio, Cologne, the nave has rectangular piers, with a nib at the back of each to support the aisle arches, whilst in the choir and transepts are tapering columns with an entasis. Even in the large Rhenish churches of the eleventh and twelfth centuries, Speier, Worms, Mainz, the columns are plain rectangles, or T-shape, or cruciform.

In France the builders found it difficult to abandon the column, to which tradition had accustomed them. Even in churches otherwise so far advanced as Nôtre Dame, Paris (c. 1160), and Laon Cathedral, they are used in the main arcades. There was not great building activity in Central France before the

French piers.

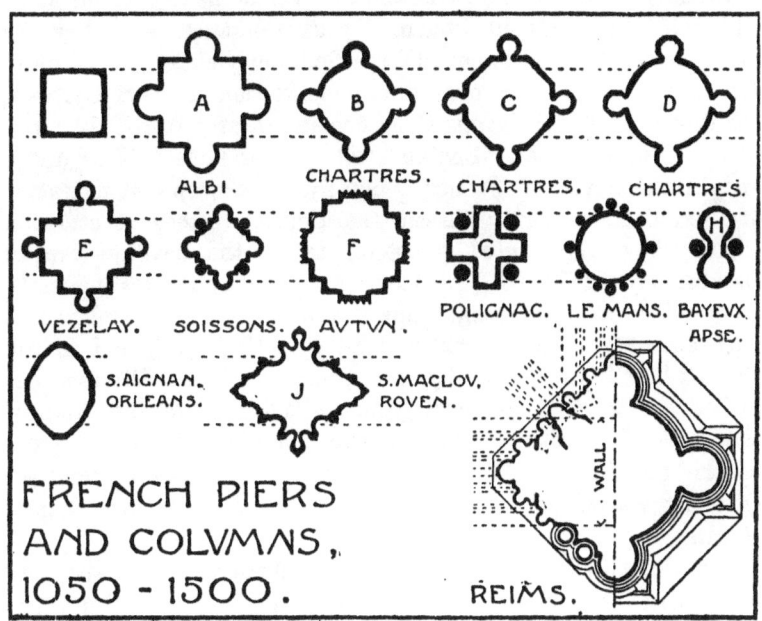

FIG. 19.

middle of the twelfth century; but in some of the few early examples, of which S. Germain des Près, Paris, is one, there are cruciform piers, of the type common elsewhere in the country, consisting of a square with an attached column on each side (A).

This developed into the most characteristic of all French forms, which was employed all through the thirteenth century, and sometimes later. In it a column is surrounded by four attached shafts, which are sometimes semicircular, but generally three-quarter round (B). Of this character are the piers of the Cathedrals of Reims, Amiens, Tours, Bordeaux, etc. In Chartres Cathedral some of the piers are octagonal, whilst others are circular. The former are surrounded by four attached three-quarter round shafts, and the latter, by four attached octagonal shafts; an excellent instance of the good effect which can be produced by counter-changing (C and D). The French, outside Normandy, did not take kindly to detached shafts; partly because they had no material so suitable as Purbeck marble, and partly, perhaps, because they regarded them as not altogether sound structurally. Still they used them occasionally, in some of the aisle columns of Nôtre Dame, Paris, and in Laon Cathedral for instance, whilst in Normandy, at Rouen, Bayeux, Coutances, etc., they are more plentiful. In the nave of the fine abbey church at Vézelay, Burgundy (c. 1126), the piers are a modification of the S. Germain des Près type, which brings them one step nearer to the clustered pier of Normandy and England (E). Other piers in Burgundy, and in the South of France generally, have a special character of their own, owing to Classic traditions. Instead of attached shafts, they have fluted pilasters, as in the nave of Autun Cathedral (c. 1132) (F). In Auvergne are many interesting early piers which are somewhat different from those generally met with elsewhere. In the nave of Le Puy Cathedral, and in the Church of Polignac, close by, are cruciform piers with four detached shafts in the corners, which stand clear of the arms of the cross (G). Still more effective and unusual are the piers at the crossing in the former church. In these a detached shaft is *recessed* on each western side with particularly happy results.

In Sens Cathedral (c. 1150) large clustered piers alternate with pairs of columns, one column being placed behind the other. This doubling of columns was a common device at the east end of French cathedrals with chevets, especially in Normandy, where it was important that the supports should be narrow and yet of sufficient depth to carry the wall above. In Bayeux and Coutances Cathedrals, double columns, which, however, are attached to one another at the back, are employed in this position, with small detached shafts partially recessed between them (H).[1]

There is not much difference between thirteenth and fourteenth century French piers, except that the latter are somewhat thinner and have often a greater number of attached shafts, as in the naves of Bourges Cathedral, S. Ouen, Rouen, Tours Cathedral, etc. In fifteenth-century work the supports, when not cylindrical columns or octagonal piers, have a number of filletted and moulded shafts worked on their face, as in S. Maclou, Rouen (J), which in most cases are continued round the arches without the intervention of capitals, as in S. Vulfran, Abbeville (c. 1490).

In continental churches of the late fourteenth and fifteenth centuries, figures are frequently placed against piers on the nave side. They stand on corbels, with canopies over them, about halfway between the floor and the springing of the arches of the arcade (see Fig. 84). Many of the corbels and canopies are delightful in design in themselves, but it is a question whether they and the figures are desirable additions. Their richness catches the eye unduly. In most churches the original figures have long since disappeared, and it is therefore difficult to say whether there is anything in the idea. When figures have been added in Classic times, as in some of the Belgian churches, there can be no doubt that the effect produced is a bad one; but that may be entirely the fault of the figures. S. Ouen, Rouen, is one of the earliest churches in which these canopied pseudo-niches appear, and it is also one in which they are managed more effectively perhaps than in any other example. *Canopied niches on piers.*

An important point in mediæval building is the relative thickness of arch and wall above to the supporting column or pier below. This depends, to some extent, on whether naves and aisles are vaulted; but not entirely. In an unvaulted church the rule is that the wall is wider than the support below, and the two are brought into harmony by the capital, as described later. There are a few exceptions to this, but not many. In vaulted churches there is by no means such uniformity; and French methods are very different from English. In the majority of English examples, the plan is the same in vaulted as in unvaulted churches. In Salisbury Cathedral, for instance, the wall is wider than the central column and detached shafts combined (see *Relative width of pier and wall.*

---

[1] The columns of the chevet of Canterbury Cathedral are double, owing to William of Sens, who was responsible for the design.

Fig. 17, A), and a similar arrangement was followed in those later examples, such as Exeter Cathedral, in which the piers consist of a cluster of attached shafts. In all typical large vaulted French churches, the opposite is found; the support, whether simple column, as in N. D., Paris, or column with attached shafts, as in Chartres Cathedral, is considerably wider than the arch and wall above. In Westminster Abbey there is an approach to a mixture of French and English methods (see Fig. 17, B). The supports are the same design as at Salisbury; but the wall above is only slightly thicker than the central column alone, the detached shafts projecting in front of it. In Salisbury Cathedral the transverse arches of the aisle vault have a small bearing on top of the capital, whilst the diagonal ribs die against the wall. In Reims and Chartres Cathedrals, the corresponding arches and ribs spring from the attached shaft which forms part of each pier, and from a portion of the pier itself (see Fig. 19, Reims). At Salisbury the vaulting shafts on the nave side start high above the column. At Chartres and Reims the shafts start from the capital of the column, and are supported partly on the cylindrical portion of the column, and partly on one of its attached shafts. The thinning of the wall in French churches has no bad effects in early work—in fact, there is much to be said for it—but in later examples it gives that wirey look which is so unsatisfactory in S. Ouen, Rouen, Auxerre Cathedral, etc. There is plenty of strength in the piers, because in these churches the vaulting shafts run down to the floor; and the walls are strong enough because they are buttressed, so to speak, by these shafts, but the arches, in nearly all instances, look deplorably thin.

Capitals. In plain rectangular piers, capitals may be dispensed with, as the pier is generally the same width as the arch and wall above; and although a moulding is advisable to mark the springing line, this is purely an ornament. In the pre-Norman Church of S. Martin, at S. Albans, and in many early examples abroad, a simple abacus is all that parts pier and arch. In a few fourteenth-century churches, and in many of the following century, capitals are omitted entirely, because the plan of the pier agrees approximately, often exactly, with the section of the arch above. But a column supporting the portion of a wall at the springing of an arch, which is wider in all directions than the column, must have a spreading capital.[1]

[1] In the naves of Gloucester Cathedral and Tewkesbury Abbey Church, the columns are so huge that little more than an abacus suffices. In some semi-Gothic,

COLUMNS, PIERS, CAPITALS, AND BASES.   35

In many of the Byzantine churches of the sixth century, and Dosserets.
in some of the early Basilican ones in which antique columns and
capitals were largely re-used, the difficulty of starting an arch from
the top of a column led to the introduction of a "dosseret," or
shaped block, between the arch and the capital proper (see Vol. I.,
Fig. 107, p. 171). The dosseret of this form is confined almost
entirely to Byzantine churches, and to early churches in Italy in
which Byzantine workmen were employed, or in which the local
masons copied Eastern methods. There is, however, a pseudo-
dosseret, or upper abacus, which, in the eleventh century and early
part of the twelfth, was largely used, not only in Italy, as in Pisa
and Torcello Cathedrals, etc. (see Vol. I., Fig. 126, p. 192), but also
in the South of France, especially in the Romanesque churches of
Burgundy and Auvergne. This upper abacus, a square-sided
moulded slab, occurs most frequently above pseudo-Corinthian
capitals. These have their own abaci, which, however, following
the classic original, are curved in plan, and are not therefore the
most suitable shape for an arch to spring from.

In more northern Romanesque work the dosseret is discarded Roman-
entirely, and the arch starts direct from the top of the capital, as esque
capitals.

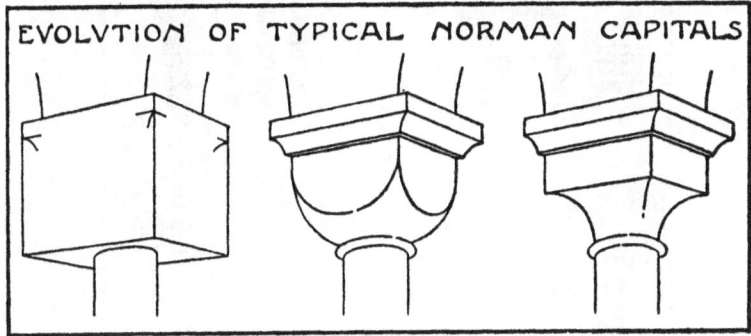

FIG. 20.

it always should do. The architects of S. Sophia, Constantinople,
in the sixth century, had the good taste to recognize this, and
to dispense with the unnecessary dosseret in the most important
parts of their church. The capital they designed became the
model for one half of the Romanesque capitals of later date. In

semi-Renaissance churches, such as S. Etienne du Mont, Paris, there are no
capitals at all, and the mouldings of the arches die into the round of the columns
below—which are the same width as the wall over—as best they can.

36 A HISTORY OF ARCHITECTURAL DEVELOPMENT.

it the portion below the abacus is convex, like the echinus moulding of the Greek Doric order. Other Romanesque capitals derived their forms from ancient Ionic and Corinthian capitals, and, apart from differences in treatment, are easily distinguishable from those of the first-mentioned type by their concave outline.

The capital a corbel.   A capital above a column really partakes of the nature of a corbel, or rather a series of corbels branching out on all sides. A square block of stone or marble is taken, the upper part moulded to form an abacus, and the corners of the lower part rounded off so that it shall "sit" satisfactorily on the column below. When the capital is of any size, the abacus is worked on a separate stone. The result, in both cases, is a capital of convex outline. If the concave form is required, rather more stone has to be cut away in the lower part, but the method followed is the same in both instances.

Convex capitals.   There can be no doubt that the convex form proclaims better than the concave the functions of a capital; namely, to support the

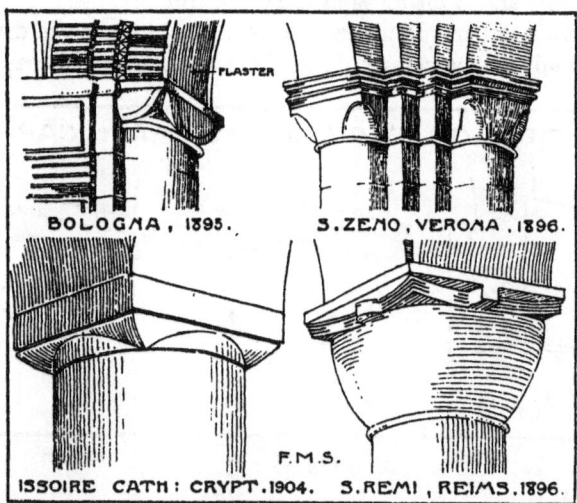

Fig. 21.

arch and transmit its thrusts to the column below. It is no wonder, therefore, that it was the favourite with Romanesque builders, whose chief aim was to find the most suitable form for every part, and then to make it. The convex capital appertains to all countries, but each has several varieties. In Normandy, England, and Germany it is generally somewhat clumsy in form—

the term often applied to it being the "cushion" capital; but in Italy and Southern France there are many charming examples of it of greater delicacy. A modification of the English variety consists of a number of cone-like forms divided from one another by sharp little ridges. This recalls strongly the egg-and-dart ornament of Classic work from which it was probably derived. Connecting links between the two occur frequently in Italian carvings of the ninth and tenth centuries in which deliberate attempts have been made to copy this best known of Classic ornaments.

Most of the capitals with a concave curve below the abacus are more or less correct imitations of the Roman Corinthian. The measure of correctness depends on the strength of Classic traditions in the locality. Thus, in Italy and Southern France the Romanesque capitals are distinguishable only from antique ones by a certain coarseness of workmanship; whereas, farther north, the differences are so great that it is sometimes difficult to trace any resemblance. In work in Central France, even as late as the thirteenth century, the capitals are modified Corinthian, but other leaves are carved instead of the acanthus, and the form and mouldings of the abacus are very different from those in Roman examples.[1] *Concave capitals.*

Each shaft of a clustered pier requires its own capital. These capitals are sometimes quite detached from one another; at other times they are joined together. In the latter case there is one capital composed of several members, which correspond with the divisions in the pier below and in the arch above, and the principle of subordination is preserved throughout. When columns and not piers support arches of more than one order, harmonious relation throughout is more difficult. At Tewkesbury and Gloucester none can be said to exist. In the choir columns of Peterboro' Cathedral an attempt has been made, and not unsuccessfully (see Fig. 16). The design, however, illustrates the difficulties, and shows how wise the mediæval men were in employing, as a rule, the clustered pier with the subordinated arch. *Subordination in capitals.*

The plan of the abacus, or upper member of a capital, changed considerably during mediæval times, and nowhere were the changes so numerous or are so clearly defined as in England. The abacus of a Romanesque capital in all countries is square in plan, because *Plan of abacus.*

---

[1] For further particulars of carved capitals, both Romanesque and Gothic, see "Carving," pp. 127-31.

the orders of the arch above are rectangular. In most continental work the square abacus continued general for many years after Gothic architecture was fully developed, the only change being that the corners were sometimes champhered off. In the typical French column surrounded by four attached shafts, the capital, in most cases, is considerably deeper round the column than round the shafts, as in the choir of Tours Cathedral. In England, when the mouldings of arches changed their character towards the end of the twelfth century, and became a series of bold rounds and deep hollows contained within a segment of a circle, the abacus and the mouldings below it changed also, and the whole became circular in form. Capitals circular in plan are not uncommon in Northern France, especially in Normandy, but they are not so characteristic a feature of French Gothic as they are of thirteenth-century English. It is a question if the change was really an advantage. Columns and arches are brought no doubt into more absolute harmony; the different parts of a church blend together more thoroughly; but it is doubtful if this completeness and harmony are sufficient compensation for the loss of the greater boldness and virility of earlier work. In English thirteenth-century architecture there are no sharp angles anywhere inside a church, and no strong contrasts. Column, shaft, arch mouldings, and capital, all are rounded, and the capital no longer breaks the vertical lines of pier and groining shaft as it did before. Moreover, the lower part of the capital loses its convex outline and becomes concave in all cases; its apparent strength and value of a support being thus considerably impaired.

FIG. 22.

Capitals, 1150–1500.

From 1150 onwards, the concave, or "bell"-shaped capital remained the characteristic form everywhere except in Italy and

Spain.[1] In France the builders wisely retained the proportions of the earlier capitals—with slight reduction—until the fifteenth century. Between early thirteenth and late fourteenth-century French capitals there is no great difference. The abacus in the latter is sometimes octagonal in plan, and the mouldings thereof slightly different from earlier ones; the carving round the bell is stiffer and less bold, but otherwise there is little change. In England, on the other hand, the progression—if progression it

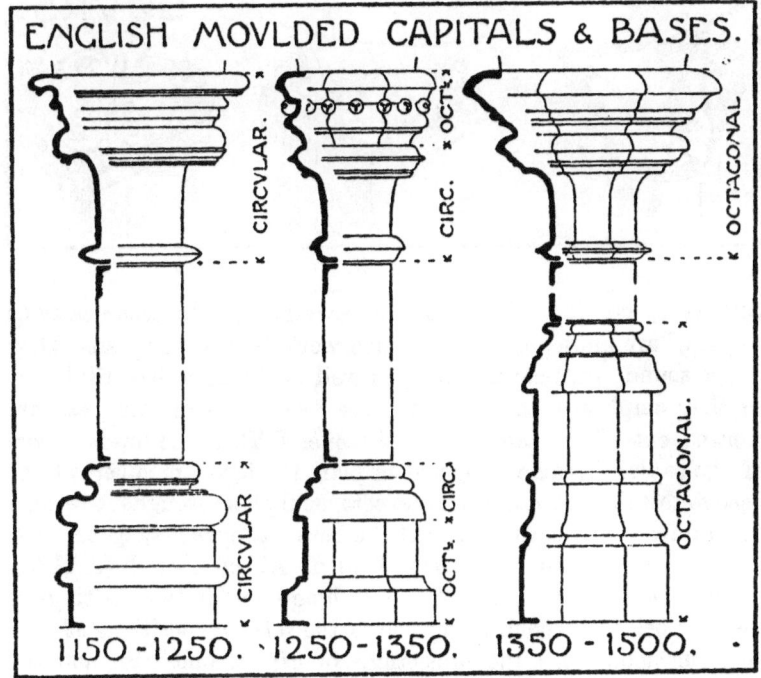

FIG. 23.

can be called, because it is very doubtful if the changes made were improvements—was continuous. About the middle of the thirteenth century the top member became octagonal, the lower members and bell remaining circular. A hundred years later all parts, even the bell itself, were made octagonal; the slight angularity which resulted being more in keeping with the sharp arrises of the arch mouldings. As time went on, capitals became

[1] These two countries never thoroughly assimilated Gothic methods, and never entirely threw over Classic ones, so it is no wonder that the developments elsewhere affected them but little.

40   A HISTORY OF ARCHITECTURAL DEVELOPMENT.

smaller and smaller, until, in the fifteenth century, they lost all importance, and were often omitted altogether.

Bases.   Bases to columns and shafts followed in all respects the same evolution as capitals. Romanesque bases are either copied exactly from classic ones, or else are modified versions of them. The upper moulded members are circular in plan and they rest on a square die, the two parts of the base being often connected at the

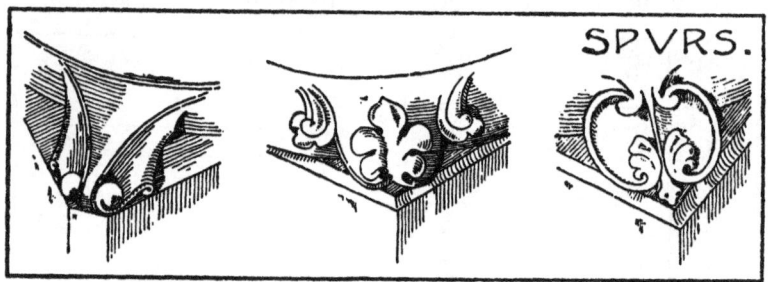

FIG. 24.

corners by carving. These bits of carving, known technically as "spurs," are more general in French work than in English. They are a sound, practical addition, as well as being a beautiful one, as they emphasize the fact that the two parts of the base are worked out of the same piece of stone. When the top members of the capital became octagonal in plan, the lower members of the base followed suit; and when the octagonal plan throughout became general for capitals, the whole of the base was made octagonal also.

Much Wenlock.   Fig. 25 is one bay of Much Wenlock Abbey Church (c. 1180), in which the three orders of the arch agree with the shaftings of the pier below. The drawing shows the relative positions of arch and pier mouldings, the projections of capital and base, and the corbel-like character of the capital.

Doorways.   There is no need to trace the development in design in doorways and other minor arched openings, because this followed on similar lines to that described above for main arches and piers. Arches of doorways are semicircular or pointed, sharp or flat; shafts are attached or detached; mouldings are large or small, numerous or few, according to the period. The capitals and bases of shafts in the jambs of openings are reproductions in miniature of the larger capitals and bases of the interior. The same development proceeded simultaneously throughout, and this can be traced as easily in the smallest fitting as in the most important structural feature (Fig. 26).

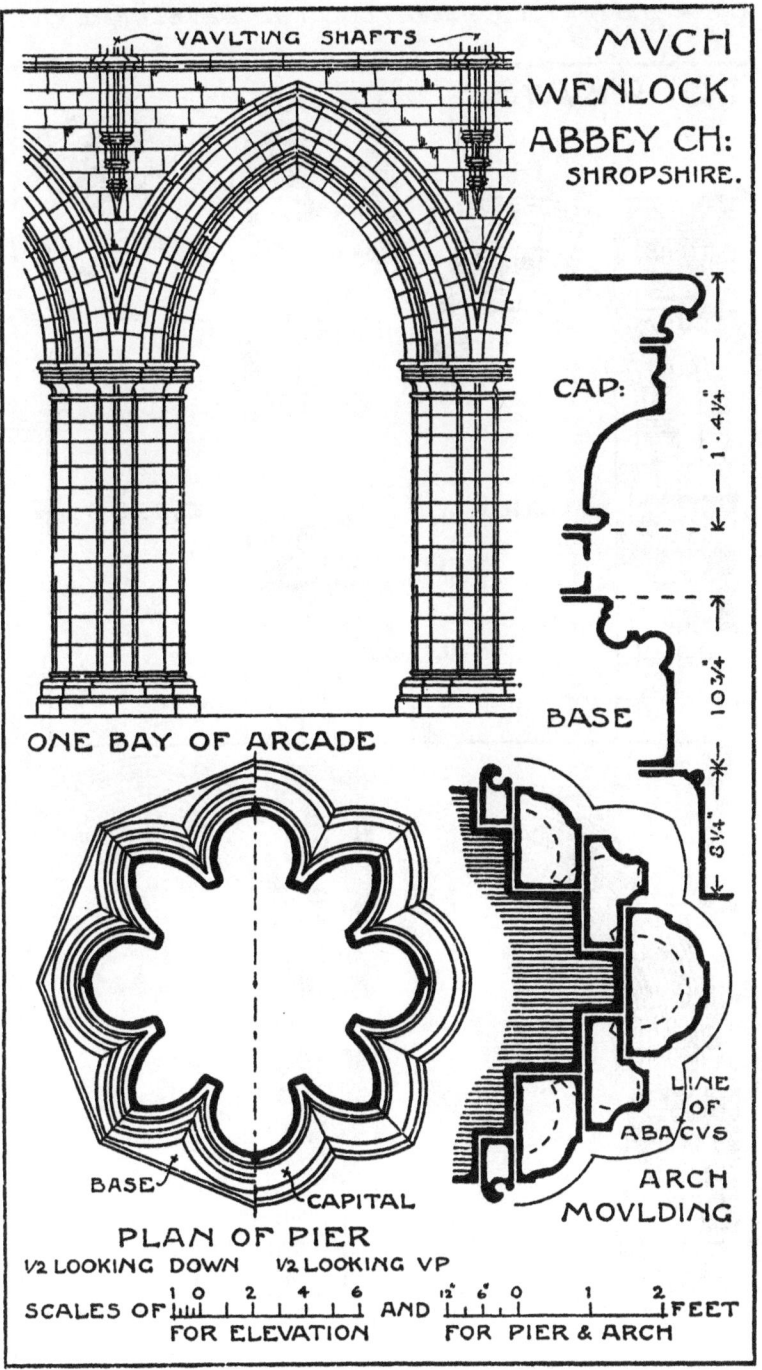

Fig. 25 (G. Langshaw).

42 A HISTORY OF ARCHITECTURAL DEVELOPMENT.

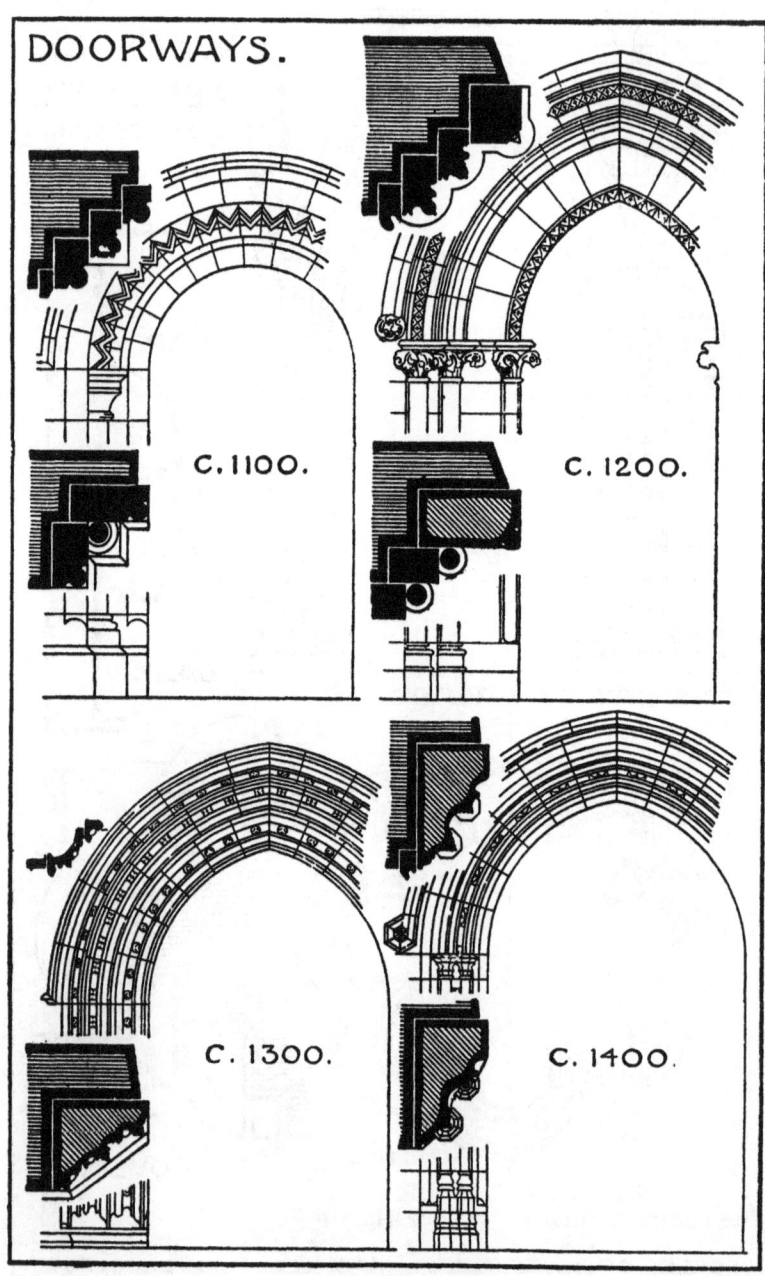

Fig. 26.

CHAPTER IV.

OUTSIDE OF CHURCHES, WALLS, BUTTRESSES, PLINTHS, ETC.

STONE was the favourite material of the mediæval builders, although marble, brick, and, in certain parts of England, flint were all used for walling. In Northern Italy a very fine effect is often produced by courses of marble, alternating with four or five courses of brick which together are about equal in height to one course of marble. In Central and Southern Italy walls are often faced entirely with marble, which in some cases is merely an applied veneer, but in others is structural. In Southern France there are many fine churches of the eleventh and later centuries built entirely of brick; and brick was the material generally employed throughout the Middle Ages in Northern Germany, Holland, and Belgium, owing to the scarcity of stone. In England, the art of brick-making, which had flourished during the Roman occupation, had died out, and was not reintroduced until the fourteenth century. Most of our brick churches are a century or two later, and they are chiefly in the Eastern Counties, Norfolk, Suffolk, and Essex, where a close intercourse with the Low Countries was maintained.[1] Churches with walls built and faced with flint, are most common in Sussex; two excellent examples being at Old and New Shoreham. Flint was also largely used in Norfolk and Suffolk, sometimes in its natural rounded form, and sometimes, especially in the fifteenth century, split smooth, and squared. In the latter case it is generally framed in by stone, and is merely a panel, as in the Chapel of Houghton le Dale, Norfolk. *Wall materials.*

In the eleventh century the craft of the mason was more advanced in some countries than in others. Italy naturally came first, as it had behind it centuries of building tradition. England was perhaps the country most behindhand of any, although in *Stone walls.*

---

[1] The tower and other eleventh-century parts of S. Albans Cathedral are built chiefly of old Roman brick taken from the ruins of Verulam close by.

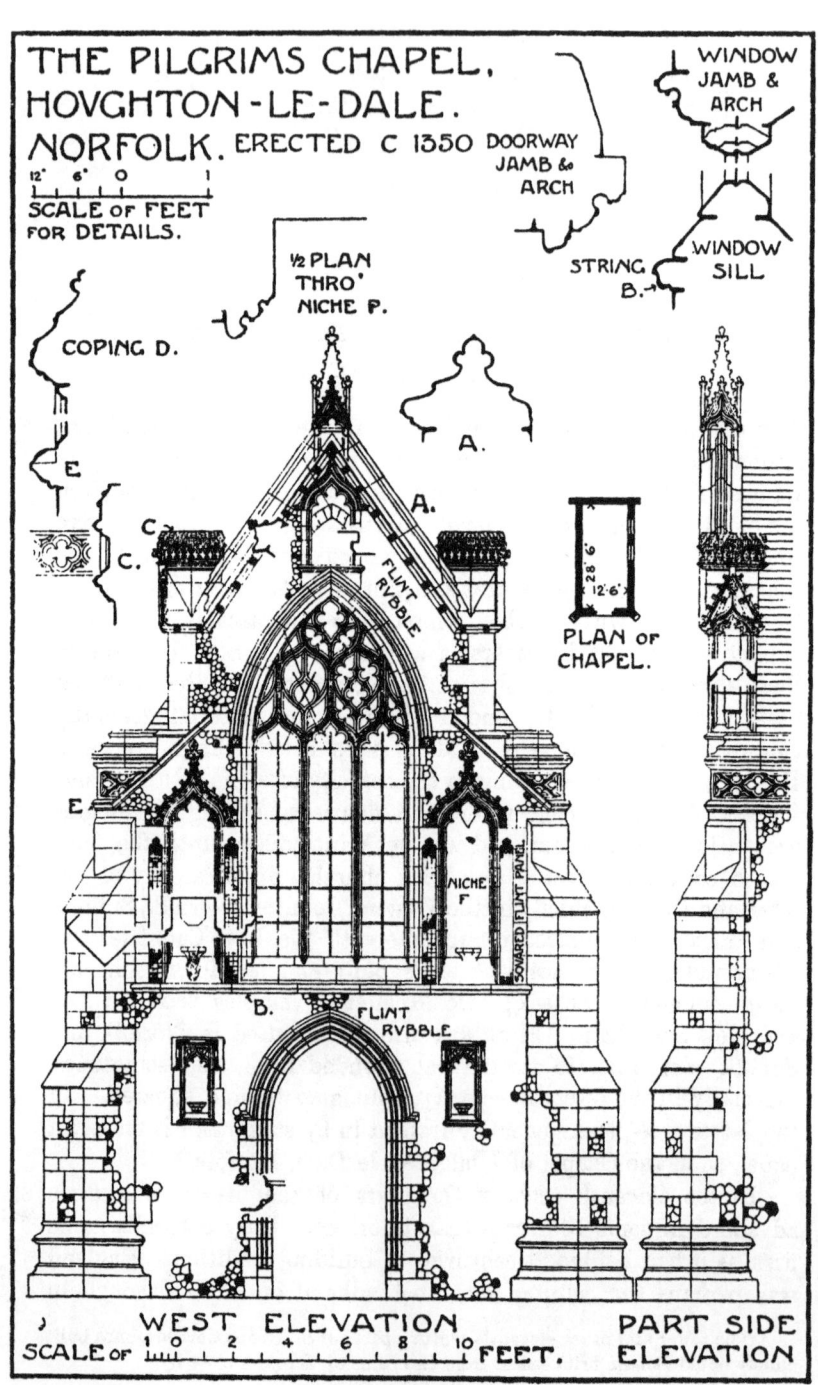

Fig. 27 (Pugin).

some of the pre-Norman work there is a finished execution and a delicacy of detail which were not equalled for nearly fifty years after the Norman Conquest. In the little Odda's Chapel, near Deerhurst Church, Gloucestershire, built in 1056, the few mouldings that remain have much more refinement than any work immediately following can show.

Many of the stone walls in England of the second half of the eleventh century were built of rubble entirely; the quoins, buttresses, and jambs and arches of doors and windows alone being of ashlar. To this their excessive thickness is due. The outside and inside faces were plastered and generally painted. Restorers have swept away the plaster from the outside—and curiously enough, often from the inside as well, leaving rough, uncoursed stonework that was never intended to show—and it is now difficult to find an English church stuccoed as it was when it was first built.[1] Although the contrast between a stuccoed wall and its stone dressings is very effective, an objection to the outer skin is that, although a preservative at first, it soon decays; and when that happens, the result is patchy restorations or damp walls. This led to the gradual disuse of random rubble, which required outside cementing, and the substitution of rubble in regular courses for buildings in which ashlar facing throughout was not obtainable, or would have been too expensive. *Walling in England.*

Many large churches, however, were faced with ashlar, both inside and out, the core alone being of rubble, but the workmanship was rough, and the mortar joints wide, until the beginning of the twelfth century. The old writer, William of Malmesbury, describing the work executed between 1115 and 1139, says, "the courses of stone being so correctly laid, that the joint deceives the eye, and leads it to imagine that the whole wall is composed of a single block."[2] A great improvement was evidently taking place in the mason's craft, and from that time onwards the walls, like the piers, gradually diminished in thickness, until, in the fifteenth century, the limit was reached. But although the walls of the latter period are thin, their strength is as great as or greater than that of the thicker, earlier work, because they are practically of ashlar throughout, the stones being worked true and square, and *Ashlar walling.*

---

[1] The church at Cefalû, in Sicily, however, built (c. 1120) by Normans (see Fig. 130), has still its stucco outside, and may be taken as a guide to what our churches were like.

[2] Parker's "Glossary of Architecture" (vol. i. p. 132).

properly bonded with one another. Moreover, additional strength is given to them by buttresses of considerable projection.

Buttresses. There is a marked difference between the Northern method of buttressing and the Southern. The Italians never took kindly to the buttress as an architectural feature. They frequently dispensed with it altogether when their churches were not vaulted, and even when obliged to use it by structural necessities, they followed, as often as not, the old Roman device, and placed it inside. In Southern France the feeling regarding buttresses was the same. It occasioned the aisleless plan of church with the necessary abutments inside, which is there so general (see Chap. XVII., p. 286). The functions of buttresses are to strengthen walls and counteract the thrusts of arches. So long as they do these satisfactorily it is immaterial, so far as mere stability is concerned, whether they are placed outside or inside a building. But the builders of England and Northern France were quick to perceive the artistic advantages of the former method. In the first place, outside buttresses give scale, and also divide the wall into bays corresponding with the divisions of the interior. Secondly, they form strong vertical lines, leading the eye upwards, and thus help to convey that impression of height which was one of the chief aims of the church-builders of the North. Lastly, they give the mason his opportunity. No part of a church, throughout the Middle Ages, received more care and thought than these strengthening props, and none can be instanced as more thoroughly characteristic of mediæval art.

1050–1150. There is little difference between buttresses of contemporary date in the different countries which favoured them, and their development proceeded on much the same lines in all. Whatever the walling might be, rubble or squared stone, they were always faced with, or built entirely of, ashlar. The typical Romanesque buttress is of great width, and has very slight projection. It runs, as a rule, from plinth to parapet without a break, and stops flush with the face of the latter. It is often absolutely plain, although sometimes an attached shaft is worked on each angle. When there is no parapet, the buttress finishes on top with a plain slope or set-off (Fig. 29).

1150–1250. With the general adoption of vaulting for naves as well as aisles, coinciding as it did with the thinning of walls and piers, came the necessity for stronger and more pronounced buttresses. The change from the wide, shallow, Romanesque buttress to the narrow but deeply projecting buttress of later work is a great one. The statical fault of the early form was that there was not sufficient projection at the base. This fault the later men remedied. The thrust exercised by an arch is represented by a line known as "the curve of pressures," which varies according to the shape and span of the arch, to the weight above its haunches, which neutralizes, to some extent, its thrust, and to other minor causes. The wall against which it is thrown may be heavy enough to counterbalance it (as A, Fig. 28), in which case buttresses are mere ornaments; on the other hand, additional abutment may be necessary. In the latter case it could be provided by a buttress of a single slope (B)—such as are often built now when appearances are of no account or expense is a consideration—provided it covers entirely the line of thrust. The mediæval builders

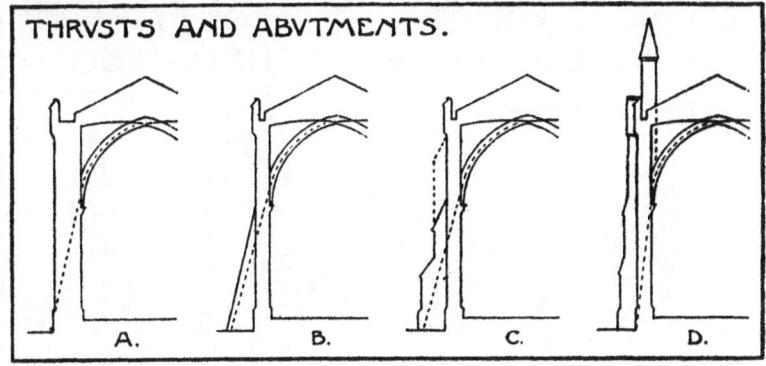

FIG. 28.

fully understood this, and to some extent acted upon it. They allowed for ample projection at the base, and then raised their buttress in stages, recessing each stage as it rose (C). This meant a little extra material, a little extra labour, especially when the buttress was carried above the haunch of the arch, as shown by dotted lines (C). But the material was not altogether wasted, as the additional weight at the top changed somewhat the direction of the thrust, and therefore permitted of less projection at the base (D). Another advantage is that the upper part of the wall is strengthened, which is not the case when the buttress is kept low.[1]

[1] In some places, especially in the southern half of France, many buttresses have the same projection, and that a considerable one, from bottom to top, as in the church of Villefranche-de-Rouergue. The effect is excellent.

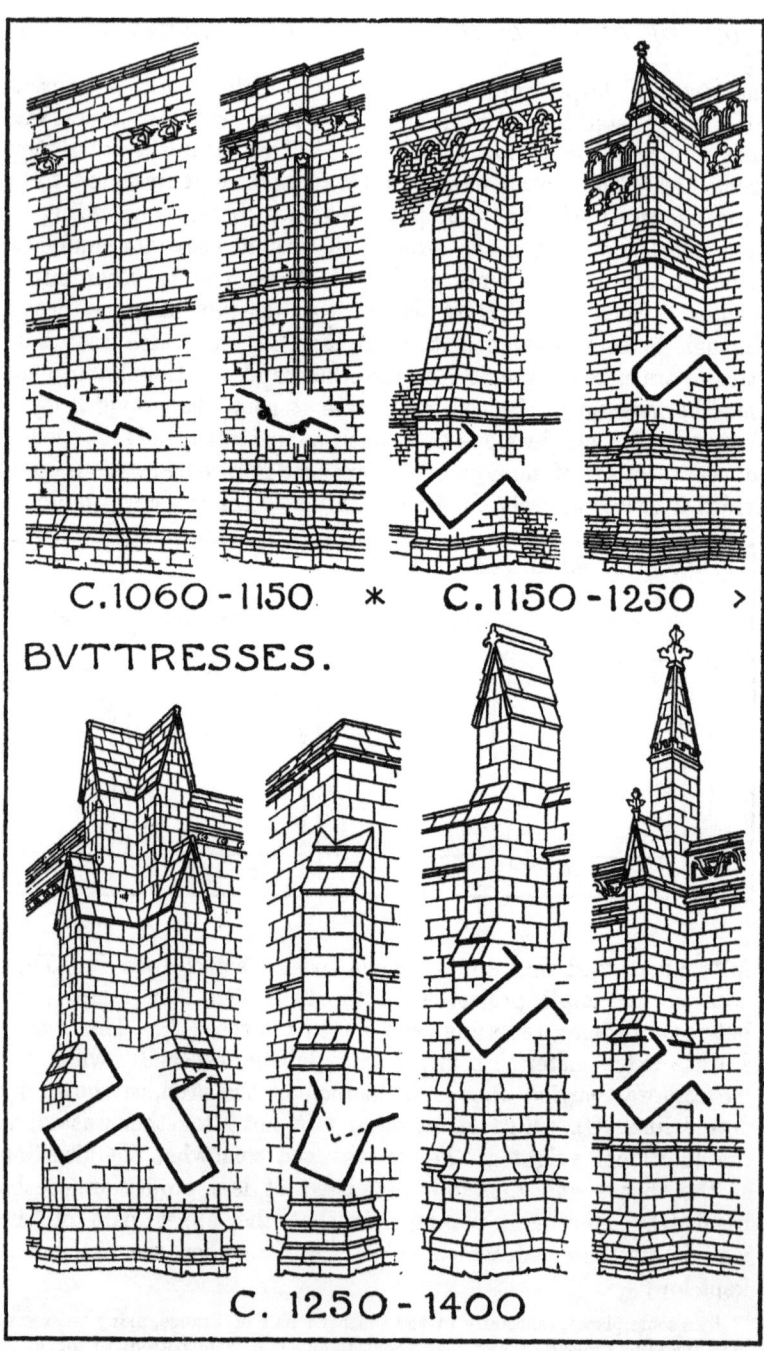

Fig. 29

OUTSIDE OF CHURCHES, WALLS, BUTTRESSES, ETC. 49

When a buttress is in different stages, these are separated from one another either by sloping weatherings, or set-offs, or else by steep-pitched gables which die against the face of the stage above. There is no rule to regulate the slope of the set-off. This differs considerably in different examples. It might have been thought that the top slopes would be steeper than the lower ones, because, being more above the eye, they would become more foreshortened. They are made so occasionally, but by no means universally. In some buttresses the top slopes are the flattest. At the top the buttress finishes much the same way as each stage finishes. When it is crowned by a gable, this may be below the parapet, or level with the top of it, or be carried considerably above it. The advantage of the last arrangement is that a considerable mass of masonry is poised above the haunches of the arch and vault (although not necessarily immediately over them), and its weight, exercising a vertical pressure, helps considerably to neutralize the side thrusts (see Fig. 28 and Fig. 29). _{Stages of a buttress.}

This is the reason for the pinnacles which play so important a part in Gothic architecture. They are not merely ornaments; they are, in some cases, absolute necessities, and are standing proof of how the mediæval architect converted a structural requirement into an ornamental feature. It is true that they are sometimes introduced in fifteenth-century work when the need for them does not exist (for instance, in churches with flat timber roofs which exercise little or no lateral thrust); also that they are frequently omitted in twelfth-century buildings. But in the latter case this happened either before their advantages were properly appreciated, or else when the mass of the buttress was so great as to render them unnecessary. [Pinnacles.]

Thirteenth-century buttresses often have shafts at the angles, which are detached like the shafts round columns of the same period. Sometimes the corners are widely champhered, so much so that the front becomes semi-octagonal. In many churches also—Salisbury Cathedral is one—the stages of the buttresses diminish in width as well as in projection, in which case weatherings occur on all sides. [Treatment of angles.]

In the middle of the thirteenth century the custom was introduced of making one buttress do the work of two at an outside corner (Fig. 29). This was placed diagonally. One buttress was really sufficient, as, although additional strength at a corner is always advisable, the only thrust worth considering likely to [Corner buttresses.]

VOL. II.   E

50   A HISTORY OF ARCHITECTURAL DEVELOPMENT.

come at this point (openings are generally too far away from corners for their arched heads to need other abutment than the wall) would be from the diagonal rib of a vault, and that is best counteracted by a buttress on the line of its thrust. Diagonal buttresses, however, never became universal; and two buttresses, at right angles to the wall and to each other, were used as often as a single one up to the very last.

Niches. Niches for figures are sometimes worked on the face of buttresses in Romanesque churches, especially in Southern France; but they were comparatively rare until the great revival of figure sculpture about the middle of the twelfth century. Then the sculptor demanded place for his figures; and, not content with the opportunities afforded him in the jambs and heads of doorways, claimed the buttresses also. Beautiful examples of niches, with cusped canopies over them which afford protection to the figures below, occur in the east end of Ely Cathedral, and on the west front of Wells. In Wells Cathedral the niches are on all sides of the buttresses, and, with their figures, produce a richness of effect unsurpassed elsewhere.

Buttresses, 1250–1500. The differences between thirteenth and fourteenth-century buttresses are slight, being merely in detail. About the middle of the latter century, the custom became general of covering both walls and buttresses with panelling. The result is that a buttress no longer stands out so boldly as before, as its outline is lost to a great extent in the general scheme of rich elaboration. Partly perhaps as a corrective to this, its upper stages are often different in plan from the lower ones. They are octagonal, hexagonal, or else a square placed lozenge-wise; the different faces being crowned by canopies, above which rises a crocketted pinnacle common to all. In the fifteenth century, especially at the angles of towers, buttresses are often octagonal in plan from top to bottom; and when all their sides are panelled, as well as the wall, they may be said to be almost non-existent, so far as appearance goes.

Batter. The face of a buttress often slopes inwards a trifle (2 inches or so in about 10 feet). This inward inclination, or "batter," helps the set-offs, and assists in producing a pyramidal, and therefore strong, effect. This refinement was undoubtedly practised by the Romanesque builders in Italy, although it is doubtful if it were employed in more northern countries until the Gothic style was fairly developed. Like the entasis of Greek columns, it is not perceptible to the eye in most cases, although in others it is more marked. It is not confined to buttresses, but occurs also in towers. In the tower of Stanton Harcourt Church, Oxfordshire, it is so unmistakable as to be almost disagreeable. Diminution in width is difficult to arrange satisfactorily in octagonal buttresses (as each set-back widens the wall space between them), and a batter is almost an impossibility. The result is that towers so buttressed often present a top-heavy appearance.[1]

Flying buttresses made their appearance above the aisle roofs which at first concealed them about the middle of the twelfth century, and rapidly became a marked feature of the outside; especially in France, where the great height of the large churches necessitated many buttresses one above another.[2] They give an appearance of vigour and active force to a building which nothing else can afford, but when employed extravagantly, as was frequently done abroad, they create a feeling of unrest which is far from satisfactory. <small>Flying buttresses.</small>

In most Romanesque churches in Italy there are not even the wide, shallow buttresses common to England and Normandy, but the walls, especially in Lombardic work, are divided into panels by narrow, vertical pilaster-strips, and by horizontal string-courses. These have no structural value unless the walling is of either rubble or brick; then they act as bonding courses, and strengthen it (see Fig. 113). Pilasters and string-courses are the descendants of the Roman columns and entablatures, the connecting links being easily traceable in late Roman buildings, such as the theatre at Orange, France, and in some early churches in Italy. <small>Pilaster buttresses.</small>

Until the fourteenth century, arcading was the favourite way of decorating the walls of mediæval churches, outside as well as inside. It was a Classic tradition which filtered through early Christian work from the buildings of Ancient Rome (see S. Apollinare-in-Classe, Vol. I., Fig. 117), and it did not disappear until large traceried windows swallowed up all the wall space and left no surface to decorate. <small>Wall arcading.</small>

In general design and in detail, arcading followed the same evolution as the structural parts of buildings; the arches being semicircular, pointed, foliated, or ogeed, and the shafts being

---

[1] This defect is particularly marked in the Victoria Tower of the Houses of Parliament when the whole tower is visible.

[2] For their development and functions, see Chap. VI., on ribbed vaults, pp. 95-100.

attached or detached, moulded or plain, according to the period when the church was built. Throughout the eleventh and twelfth centuries intersecting arches are common (see Fig. 4). In the North these are always semicircular, but in Southern Italy and Sicily, as at Amalfi, Monreale, near Palermo, etc., they are pointed. Between 1280 and 1350 walls are seldom arcaded, for the reason just given; but after the latter date the desire for over-elaboration which possessed the people, produced the flat panelling, already referred to, which covers walls, buttresses, piers, and even arches.

Horizontal lines.

Plinths, string-courses, oversailing-courses, and parapets form the horizontal lines outside. The main horizontal line of a church, of course, is its roof (except in fifteenth-century examples, when it is often hidden behind the top parapet); and the great, quiet mass of the high-pitched roof in many a Gothic cathedral and church exercises a steadying influence on, and forms an admirable background to, the silhouettes of pinnacle and flying buttress below. Horizontal lines could not be dispensed with altogether in mediæval work, but in the main they are kept subordinate to vertical ones. They are stronger in French Gothic than in English, especially in the western fronts of the great Cathedrals of Laon, Paris, Reims, etc. (see Figs. 196 and 197).

Plinths.

The mediæval builders showed their wisdom in starting all but their smallest buildings from a moulded plinth. The Greeks felt the need for something below their columns and walls to give their temples the effect of rising from the ground, and not of sinking into it, and devised the stylobate. The Romans raised their columns on bases and pedestals, and their buildings on a high podium. It was, however, left to the mediæval men to develop the moulded plinth, which, in a series of stages, some moulded, some plain, affords a visible footing from which the wall can start.

String-courses.

String-courses in both Romanesque and Gothic are always placed immediately below windows on the outside, and often on the inside as well. In these positions their chief office is to separate the pierced portion of the wall from the unpierced; as their small projection outside affords but little protection to the wall below. Externally they either stop against the buttresses, or else break round them. In Romanesque churches the abacus which marks the springing line of the window arch (it is often the abacus of the capital of the shaft in the jamb) and from which the label of the arch starts, is often continued horizontally as a string; and in early Gothic it is the label itself which is returned at the springing for the same purpose. Later, when windows reached from buttress to buttress, no room was left for a string in this position, and that under the windows is the only one.[1]

In small churches roofs are often carried down to the eaves, and their timbers rest on a projecting course which is moulded according to the fashion of the day, and sometimes carved. In large churches they generally stop behind parapets. Considerable thought was given to the designing of these. The parapet projects in nearly all cases in front of the wall below, and in work of the eleventh and twelfth centuries is generally carried on corbels, which, more often than not, are carved as grotesque heads. These corbels frequently support small trefoil or pointed arches (see Fig. 29), which form a rich band under the plain masonry of the parapet above. About the middle of the thirteenth century, the corbel course and arches were discarded in favour of an "oversailing" course, which, besides being moulded, was frequently carved. The large square flowers in fifteenth-century examples are particularly striking. The parapet at first was quite plain, and so it continued until about the end of the twelfth century. Then panels were either sunk on its face or pierced through it. The designs of these changed from time to time. Stiff and geometric to begin with, the lines later became flowing, as in Malmesbury Abbey Church, and then stiffened again towards the fifteenth century, following much the same development as the traceried heads of windows (see Chap. V., pp. 60-64). In the fifteenth-century, battlementing, which had been introduced some time previously, became general, and was either plain, or panelled, or pierced.

Parapets, etc.

The reason for the projection of the parapet was to provide more space behind for the gutter and flashings, and also to act, to some extent, as a protection to the wall below. The parapet certainly affords a more dignified finish than the eaves-gutter, and therefore possesses æsthetic advantages as well as mere practical ones. But it has its disadvantages. Defective leadwork in gutterings has caused the timbers to rot in many a roof, and has let in damp to many a wall.

[1] The mouldings of strings are much the same as labels over openings (see Fig. 14).

54 A HISTORY OF ARCHITECTURAL DEVELOPMENT.

Gurgoyles.

The mediæval builders employed long stone spouts for carrying off the rain from the gutters, and many of these gurgoyles are carved most grotesquely. They are effective as ornaments; but are otherwise objectionable, inasmuch as they discharge large volumes of water on to the ground at given points. They have in consequence been superseded in modern churches by the often unsightly but more practical rain-water pipe. The gurgoyles are not always in stone; some of the most effective are in lead. The latter are rare on churches, and are generally found on mediæval, or early Renaissance, domestic buildings.

FIG. 30.

CHAPTER V.

DEVELOPMENT OF WINDOWS.

WINDOWS in Byzantine and early basilican churches are, as a rule, numerous and large; but in Romanesque churches, especially in the early ones, they are few in number and generally small.[1] The change occurred in Italy in the ninth century, when the Eastern custom, until then prevalent there, of filling windows with pierced slabs was discontinued (see p. 181, and Vol. I. p. 222). These slabs obstructed a considerable amount of light; when they were done away with one reason for large openings disappeared. Some writers ascribe the change to the temper of the people, who, about that time, discovered that a dim religious light was necessary for their devotions. But apart from this are the practical considerations that much light was no longer needed—as the old methods of decorating walls with mosaics had fallen into general disuse, and fresco painting had hardly taken its place—and that the fewer and smaller the windows the better, since the builders required far stronger abutments for their vaults than had been imperative in the days of timber roofs. Soon it was found that thrusts of vaults could be transmitted by flying buttresses, that walls could be reduced in bulk, and windows, in consequence, became larger than ever.

Romanesque windows are generally placed singly, but in domestic work, in church belfries, and in the east ends of churches especially, two or more are often grouped together. When in groups the lights are divided from one another by either walling or shafts. In the former case they appear from the outside as though they were separate windows, connected only by a hood moulding, and not always by that; whereas from the inside, {Windows, 1000–1150.}

---

[1] Some Romanesque windows in large churches are of considerable size, especially in England and Northern France, where more light was required than in the south. In many English cathedrals such windows have, at a subsequent period, been divided in two by a central mullion, and tracery has been inserted in their heads, as at Peterboro' Cathedral.

owing to the wide splaying of the jambs, they unite to form one window. The outer jambs are sometimes plain or merely champhered, but more often they are enriched by shafts, from which spring arches concentric with the window-head. In walls arcaded on the outside, the practice was general to pierce some of the bays of the arcading for light, and this continued the custom so long as walls remained arcaded.

The division by shafts is the more usual one in Italy, Germany, Switzerland, and Southern France. The shafts are often placed in the centre of the wall, in which case their capitals have con-

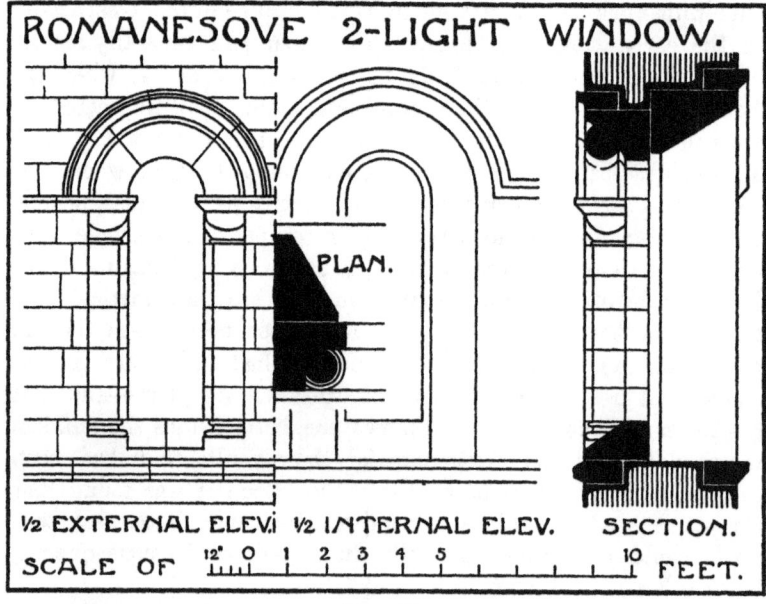

Fig. 81.

siderable projection in front and at the back, but very little at the sides, like many Byzantine ones of earlier and contemporary date (see Vol. I., Figs. 145 and 149). In English work before 1066 the central position for the shaft was generally adopted; but after that date (in Northern France as well as in England) the shafts are nearer the outside face of the wall, so as to leave more room for splayed jambs on the inside.

Windows, 1150–1250.
In Romanesque windows the lights are seldom more than thrice their width in height, and sometimes are considerably less.[1]

[1] In S. Mary Buildwas Abbey Church, the clerestory windows are about twice their width high, although the east windows are nine times.

DEVELOPMENT OF WINDOWS.

When the pointed arch supplanted the semicircular, the lights elongated considerably, and to some extent narrowed also. In Kirkstall Abbey Church west front (c. 1160), in Tynemouth and Hexham Priory Churches, and elsewhere, are early instances of

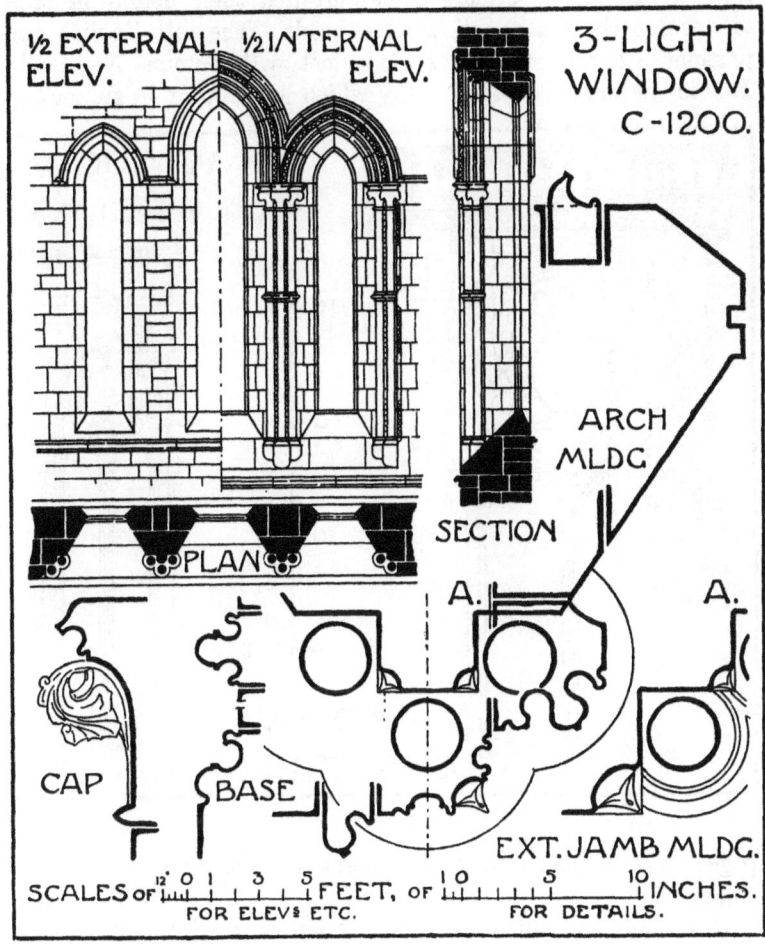

Fig. 32.

the tall proportions which afterwards became so characteristic a feature of English work. In Hexham Priory Church the lights of the transept are 2·6 feet wide by 24·6 feet high; in Brinkburn Priory Church, Northumberland, the lights of the west window are each 1 foot 10 inches wide by 19 feet high; in the

58 A HISTORY OF ARCHITECTURAL DEVELOPMENT.

west end of Romsey Abbey Church they are 2 feet wide and as much as 30 feet high from sill to apex. The famous "five sisters" window in the north transept of York Cathedral has the proportion of about 9 to 1. In France much wider lights are the rule, and the builders early curtailed their height in order to develop the tracery of window-heads. The tall English proportions are consequently seldom met with outside Normandy. This is one instance out of many which will appear in subsequent

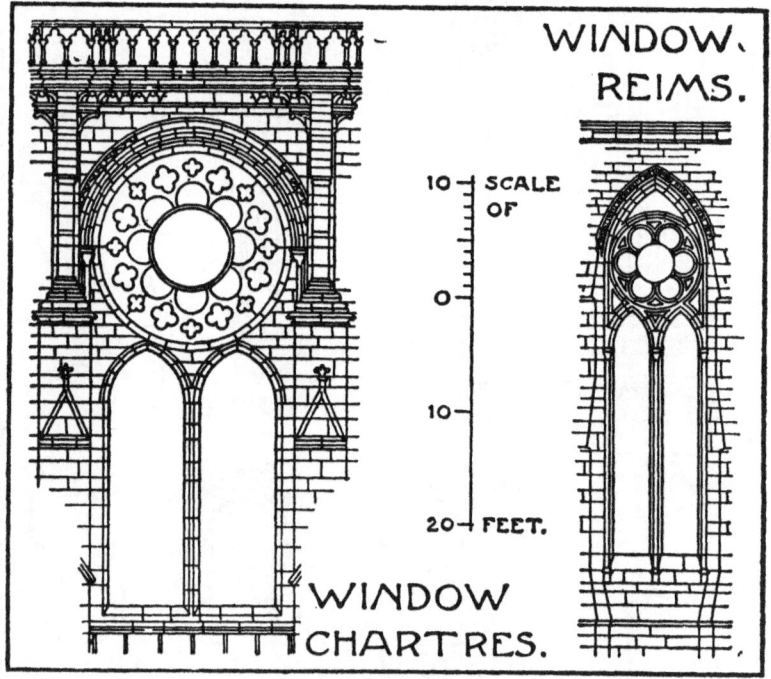

Fig. 33.

pages of differences in development on the two sides of the Channel.[1]

The lights of thirteenth-century lancet windows are grouped

---

[1] In Soissons Cathedral (c. 1210) the single lancet lights of the aisles are each 7 feet wide, and each bay of the clerestory has a pair of lancets, only a little narrower than the aisle windows, with a foliated circle pierced through the tympanum above. The great width of the lights in early French Gothic and their comparative stumpiness are especially marked in the stately desecrated Church of S. Frambourg, Senlis (c. 1177), one of the finest of the smaller examples of early Gothic in France. The church is aisleless, about 30 feet wide by 130 feet long, exclusive of the semicircular apse, and is vaulted throughout.

DEVELOPMENT OF WINDOWS. 59

in much the same way as Romanesque ones, although a greater number than before are in many instances united under one hood moulding, five and even seven being not unusual. In the jambs outside and on the splays inside are often many detached shafts, and there is an increased richness in mouldings and ornament. Sometimes the lights are so close together that they are separated merely by wide mullions of ashlar, as in Oakham Church, Surrey (c. 1230), and literally form one window. Mullions, however, are more distinctive of windows of later date with traceried heads.

As stated above, the Frenchmen were engaged in the development of tracery whilst we were mainly concerned with perfecting the proportions of the long lancet light. Most of the early French

Plate and bar tracery.

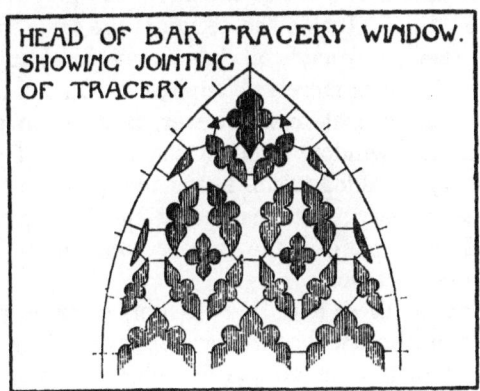

Fig. 34.

tracery is of the kind known as "plate," which is composed of circles, quatrefoils, and other geometrical figures, pierced through slabs of stone, which fill the window-heads. In Chartres Cathedral, N. D., Paris, and in other large French churches of the end of the twelfth century, there are many such windows. "Bar" tracery, as it is sometimes called, in which the design is worked in different pieces of stone cut to the required shape and often dowelled together, was a somewhat later creation. The latter does not seem to have been employed in England before 1250—the date of the Chapter House of Westminster Abbey—or at all events not to any extent; but in France it was general for some years before. The windows of La Sainte Chapelle, Paris, finished 1248, have bar-tracery heads throughout.

60 A HISTORY OF ARCHITECTURAL DEVELOPMENT.

Origin of tracery.

But it does not follow necessarily that tracery was introduced into England from abroad. The germ of it had existed in this country for nearly a couple of centuries before the French first brought it to a logical conclusion. In Romanesque work it is no uncommon occurrence to find two lights side by side and over them a circular window; and when the pointed arch appeared the arrrangement became more and more common, and the lights and the circle were brought closer together. The next step was to enclose them under one hood moulding. When this is done, especially when both lights and circle over are foliated or cusped, the result is a plate-tracery window. An interesting attempt at tracery occurs in the north aisle of Stone Church, Kent (c. 1240). Here there are three windows side by side. Outside they are all alike, each consisting of two lights with a quatrefoil above enclosed by a hood moulding. Inside the design is the same in two, except that in one case the quatrefoil has many mouldings round it, whilst in the other it is merely champhered. On the inside face of the third, or easternmost one, however, is an open screen, quite detached from the window itself, which consists of a cylindrical shaft with richly moulded trefoil heads and quatrefoil over. It is partially plate tracery; but the mouldings intersect, and if the spandrils had been pierced, the tracery could have been formed entirely by bars of stone.

Early circular windows.

In addition to these tentative attempts at tracery in windows with two or more lights, the circular windows, which occur singly in so many English Romanesque churches, are often filled with shafts which radiate from the centre and divide each window into many lights, the heads of which are foliated. They are known as wheel windows. In Barfreston and Patrixbourne Churches, both in Kent, are fine early examples, and in the gables of the west front of Peterboro' Cathedral and in the south transept of York Cathedral are others, similar in character, but larger and later in date.

Early French traceried windows.

One characteristic trait of early French traceried windows, which does not occur in English examples, is that the arches of the window-heads, especially those in the clerestories, are much stilted, or, in other words, the tracery comes down far below their springing line. The whole of the window-head proper is filled by a large circle, sometimes cusped, at other times plain, which is the full width of the lights below (see Fig. 33, Reims). Such windows, generally of two lights, occur most frequently round eastern apses,

Fig. 35 (A. H. Kersey).

62   *A HISTORY OF ARCHITECTURAL DEVELOPMENT.*

because the spaces available for windows there are much narrower than in the bays of the choir west of the apse and in the nave.[1]

1250–1350.

With the exception just mentioned, there is little difference between English and French tracery from 1250 to about 1300. The designs always consist of geometrical figures, circles, quatrefoils, trefoils, spherical triangles, etc., a tendency towards an elongation of the figures being noticeable at the end of the thirteenth century. Early in the following century, however, in England the designs lost all stiffness and the tracery lines became flowing. There can be no doubt that whatever credit is due

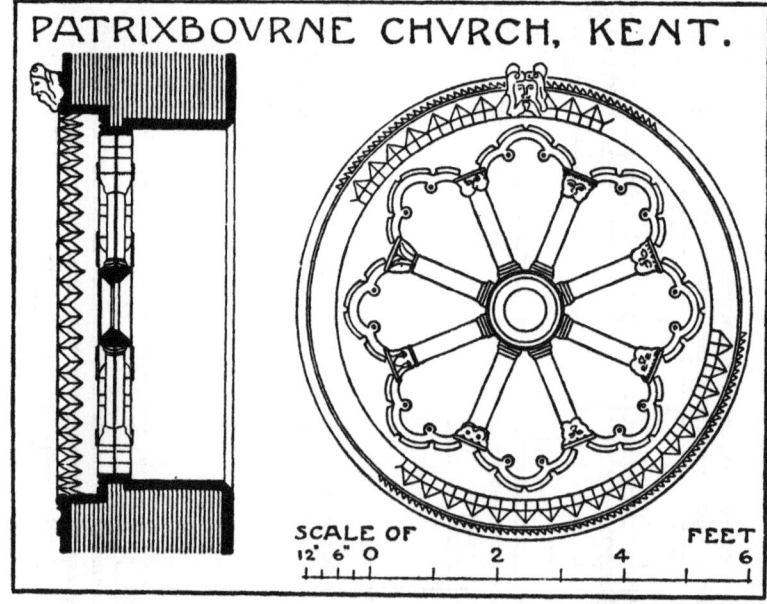

Fig. 36.

for this departure belongs to the English masons. The French examples of curvilinear tracery, as it is sometimes called, are, with very few exceptions, of much later date. Amongst the most beautiful windows in England of this type may be mentioned the east window of Carlisle Cathedral (c. 1330–1380), which still retains a trace of geometric formality, the west window of York Cathedral (c. 1330), and the windows of Boston Church, Lincolnshire, Cottingham, Beverley, Selby, and other large churches in Yorkshire.

[1] Stilted window-heads are not confined to apses alone. In many French churches all the window-heads are stilted.

Fig. 37.

64   A HISTORY OF ARCHITECTURAL DEVELOPMENT.

1350–1500.

Fifty years later England and the Continent definitely parted company. The English straightened the bars of their tracery, until the entire heads of windows became filled with a series of long, straight-sided, pierced panels; whereas the French adopted and carried to excess the flowing lines, producing flame-shaped openings, hence the term "flamboyant" generally applied to French traceried windows of the latter part of the fourteenth and the following century. One instance of flamboyant design crossing the Channel is in Brede Church, near Hastings, where not only the tracery but the mouldings as well are curiously French.

The transition from flowing lines to straight seems to have come suddenly in England, and it coincides with the devastating Black Death of 1348–1350. Other changes in design, from lancet lights

Fig. 38.

to traceried windows, from geometrical forms to curvilinear, came gradually. There are many examples which are neither one thing nor exactly another; but there are few windows in England combining both flowing and vertical lines. The west windows of Monmouth Church and the little chapel of Houghton-le-dale, Norfolk (c. 1350) (see Fig. 27), and the east window of Claypole Church, Lincolnshire, are instances. One reason for the change was that perpendicular tracery requires less stone, less work, and less skill in setting out than either of the earlier forms. Workmen and clients were both in a hurry. They wanted to make up for the loss of time which the Black Death and the general distress which followed had caused, and, besides building quickly, wished to build economically.

Transoms.   In nearly all large fifteenth-century windows the lights are divided horizontally by transoms, of which there are sometimes two or more to each light, as in the west window of Winchester Cathedral, the windows of Bath Abbey Church, etc. Transoms first began to be inserted to any extent about the middle of the previous century, but they are not unknown in earlier work, especially in domestic buildings. The windows of the Banqueting Hall in the Bishop's Palace, Wells (c. 1230), for instance, are divided by them. They were of some advantage to the stained glass designer, inasmuch as each of his figures could be framed in top and bottom, as well as at the sides, and this is sometimes stated as the reason for their introduction. But it is doubtful if his wishes would have had much effect on the mason if the latter had not desired cross-stays to his tall, thin mullions.[1] It may be urged that the increased popularity of transoms was due to a desire to bring the window into unison with the panelled wall; but the converse is more probable. The panelled wall was more likely the result of the panelled window.

Much of the beauty of traceried windows is due to the emphasis given to certain parts of each. Some mullions and tracery bars are wider than others, and have a greater number of mouldings worked on them. The lights and the heads are consequently grouped. There is no hard-and-fast rule as to which mullions shall be emphasized, but in four- and six-light windows the centre one is generally thicker than the others; or in the latter there may be two thick mullions dividing the window into three divisions of two lights each. In a five-light window the two central mullions generally have extra mouldings, and in a seven-light either the central ones or the second from either side.[2] In windows of many lights, mullions of three different sizes are not uncommon, the largest being of three "orders," the next size of two, and the smallest only of one. The same scheme runs through window-heads. The main and secondary divisions are emphasized by similar means, and great delicacy is often given to a design by the slightness of the bars which surround

Subordination of window mouldings.

---

[1] Each light is by no means always filled by one figure. In the great east window of York Cathedral (filled with glass in 1405–1408) there are several figures in each; and in many fifteenth-century windows without transoms, the lights of which are much longer in proportion than in any window with them, the glass stainer has shown how he could employ one figure only, and yet fill the whole space by the aid of elaborate canopy work.

[2] This is not a universal rule. Many windows of several lights have all their mullions the same thickness.

VOL. II. F

66 A HISTORY OF ARCHITECTURAL DEVELOPMENT.

the smaller openings. In most large windows, and in some small ones, the central light (or lights) is wider that the side ones, partly because of the stronger mullions which frame it, and partly because, even when all mullions are of the same thickness, a central light has a tendency to look narrower than the side lights if all are of the same width.[1]

Mullions. There is an enormous difference in proportion and detail between mullions and bars in early and late traceried windows. Early mullions are very wide, but have small projection from the face of the glass; the later ones have greater depth, but are much thinner. There is not really very much difference in superficial area between the two—the early ones are a trifle heavier—and the appearance of strength is much the same, especially when

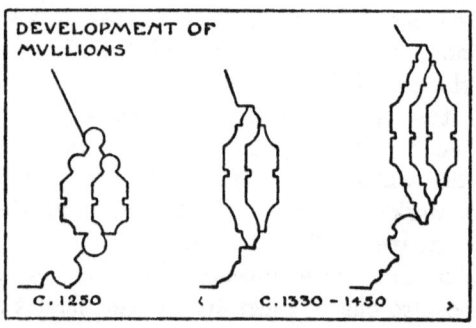

Fig. 39.

the window is viewed sideways. As regards the contours of the mouldings at different periods, when the design is geometrical the principal mouldings of mullions, jambs, and tracery are segments of circles, generally three-quarter rounds, although sometimes the curve is broken by a fillet. When the lines of the tracery are flowing, the mouldings are mainly ogees, and the ogee continued general after the lines straightened. Thus, much in the same way as arch mouldings altered as the arch form changed, so the mouldings of tracery changed to agree with its lines.

Cuspings. In most plate-tracery windows, and in a few early ones of the other class, the cusps spring from the flat soffit alone, not from the splayed or moulded part of the tracery at all. Such cusps are

[1] For the same reason the central openings in a Greek peristyle are often wider than the side ones (see Vol. I. p. 91).

either worked on the solid, or else are in separate pieces of stone which are tenoned into the head of a light or into a circle, or whatever the opening may be. Many of these have dropped out, and have not been reinstated in "restoration." This "soffit," cusping, as it is called, disappeared as bar tracery developed, but it occurs in the heads of the triforium openings of the Angel Choir, Lincoln (c. 1260), and Westminster Abbey; and as late as the fourteenth century in the highly enriched windows of Leominster Church (c. 1310). In most windows from 1250 onwards the cusping either starts from a fillet or else cuts into the moulding below.

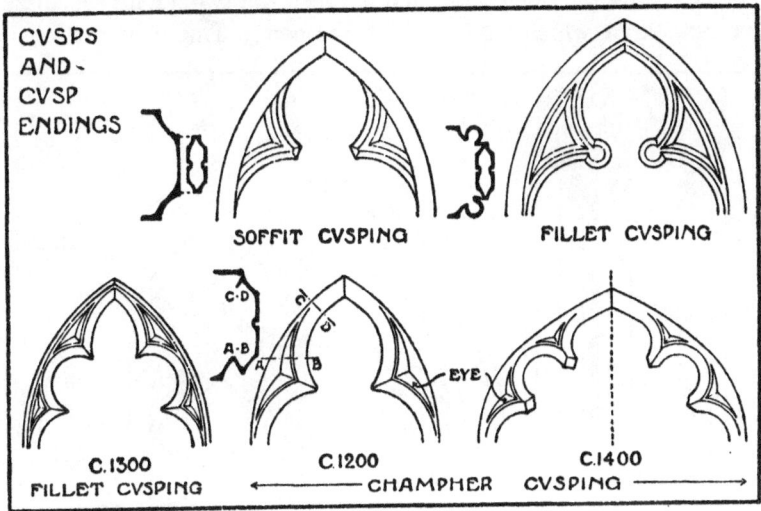

Fig. 40.

The back of the cusp is champhered so as to form an "eye," which is sometimes merely sunk, sometimes pierced and glazed.

The cusp terminations in the different centuries vary considerably. In the thirteenth century they finish square or with a blob; in the fourteenth they come to a sharp point, and in the fifteenth to a broad point. An examination of the windows of the different periods shows how well suited each form is to the shape of the cusped opening in which it occurs.

In the windows of the eleventh, twelfth, and early thirteenth centuries the arch on the inside face of the wall over each light is generally concentric with the window-head, but rises high above it because of the wide splaying of the jambs (see Figs. 31-2). When many lights are grouped together to form one window, *Window arch construction.*

being divided from one another merely by mullions, another treatment becomes necessary. The inside arch is made much flatter than the outside one, and, notwithstanding that it is far wider, it is in consequence very little, if any, higher; sometimes it is actually lower. Late thirteenth, fourteenth, and fifteenth-century window openings have, in most cases, three arches over them, which are struck from different centres. On the outside is the window arch, which includes the jamb mouldings, if there are any, and the tracery, its duty being to carry the outer face of the wall; on the inside is another arch, called the "scoinson," which carries the inner face; and between the two, an intermediate, or rear, arch which comes under the core. This construction is

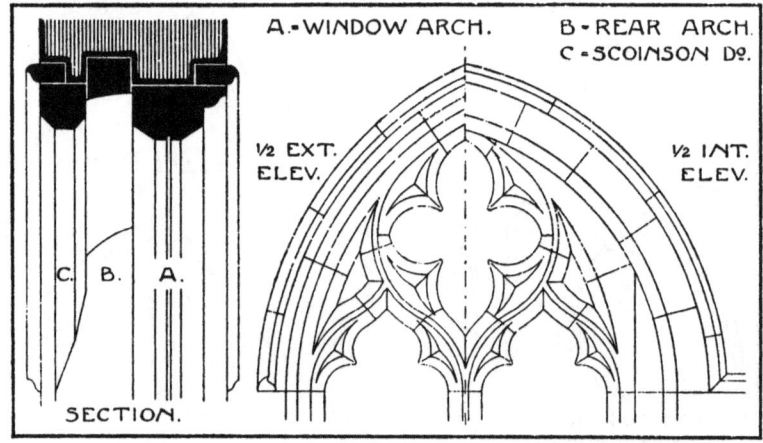

FIG. 41.

another instance of the desire of mediæval builders, mentioned before, to give elasticity to their work, and so, by not connecting all parts together too rigidly, prevent the possibility of cracks if settlements occurred. The lowering of the inner arch was right for another reason. Tops of windows are always above the eye; in most cases considerably above it; and the eye consequently sees under an inner arch. The top of the tracery may be above the apex of this arch and yet the whole of it be visible from below. Besides, two arches of different curvature form pleasant contrasts.

Circular windows.   The early wheel windows, mentioned on a previous page, are the forerunners of the large "rose" windows which form such effective features in the great cathedrals abroad. Mediæval builders in England never took kindly to them. There is a traceried circular window of fair size in the south transept of Lincoln Cathedral, and a somewhat larger one in the Chapel of the Nine Altars at Durham. In the transepts of Westminster Abbey are similar windows, the design of which has been altered more than once. Apart from these there are few of any size in England. On the continent it is different. Hardly an important cathedral is without its circular window, either in the west front or in one or both of the transepts. The design of these varies according to date, and the whole gamut of French tracery can be studied from circular windows alone; from the plate-tracery examples in the west fronts of Laon and Chartres, through the geometric ones of Paris and Reims, down to the ones filled with flowing lines, of which the finest is probably that in the south transept of S. Ouen, Rouen. Even when a French western or transeptal window has vertical lights, an enormous traceried circle often fills not only the head but halfway down the sides as well, as in the south transept of Beauvais Cathedral. This design is the natural development from the earlier windows in which the arch is stilted to allow of a circle the full width of the lights below it, as shown in Fig. 33.

CHAPTER VI.

VAULTING.

Introduction. THE most characteristic trait of mediæval architecture is vaulting, and yet it is by no means universal in either Romanesque or Gothic churches. In Italy, the traditions of the wood-ceiled basilican church account for its absence during the eleventh and twelfth centuries, and even in later ones. Elsewhere in Europe, in England, Normandy, and Germany, it was not so much tradition as the difficulty of vaulting wide spans which caused many of the large churches to have timber roofs over their naves. The aisles could easily be vaulted, and generally were; but the workmen were not always sufficiently skilled at first to attack the more difficult problem of vaulting the naves, choirs, and transepts.

The vault was no invention of the Middle Ages. Of the two forms of vault, the barrel, or cradle, vault and the intersecting vault, the former was well known to the Egyptians and Assyrians, and both were extensively used by the Romans. But although the forms remained much the same, the methods of construction finally adopted by mediæval builders—especially as regards the intersecting vault—are in many respects different from those of earlier work. The steps by which they reached the solution of the difficulties which beset them, and the further modifications which they introduced, form the subject-matter of most of this chapter.

Barrel vaults. Some mediæval barrel vaults, like Roman ones, are solid; and the outer covering, generally tiles, is bedded on top of the vault itself. In the majority of cases, however, they are only a foot or so thick, and are covered by a protecting timber roof, in the same way as intersecting vaults are covered and protected. One practical disadvantage of a barrel vault over an aisled church, is that, being continuous, it presses equally on voids and solids, on arches as well as on piers. In the words of Sir G. G. Scott, it entails "an illogical arrangement of divided substructure and continuous superstructure." This, so far as it affects appearances merely, is partly overcome in many twelfth-century churches, especially in Burgundy and Auvergne, by placing transverse arches above the piers, as in Autun Cathedral (see Fig. 161). These, however, are of little use structurally, although they do strengthen the vault slightly at these points. The vault is not carried on them, as in the Roman building known as the Baths of Diana, Nîmes (see Vol. I., Fig. 75, p. 122); they are too far apart.[1] Another objection sometimes urged against a barrel vault is that, unless a church is of great height, clerestories are impossible, as all upper windows at the sides have to be kept below its springing. As a matter of fact, this is really a blessing in disguise, because the principal light to a church should come from the west end, and obtrusive side light is a nuisance.

Barrel vaults were never popular in England in either Romanesque or later times. Early examples are over the nave and galleries of S. John's Chapel in the Tower of London (c. 1080), the vaults being semicircular ones. Later vaults occur over Roslyn Chapel, Scotland, and the little S. Catherine's Chapel, Abbotsbury, Dorset. In the latter building the vault is a pointed one, and the whole is pannelled in stone, with excellent results.

The intersecting vault permits of windows at the sides, as high as its apex, but that is not the reason why it was preferred. Its great advantage is that it concentrates the thrusts and weight of a vault over the points best capable of receiving them, namely, the piers; a fact that was known to and thoroughly appreciated by the Romans. *Advantages of intersecting vault.*

The earliest Romanesque intersecting vaults, like Roman ones, are continuous, as in the nave aisles of the Abbaye-aux-Dames, Caen, and the crypt of Rochester Cathedral. The first modification made by the eleventh-century builders was to divide the vault into bays by transverse arches and longitudinal arches (or wall ribs, when the vault is enclosed on two of its sides by walls). These arches spring from pilasters or attached columns projecting in front of wall or pier, and as their span is less than that of the vault enclosed by them they show below *Development of vault; transverse arches.*

---

[1] With steel and reinforced concrete there is no reason why the barrel vault, with transverse ribs to mark the bays, should not come again into favour, and be built on sounder principles. Its form is to some far more beautiful than the intersecting vault.

72 A HISTORY OF ARCHITECTURAL DEVELOPMENT.

it. The infilling of each bay (or severy, to use the more architectural term), now rests on these arches, thus removing still more the weight of the vault off the voids below, and concentrating it above the piers.[1]

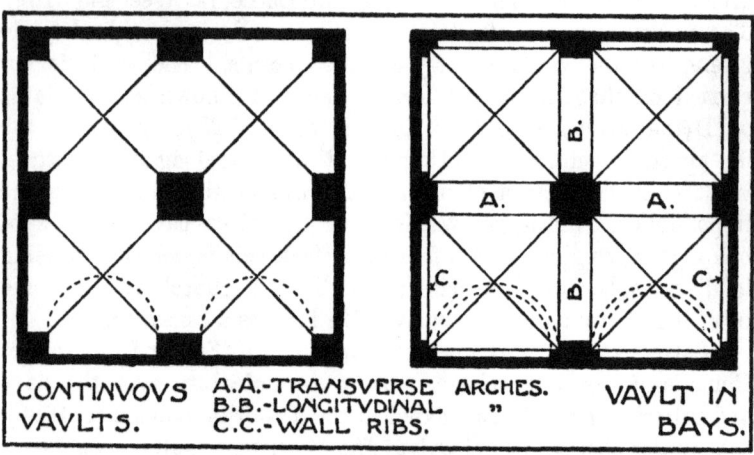

FIG. 42.

Diagonal ribs.

The next development carried the system one step further. This was the introduction of diagonal ribs below the lines of intersection, or "groin" lines of the vault. The vault now becomes a ribbed vault, in contradistinction to a groined or intersecting vault, and each severy consists of two distinct parts, (1) the constructional frame, composed of transverse arches, longitudinal arches or ribs,[2] and diagonal ribs; and (2) the infilling, or web, which rests on the frame. The latter, as it has only its own weight to carry, can be made merely a few inches thick, and practically no part of it bears on the walls. The principle of a combination of thrusts concentrated at given points is now complete, and this concentration facilitated their neutralization, as will be seen later when dealing with flying buttresses. The structural value of ribs has been so emphasized that their æsthetic value is sometimes forgotten. It is on them the eye rests; and not on the infilling,

[1] The Byzantines used transverse arches occasionally, as, for instance, in the vaults over the narthex, outer narthex, and aisles of S. Sophia, Constantinople; but there is this difference, the arches do not spring from projections, and would not show at all if it were not that the vaults are domical.

[2] In many early vaults in England and France wall ribs are omitted, as the great thickness of the walls below rendered them unnecessary.

VAULTING. 73

the curves of which are, to a great extent, lost in most instances, owing to distance and insufficient lighting. The Englishman possibly felt their æsthetic value more than the Frenchman, whose attention was mainly concentrated on structural considerations, and this, to some extent, accounts for the differences between English and French vaulting mentioned in the following pages.

Diagonal ribs first appeared in churches towards the end of the eleventh century, but they did not become general for some fifty years. Most Romanesque vaults of the first quarter of the twelfth century are without them, and in Burgundy, owing to the conservative instincts of the Monastic orders which were especially

Early ribbed vaults.

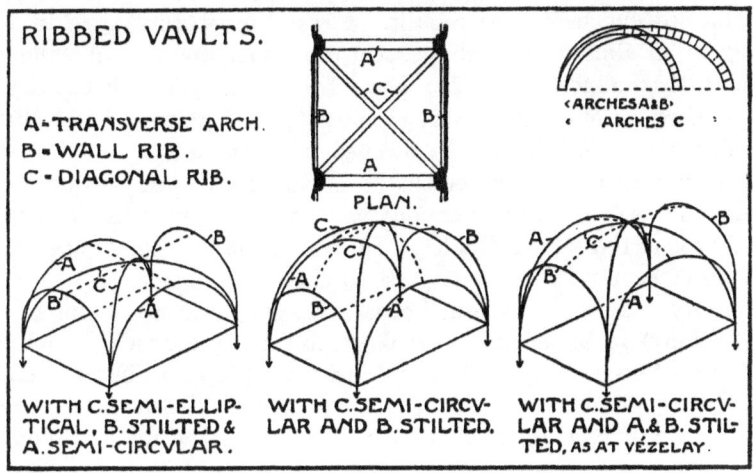

Fig. 43.

powerful there, they are often omitted in later work. There can be no doubt that they simplified considerably the building of vaults of wide span, and the Romanesque builders therefore deserve great praise for realizing their advantages. But did they, strictly speaking, originate diagonal ribs? Did they not really merely reintroduce them in a modified form? In Roman intersecting vaults there are diagonal ribs of brickwork (see Vol. I., Fig. 74, p. 120). These, however, do not project below the surface of the vault. Moreover, as successive layers of concrete were added, they lost their independent functions, and became imbedded in, and part and parcel of, the vault. Still they are there, and the Romans used them for much the same reason as they were used later; namely, as permanent centers to carry the infilling.[1] It is quite possible that by the eleventh century the old methods had been entirely forgotten, but, even admitting that as proved, the builders of the Middle Ages cannot be credited with an entirely new invention.

The date of a vault is always difficult to fix, partly because it is the last part of a church to be built. When a church was commenced may be known exactly, but there is very seldom documentary evidence to show that work proceeded without a break; and where documentary or other evidence does exist, it generally proves the contrary. Besides, builders were inexperienced at the beginning, and many early vaults undoubtedly collapsed and had to be rebuilt. Fires also necessitated rebuilding to an almost incredible extent, and in a fire a vault suffers more than almost any other part of a church. Which country, therefore, deserves the credit of being the first to use visible ribs below the groins cannot be decided with certainty. Still less can an authoritative statement be made regarding any particular church. All countries were engaged trying to find a satisfactory solution of the same difficulty. In France, ribbed vaults appeared simultaneously in different parts at the beginning of the twelfth century: at Bordeaux and Poitiers in the south, at Quimperlé (Brittany) in the north, round Beauvais, and in the valleys of the Seine, Marne, Oise, etc.[2] At Morienval (Oise), a narrow ambulatory round the eastern apse is covered by ribbed vaults, and the date of these is said to be c. 1120.[3] In the district round Beauvais and Soissons many churches of about this date have aisles vaulted with diagonal ribs. The nave of S. Etienne, Beauvais, is also vaulted in this manner, but the vaults are

---

[1] In Roman intersecting vaults, such as those of the Basilica of Constantine, etc., the weight of the vault was concentrated over the piers quite as much as in mediæval vaults.

[2] M. Corroyer's theory (see his "Gothic Architecture," translated) is that diagonal ribs were first used in Aquitaine under vaults built in rings like a dome, but this receives little support from his own countrymen, and from others.

[3] The east end of the church at Morienval has been altered so often that it is difficult to give a date to any part. The chancel was evidently originally barrel vaulted—springers of the vault remain on both sides—and ended with a semi-dome over the apse. The present semi-dome starts higher than the original one, is pointed, and has two ribs under it, although built dome fashion with concentric courses. The ambulatory beyond is an addition, and although its correct date may be 1120, the work is so rough that it may be earlier. The transverse arches (semicircular) across the ambulatory are only about 2 feet 6 inches wide.

VAULTING. 75

certainly later than the original date of the church (1120–1123), and were probably rebuilt after a fire in 1180.[1] Some of the aisle vaults, which are ribbed, date from before the fire.

The claim of priority for Italy rests chiefly on S. Ambrogio, Milan, the wide nave of which has ribbed vaults. The east end of this church is ninth century. The nave, according to Cattaneo, was built "in the second half of the eleventh century." If this date is correct, one of the widest of Romanesque vaults—its width is 44 feet—and also one of the most effective (see Fig. 112), was built twenty years or more before the similar smaller vaults of France. It is difficult to believe this, although it may be true. Cattaneo continues, "In 1129 the second belfry was erected, and in 1196 they repaired the damage done to the edifice by the fall of an arch in the principal nave." This sentence mentions two dates when building operations were in progress. The first rebuilding of the nave may have merely preceded the building of the campanile tower by a few years, which would give c. 1120 for the nave vault. But "the fall of an arch," if that were a transverse arch, means the collapse of two bays; and there are only three vaulted bays to the nave of S. Ambrogio. Cattaneo's own statement therefore shows that part of the nave vault must have been rebuilt after 1196; perhaps the whole of it was. On the other hand, the angle shafts which carry the diagonals are so important that they must be part and parcel of the original design in the first rebuilding (see Figs. 15 and 112). They would never have been made so large if they had been intended merely to carry groin lines. One may, therefore, fairly assume that diagonal ribs were intended from the first, and the real question is, was the nave built forty or fifty years before the tower—the date of which is known to be 1129—or at about the same time? This vault was not so difficult to build as many later ones in England and France, because, although its span is considerable, it springs low down, only a few feet above the crown of the arches of the main arcades.

S. Ambrogio, Milan.

Angle shafts, on a smaller scale than those in S. Ambrogio, are not conclusive evidence that the vaults over had diagonal ribs. There are angle shafts to the vault under the gallery of the north

Angle shafts and ribbed vaulting.

---

[1] Mr. Moore, in his "Gothic Architecture," states that the present vaults were copied from the original ones, which also had ribs. I was at Beauvais this year (July, 1907), but was unable to discover any signs which would prove this, as the church is under restoration, now nearly completed, and the greater part of the stonework inside, especially the capitals of the piers which might have supplied a clue, appears to be quite new.

transept, Winchester, but no diagonal ribs (see Fig. 44). Angle shafts were introduced before diagonal ribs were thought of, because the groin lines of the vault otherwise had to start from the

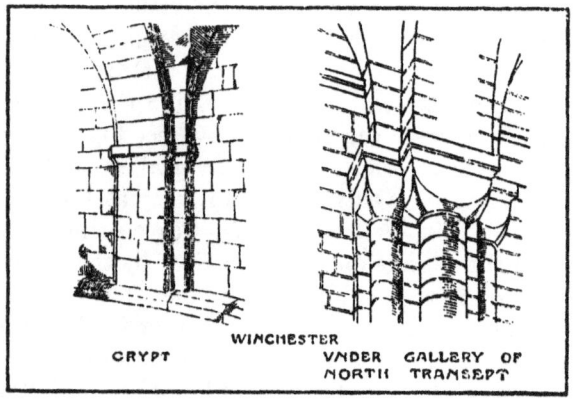

FIG. 44 (J. Bilson).

inner angle of the pier carrying the transverse arch, which did not provide satisfactory springing.

Durham Cathedral. For England a strong claim can be made for priority; but even that cannot be entirely substantiated. In Durham Cathedral, the small vaults over the aisles of choir and transept are ribbed vaults, and these Mr. Bilson places as early as 1093–1096.[1] The period given by him for the nave vaults is between 1128 and 1133 (see Fig. 176). These vaults will be referred to later (see p. 251). It is natural that the question of priority regarding diagonal ribs should arouse considerable controversy, because they went a long way towards solving the problem of vaulting large spaces, and thus greatly assisted the development of mediæval art.

Early difficulties. Diagonal ribs were a great advance, but they caused a difficulty which had not existed before. In a square vault without ribs, the arches of which are semicircular, the groins are semi-elliptical and therefore weak in form. This weakness does not matter in vaults of this description, as the groin lines are unconstructional and, so to speak, accidental. But when diagonal ribs are added,

[1] See "The Beginnings of Gothic Architecture," by Mr. John Bilson, in *The R.I.B.A. Journal*, vol. vi., Nos. 9 and 10. Part II. should be read for the arguments regarding these vaults and other early ribbed ones at Winchester and Peterboro', and Part I. for an interesting summary of the pros and cons for continental priority.

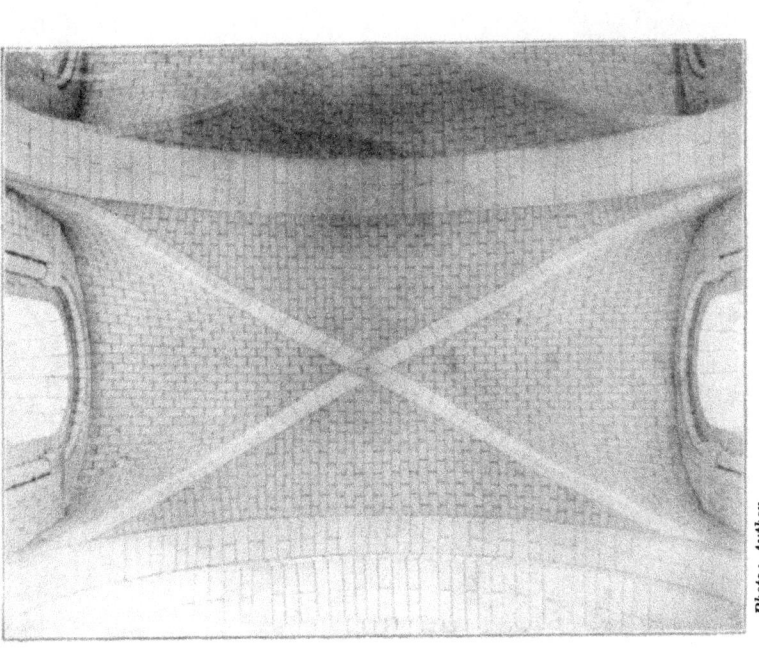

Photo: Author.

Fig. 46.—S. Georges de Boscherville: One Bay of Choir Vault. There are no Diagonal Ribs; Lines are only Painted.

Photo: Author.

Fig. 47.—Angers Cathedral: Nave.

[*To face p.* 78.

these cannot well be built on the same lines, as they have to carry a great part of the weight of the infilling and must therefore be strong. The Romanesque builders tried making the ribs segmental, as in Durham Cathedral, or else semicircular (see Fig. 43). The latter form was strong, but when the other arches of the vault were semicircular also the result was practically a dome, and should have been built as such.[1] The domical form was avoided in some cases by stilting considerably the transverse and longitudinal arches so that their crowns should be on about the same level as the apex of the diagonal ribs. A better expedient still was followed at Ouistreham Church, near Caen, where the arches are semi-elliptical; and this was also sometimes done in early English examples. Most early ribbed vaults are over aisles; their spans are consequently small, and the builders could "cook" the curves without producing weakness or ugly lines. Exact setting out of these vaults was also rendered difficult by the fact that, in England certainly, although many side vaults are approximately square, few are exactly so, and some are unmistakably oblong.

These rough and ready devices were all very well over aisles, but they were unsuitable for wide spans. Nave vaults required more scientific treatment. Searching about for a remedy, the workmen bethought themselves of the pointed arch, which had, some years previously, lessened the difficulty of the barrel vault. The solution of the difficulty was found. There was no longer any occasion for stilting arches or for weak diagonal ribs; there was no longer any need for a domical form, although for many years, it must be admitted, especially in Southern France, the latter prevailed in vaults built entirely with pointed arches, and arches, especially wall ribs, continued to be stilted when there was often little reason why they should be. Fig. 45 shows how transverse and longitudinal arches and diagonal ribs can, by the aid of the pointed arch, all be of the same height, no matter what the shape of the vault may be, or how wide its span. In most French vaults, in which the system is complete, the diagonal ribs are made semicircular, and the radius of these dictates the height and consequently the forms of the other arches. In England they are generally slightly pointed.

<small>Difficulties solved by pointed arches.</small>

The Normans were the pioneers in vaulting in Northern Europe, but they clung to the semicircular arch, and their fame

<small>Early ribbed vaults with pointed arches.</small>

[1] M. Corroyer says that in the church of S. Avit Senieur, in Southern France, it is a dome, the stones being laid in rings, and the ribs acting merely as stiffeners.

rests more on their eleventh-century work than on their twelfth. In Germany and Italy also, traditions were too strong to allow of early change, and the "round arched Gothic," as it is sometimes called, of the former country is amongst the finest in Europe.[1] France and England were the first to adopt generally the pointed form. The vaults over the aisles of Malmesbury Abbey Church (c. 1140–1150) are amongst the earliest ribbed vaults in this country in which the transverse arches, and the arches of the nave arcade alongside them, are pointed. The diagonal ribs are semicircular. In Durham nave the transverse arches are also pointed and, if Mr. Bilson's dates are correct (1128–1133), these arches are earlier than the Malmesbury ones. These vaults have no wall ribs. In

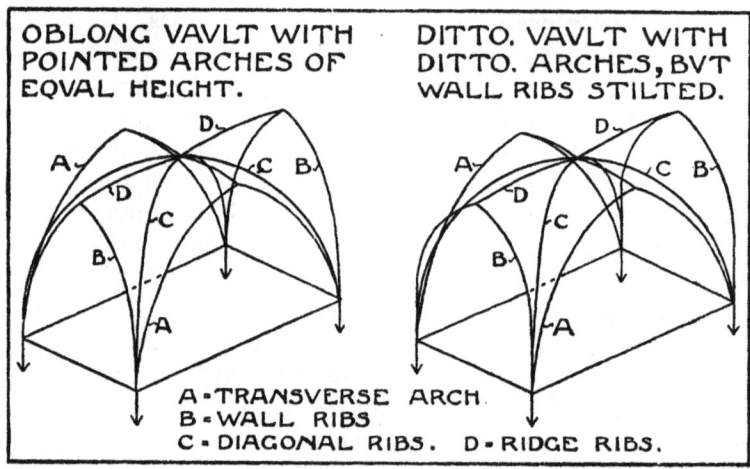

Fig. 45.

France the pointed arch was employed in vaults almost as early as diagonal ribs. Many small churches round Amiens, Beauvais, Soissons, etc., have pointed ribbed vaults, which are attributed to 1120–1130. The first large church with vaults of this description, the date of which is known, is S. Denis, near Paris. The narthex was finished 1140, the choir in 1144. In S. Maurice, Angers (the cathedral), the magnificent vault of about fifty-four feet span is pointed throughout, and cannot be later than 1150–1153. The dates of the above examples show that the pointed arch was used

[1] It must not be forgotten that at first the pointed arch was only used for arches of arcades and for vaults. Windows continued to be semicircular headed until near the end of the twelfth century.

VAULTING. 79

for vaulting almost simultaneously in France and England; although the Frenchmen had the advantage of a few years.

One important difference between early and late ribbed vaults is the great width of the tranverse arches in the former. This is especially marked in churches of the South of France, such as S. Radegonde, and the Cathedral, Poitiers, S. Pierre, Saumur, S. Trinité, Angers; in S. Ambrogio, Milan, and in most German churches of the twelfth century. It is also noticeable, though to a less extent, in the somewhat later great churches of Northern France, such as N. D., Paris, Laon Cathedral, etc. The transverse arches in Romanesque vaults in this country are also heavy, but then so are all the other ribs. In the churches of Poitiers and Saumur, etc., the diagonal ribs are exceptionally slight. The wide transverse arch possesses one great advantage: it unmistakably divides the vault into bays corresponding to the bays below, and prevents the somewhat monotonous effect which a vault with all its ribs about equal in size presents. In the churches of Southern France it was a necessity because of the domical character of the vaults. It was needed for strength, and it was required for appearance (see Fig. 164). In England even the earliest vaults are only slightly domical in form, the later ones not at all, and, consequently, wide transverse arches, except in quite early work, are practically unknown. *Transverse arches very wide.*

The pointed arch not only solved the difficulty occasioned by the use of diagonal ribs, but it also facilitated the vaulting of oblong spaces. Such spaces, it is true, had been vaulted before diagonal ribs and pointed arches were thought of. Some of the vaults in Caracalla's Baths, Rome, for instance, are not square. The best instances in Romanesque times of oblong vaults without ribs and with semicircular arches occur over the nave of Vézelay Abbey Church and the choir of S. Georges de Boscherville, Normandy (c. 1120) (see Fig. 46). Here the wall ribs are much stilted and the transverse arches slightly stilted, so that their crowns are nearly straight. The result is not altogether satisfactory, as the weight of the vault comes too much on the transverse arches and too little on the walls. It may be asked, why should not all vaults be square? In the majority of churches the nave is about double the width of each aisle, and, consequently, if a bay of one be square the corresponding bay of the other must be oblong. Before the pointed arch became general the oblong form was avoided, as in S. Ambrogio, Milan, and in many early French and *Vaulting of oblong spaces.*

German churches vaulted with semicircular transverse arches, by making one bay of the nave vault correspond to two bays of the aisle on either side; all bays being thus approximately square. But the objection to this plan is that each bay of the central vault is enormous, and the span of its diagonal ribs, in particular, immense (see Fig. 51).

Sexpartite vaults. As a corrective to this the French designed what is known as the sexpartite vault. All early ribbed vaults are quadripartite, that is to say, each bay is divided into four compartments by the diagonal ribs. In the sexpartite vault an intermediate transverse arch is introduced, which cuts the diagonal ribs at their

Fig. 48.

intersection and thus supports them. This, in the early essays, was simply an arch built under the web, which was formed independently of it. Examples are in the nave of the Abbaye-aux-Dames, Caen, and the church of Bernières-sur-mer, both in Normandy. The next step was to let these intermediate arches take their share in supporting the web. The result was the sexpartite vault, *i.e.* a vault divided into six compartments. It was a great favourite in France for some thirty or forty years, but it was definitely abandoned early in the thirteenth century. Æsthetically it is unsatisfactory, as it leads to many twisted curves in the web, which, at the back of the intermediate arches, is often no wider than the arches themselves for a considerable height above the springing. In some French examples the bad

Photo: Author.
FIG. 49.—S. PIERRE, LISIEUX: QUADRIPARTITE VAULT OF CHOIR.

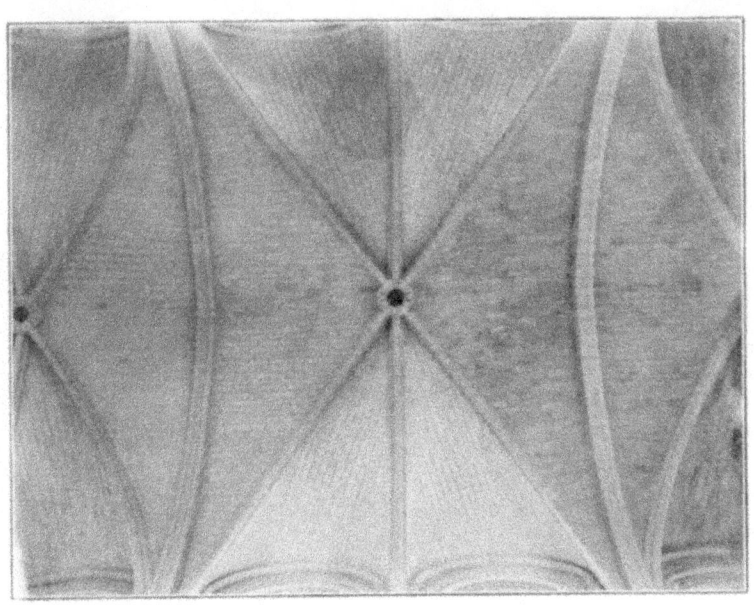

Photo: Author.
FIG. 50.—LAON CATHEDRAL: SEXPARTITE VAULT OF NAVE.

[*To face p.* 80.

effect is minimized by starting the intermediate arches some feet above the other arches of the vault. Nearly all these sexpartite vaults are much scooped; the intermediate arches have therefore to rise considerably higher than the main transverse arches, which is an additional reason for stilting them. In the church of La Trinité, Angers, the intermediate arches are stilted as much as eight feet. The following French cathedrals, amongst others, have sexpartite vaults: Laon, Paris, Bourges, etc. Noyon was

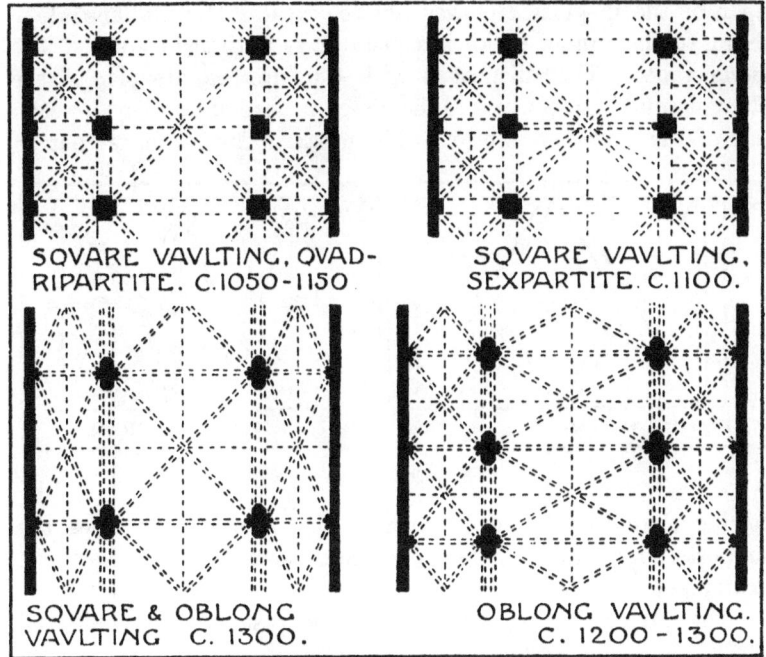

Fig. 51.

designed for sexpartite vaults, but the present ones are quadripartite. In England there are few examples of the sexpartite form. The choir of Canterbury Cathedral (the work of William of Sens, a Burgundian) and the south transept of Lincoln Cathedral, however, are vaulted in this manner.[1]

---

[1] In early sexpartite vaulted churches the columns are alternately large and small—which is logical—but in some of the later examples—Paris, Laon, etc.—the columns are, with some exceptions, of the same size. At Noyon columns alternate with larger piers.

82 A HISTORY OF ARCHITECTURAL DEVELOPMENT.

Oblong vaults.

The difficulty of vaulting wide square bays with quadripartite vaults, and the unsuitability of the sexpartite form forced the builders in most countries to make their nave bays oblong, the length being from north to south, and to make each bay of the nave the width of an aisle bay each side. The aisle bays took their chance. They are sometimes approximately square, at other times oblong, their length being from north to south or from east to west as was necessary. Owing to the pointed arch, the shape of the plan of a vault was immaterial, provided the span of the diagonal ribs was not too great. The Italians alone clung to the square for their central bays until the advent of the Renaissance. They dispensed with the intermediate pier of the Romanesque builders, and in the aisles, instead of two bays to each bay of the nave, had one long oblong bay. The result is that in

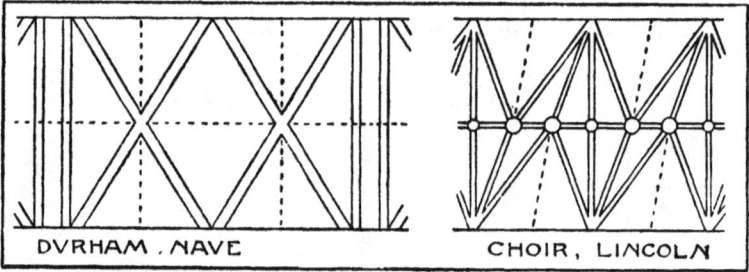

FIG. 52.

Italian churches of the fourteenth and fifteenth centuries the supports are always far less numerous than in more northern examples.[1]

The French having returned to the quadripartite vault and perfected it—the credit for this is undoubtedly theirs—stopped satisfied. Even in their fifteenth-century churches the vaults are of this simple character, with very few exceptions, the only ribs being the transverse, diagonal, and wall ribs, with occasionally a ridge rib. But the English were restless. They had shown in the early vault over Durham nave—which differs from other vaults in being in seven compartments, there being no transverse arch above the intermediate piers, where one might naturally have been expected—that they liked something different from other

---

[1] The builders were doubtless influenced by the old Roman plan of few supports, but they forgot that the Roman supports are exceptionally large. Hence is owing, to a great extent, the unsatisfactory character of Italian Gothic.

VAULTING.

people, and this feeling is shown again in the choir vault of Lincoln Cathedral, where the diagonal ribs do not run from corner to corner (see Fig. 52), and in subsequent developments.

Before considering these, however, it is best to deal briefly with the methods of building the infilling or web. In early vaults this was often little more than rubble, plastered on the underside, but in later work it was coursed stone. Whichever method is adopted, its surface is slightly concave, so that it forms a

The web.

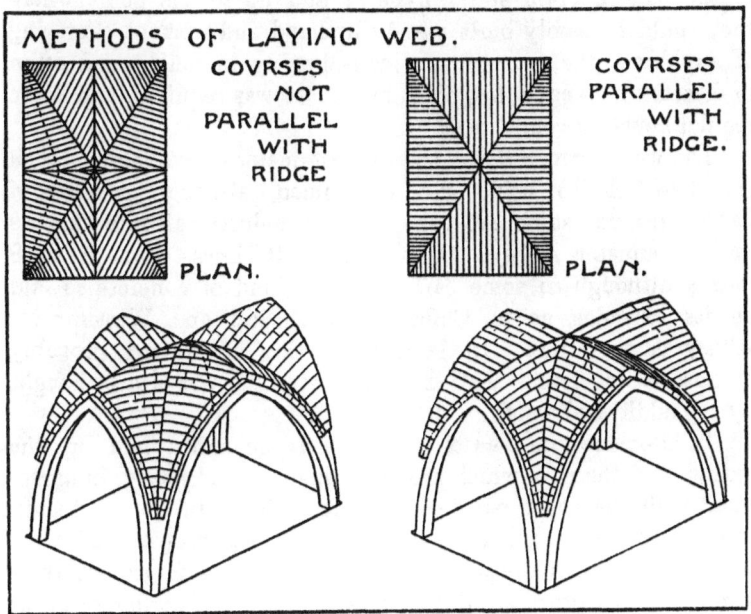

Fig. 53.

flat segmental arch from rib to rib. Viollet-le-Duc, in his "Dictionnaire Raisonné," describes two methods for coursed stone, one which he dubs French, and the other English. In France, he says, the stones were always built parallel to the ridge, and in England and in the semi-English work of Southern France, they were placed either at right angles to the diagonal ribs, or else at right angles to an imaginary line drawn between the diagonals and the transverse arch, or the diagonals and the wall rib. But this is not quite correct. The so-called French method is, it is true, general in Northern France; but it is also not uncommon in England. The two methods occur, side by side, in the vault over the cloisters on the north side of Westminster Abbey. In Westminster Abbey there may be strong suspicion of French influence, but there can be none in the Lady Chapel of Chichester, or at Fountains Abbey; and yet in the vault of the former, and in that over the huge cellar of the latter, the stones are laid, to all intents and purposes, parallel with the ridge.[1] The truth is that in nearly all examples, French as well as English, the web is by no means built throughout in exact accordance with any hard-and-fast rule. The stones at the bottom often start anyhow; and up to the point where they could be safely built merely by hand and without centering of any kind, the courses vary considerably in height and often in direction. Above that point more care was required, and more regular coursing commences.

The web is generally of the lightest material available, clunch (*i.e.* hard chalk) being not uncommon, although courses of harder, heavier stone are sometimes introduced at intervals, as in Westminster Abbey. It varies in thickness from 4 to 8 inches, although in some early vaults a kind of concrete is laid on its extrados, as in Chichester Cathedral and Westminster Abbey nave vaults. In later work this is omitted, probably because it was found that the added strength was dearly bought by the additional weight.[2]

Sections of ribs.

In Romanesque vaults the web is generally laid on the extrados of the ribs, which are wide, shallow, and heavy, in agreement with the other parts of a church. Early in the thirteenth century, however, the ribs were made much deeper, and were rebated to receive the web. They are also far thinner, but their strength is as great as, if not greater than, the earlier ones, as their depth is increased by an amount equal to the thickness of the web. The joints were often strengthened by metal or slate dowels, especially in late work. Many of the later ribs are not

---

[1] In one of the bays of the choir aisle of Tewkesbury Abbey, one side is built French fashion, and the other in so-called English fashion, but one or other may have been restored.

[2] In Chichester Cathedral the concrete is a foot thick, the chalk below 6 inches. In Westminster Abbey the vaults over the eastern part of the church and over about two-thirds of the nave have about 9 inches of concrete above them. The remaining bays to the west, which are a century or two later in date, have none. The Roman tradition of layer upon layer of concrete may possibly have suggested this covering; but it is more probable that the old traditions were lost, and that the early mediæval builders added the layers because they were afraid of the strength of their thin shells.

only elaborately moulded, but are also enriched with carved ornament.

The task of building the web was by no means an easy one in some of the wide, lofty churches of Central and Northern France. The Englishmen never mastered the *science* of vaulting so thoroughly as the French, although in beauty English examples more than hold their own, and present greater variety than continental ones. The mediæval builders were confronted with much the same difficulty as the Romans centuries before. Although wood was plentiful in Europe in the Middle Ages, the cost of scaffolding and ordinary centering for a vault, such as that over Amiens Cathedral, would have been a serious item if special devices had not been adopted. According to Viollet-le-Duc, in the Isle-de-France at least, the workmen employed hand-centers, consisting of two planks of wood, curved on top, to give the desired concave surface. A slot was cut along each, and the

FIG. 54 (Viollet-le-Duc).

two were loosely joined together by wedges. At the ends were angle-irons, which rested on the ribs. Where the space to be filled was narrow, *i.e.* at a few feet only above the springing, the planks lay side by side; as the space widened they were lengthened out until they were almost end to end. Two men working together could easily manage such a center. The objection, however, to this theory is that, although possible when the length of a course of infilling does not exceed, say, 10 feet, the top courses of many of the great French vaults are more than double that. This would entail a center too heavy to be managed by hand.[1] Moreover, it is the top courses which most require

---

[1] The upper courses were very likely laid on single boards, propped up temporarily from a light scaffolding below. Quick-setting mortar would be used, and workmen after setting a course in one compartment could pass on to a course in another, giving the first time to set. It must be remembered that the web is often very thin. Viollet-le-Duc says that in the vaults of Nôtre Dame, Paris, it is only 10 centimetres, less than 4 inches, thick.

86 A HISTORY OF ARCHITECTURAL DEVELOPMENT.

support when building; the joints of the lower ones are more horizontal, and the stones, in consequence, rest more on the ones below. The adhesive power of the mortar alone almost keeps the latter in their places.

Extra ribs. It is more than probable that it was the desire to avoid long courses which led the English architects to adopt the intermediate ribs (see p. 88, tierceron) termed superfluous by some French and American writers, and so reduce by more than half the width of the compartments of the web. Thus, in Exeter Cathedral and in the nave of Westminster Abbey, the top courses of the web are not 8 feet long. That intermediate ribs were introduced to facilitate the building of the web is, to some extent, proved by the many churches in which the nave vaults have them, while the aisles have them not. Westminster Abbey and Lichfield Cathedral are cases in point.

Extra ribs began to appear in English vaults early in the thirteenth century. The first was the ridge rib, sometimes called the lierne; and this was rapidly followed by intermediate ribs, or tiercerons, which spring from the same spot as the diagonals, and divide the four big compartments of each vault into several smaller ones. Viollet-le-Duc attributes the introduction of the ridge rib to the desire of the English to cover the ugly joint at the summit of a vault which results when the courses of stone on each side are not parallel. But it has already been pointed out that in many English vaults the courses are parallel; and it should also be remembered that even when such is the case, some coaking is required to make the two sides meet satisfactorily, because the surface of the web is not straight, but concave. Moreover, in so many vaults the stones were not intended to show, but were plastered and painted, that another reason may be suggested.

Reason for ridge ribs. When vaults are constructed with semicircular or semi-elliptical arches there is no ridge line; with the pointed arch there is. The suggestion is consequently not unnatural, that the need for emphasizing this soon became evident to the artistic mind of the English builder, and he therefore introduced the ridge rib, irrespective of how the stones of the web were laid. Early examples of it in England are in Lincoln and Chester Cathedrals, Westminster Abbey, etc. In Southern France it was common in the vaulted churches of the end of the twelfth century, such as S. Pierre, Saumur (see Fig. 164), S. Radegonde, Poitiers, Poitiers Cathedral, etc. The three great bays of the nave of Angers

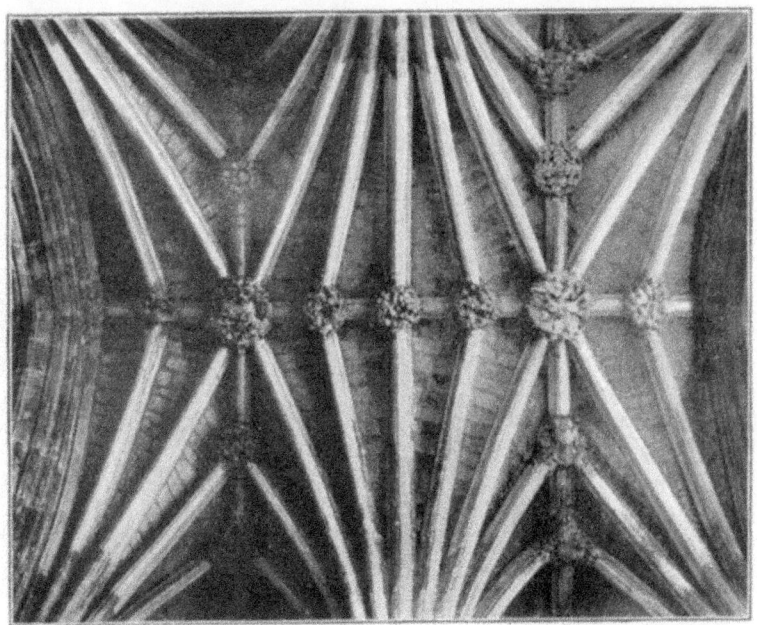

Photo: E. K. Prideaux.
FIG. 55.—TIERCERON VAULT OF S. JOHN'S CHAPEL, EXETER CATHEDRAL.

Photo: E. K. Prideaux.
FIG. 56.—EXETER CATHEDRAL: VAULT OF NAVE.

[*To face p.* 86.

VAULTING. 87

Cathedral (c. 1150) are without ridge ribs, but the later choir vaults have them. In the above-mentioned foreign examples the ridge ribs (like the diagonals) are extremely slender, and were probably made so because otherwise they would have emphasized disagreeably the dome form of the vaults. In England this had

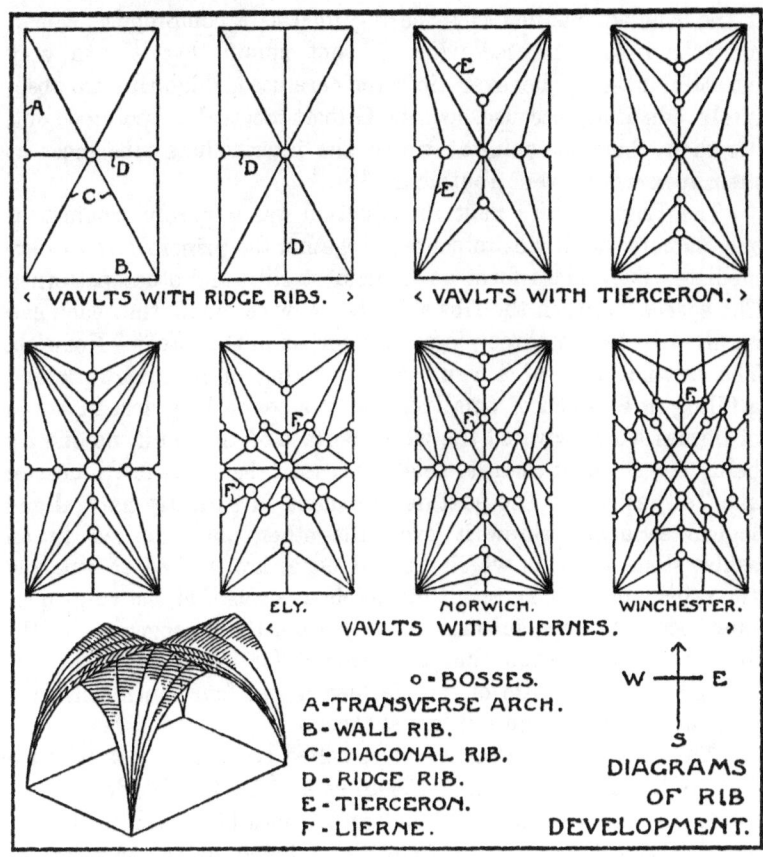

Fig. 57.

not to be guarded against, as the ridges are straight in most Gothic examples, the exceptions being mainly those in which they slope *upwards* from the central boss to the sides, in order to provide greater height for windows. The architects of Northern France used ridge ribs sparingly, and to the last regarded them as not absolutely necessary.

Tiercerons.

In oblong bays of vaulting, one tierceron is generally introduced in each central compartment, and two or more in each side one. The French, who delighted in overcoming structural difficulties by sheer *tours de force*, and to whom compromise was distasteful, rejected these ribs as useless and unconstructional. But they are not so really. Their function has already been indicated; and if the English method is to be regarded as a compromise, a man must be indeed bigoted who will not admit that it is a very beautiful one. Whenever tiercerons are used, ridge ribs are absolutely essential, because, as Sir Gilbert Scott has pointed out, "without them the point at which the intermediate ribs meet at their apex would want abutment."[1]

Liernes.

The Englishman's next introduction was a purely ornamental one, namely, small ribs to connect together the principal and intermediate ribs, and so form with them starlike and other patterns.[2] The spaces between the ribs are often now so small that each can be filled by two or three pieces of stone, as in the nave of Norwich. The original idea of a vault as consisting of a framework and a filling-in between of small stones, was before long lost in a web of liernes which covered the whole surface of the vault, no one rib being any stronger than its neighbour, as in the choirs of Gloucester and Tewkesbury. The next development, in perfectly natural and logical sequence, threw it over altogether, and resulted in an ashlar stone vault, in which rib and panel are worked on one and the same stone. One result of the change was that the vault once more became of one substance. It had not the homogeniety of the Roman concrete vault, but it exercised far less thrust than the strongly-ribbed vaults of the thirteenth and fourteenth centuries, and consequently required less abutment.

Fan-vault.

Thus was born the van-vault, so called because its ribs take the form of a half-opened fan. It is an essentially English design, and an appropriate and beautiful ending to centuries of vault development. The earliest example of it is found in the cloisters of Gloucester Cathedral (c. 1370), the main arches being pointed. In nearly all other examples of fan vaulting, Henry VII.'s Chapel, Westminster, S. George's Chapel, Windsor, Eton College

---

[1] In his lectures on "The Rise and Development of Mediæval Architecture," vol. ii. p. 208. Ridge ribs are sometimes omitted in English vaults between the tiercerons and the wall ribs, as in Lincoln Cathedral.

[2] These small ribs are generally also called "liernes." The term is applied to any ribs which do not start from the springing.

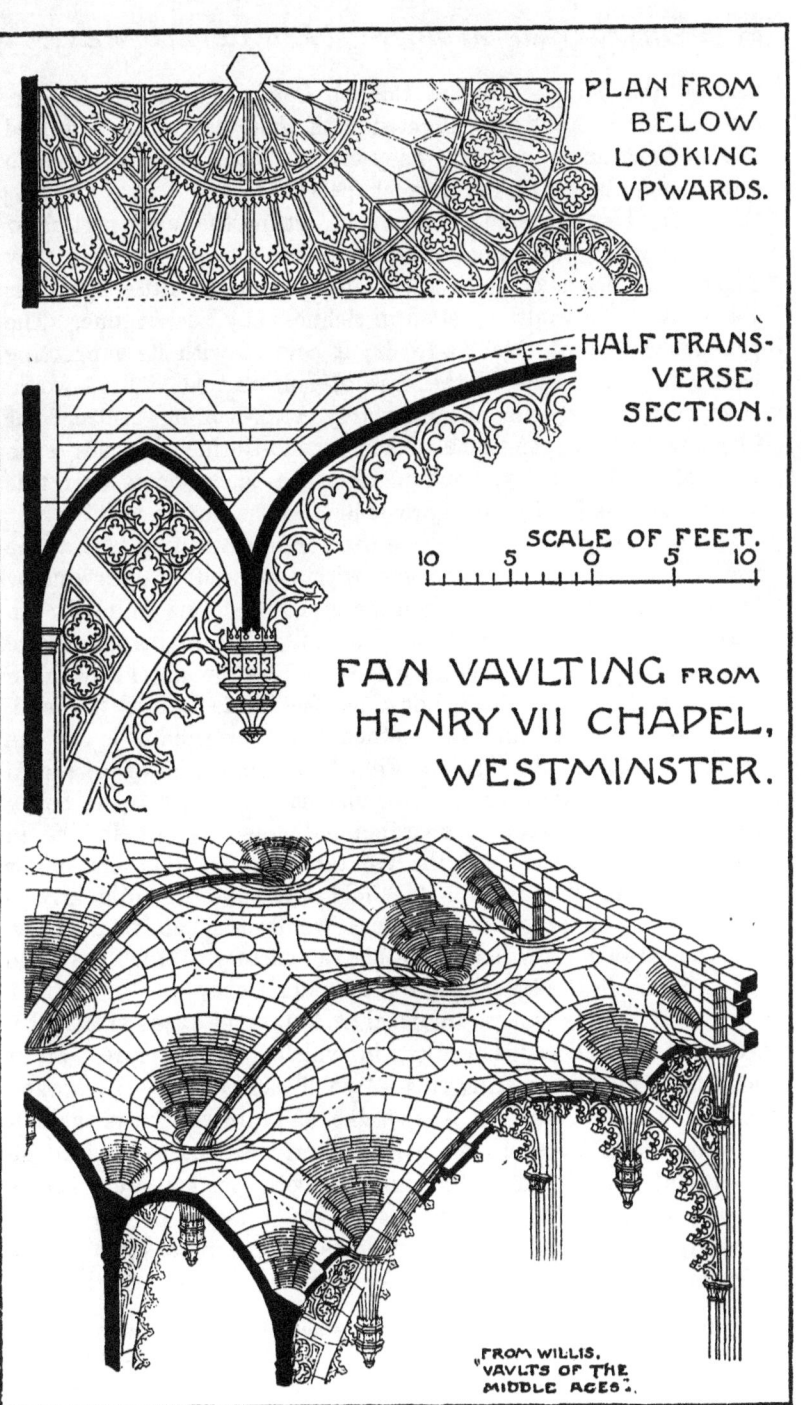

Fig. 58.

Chapel and King's College Chapel, Cambridge, they are four-centred. The builders, delighted with their new form, indulged in many charming fancies. They carried down the ribs so as to form pendants, as in the side chapels of Henry VII.'s Chapel; they started strong transverse arches, letting the lower part show and concealing the upper part, as in the central portion; they cusped the heads of the panels and carved the little spandrils above, until the vaults excelled in richness any Eastern one. The pendant was by no means a freak; it covered with its supporting bars what otherwise—in the case of four-centred vaults—would have been a flat and uncomfortably weak-looking centre. Sir Christopher Wren, in some of his pseudo-Gothic churches, such as S. Mary Aldermary, London, formed a saucer-dome over this space, but it is hardly an improvement on the earlier form.

Relation of wall rib to window. One advantage of the four-centred arch in vaulting is that the wall rib can be made concentric with the head of the window below it more easily than when more pointed forms are used. In earlier vaults there was often a difficulty in bringing these two into harmony. In some cases it is solved by the aid of a sçoinson arch (see p. 68) over the window on the inside face of the wall, and this is the most natural method when the window is not the full width of the bay. In late French cathedrals, however, and in a few English ones (York nave, for instance), the entire space below the vault down to about the springing line of the wall rib is filled by the window-head, and the rib then forms its natural outer member.[1] In the nave of Lichfield Cathedral the difficulty is overcome by making the clerestory windows spherical triangles, but the experiment is not altogether satisfactory. Much the same thing occurs in the triforia of Westminster Abbey.

Bosses. Bosses, or key stones, are usual at the intersections of all ribs, except in Romanesque vaults, in which they are rare. Short lengths of all the meeting ribs—4 to 6 inches long—are worked on the boss, so as to form skewbacks, and the web butts against, or more often rests on, the solid central mass, so that thorough abutment is provided at the apex for both ribs and web. Some of the finest of Gothic carvings are on bosses. In the simple quadripartite vault, bosses only come at the intersection of the diagonals, as in the naves of Chichester and Salisbury Cathedrals,

---

[1] In French work this was all the easier because the springing line of the wall rib is always far above that of the main ribs, which is not so general in England. It is so at York, however.

where they appear as jewels in an immense setting. As soon as ridge ribs were introduced they became necessary at the apex of transverse arches; and with the advent of tiercerons, at the points where these cut the ridges (Fig. 55). With liernes connecting together the main ribs, they multiplied enormously, and also varied considerably in size, there being great difference in this respect between the bosses at main intersections and those at subordinate ones. In the latter positions they could not have been dispensed with, because the liernes often cut so awkwardly into the sides of larger ribs, that but for the bosses the junctions would have been exceedingly ugly.

The following list states the character of the vaulting, etc., in some of the English cathedrals, etc. :— *Summary of English examples.*

Timber roof.—(Ceiled) Naves of Ely, Peterboro', S. Albans; (open) Rochester.

Barrel vault.—S. John's Chapel, Tower of London, S. Catherine's Chapel, Abbotsbury.

Quadrant barrel vault.—Gloucester choir triforium.

Intersecting vault.—(Plain) Rochester, crypt; (with transverse arches) Durham Castle, crypt; Gloucester, aisle of choir; S. Albans, aisle of nave; S. John's Chapel, London, aisle.

Ribbed vaults—
(1) Simple four-tite. Durham, nave and aisles; Chichester; Fountains' Abbey, cloisters; Salisbury, nave, choir, cloisters, etc.; S. Saviour's, Southwark; Wells, nave; S. Cross, Hampshire, chancel (vault is domical); Boxgrove Priory.
(2) With ridge ribs. Chester, choir; Gloucester, nave; Westminster Abbey, choir; Worcester, choir.
(3) Six-tite vaults. Canterbury, choir; Lincoln, south transept (with ridge rib).
(4) Tierceron vaults. Ely, presbytery; Exeter, nave and choir; Hereford; Lichfield; Lincoln, presbytery and nave; Westminster Abbey, nave; Worcester, nave.
(5) Tierceron and lierne vaults. Chester, nave; Ely, choir and Lady chapel; Winchester, nave; York, choir; Worcester, cloisters; Norwich, nave; S. Mary Redcliffe, Bristol.
(6) Liernes. Tewkesbury, choir and crossing; Gloucester, choir; Wells, choir. Christ Church, Oxford, constructed much like central vault Henry VII.'s Chapel,

92 A HISTORY OF ARCHITECTURAL DEVELOPMENT.

Westminster, and Sherborne Abbey Church, form connecting links between lierne and fan vaults.[1]

Fan vaults.—(With pendants) Henry VII.'s Chapel, central portion and side chapels; (without pendants) King's College Chapel, Cambridge; Bath Abbey Church; Gloucester, cloisters; Winchester, Bishop Waynflete's Chantry Chapel.

The next points to consider are the setting out of the ribs at the springing of a vault; the counterpoise necessary to resist their thrusts; and the disposition of the shafts from which the ribs spring.

Setting out of ribs.
In Romanesque work the different ribs are independent of one another, and each has its separate skewback. In Gothic

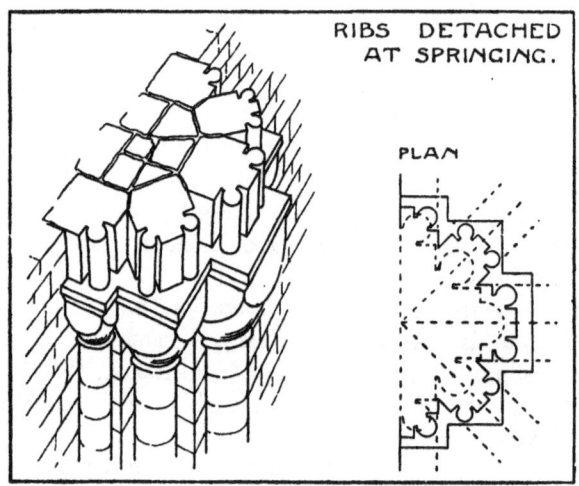

FIG. 59.

work this was impossible, because, in English work at least, the ribs are more numerous, and all the parts of a church below the vaults so much smaller. Nor did the builders desire it. They realized that concentration of all thrusts was the first essential; and that so long as each rib acted independently, the satisfactory neutralization of their thrusts was extremely difficult. They therefore united all the ribs together, for a certain number of courses above the springing, up to a point at which their separation became imperative. These courses are all built with

[1] The Sherborne vaults are practically fan shape, but the liernes are not curved as in fan vaults, they are straight.

VAULTING.

horizontal beds, the top surface of the top course being splayed to the necessary angle to give each rib a skewback to spring from. The number of courses varies in different examples according to the shape of the vault, and its pitch. In Westminster Abbey there are seven courses; in Lincoln Cathedral choir as many as ten; in other examples only three or four. In a square vault the ribs separate from one another much sooner that in an oblong; and in a steep or much stilted vault they remain in contact longer than in one of flatter pitch. The number also depends, to a considerable extent, on the point from which the diagonals start. In many vaults the centre line of each diagonal meets the centre line of the transverse arch on the wall plane (as shown on Fig. 60); sometimes the lines meet considerably behind it, and occasionally even in front of it. There is no hard-and-fast rule as to this. The meeting point depends entirely on whether it is desired to compress the ribs at the springing into the narrowest possible compass, or to spread them out.

These bottom courses of the vault are collectively called the "tas-de-charge." The principle it embodied was not new. In Egyptian, Byzantine, and Sasanian barrel vaults the bottom courses are often laid with horizontal beds up to an angle of about 30°. In Roman intersecting vaults the diagonal ribs, mentioned in Vol. I. (Fig. 74), spring from a tas-de-charge of concrete; and in some Romanesque ones without ribs, the groin lines start from one of stone, as in portions of Winchester Cathedral (see Fig. 44). But to the Gothic men belongs the credit of applying it to ribbed vaults.[1] The merits of the tas-de-charge are: (1) that it unites all thrusts and simplifies the question of counterpoise; (2) that it reduces to a minimum the danger of the slipping or crushing of any one rib at its springing, and the consequent fracture of the vault; (3) that it lessens both the span and the rise of the active portion of the vault, viz. that built with separate voussoirs, and therefore the amount of centering required; (4) that it brings the thrusts well *within* the wall, the tas-de-charge itself acting as an abutment, and taking a good deal of the thrust.

Tas-de-charge.

In all early French Gothic vaults the wall ribs do not start from the same springing line as the other ribs, but from a point

French and English wall ribs.

[1] To determine the point at which the tas-de-charge ends and independent voussoirs commence, draw lines from the points at which the ribs intersect on plan, at right angles to the direction of each. Where these lines cut the extrados of the ribs is (approximately only when the ribs are of different depths) the top of the tas-de-charge.

94 A HISTORY OF ARCHITECTURAL DEVELOPMENT.

far above it; a shaft, detached in most cases, resting on top of

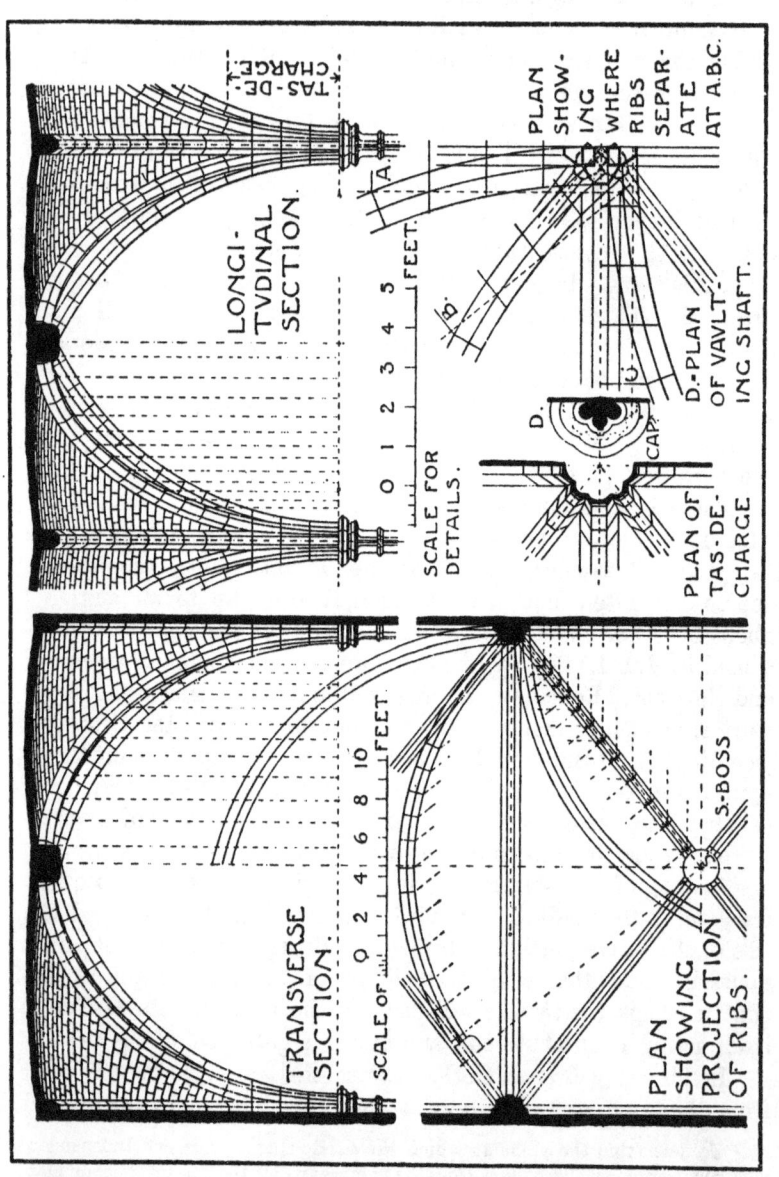

Fig. 60.

the capital of the main vaulting shaft, and carrying the rib. The English never employed the upper shaft, and in many of their early vaults the wall ribs spring from the same point as the others. In nearly all later ones, however, the rib is much stilted, as in the nave of York Cathedral, and the result, therefore, is the same as in French work. There can be no doubt that the principle of separating the wall ribs from the others is a sound one. Their thrusts, unlike those of other ribs, are contained within the building; none passes to the outside, and has to be neutralized. The thrust of one rib is met by the counter thrust of the next, and when these thrusts meet above the point where the other thrusts are focussed, they exercise a downward pressure which has a steadying influence. Moreover, the absence of wall ribs from the tas-de-charge undoubtedly facilitates the concentration of the thrusts of the others, as the area of thrust is lessened. Statically, therefore, it is right, but æsthetically it is of doubtful advantage; as it occasions considerable cutting back of the web, in order that this shall not come in front of the wall rib.

There is no difficulty in providing sufficient resistance to the thrust of a barrel vault, especially in a building of a single span. The wall being continuous below the vault, all that is needed is that it shall be sufficiently thick. In a building divided into nave and aisles the continuous thrust of the central vault is counteracted by continuous aisle vaults, either semicircular, as in S. John's Chapel, Tower of London, and the church at Carcassonne, etc., or of quadrant shape, as in the narthex of S. Philibert, Tournus, and many other churches in Southern France (see Figs. 150 and 151). When the central vault is divided into bays by ribs, corresponding ribs are often built under the side vaults, and on the outside of the aisle walls are flat buttresses, which, however, are not much more than complimentary, owing to their slight projection. *Counterpoise barrel vaults.*

The task of counteracting the thrusts of intersecting vaults, especially ribbed ones, is not so easy, and it is no wonder that the early mediæval builders did not solve the problem straight away. All the thrusts being concentrated at given points, the wall in between these points is of little assistance. This was recognized so thoroughly after the twelfth century, that, in France especially, the wall became window. For the same reason a series of supports was substituted for continuous abutment. These stretched across from the back of the nave wall to the inside face of the aisle wall, under the aisle roof. They are not solid walls, for that would have weighted unnecessarily the *Counterpoise intersecting vaults.*

transverse arches over the aisle below, and also have interfered with free passage in the triforium, but are, as a rule, quadrant arches. They are, in fact, flying buttresses, although hidden.[1]

The hidden buttress possesses one advantage over the exposed one, that it is less liable to decay. It was sufficient so long as the churches were comparatively low, or when the triforium above

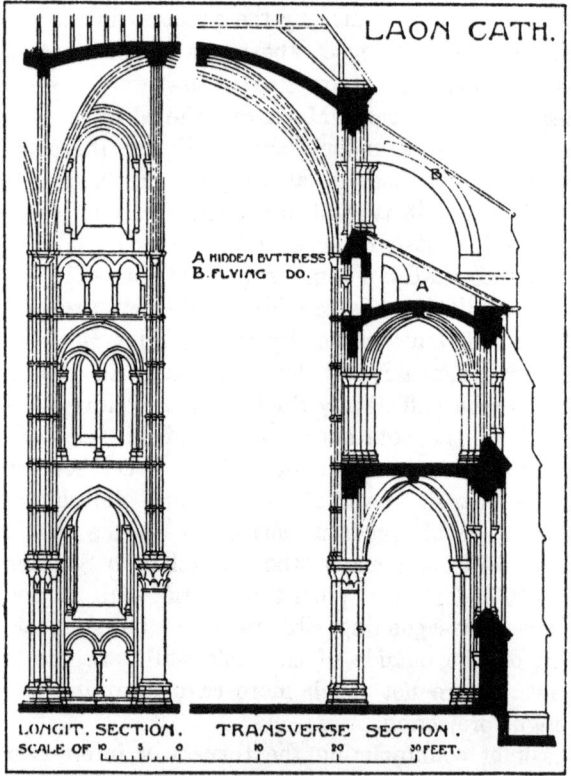

Fig. 61.

the aisles was a spacious gallery, and the roof over consequently as high as the springing of the nave vault, as at Laon, in Northern France; but it ceased to be effective when the upper gallery was omitted, and the soaring ambition of the French architects led to greatly increased height for all parts of a church, the central nave especially.

[1] Exactly the same abutment was provided by the Romans in their great vaulted buildings, such as the Basilica of Constantine.

VAULTING.

The builders did not trust entirely to these hidden buttresses to counteract the vault pressure. As a matter of fact they relied more on the thickness of their walls, and on the height that these were carried above the springing of the vault to the underside of the tie-beam of the timber roof above. They knew that any weight above a point on which there is a side thrust neutralizes, to some extent, that thrust, and directs it downwards. They also, as an additional precaution, weighted the extrados of the vault above the tas-de-charge, so as to keep the thrusts still more within the walls.

With the modest dimensions of our cathedrals these hidden buttresses, coupled with the other precautions mentioned, sufficed; at all events at first, as at Worcester and portions of Lincoln, Salisbury, etc. But the failure and sometimes complete collapse of early vaults soon showed that more direct resistance was required. In many cathedrals, both in England and abroad, extra buttresses have been added which rise above the aisle roofs. In all large churches abroad, commenced after the latter part of the twelfth century, visible flying buttresses form part of the original design. *Flying buttresses.*

Flying buttresses transmit thrusts rather than resist them. Starting from the upper part of the nave wall—as a rule, from slightly projecting buttresses—they conduct the thrusts to buttresses built out from the aisle wall. In Nôtre Dame, Paris, which has double aisles, the principal flying buttresses are in single spans. As a rule, however, in double-aisled churches, the portion of the wall over each pier between the aisles is carried up to form an intermediate buttress, so that each flying buttress consists of two arches. The first arch transmits the thrust of the vault from the nave wall to the intermediate buttress, and the second carries it over to the outer buttress. This has to be sufficiently strong to resist the thrust of the flying buttress itself, and such transmitted vault thrusts as have not been neutralized on the way. *Buttresses transmit thrusts.*

There was evidently no hard-and-fast rule to determine the relative position of the flying buttress to the vault. This differs considerably in the various examples. The builders evidently did not make careful calculations to ascertain the amount of pressure exercised, the exact direction it took, or the precise point from which it started. They judged from experience, from failures, and from successes. It is a question whether such calculation, if made now, would be of any use, because, given one single *Relative position of flying buttresses to vault.*

VOL. II. H

instance of bad workmanship, or of defective material, and the calculations are upset, unless an enormous margin of safety is allowed (see Figs. 61 and 62).

In the majority of examples the top of the intrados of the arch of the flying buttress—or of the most important one when there are several—*i.e.* where it butts against the nave or choir wall, is, approximately, on a line with the top of the tas-de-charge. Its position varies, however; sometimes it is above it, at other times below it, the latter being most general in early, unsatisfactory examples. The pitch of the vault (the thrust of a steep vault is more vertical than that of a flatter one), the height of the tas-de-charge (this varies, as already stated), and the weight of the wall above the springing line of the vault, all these must be taken into account in determining the exact position of the flying buttress. Again, the depth of the buttress from soffit to top of coping, and the slope of the coping, make considerable difference. In early buttresses the bottom curve is often a quadrant, and the top slope of flat pitch. The mass of masonry against the wall which offers resistance to the vault thrust is consequently small. Experience showed that this form was not satisfactory, and the tops of later buttresses are consequently of steeper pitch, and the underside curves are equivalent to half a pointed arch. The early form was most unsatisfactory when the flying buttress was low down; for then, if the upper part of the wall ceased to be perpendicular, owing to the thrust of the vault or other causes, the top of the flying buttress dropped and began to press hard against the wall, with the result that it soon collapsed, being subjected to a thrust outward above and to a thrust inward below. In many later buttresses, and in some earlier ones, there is often a considerable space between the top of the voussoirs composing the soffit curve and the bottom of the coping. This was sometimes solid, and was plain or had sunk panels on its face, sometimes, especially in late work, it was pierced. Such a buttress provides a considerable margin when any uncertainty exists as to the exact direction of the vault thrusts. Moreover, it acts over a large surface, and consequently affords greater support to the wall.

Flying buttresses as stiffeners.

Flying buttresses are not used merely to resist or transmit vault thrusts. In the lofty cathedrals of Northern France, such as Reims, Amiens, etc., where two flying buttresses come one above the other, the upper one has no relation whatsoever to the vault. Its function is simply to aid in supporting the high wall

VAULTING.

of the clerestory and to take the thrust of the timber roof above the vault, which, owing to its construction, is often considerable. At Beauvais, where there are three tiers of buttresses, the lowest is far below the vault, the middle one slightly above the tas-de-charge, and the top one close under the top parapet. The first and

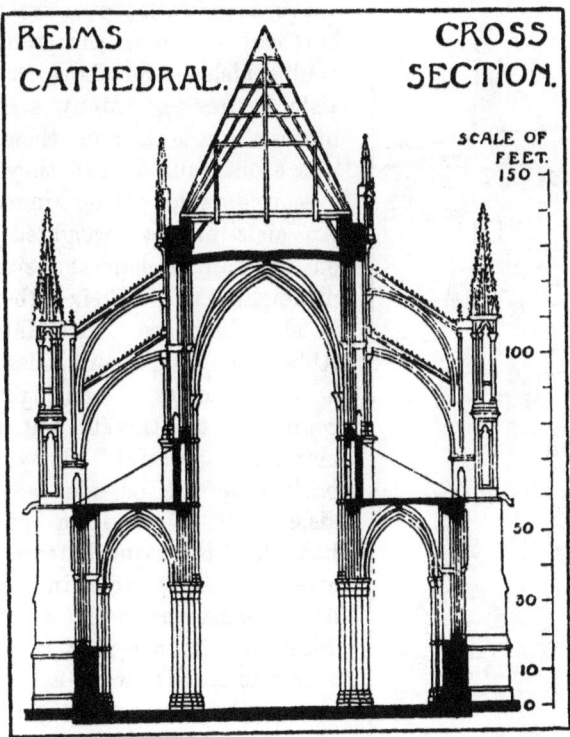

Fig. 62.

last have nothing to do with the vault, they are merely stiffeners to the wall.

It must not be supposed that the builders, when they adopted flying buttresses, dispensed with the other methods of counteracting the thrusts mentioned on a previous page. On the contrary, they developed them. The side walls of the nave were still carried up above the vault, in many cases far higher than before. In Reims Cathedral there are several feet between the top of the vault and the bottom of the tie-beam, and this means the same

100   A HISTORY OF ARCHITECTURAL DEVELOPMENT.

amount of extra wall at the sides and a large increase in the weight pressing on the vault thrusts.[1]

Pinnacles.

Fig. 63.

In addition, the builders multiplied pinnacles, the statical advantages of which have already been mentioned (see p. 49). They placed them above nave walls; over intermediate buttresses — when the church had double aisles—and above the outside aisle buttresses. Many early flying buttresses are without them, but it was soon realized that they effected a considerable saving in material. An aisle buttress weighted heavily on top can be half the size of an unweighted one. Their æsthetic value is also immense. In Malmesbury Abbey Church the pinnacles are not only particularly well placed to counteract the thrusts, but are also extremely graceful. They are set back from the outside face of the aisle wall, start from above the haunch of the flying buttress, and are strengthened by gables in front which add beauty as well as stability. Pinnacles did not play so important a part in English work as in French, where the greater height of the churches, the apsidal east ends, and the frequency of double aisles led to multiplication of flying buttresses and consequent multiplication of pinnacles. In the opinion of some, the number abroad is sometimes too great, and the effect over-done; but there can be little doubt about the

[1] This additional height was probably chiefly for effect. In England, where great height was not desired, there is no great space between the vault and tie-beam; sometimes the tie-beam rests on the vault.

success of the abside of Le Mans Cathedral, where flying buttresses and pinnacles combine in unusual profusion, owing to the forking of the buttresses between the projecting apses (Fig. 97).

The principle of thrust and counterpoise may be briefly summed up as follows:— *Summary.*

1. The tas-de-charge unites all thrusts and consolidates them at given points.

2. The tas-de-charge itself offers resistance to thrusts and also decreases the amount of thrust, inasmuch as the span and height of the "live" portion of the vault are lessened.

3. A high wall above the point of pressure tends to divert a lateral thrust into a vertical.

4. Pinnacles act in the same way.

5. Flying buttresses transmit thrusts to abutments.

6. Abutments weighted by pinnacles can be smaller than when unweighted.

Only two points remain for consideration: one, the arrangement of the vaulting shaft; the other, the different points from which the vaults spring.

In early mediæval work the vaulting shaft starts from the floor and, forming part of the pier, passes through the triforium to the springing of the vault. This is the arrangement at Durham, Chichester, the Abbaye-aux-hommes, Caen, and in most vaulted Romanesque churches of Italy, France, and Germany. *Vaulting shaft.*

As the desire grew for greater lightness and smaller piers, this method was abandoned in England in the thirteenth century and never again became general here, although in parts of Lincoln and Lichfield Cathedrals, and in the fourteenth and fifteenth-century work in the naves of Winchester, Canterbury, and York the old plan is followed (see Fig. 219).[1] At Exeter, Ely, Chester, the choir of Lincoln, etc., is seen the typical English arrangement. In these cathedrals each vaulting shaft springs from a carved or moulded corbel, which nestles between the arches of the nave arcade, immediately above the capitals of the piers. It is a beautiful and at the same time a perfectly sound structural device. Sometimes the shaft starts higher up, from the stringcourse under the triforium, as at Carlisle, with merely a very small corbel below. In Salisbury and Wells Cathedrals it starts higher still, from above the triforium, and possesses little importance. *English method.*

[1] In Winchester Cathedral the old Romanesque piers were remodelled, which, to some extent, accounts for the shafts starting from the floor.

The arrangement in these last two churches emphasizes the fact that verticality was not the sole aim of English workers. By the omission, practically, of the shaft they lost the appearance of height which vertical lines give, but the gain in breadth of effect was ample compensation.

<small>French methods.</small> In France the design depends somewhat on whether the supports are simple columns, as in Nôtre Dame, Paris, and Laon Cathedral, or whether they are columns with attached shafts, as at Reims and Chartres. In the former case the shafts, either three or five in number, start from the top of the capital of each column. To allow space for these the wall has to be considerably thinner than the diameter of the column below, as already mentioned (see pp. 33 and 34). The shafts in these two examples could not have started from the floor without disturbing the cylindrical form of the column which the architects were anxious to retain. In Sées Cathedral a detached shaft is carried down in front of the column, the effect produced being particularly good. In the choir of Canterbury Cathedral, the work of William of Sens, the same arrangement is followed as at Paris. In cathedrals with shafted columns, the shaft on the nave side is sometimes carried up its full size, as in Amiens Cathedral, with merely the abacus of the capital carried round it; a subordinate shaft on each side of it starting from the top of the capital to support the diagonal ribs. In Reims Cathedral this shaft is stopped by the capital, and the vaulting shaft above it is more slender. In later work, however, no attempt is made to lessen the feeling of verticality. In S. Ouen, Rouen, and in the naves of Auxerre and Tours Cathedrals, three or more grouped shafts form part of each pier and, starting from the floor, run without a break to the springing of the vault, thus adding considerably to the apparent height of the church in each case.

<small>Springing of vaults.</small> There is no hard-and-fast rule to denote the point at which the vaulting shaft shall end and the vault begin. In the Cathedrals of Salisbury, Exeter, Ely, Lichfield, Bourges, Paris, Laon, etc., the vault springs from the string between the clerestory and triforium. At Durham and Lincoln it springs from below it, and from above it at Chichester, Chester, Wells, etc. At Amiens and Beauvais Cathedrals the springing line is nearly halfway between the string and the top of the clerestory windows, which accounts, to some extent, for the great height of these two examples. As a general rule, late French churches follow the example of the two last-mentioned cathedrals.

Photo: Author. Fig. 65.—Sées Cathedral: Nave.

[*To face p. 102.*

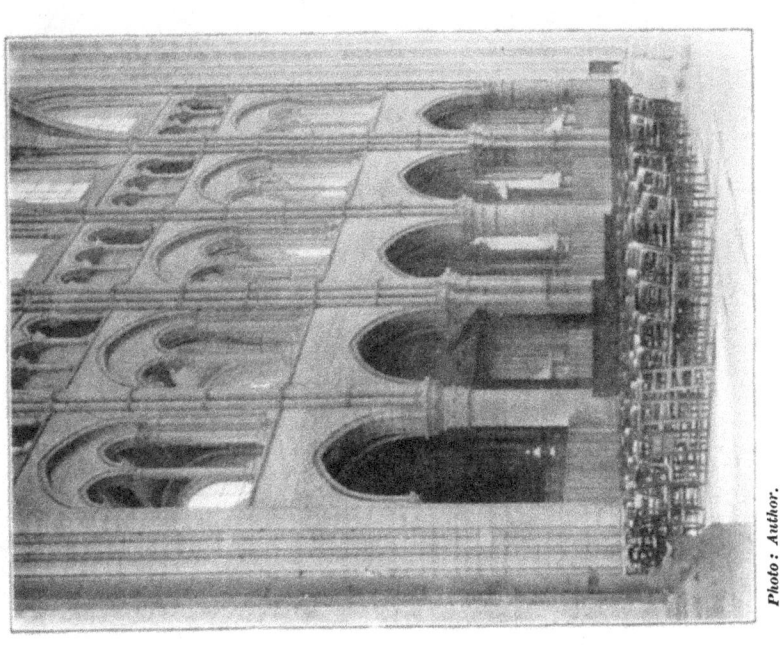

Photo: Author. Fig. 64.—Laon Cathedral: Nave.

CHAPTER VII.

TOWERS AND SPIRES.

CHURCH towers may be placed singly—(*a*) over crossings, (*b*) at west ends, central with a nave, (*c*) at either side, sometimes near the west end, sometimes near the east, in some cases starting from the nave walls and spanning the aisles, in others attached to the aisle walls only, and (*d*) detached entirely from the church to which they belong. They may be in pairs—(*a*) at west ends, (*b*) at ends of transepts, (*c*) over transepts, (*d*) flanking either eastern or lateral apses, (*e*) at the extreme east end, as at S. Nicolo, Bari, although this position is very rare (Fig. 123). {Position of towers.}

A central tower over the crossing in a cruciform church gives the roofs of nave, choir, and transepts something to stop against. One in a church without transepts allows the roofs over the western and eastern ends to start from and rise to different levels without an ugly break resulting. There is, therefore, a sound æsthetic reason for a central tower, except when a church is so lofty as to render it an undesirable addition, as in the majority of large French churches. In England central towers are the rule in cathedrals, and there are also some striking examples in Normandy. The Germans seldom built them; they preferred octagonal cupolas over crossings, like those in Northern Italy. In their Romanesque work they excelled in the grouping of these cupolas with circular turrets, of which there are generally two at least, and often as many as four, in a large church (see Fig. 134). {Central towers.}

A possible objection to a central tower is that it requires piers to support it considerably larger than are needed elsewhere. But in a cruciform church with transepts as high as the nave and choir, even when there is no central tower, the piers at the crossing still have to be stronger than other piers in order to resist the thrusts of the arches of the arcades. In the eastern transepts of Salisbury Cathedral the arcades are continued across, and over each arch is an inverted arch, thus obviating the necessity for stronger piers. When the nave and choir are sufficiently wide, and are also long, larger piers at a crossing are sometimes an advantage, as the deeper arches they carry form pleasant breaks in a vault, and these, coupled with the projection of the piers, improve the perspective and tend to heighten the mystery of the interior. Central towers are most effective from inside, when they are also lanterns, *i.e.* so arranged that the roof or vault over each is sufficiently high to allow of windows in their sides above the adjoining roofs, which windows throw a flood of light into the middle of a church. Romanesque central towers, so far as can be gathered from existing remains, were generally lanterns, although many, like Tewkesbury Abbey, now have later vaults under their windows at about the level of the main vaults. The central towers of Lincoln, Canterbury, and York Cathedrals, and Pershore Abbey Church, are lanterns, and amongst continental examples, four of the finest are at Coutances and Evreux Cathedrals, S. Maclou, Rouen, all in Normandy, and Braisne Church, between Soissons and Reims.

Western towers. The most effective and suitable position for a pair of towers is at the west end. They frame in the principal doorway and the central part of the front, and, in addition, they mask the aisles at the sides. The end elevation of an aisled church is seldom satisfactory when its lines follow truthfully the sectional outline behind it. To conceal this was one of the chief aims of the mediæval builders, and in choosing a pair of towers for this purpose they showed sound judgment. For the same reason, the transepts of many French churches, which have an aisle on each side, were flanked by twin towers until, for circumstances which are suggested later (see p. 277), they were finally abandoned.

Towers over transepts. Towers over transepts are far from common, and yet this position has many advantages. The towers can rise from solid walls, and have not to be balanced aloft on piers and arches; they can be built independently of the rest of the church, and can be allowed to settle as they please; their full height shows; they cause no cramping of the width at the crossing; and they add considerable stability instead of being, as is often the case with a central tower, a source of weakness, at times even a positive danger. Moreover, provided they are of fair height and not too far apart—they should start close against the aisles—they provide more striking grouping than even twin towers at a west end. Towers come over the transepts in Angoulême Cathedral, in a few other churches in Southern France, and in Tréguier Cathedral,

Photo: Author.

Fig. 66.—Coutances Cathedral: Lantern.

Photo: Author.

Fig. 67.—Evreux Cathedral: Lantern.

[*To face p.* 104.

Photo: Author.

FIG. 68.— BRAISNE CHURCH: LANTERN.

Photo: Author.

FIG. 69.—S. MACLOU, ROUEN: LANTERN.

[*To face p.* 104.

Brittany, where there is a central tower in addition. Exeter Cathedral alone in England has towers in this position. The two are practically all that remains of the Romanesque church. In early days a pair of towers so placed was probably not uncommon, but beyond the examples mentioned there are but few others existing now. In later work they are still rarer, the largest and most striking examples being those of Vienna Cathedral.

There are not many churches in which the eastern apses are flanked by towers, except in Germany where, however, they are mostly more turrets than towers. S. Abbondio, Como, is an Italian example, the two towers rising above the aisle roofs at the junction

Fig. 70.

of the nave and choir. In the church of Morienval, France, the towers are somewhat similarly placed at the east end of aisles which are cut off from the chancel by walls. In Tournai Cathedral towers crowned by spires flank the apsidal transepts with striking effect (see Fig. 140). No statement can be made regarding the most usual positions of detached towers. Some are close up to a church, others many feet away from it, as at S. Zeno, Verona.

In France few large churches have single towers at the west end, S. Ricquier, near Abbeville, being one of the chief exceptions. In England a single tower at the west end is an old tradition. The number of Anglo-Saxon examples still remaining is proof that before

Towers in other positions.

Western towers in England.

the Conquest this position was general, which is all the more interesting as single western towers are rare in early work abroad. The Italian basilican church had a narthex at the west end, never a tower. Byzantine churches have no towers at all, and although Ravenna boasts many early ones belonging to its basilican churches they are not central western ones. In Normandy, in the eleventh century, towers over crossings were the rule, and western ones, except in pairs, the exception. In the centuries immediately following S. Augustine's mission to England, a tower attached to a church was almost a necessity in this country; not so much for appearance as for refuge. In most villages the church occupied the most central and highest point, and it was therefore only natural that attached to it should be the stronghold. A tower provided refuge for both people and priests, and although there was no particular reason for choosing a western position, this was at least as convenient as any other and had æsthetic advantages as well. Fortified towers attached to churches, and churches fortified throughout, are neither rare abroad. Albi Cathedral is an example of the first; the church at Royat, Auvergne, with its machicolations all round, of the second. In England, in the debatable land on the Scottish border, there is at least one church, Burgh-by-Sands, Cumberland, which has a fortified tower, the only approach to which is from the church by a narrow opening, projected by a strong iron door. Whatever was the reason why the English so early adopted single western towers, they never tired of them. Ely is the only cathedral with one tower at the west end, but there are thousands of parish churches, of all dates and in all parts of the country, with this feature. In fact, it remained the rule long after Gothic had passed away.

English towers.

Before the Conquest some central towers had been built over crossings in England, as at Dover Castle, and after it very few large churches were designed without them. Amongst Romanesque examples, the finest are those of S. Albans Cathedral, built with Roman bricks from the ruins of Verulam close by; Tewkesbury Abbey, exceedingly massive and bold; and Norwich Cathedral, more slender, and crowned by a later spire. The small height of our Gothic cathedrals, *i.e.* small as compared with continental examples, rendered the building of a central tower comparatively easy. The result is that this feature, sometimes crowned by a spire, and sometimes not, is one of the most characteristic features of English church architecture. The pair of towers at the west end were not abandoned, but some early cathedrals, like Salisbury, and some later ones, like Winchester, are without them. Amongst cathedrals with both central and western towers are Durham, Canterbury, York, Lincoln, Wells, and Peterborough; the western towers of the last-named, however, are small. Lichfield Cathedral is unique in England in having three towers crowned by spires. At Chichester only the central tower has a spire, not either of the end ones. Cathedrals with a central tower and spire, but no west towers, are Salisbury and Norwich, and to these at one time could be added Old S. Paul's, London. Gloucester, Hereford, Worcester, and some others, have now central towers only. Some English towers at present without spires were intended originally to have them, and in a few cases did have them, but they have disappeared. The highest tower is the central one of Lincoln, which rises 262 feet above the ground, over 50 feet more than the western towers, which are also unusually high. The tower of Gloucester Cathedral, early fifteenth century, comes next in height, 225 feet. In beauty of design it is only surpassed in contemporary work by the central tower of Canterbury.

Italy is the land of towers, and yet the Italians never appreciated their full value as important integral parts of a design. They are generally detached entirely, like Giotto's Campanile at Florence, and even when attached often appear like afterthoughts. The one touching the side wall of the Cathedral at Trani has a roadway running through it. Fear of earthquakes accounts largely for the number of detached towers in Italy, but the fact that in the Eastern church towers were omitted altogether possibly also had some weight in determining the Italians not to make them part and parcel of their designs. A central tower over the crossing is almost unknown in the country, although there are frequently low cupola turrets at that point; and twin towers at the west end are exceedingly rare. The earliest church towers in Italy, and therefore in Europe, are those of Ravenna. A few are square, but most are circular, one or two of the smallest of the latter starting from square bases. The oldest is the one near the cathedral, which dates from the fifth century. The towers of S. Apollinare in Classe and S. Apollinare Nuovo belong to the middle of the following one. That these towers were belfries seems certain. Cattaneo says that bells were undoubtedly used in the sixth century, but judging from the number of their windows, especially in the upper storeys, they may also have been

Italian towers.

watch or beacon towers, and perhaps have served as places of refuge. There are seven storeys in the In Classe church and each has six windows. In the bottom storey these are merely slits; in the next two storeys are single lights; then come double lights; above them triple lights; with double lights again in the two top storeys. There does not seem to have been any particular reason why these towers should have been round, or why the Irish towers, built three or four centuries later, were of similar form. There was a reason for the circular towers of Sussex and some of the eastern counties. Flint was the building material there, stone was scarce, and the builders wished to save quoins. In Sussex there are three or four on the banks of the small river Ouse, which runs from Lewes to Newhaven, and passes through Piddinghoe, Southease, etc.

Campanile towers. Square towers in Italy are mostly very tall and slender, and of the type known as "campanile." The term signifies literally a bell-tower, but by common usage it is applied only to towers without buttresses. Although campanile towers have not the buttresses at the corners, diminishing in stages, which give the northern towers their slightly pyramidal outline, a similar effect is obtained in them by the "batter" or inward inclination given to the walls. The tower of S. Mark's, Venice, which collapsed on July 14, 1902, was 35 feet wide at the base and 32 feet at the top, its height to the cornice over the bell loggia being about 200 feet. Its batter, therefore, was $1\frac{4}{5}$ inch in 10 feet, which is about the customary rake.[1]

Venetian towers. There may be said to be three distinct schools of tower design in Italy, excluding the Ravenna towers, and those in the South which were mainly due to foreigners: (1) Venetian, (2) Lombardic, (3) Roman. Each possesses distinctive characteristics. Towers of the Venetian type are frankly belfries, with an open loggia at the top of each which forms the bell chamber. They are without openings, except small slits which light the staircases. At the angles and in between are pilasters of slight projection, which start from the base and run up the face without a break to support arches immediately under the bell loft. There are no horizontal

[1] The fall of the tower appears to have been due to its walls having been weakened by alterations, and not to any fault in its foundations. These consisted of piles of poplar, on which was laid a platform of two layers of oak beams crossing one another, above which came several courses of stone. The upper courses originally showed above the pavement of the piazza. The tower itself, except the upper loggia, pyramid, spire, etc., was built entirely of bricks, many being old Roman ones.

FIG. 71.—S. ZENO, VERONA.

Photo: Alinari.
FIG. 72.—TOWER OF SS. GIOVANNI E PAOLO, ROME.
[*To face p.* 108.

bands or string-courses. The tower of S. Zeno, Verona, is of the Venetian type, but it has two open loggie, instead of a single loggia, and it is built in alternating courses of brick and marble. The conical spire which crowns it is of brick.¹

Lombardic towers differ chiefly from Venetian in that each storey has windows and is marked by a horizontal string-course, of the usual Lombardic type, which stops against pilasters at the angles. The tower of S. Satiro, Milan (c. 879), is probably the oldest square church tower in Northern Italy. It has four storeys, and the windows increase in size from narrow slits immediately above the ground, to two very wide openings on each side at the belfry level. The tower of S. Ambrogio, Milan, built 240 years later, is similar in design, but richer (see Fig. 113).

FIG. 73.

Lombardic towers.

Roman towers are without pilasters, but solidity is given to the angles by keeping the windows well in the centre. They are divided by cornices which gird them, and take the place of the string-courses which in other towers generally stop against angle pilasters. The finest are those of SS. Giovanni e Paolo and S. Maria in Cosmedin, both of the twelfth century. In both towers the number of lights is the same in each of the four or five upper storeys. The tower of SS. Giovanni e Paolo is of brick, but the window shafts and capitals and the little corbels in the cornices are of white marble. As in other towers in Rome, roundels of green marble and porphyry are inserted in different places with excellent effect.

Roman towers.

A tower, unique in many respects, is the circular one at Pisa, which leans 13 feet out of the perpendicular. The generally accepted theory regarding its non-verticality is that this is the

Pisa.

¹ Many Italian spires are built of glazed brick of different colours; the spire above the square tower of S. Giovanni Evangelista, Ravenna, being in alternating bands of green and white.

110 A HISTORY OF ARCHITECTURAL DEVELOPMENT.

result of bad foundations, or of earthquakes. This view, however, is combated by Mr. Goodyear,[1] who holds that it was intentional from the first. The ground storey has a blind arcade, like the cathedral, and above it are six tiers of shafted and arcaded galleries with a belfry of smaller diameter on top. The upper storeys and belfry are nearer the perpendicular than the lower ones, showing either that an attempt was made when the tower was half built to correct the inclination, or else, as Mr. Goodyear claims, to give an entasis to the outline. It is difficult to endorse his theory, as it seems incredible that any architect could wilfully perpetrate so mad a design, or that any people should be so insane as to allow him to carry it out. That the tower has stood so long and so steadily is owing to the great thickness of the wall, which at the base is about 14 feet thick, and yet the internal diameter of the tower is only 25 feet. The galleries project about 3 feet, leaving 8 or 9 feet for the thickness of the wall above the ground storey.

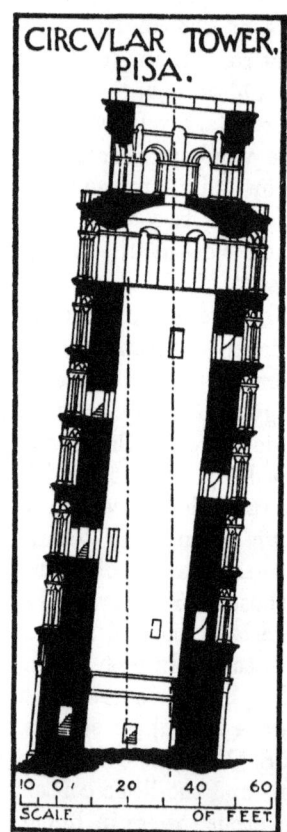

Fig. 74.

The Lombardic type of tower was the one at first followed in other countries, but more pronounced buttressing soon led to modifications of it. Campanile towers pure and simple are rare in both England and France. A small but graceful example is at Yatton Keynell, North Wilts. The sides batter as in Italian examples. Most Romanesque towers have at the angles the wide buttresses of slight projection typical of the period, and otherwise are quite plain except at the top, where there are often one or more bands of arcading. The two small ones on the west side of the transepts of Canterbury Cathedral are particularly well-proportioned. There is no need to trace the variations introduced from century

[1] In the *Architectural Record* for January, 1898.

Photo: Author.
FIG. 75.—JUMIÈGES ABBEY CHURCH.

Photo: Neurdein.
FIG. 76.—COUTANCES CATHEDRAL: CENTRAL LANTERN TOWER.

[*To face p.* 111.

to century in tower design in England, as they are similar to those already described when dealing with other parts of churches. The finest late towers we have are those in the west, in Somerset, Gloucester, etc. Distinction is given to many of these by the pierced stone panels which fill the windows and take the place of the wood louvres which are customary elsewhere.[1] These panels bear a strong resemblance to the slabs in the windows of Byzantine churches, and are the only instances in which the custom prevailed in Gothic work. Examples are in the towers of S. Mary Magdalene, Taunton, and Huish Episcopi, Somerset; Tiverton, Devon; and Coleshill, Berks.

A characteristic French form of tower is that in which (the lower part being square) the upper part is octagonal. In front of the canted sides are turrets, which preserve the square form to some extent. At Jumièges Abbey Church, Normandy, and S. Germain, Auxerre, are Romanesque examples. The majority of towers of this type, however, belong to the thirteenth century, whilst a few are later, like the west towers of Reims Cathedral. The object undoubtedly was to facilitate the starting of the spire, and prevent the somewhat abrupt change which takes place when a tower is continued square to the top and an octagonal spire springs directly from it. This plan is followed in the south-west tower and spire of Chartres Cathedral, and in the famous towers at Laon, where niches, which start from the buttresses below, project at right angles to the canted sides (see Fig. 196). The finest towers of this type are the three at Coutances. The angle pinnacles of the central tower are octagonal, and reach nearly to the parapet; those of the two western towers are square, and are carried far above it. Although many French towers are now without spires, it seems probable that wood ones at least were intended in most cases. The spire of the south-west tower of Chartres is stone, and so are the spires of the two western towers of Coutances. At Reims a spire of the same material has been started over one of the western towers, but was never finished.

Characteristic French form.

An excellent way of finishing a tower, when funds do not admit of its being carried high, is in the Church of S. Nicolas, Caen. The east and west ends of it have gables, with a roof between. These saddle-back towers are numerous round Soissons, France, and are far from uncommon in some parts of England, notably

Saddle-back towers.

---

[1] In France the louvres of tower windows are larger than in England, and are frequently covered with small slates.

112 A HISTORY OF ARCHITECTURAL DEVELOPMENT.

Herefordshire. The tower of Braisne Church, near Soissons, has a gable on each of its four sides, and this was the general custom in German towers crowned by spires.

There will always be differences of opinion as to whether the campanile towers of Italy, or the buttressed towers of more northern countries, are the finer. The former are certainly the more graceful, the latter the more robust. In a less clear atmosphere than that of Italy, the delicacy of such a tower as the S. Zeno one would be lost; and in that atmosphere the shadows cast by buttresses like those of the west towers of Canterbury Cathedral would be too strong. A tower of unbroken lines is

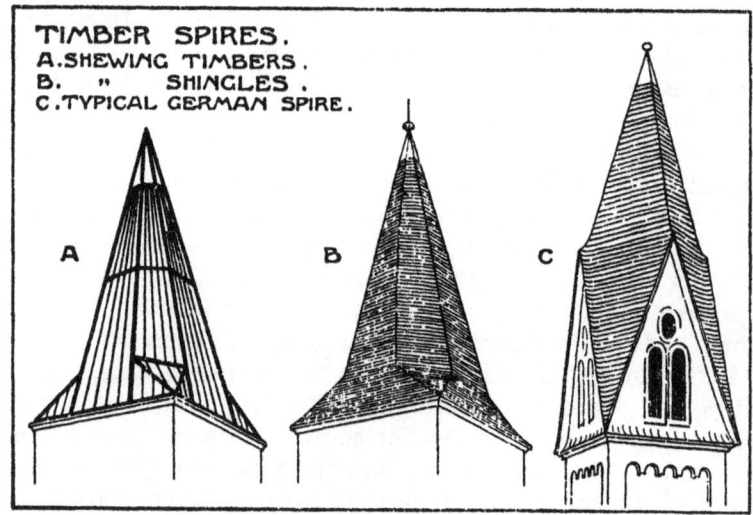

FIG. 77.

undoubtedly best for Italy; one with bold projections has so far been regarded as most suitable for our climate. But it does not follow that such will always be the opinion; and as Classic feeling gains ground in England, we may ere long see the abandonment of features which in the North of Europe in mediæval days were considered essential.

Spires. The majority of Romanesque towers were merely crowned by steep-pitched timber roofs, which gradually were elongated into spires. These were mostly square in plan, like those over the towers of Tournai Cathedral (see Fig. 140). Nearly all later spires, whether in wood or stone, are octagonal. The usual way in which an octagonal timber spire sits down on a square tower is very simple. A trimmer is inserted between each pair of hip rafters near the base, and from its junctions small trimming rafters are carried to the corner, with ordinary rafters in between. The triangle thus formed covers what would otherwise be an exposed angle. The same form is occasionally worked in stone, but it is most appropriate to wood.[1] In most stone spires of the thirteenth century in England, each angle is bridged by a "broach,"

Fig. 78.

the top of which dies into one of the canted sides, whilst the bottom completes the square. The canted sides of a spire are carried on squinch arches thrown across from side to side of the tower to form the necessary octagon. Until near the end of the thirteenth century all spires in England started slightly in front of the face of the wall from projecting oversailing courses. In the

---

[1] Wood spires are covered by lead, slates, tiles, or oak "shingles," according to the locality. The old shingled spires of Sussex, which have toned down to a soft grey, are particularly pleasing.

VOL. II. I

114 *A HISTORY OF ARCHITECTURAL DEVELOPMENT.*

fourteenth century the custom became general of finishing a tower by a parapet, with the result that the spire started behind it. The buttresses at the angles, which hitherto had usually stopped under the oversailing course, were now continued above the parapet, generally in the form of pinnacles, and in some cases flying buttresses were thrown across from the pinnacles to the canted sides of the spire. A broach was sometimes retained, but more often a flat slab covered each angle, leaving the passage-way clear.

Construction of stone spires. The sides of a stone spire are not more than from 6 inches to 9 inches thick, according to size. Near the top they are often thinned down to 4 or 5 inches. The actual top for a few feet is solid, and finishes with a finial. All joints are horizontal, a spire being really built up in a series of corbels, and consequently exercising no side thrust, only vertical pressure. All spires ought to have a slight entasis to prevent the sides appearing concave, and many English ones have this refinement, although it is not universal. In the stumpy spires of Italy, the entasis is often so strong as to be disagreeable, and in early examples in France it is more marked than in this country.

Angle of spires. The later the spire the steeper its slope. In English spires of the thirteenth century, their angle is often not more than 73° to 75°; the timber ones being generally less steep than the stone. The spires of Salisbury, Norwich, and Lichfield are about 80°, the Coutances spires 82°, the spire of Patrington Church, Yorkshire, is a trifle more (Fig. 251), whilst the spire of Louth Church, Lincolnshire, is as much as 85°. In England richly ornamented spires are rare. The Patrington Church spire has some arcading round its base, but as a rule the simple lines are allowed to show from parapet to finial, banded in places and crocketed at the angles in fourteenth-century examples, but otherwise plain. The windows, or lucarnes, vary in design according to date, but are seldom more than single lights or pairs of lights, crowned by a gable. On the continent the spires are often more elaborate. The French generally covered their early ones with scalloping, etc., cut in the stone, and in the fifteenth century sometimes nearly concealed the whole of a spire under a network of little buttresses, carved panels, niches, and crocketed canopies. The two western spires of Chartres Cathedral are examples of the two periods, the south-west spire being early, and the north-west one late.

German spires. The Germans paid especial attention to spires, and although they built few stone ones, the designs of their timber ones show considerable variety. Many are similar to the English tiled or shingle-covered spire. In the most typical form, however, the tower below is gabled on all four sides, and the spire starts from the apexes of these gables, and is continued down between them to their springing. The same is done over octagonal towers, the spires then being also octagonal. Sometimes the spire is octagonal above a square tower and sixteen-sided above an octagon.

The question as to whether a tower alone or a tower and spire combined is the more effective depends on circumstances. In mountainous districts spires are a mistake, unless they stand in a wide valley. At the foot or side of a hill their height is dwarfed by the mass rising above them, and on a summit they appear thin and their outline becomes blurred by distance. In the Lake district in England most of the towers are without spires and are broad and stumpy. Spires are most telling on flat or undulating country, and for this reason are especially numerous in the shires, in Leicestershire, Northamptonshire, Rutlandshire, etc. The home counties, Kent, Sussex, and Surrey, have also several. Towers abound in England in the north and west, although portions of the latter are flat. Boston "stump" is also a landmark for miles round in the Fen district, and is probably more striking than if it had a spire. The fine effect both towers alone and towers with spires produce in towns, especially from a distance, may be well seen at Oxford, Rouen, etc. In mediæval days, when cities were surrounded by walls, they were the only features that showed above them. S. Bernard was wrong when he forebad towers in Cistercian churches, and the Benedictines were right in always adding them to theirs. For a church without a tower can be hidden completely by trees in the country, by houses in a town; and what is out of sight is too often out of mind.

<small>Tower or spire.</small>

CHAPTER VIII.

MURAL DECORATION—SCULPTURE, CARVING, STAINED GLASS.

THE interiors of many mediæval churches, as seen to-day—as clean and colourless as a hospital ward—give but a faint idea of what their appearance was originally. When built they were a blaze of colour from floor to roof. The windows were filled with stained glass, just sufficient clear glass being left to admit light and to frame the dazzling figures of saints, apostles, and martyrs; the walls were painted, and the mouldings of arches picked out with colour and often gilding; the floors were covered with encaustic tiles, yellow, red, and brown. Puritanism, sanitary considerations, and restoration have changed all that. In place of coloured wall, we too often have now newly scraped stone, clean new plaster, or, worse still, rubble walling with the joints picked out, sometimes in black mortar. The brilliant glass has, in many cases, disappeared altogether, making our churches, especially fifteenth-century ones, more like conservatories than places of worship. The difference is as great as between a painting and an engraving; the composition remains the same, the colour is absent. Continental methods have been even more drastic than those of this country. To give one example only. The east end of Laon Cathedral, a few years back, contained most interesting remains of early thirteenth-century and later decorations. The first was applied direct on to the stone, and this, in the fifteenth century, had been covered by a thin layer of stucco, which in its turn had been painted. The work afforded valuable examples of the methods employed in both centuries and of the disregard which later workmen showed for the efforts of their predecessors. The little that remained was only a small portion of what formerly existed there, but even that was doomed. It had to go, said a workman, "pour le faire propre."[1] Cleanliness may be next to godliness, but if not tempered by judgment and respect for the past, it tends to destroy both art and history. What is wanted in old churches is the cleanliness of the painter, not that of the charwoman or "restorer."

Colour can be introduced in a church either in the form of applied decoration, such as marble veneer, mosaics or paint, or by the employment of different materials structurally. In the north of Italy brick and marble or brick and stone are interchanged with the happiest results. Farther south brick is abandoned, and marbles of different colours alternate, the effect being most satisfactory when one colour predominates, and not, as at Siena, when bands of black and white marble are about equal in height. The old Roman custom of covering walls with a thin veneer of marble, which was practised so successfully by the Byzantines, was also frequently followed in central and southern Italy. S. Miniato, Florence (Figs. 117 and 118), shows a particularly good example of this treatment, the slabs being small and the patterns varied. In France and Germany materials of different colours were seldom used. In England also stone facings inside are generally of one colour, although in parts of the country where red and yellow stone exist side by side, often in the same quarry, arches and piers are sometimes of one and the walling of the other. English work, however, especially that of the thirteenth century, is often marked by strong contrasts, owing to the use of detached shafts of marble in combination with white stone. In the south of England these shafts are generally from the quarries in the isle of Purbeck, Dorset, and in the north from Frosterley, near Durham, and elsewhere. In the nave of Salisbury Cathedral and throughout the whole of Westminster Abbey the columns, surrounding shafts, and the capitals and bases are all marble. At Worcester only the shafts, the abacus of each capital, and top members of each base are of that material, the remainder being stone. The shafts in jambs of triforia, clerestory and aisle windows, doorways and porches are also frequently of marble. The contrasts now are in many cases too marked, especially at Salisbury, where the jump from the dark Purbeck of the piers to the white stone of the arches is too abrupt, and the general effect disagreeably cold. That this

Methods of decoration.

---

[1] My first visit to Laon was in 1896, when the scraping tool was getting perilously near the east end. I was there again last year (1907), after the above was written, and was glad to find that something had been spared. In La Trinité Angers, so far as can be seen, not a vestige of old stone or colour remains.

frigidity is part and parcel of the original design is extremely doubtful. The white stone of arches and wall was most likely painted, probably in rich reds and occasional yellows, and the effect in mediæval days was entirely different. Some of the most striking schemes of decoration in materials of different colours are in the volcanic district of the Puy-de-Dome, France, and in Romanesque churches elsewhere, but these are mainly confined to exteriors, and are referred to later in the chapter dealing with the churches of Auvergne. A similar treatment occurs in Chichester Cathedral in the tympana over the openings of the triforia, which in some cases are filled with lozenge-shaped stones of different colours.

Mosaics. Whether mosaic work originated in the East, and thence was carried to Rome, or in Italy, is a disputed point; but it seems likely that although the Romans were early workers in marble mosaic for floors, the art of glass mosaic commenced elsewhere. The latter certainly reached perfection under the Byzantine Greeks of the sixth century, and much subsequent work in Italy, down to the end of the twelfth century, was executed by Greek workmen. Amongst noted late examples of it are the blue Madonna in the apse of Torcello Cathedral, the head and shoulders of Christ in the apse of Cefalû Cathedral, the same design in a similar position in Monreale Cathedral, both in Sicily, and the wonderful band of figures round the nave, under the clerestory windows, in the last-named church. In S. Mark's, Venice, are also remarkable mosaics of the eleventh and twelfth centuries; but these and other contemporary examples in Greece and Constantinople have already been dealt with in the first volume. In the thirteenth century the art died, except in the East, where it lingered in places a short time longer. One reason why it was abandoned is that Romanesque and Gothic churches do not lend themselves so well to applied decoration as basilican churches. The triumphal arch of the latter, with its fine expanse of wall over it, crying aloud for colour, disappeared in the desire to carry the vault from end to end without a break; and the open triforium galleries at the sides occupied the space over the arcades formerly available for mosaics. A revival has taken place of late years, as the fine work in Westminster Cathedral shows, and there is no reason why this most durable form of mural decoration should not again become general.[1]

[1] Although so largely used by the Byzantine Greeks on domes, mosaics were

Photo: Author.

FIG. 79.—CHICHESTER CATHEDRAL: TRIFORIUM.

[*To face p.* 118.

MURAL DECORATION, ETC.

The remains of early fresco paintings are not numerous, but there can be little doubt that the art was practised in Italy through the first centuries of church-building. In the underground church of S. Clemente, Rome, are fresco paintings of all periods, some as early as the fourth century, others as late as the beginning of the twelfth, when the present upper church was built. Examples in Romanesque churches are few. The Romanesque workman was a builder, he revelled in his bricks and mortar and stone; as a decorator he was inferior; but the absence now of paintings in his churches does not necessarily mean that none ever existed there. Many have doubtless been destroyed. These probably were not great works of art. Until towards the end of the thirteenth century the fresco painters produced little worthy to compare with the figures of the mosaic worker. Then came a Renaissance, and in the work of Cimabue, Giotto, etc., in the Franciscan church at Assisi, in S. Croce, Florence, etc., the art reached its highest level.

Fresco painting.

Before oil became the general medium for mural decoration early in the fourteenth century, work not executed in fresco was done in tempera, fixed sometimes by a final coat of oil. Tempera differs mainly from fresco in being applied to a dry surface and not to a damp one. Sometimes the work was done direct on stone, but more often a thin coat of stucco was laid first, as this afforded a more even and satisfactory surface to work on and prevented absorption. The process is an exceedingly ancient one, extending back to the days of Egypt, Greece, and Rome, and was practised all through the Middle Ages in all countries. The palette was an extremely limited one until the end of the thirteenth century, and consisted of little more than reds and yellows. There are many fragments of pictures painted in this medium in England, but all are more or less damaged. Many have been covered by later paintings, or by plaster, to form a key for which the earlier surface, plaster or stone, has been hacked. Others have been hidden by whitewash, applied either in the days when whatever was beautiful was held to be idolatrous, or during periods of great sickness. After the plague visitations, which were so frequent in the Middle Ages, disinfection of churches was as necessary as disinfection of houses, and much

Distemper and oil paintings.

never, so far as I know, applied to the compartments of ribbed vaults. The art was moribund before they were invented, and the idea of applied decoration (save paint) was altogether repugnant to the mediæval mason.

of the whitewashing generally attributed to the Puritans was very likely a precautionary method taken much earlier to prevent the spread of disease. Whatever the reason, the damage done was irreparable. Whitewashing mosaics only preserves them, but it spells ruin to both fresco and distemper. The paintings on the western sides of the nave piers of S. Albans Cathedral are fair examples of early work. So far as can be judged from somewhat scanty existing remains, such pictures only came at intervals, or in bands, the walling in between, above, and below them being coloured a plain tint, generally red in the thirteenth century, or else whitened, with double lines of red or yellow forming rectangular spaces, which corresponded approximately to the joints in the walling behind. There was, however, no attempt at imitation jointing, and in the centre of each oblong was frequently painted a four- or five-leaved flower.

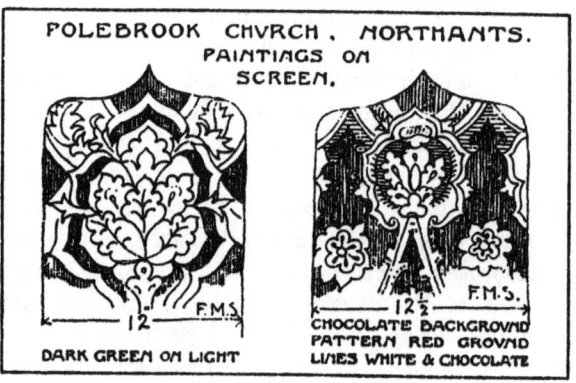

Fig. 80.

Fifteenth-century mural paintings. With the introduction of oil as the usual medium, greens and blues were added and predominated, and mural decoration became far more elaborate. Pictures on the walls do not appear to have been so general as in the thirteenth century, but many in this medium have survived on wood fittings, on triptychs, panels of pulpits, screens, etc. Walls were frequently covered with large diaper patterns, sometimes consisting of single sprigs of flowers—variety being obtained by turning the stalks and flowers different ways—and sometimes of elaborate conventional designs in imitation of Florentine hangings. The mouldings of arches especially were all painted, the fillets being frequently

Photo: Author.

FIG. 81.—S. VULFRAN, ABBEVILLE.

Photo: Author.

FIG. 82.—S. JACQUES, LISIEUX: PAINTING, 1552.

[*To face p.* 121.

gilded. Not very much of this work remains on walls in England, but there are many examples of it on screens, stalls, pulpits, tombs, timber roofs, etc., especially in the Eastern Counties, Norfolk, Suffolk, etc., and in the west. The mediæval builder had no respect for the natural colour or grain of oak. That feeling is a modern fancy entirely. Oak was the common, the only wood for all fittings, and for all structural parts of churches requiring to be in timber. These were painted and gilded, so that in many cases not a square inch of the natural material showed, and the grain was obliterated entirely. In S. Albans Cathedral the shrine of S. Alban, although of Purbeck marble, is painted blue and green, the tracery and mullions being gilded. The painting on the mouldings of many a fifteenth-century oak screen affords an excellent guide to what the painting on stone mouldings was like, and enough remains on the latter in different churches, at home and abroad, to prove that both were treated alike. In stone vaults the carvings of bosses were generally gilded, and between the leaves or figures, as the case might be, was colour to emphasize them further. The ribs were painted, sometimes merely for a short distance from the bosses, and the infilling, when plastered, was treated in the same way, although few remains exist of mediæval work on webs in northern countries. The fine decoration in S. Anastasia, Verona, is Gothic in feeling, but was executed after the Renaissance had begun; and the paintings on the vaults of S. Vulfran, Abbeville, and S. Jacques, Lisieux, are sixteenth century, the latter being dated 1552.

In no country can such extensive remains of old colour be seen as in Germany, and in none are modern redecorations and restorations—not always successful—so plentiful. The churches of Cologne, for instance, S. Martin, S. Gereon, etc., are extensively painted inside. One of the most satisfactory redecorations is in the porch of the Liebfrauenkirche, Nürnberg, which is a mass of colour, the figures and other portions being gilded solid. Such decorative schemes are not confined to churches. Restaurants, hotels, private houses, etc., are often painted much in the same way as buildings were in the time of Dürer. As in printing, the Germans have preserved mediæval traditions in decoration, and black-letter inscriptions on walls, especially in the smaller towns, are almost as common now as they ever were. *Colour in Germany.*

The colour schemes of the mediæval painters are a succession of contrasts. A broad effect is obtained, not by the use of one *Colour schemes.*

single colour, but by the juxtaposition of many colours, no one being allowed to prevail over the others. One moulding may be green, the next red or blue, or white with small sprigs of flowers painted on it—the last is reserved for hollows—and the dividing fillets either gilded or painted a strong yellow. A complete accord must have existed between mason and painter, otherwise such schemes would have been impossible, as colour completely changes the appearance of mouldings. By its aid some can be emphasized, others almost obliterated.

Quality of colour.
Considerable controversy at times has arisen over the quality of the colours used. Some have held that it was crude in the extreme, and the present fine tones they attribute to time alone. As proof, they point to examples from which whitewash or plaster has recently been removed. In[1] thirteenth-century work the colours possibly were crude, although the linseed oil that was often the final coat must have toned them down somewhat. The late G. F. Bodley always maintained that, in the fifteenth century at least, although crude colours were applied first, a semi-transparent glazing colour was added as a finish. His contention was that when whitewash has been removed from old work, the glazing coat has unfortunately been removed also, and that the colour remaining is very different in tone from the work when the painters left it. The patchy appearance of much old painting may be advanced in support of this, and even if absolute proof is not forthcoming, his suggestion is such a reasonable one that it may well be accepted.

Colour externally.
Fragments alone remain to enable one to judge of the extent to which colour was employed externally on churches, but these are sufficient to show that in most cases both it and gilding were applied to the figures, canopy work, and walling behind in porches and doorways. Colour has to be sought for in churches for the entire renovation of which funds were luckily not available. The less renowned the church, the greater the likelihood of finding remains of decoration. The north and south porches of Chartres Cathedral are famous throughout the civilized world, and it is useless to search for colour in them. And yet there can be no doubt whatsoever that they were painted and gilded originally, but both paint and gold have been cleaned off with a thoroughness worthy of a better cause. It is only in the crevices that anything can be discovered at all, and even in these the patches are so minute that their nature is not clear. Over the west door

FIG. 83.—AUTUN CATHEDRAL: OPEN NARTHEX.

[*To face p.* 122.

Photo: Author.

FIG. 84.—S. OUEN, ROUEN: NICHES ON PIERS.

[*To face p.* 123.

of Angers Cathedral a considerable amount of colour, red, blue, and green, remains; and the bands, etc., on the garments of the figures, the wings of the angels, and the animals, of which there are several, are gilded solid. In the triple western porch of Sées Cathedral, Normandy, the same three colours were used extensively, mainly on the mouldings and on the walling behind the figures. A good deal of this decoration still exists, because the restoration has not yet reached the west front.

All through the Middle Ages, and especially in the eleventh and twelfth centuries, the sculptured pictures were the books of the people. They read in stone the stories the monks, and a few others alone, could read on parchments. The wicked descending to hell, the righteous being carried up to heaven in chariots similar in form to those which they saw every day in the street, were pictures all could understand. The angels on the one side, the devils on the other, and the Saviour enthroned between, as over the doorway of Autun Cathedral, expressed in concrete form their belief. The Lamb suspended by a cord, the Figure on the Cross, conveyed far more to them than the words of the preacher; and the monks of the eleventh and twelfth centuries were wise in their generation in choosing such subjects. Sometimes the carvings illustrate a biblical incident, as over the north-west doorway of Rouen Cathedral, where the daughter of Herodias is shown dancing—or rather tumbling, as an old Bible expresses it—before Herod. Elsewhere, the skill of the sculptors is shown in representations of domestic animals, oxen and sheep, as at Laon Cathedral, which made a homely appeal to an agricultural community, or in fantastic forms, as at Paris, and Nôtre Dame, Dijon. Early in the thirteenth century symbolic sculpture and biblical pictures became rarer, and the finest work was devoted to the glorification of apostles, saints, and kings. *Sculpture*

Apart from the intrinsic beauty of mediæval sculpture, two reasons account for its especial effectiveness. The first is that it was executed by men thoroughly in harmony with the work surrounding it, and in close touch with those who carried that out, and secondly, that the sculpture in most cases is framed in. Occasionally, in fourteenth-century work, a figure stands on a corbel against a wall outside, or in front of a pier inside, as originally at S. Ouen, Rouen, without any, or with but slight, surroundings; but figures so placed are exceptions. As a rule they stand in niches with canopies or arches over them, or else *Mediæval sculpture framed.*

are carved on the tympana of entrance doorways, in which position they are still framed by an arch. In Paris, Chartres, Amiens, and other great French cathedrals, they occur in bands of arcading along the west fronts. In jambs of doorways they often partially take the place of shafts, and in the orders of the arches over they, with their canopies, form concentric bands of great richness. In the fronts and sides of the buttresses on the west front of Wells Cathedral they are in profusion, standing in niches, or seated or crouching inside quatrefoils or trefoils. Inside, save in S. Ouen, Rouen, and in some later churches, they rarely touch the structure. They are reserved mainly for reredoses, as in Winchester Cathedral, and Christ Church, Hampshire; for screens round choirs, as at Chartres Cathedral; for tombs, pulpits, fonts, and other fittings. There are exceptions. On the inside face of the west wall of Reims Cathedral is some fine sculpture and still finer carving in panels. The angels in the spandrils over the triforium arches in the eastern arm of Lincoln Cathedral have earned it its title of the Angel Choir. Even finer than these, although much smaller, are the figures over the seats in the Lady Chapel of Ely Cathedral. In pose and in drapery treatment they are as perfect as Greek sculpture.

England has little sculpture that it can pit against the sculpture of France, with the exception of that at Wells. The west front of that cathedral is unusually wide, owing to the positions of the towers (see p. 305), and the whole front forms an immense screen, specially designed to contain as many figures as possible, and to show them off to the best possible advantage. No French cathedral west front can boast so fine an array. On the other hand, the greater size and magnificence of French doorways and porches gave the sculptors abroad a far finer opportunity than their brethren as a rule enjoyed here, which they turned to excellent account.

Schools of sculpture. Viollet-le-Duc says there were five schools of sculpture in France in Romanesque times—those of Toulouse, Limoges, Provence, the Rhenish, and Clunisian. Of these by far the most fascinating is the last, or Burgundian school, of which such magnificent examples exist under the porch of Autun Cathedral and over the doorway leading from the narthex into the nave of Vézelay Abbey Church. One of the chief peculiarities in these two examples is the smallness of the heads of the figures. In all other Romanesque work the heads are unnaturally large, and like

FIG. 85.—FIGURES FROM WESTERN DOORWAY, CHARTRES CATHEDRAL.

[*To face p.* 124.

proportions extended, to some extent, all through Gothic times. The folds of drapery on Clunisian figures bear a close resemblance to archaic Greek sculpture of the seventh and sixth centuries B.C.; and the resemblance is interesting as showing how early workers at different periods expressed themselves in similar fashion, although many centuries intervened. Viollet-le-Duc's theory is that the special characteristics of this school of sculpture are taken from Byzantine Greek paintings, which, he claims, the work greatly resembles, especially in the treatment of drapery. On the other hand, it is not impossible that craftsmen from the East were employed on it. To what extent Byzantine Greeks penetrated into France and Germany in the tenth and eleventh centuries is a point that has never been decided, perhaps never will be; but it is one that well deserves thorough investigation. The Abbots of Cluny certainly had close relations with the East, and not only sent missions to Antioch and other parts of Syria, but also imported works of art from there—silk hangings, carved ivories, paintings, etc. It is quite possible that the monks persuaded workmen to return with them. This Clunisian School spread as far as Chartres and Le Mans. The figures flanking the west doorway of the former and the south porch of the latter are almost identical in treatment with those at Vermenton Church, Burgundy (c. 1130). The figures themselves stand on high bases and form the shafts at the sides, their heads projecting forward, whilst behind each head rises a short portion of a cylindrical shaft, which is crowned by a capital. This was the customary design in the first half of the twelfth century. By the end of the century much of the archaic feeling noticeable in all early sculpture had disappeared, and the faces and forms had become more realistic and the lines of drapery more flowing. The sculpture on the north and south porches of Chartres is representative of the work that followed. That on the south is earlier and finer than that on the north, and its restraint and architectural suitability are greater. Both porches are mines of wealth; but whilst giving them due praise it is possible to have a sneaking preference for the earlier and more conventional rendering found in the figures of the west doorway of the same cathedral. The work of the pioneers of a movement is often more fascinating than that of those who have carried that movement to what one is pleased to call perfection. It is more individualistic. It may have more faults, be more open to criticism, but being less correct it is often less cold.

Romanesque carving.

The source of most carving executed before the middle of the twelfth century is found in Classic or in Byzantine art. Mention has already been made of twelfth-century Corinthian capitals, which differ but slightly from second-century ones, and of corbel capitals of the former date, which recall those of the sixth century. The farther one proceeds away from the centres of Classic and Byzantine art the less skilful and refined is the carving, and the greater the departure from old traditions. In Southern Italy and Sicily the carvers were undoubtedly Byzantine Greeks, and their work is distinguished by a delicacy which is never found more to the north. The Byzantine carvers of the sixth century confined themselves mainly to representations of foliage or to patterns

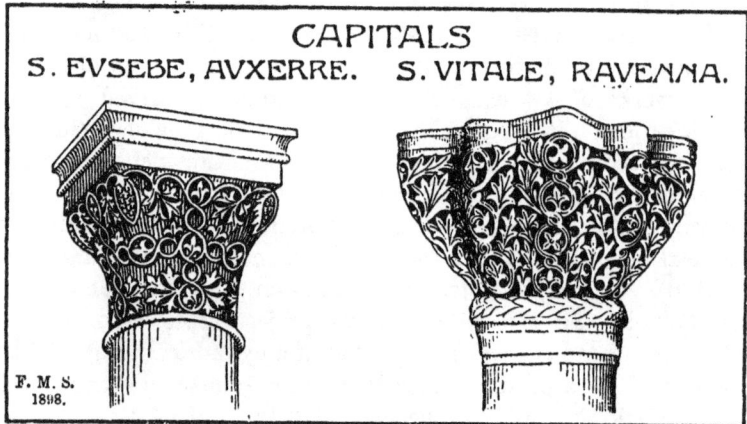

FIG. 86.

formed of interlacing strands resembling open basketwork. Their descendants of the eleventh and twelfth centuries introduced animals more freely, especially birds. The carving of the capitals in the cloisters of Monreale Cathedral, Sicily, is especially fine; and birds, half hidden by leaves, pecking at bunches of grapes are frequent. In Southern France and Burgundy the feeling is sometimes the same, but the workmanship is rougher. The carving may have been executed by Byzantine Greeks, and its inferiority be due to the fact that the workmen who found their way to the west of the Mediterranean were less skilled than their brethren who found employment nearer home. On the other hand, it may well have been carried out by local men who tried to represent detail with which they were only slightly acquainted. The mediæval craftsman was a great traveller; and many churches show evidence that at least two, and possibly more, schools of carvers were employed. The well-known capitals in the cloisters of the Abbey of Moissac are probably all native workmanship, as, although they vary considerably in design, the executive skill shown is the same throughout. Some betray a striving after Byzantine ideals, but this, in many cases, is combined with Northern mythical representations. In Burgundy there is great variety. In the church of Saulieu (c. 1119), a town which at one time was of considerable importance, the numerous capitals are marked by much free handling of the chisel and by considerable originality in design. Hardly Byzantine in feeling, they are decidedly unlike the usual Romanesque carvings. In the Church of S. Eusèbe, Auxerre, some of the capitals are quite ordinary, whilst others are decidedly the reverse. The capital illustrated resembles closely one in S. Ambrogio, Milan, and others in S. Mark's, Venice, S. Vitale, Ravenna, etc., and has the drilled holes and sharp acanthus leaves typical of Byzantine workmanship. In Germany, Normandy, and England the carving is always robust and strong, often coarse, but otherwise it differs little in design from carved work elsewhere.

Romanesque carved enrichments on arches, ribs, string-courses, etc., are primæval. The most common of all, the chevron or zigzag, was the favourite with the Egyptians, and the others also filtered through from the East. In the scalloped capital so common in English and German work of the early part of the twelfth century, the scallops, or cones, with their dividing tongues, are direct descendants of the eggs and darts of Greek and Roman times, which, in their turn, were derived from the lotus bud of Egypt. In one respect the Romanesque carvers departed somewhat from tradition. They introduced symbolism to a far greater extent than their predecessors, either Eastern or Western. It is possible that a symbolic meaning has in modern times been attributed in cases when none was intended by the craftsman—as a critic will often discover hidden meanings in a painting never dreamt of by the artist—but many carvings undoubtedly fulfilled a double object; they added beauty and they told a story. *Enrichments.*

With the change from the semicircular arch to the pointed, new schools of carvers arose, chiefly laymen, not monks, who discarded, to a great extent, Classic tradition and went direct to *Carvings, 1150-1250.*

nature for inspiration. This they rendered with considerable realism, never overstepping, however, the limitations which the material imposed. In some French carvings executed between 1150 and 1250 there is a certain dependence on old tradition, especially in capitals. Those of Nôtre Dame, Paris, for instance, although full of freshness and immense vigour and thoroughly original in treatment, are undoubtedly descendants of Corinthian capitals. Almost down to the end of the fifteenth century capitals in France show traces of the influence of this Order—a compliment to the Romans and a credit to French mediæval carvers—which only disappeared when capitals became diminutive or were omitted altogether. Otherwise, the Frenchman, like the Englishman, went to nature. Whilst the source was the same, the results, however, are very different. Nobody who knows the work in both countries will ever mistake an English thirteenth-century carving for one from the Isle de France. French carvings are bigger in scale than English ones—even allowing for the greater size of French churches—and the treatment, as a rule, is simpler and broader, probably because the stone generally used was hard and coarse. Most English carvings are small and delicate by comparison, because they are executed in soft, easily worked stone of fine grain. They are like Normandy ones, for which the same, or similar, stone was used. In English capitals from 1150 to 1250, stalks spring from the necking of each, and, shooting up the bell, end in bunches of crisp, compact, stiff-leaved foliage. The same crispness and "tightness" and the predominance of trefoil leaves are equally noticeable in the bunches at the ends of cusps, in crockets and finials, and in the carvings of spandrils.

1250-1500. In the middle of the thirteenth century carving lost the stiffness which characterizes the earlier work in both England and France, and became as exact a rendering of nature as was obtainable in stone. In some cases realism was carried too far, and the work, although beautiful, is lacking in strength. The desire to be realistic imparts a curious crumpled character to much of the foliage, notably to crockets, as in Prior Crauden's Chapel, Ely. About the last quarter of the thirteenth century the carving in capitals ceased to spring from the necking and cluster under the abacus, and twined round the bell in a compact mass, the stalks being smaller and much less pronounced, and either hidden entirely or else tucked away under the foliage so that very little of them showed. The effect was naturalistic, but it was neither so decorative nor so forcible as the earlier manner. The best carvings in England of this period are in Southwell Minster, Exeter Cathedral (in the corbels carrying the vaulting shafts), and in S. Mary's, Beverley, Yorks. After the Black Death considerable deterioration is apparent. The carving is cramped and knotty. It has neither the vigour and pleasant convention of the thirteenth century, nor the realistic beauty of the first half of the following one. Its angular stiffness— very different from the rounded stiffness of early Gothic—shows that the carvers were losing their skill, were neglecting the study of nature, and were settling down into a conventional groove. The work improved again before the end came, and late fifteenth-century carvings often show considerable vigour.

The most characteristic ornament in English work between 1150 and 1250 is termed the "Dogtooth." It is fairly common also in Normandy, even as far south as Le Mans, where it occurs in the window over the doorway of the south tower of the cathedral, and it is met with occasionally in other French cathedrals, notably Laon. The usual statement is that this feature is derived from the "nail-head" of Romanesque times, elongated and elaborated; but it is much more likely to be a modified version of the chevron, no longer continuous but split up into separate ornaments. During the above-named period the dogtooth was almost the only ornament the builders permitted themselves. They placed it between shafts, half buried it in hollows, or allowed it to stand out boldly in front of surrounding work. They used it in arches, piers, labels, string-courses, jambs of windows and doorways, ribs of vaulting— in fact, everywhere. <small>Dogtooth.</small>

Towards the end of the thirteenth century the dogtooth disappeared and was replaced by the so-called "Ball flower," which consists of a calyx of three or four leaves, slightly open so as to show in the centre an unopened flower. Absolute monotony is avoided by varying the "hang" of the flowers, but at best the ornament is but a hard and unsympathetic rendering of nature, even after due allowances are made for the nature of the material it is carved in. It is most satisfactory when it alternates with a square four-leaved open flower, especially when, as often happens, the two are connected by a stalk so that a running <small>Ball flower, etc.</small>

130 A HISTORY OF ARCHITECTURAL DEVELOPMENT.

Fig. 87.

pattern is formed. In the aisle windows of Gloucester Cathedral and Leominster Church the jambs, heads, mullions, and tracery are all peppered thick with ball flowers, the number of which the curious have counted and recorded.[1] In the great circular west window of Chartres Cathedral the ornament carved round its openings (and in the labels over it and the side windows of the front) is a species of ball flower earlier in date and more beautiful than the English variety. The leaves are folded back, not brought forward, and the whole of each flower (not merely the centre) resembles a ball. In the Church of S. Pierre de la Couture, Le Mans (c. 1150), in the labels over the arches of the windows, are flowers which are also earlier than the English ones. In some of these the flower is quite open, in others only half open, and the effect produced by the variations is exceedingly good.

Before the wars between the Houses of York and Lancaster the rose usually carved in English work was the simple five-petalled briar or wild rose. When the Houses were united, to symbolize the union, roses were carved with ten and sometimes fifteen petals. This form, in consequence of the extensive use of it by Henry VII. and Henry VIII., has been termed the Tudor rose, and, with the portcullis, forms the most distinctive badge in the chapel of the first-named at Westminster. *Tudor rose, etc.*

Few remains of twelfth-century glass exist; partly because it was not until a century later that stained glass was employed extensively, and partly because early glass was rarely fitted into stonework, but into wooden frames, which were easily removable. What little there is shows that the designs were similar to the designs for carvings, and that scroll work founded on the classic acanthus was the prevailing motive. In the thirteenth century figures were first introduced to any extent. As a rule, they are small, and are grouped together to represent scenes, sometimes biblical, sometimes pastoral. Each light consists of many of these pictures placed inside geometrical forms, such as circles, quatrefoils, squares, etc. The effect is generally very dark, as there is little white glass, and often not much yellow, the prevailing colours being red, blue, green and purple, which are worked together in wondrous harmony and rival in colour the richest of Persian rugs. Amongst English examples of this type is the famous "Five Sisters" *Glass.*

---

[1] Sharpe says that each window of Leominster Church has 820 ball flowers of different sizes.

window in the north transept of York Cathedral. In France similar contemporary windows are in the aisles of Chartres Cathedral, the choir aisles of Le Mans Cathedral, etc. In the clerestory windows of both, however, the design is different. The figures are large, and are no longer grouped and confined within geometric forms. In Chartres Cathedral each light has often only one large figure, although sometimes there are more. No attempt has been made to obtain uniformity throughout. The figures by no means all start from the same level, and some are much larger than others. In fifteenth-century glass, as a rule, the figures all toe the line, are about equal in height, and the canopies above them alike in size, although they differ somewhat in detail. There is no such exactness about the glass at Chartres. The canopies there, when they occur at all, are small and in absolute subjection to the figures. To these irregularities is largely due the unrivalled reputation that the Chartres glass enjoys. If it has a fault it is that it is too dark, owing to blue being the predominating colour. In the clerestory windows of Le Mans Cathedral there is very little blue. Some of the figures, of which there are generally two to each light, one over another, are mostly yellow, whilst others are green or red.

In fourteenth-century glass single figures, one to each light, are the rule, but they do not generally completely fill the space. Medium in size, each stands out a mass of rich colour in a setting of almost clear glass, on the small lozenge-shaped panes of which a diaper pattern, usually in yellow, is painted. Round the outside of each light is a border of delicate patterns, in colour matching the central figure, which is separated from the mullions by an inch, sometimes less, of absolutely clear glass. This edging of white glass is of great value. It separates the glass from the stone and forms the finest frame imaginable. The fifteenth-century glass stainers followed fairly closely the workers of the previous one, but they frequently omitted the border, made the figures larger, and gave greater importance to the canopies over the heads of saints, apostles, and kings. These canopies are invariably copies on the flat of the carved canopies on tombs, tabernacles, etc., and although they are of some use in lengthening the design and filling the foliated heads of lights, they are often unnecessarily large and elaborate, and somewhat overpower the figures below. The artists of Chartres did without them entirely, or introduced them sparingly. That so many of the glass designers of the fifteenth century could not, in the surroundings of their figures, tear themselves away from the designs of the mason is evidence of the decline in art which is apparent at that time in all the other crafts.[1] Stained glass possessed such virility in the thirteenth and fourteenth centuries, and exercised so powerful an influence on architectural development, that as its use increased (as it undoubtedly did towards the end of Gothic art), one might have expected more independence on the part of the artists who produced it, and a special treatment for the accessories of their figures, different from that appertaining to carved stone and better suited to the material in which they worked. That in many cases they did not succeed in originating this constitutes the chief blot, perhaps the only one, on a great deal of otherwise beautiful glass of the late Middle Ages. No fault can be found with the figures themselves; these compare favourably with the earlier ones, and evince also considerable advance in technical skill. Neither does all fifteenth-century glass show extravagance in canopy work, nor can all be included under the above generalization. In some instances the design is arranged to fill a whole window with many figures, which are grouped in such a manner that, although separated from one another by mullions, they form one picture. In other examples the figures are smaller and there are many to each light, the scale and arrangement approaching nearer to thirteenth-century glass without the enclosing geometrical forms. Of this character is the east window of York Cathedral, which was executed by John Thornton, a glazier of Coventry, in 1405. York has also fine fourteenth-century windows in the nave, and the east window of Gloucester Cathedral is of that date. The finest of late windows in England are possibly those of Fairford Church, Gloucestershire (c. 1500), and King's College, Cambridge (c. 1530). Many parish churches in England contain fragments of old glass, and in some cases windows are completely filled with it; but there is not the wealth in England that exists in France. In addition to Chartres, the Cathedrals of Bourges and Reims are full of fine glass, mostly early fourteenth century, and examples of the work of the century following are exceedingly numerous.

Modern glass is often held to be inferior to old in colour, but it is a question whether the best of the former cannot hold its own in this respect with the examples of the Middle Ages. Time

Colour in glass.

---

[1] It is seen in monumental slabs and brasses. Fifteenth-century ones are far more masonic in treatment than any of the previous centuries.

and dirt are valuable allies. Although glass is a wonderfully tough material it is certain that it is acted upon to a small extent by the atmosphere. The acids in the air affect its surface, especially in south-west aspects, and roughen it, at times make small holes in it, forming something in or on which dirt can lodge. Much of the deepness of the blues and the richness of the reds in old glass is due to dirt, especially in clerestory windows of large cathedrals which cannot easily be periodically cleaned.

The term "stained glass."
The term " stained glass " is, to some extent, a misnomer. In the finest glass there is very little staining or painting except on faces, hands, and flesh generally. The patterns on the rich robes of kings and bishops, and in the borders of fourteenth-century windows, are not in most cases painted. The glass used for these is mainly flashed glass, *i.e.* one side of a piece of glass of one colour is covered by a thin film of glass of either another colour or a darker shade of the same, and the patterns are formed by eating away with acid the flashed coat, so that in places the original colour shows. Sometimes it is the ground that is eaten away, sometimes the pattern itself. This, there can be little doubt, is the right and legitimate treatment for glass; and the more modern designers employ it, and the less they rely on applied pigments, the brighter is the future for this most beautiful and permanent form of colour decoration.

CHAPTER IX.

PLANS, ETC., OF EARLY CHURCHES IN FRANCE AND GERMANY.

THE development of the Eastern, or Byzantine, church plan from the sixth century to the twelfth, and the gradual growth of the Western, or Basilican, plan, until about the beginning of the eleventh century, as exemplified in certain Eastern countries and in Italy, have already been traced in the previous volume. No mention was made in that of early examples elsewhere in Europe, partly because these are neither numerous nor important, and partly so that the thread of continuity could be better preserved when dealing with the work in other countries. The investigations of archæologists have somewhat disposed of the old theory that during the last few years of the tenth century church building was at a complete standstill (owing to the vulgar superstition that the year 1000 A.D. was to see the end of the world); but it is still a fact that the number of churches commenced or rebuilt in the eleventh century was enormously in advance of the number in the previous one. The greatest activity was in the second half. Up to about 1050 there is little change to chronicle in either plan or general ordinance. Afterwards, advance was general and rapid throughout Europe, especially in the Western and Northern countries, and the plans show a uniform development, and, in addition, special characteristics, which separate unmistakably the later churches from the earlier ones.

The only countries which will be referred to in this chapter dealing with plans of early churches, *i.e.* those built between 850 and 1050, are France and Germany. Some contemporary churches in Italy have already been mentioned in Vol. I., and those of England will be dealt with in a subsequent chapter. Spain has few such examples, as, with the exception of the northern frontier, it was in the hands of the Moors until the eleventh century was far advanced; and in other countries,

136   A HISTORY OF ARCHITECTURAL DEVELOPMENT.

Norway, Sweden, Russia, etc., early work is almost non-existent, as Christianity, although it had taken root, had not yet borne architectural fruit.

Basilican plan.
Most of the early French and German churches undoubtedly followed the typical Italian basilican plan. The majority have disappeared. They have either been razed to the ground entirely, or else have been so altered and added to, like S. Remi, Reims, that their original designs are difficult to make out. But a sufficient number remain to show that the most usual plan was a nave with single aisles, with, as a rule, one apse only at the east end; a proof that the clergy and people, still simple in their devotions, clung to the primitive idea of only one altar. Some of the churches, however, are triapsal, and in a few examples the apses are divided from the nave and aisles by the unbroken transept, stretching from north to south, which occurs in many of the large early basilican churches in Rome, such as S. Paolo fuori le Mura, S. Maria in Trastevere (Vol. I., Fig. 111), etc. According to Viollet-le-Duc, the original church of S. Denis, near Paris (c. fourth century) had an eastern transept of this type.

Basse Œuvre, Beauvais.
The church known as the " Basse Œuvre," Beauvais (c. 997), three bays of which alone remain, gives a fair idea of the simplicity of these early examples. In plan it follows Italian traditions, but such decorative features as it possesses belong more to the East, as is often the case in early eleventh-century churches in France. In this church (and in most other contemporary examples) the arcades inside are low, the piers being plain rectangular ones, and the arches, of course, semicircular; the windows, one to each bay in the aisles and above the arcades, are large, because they were probably originally filled with pierced slabs, as in Byzantine churches; and the space between the arcade and clerestory, which is considerable, left plain, although it was possibly originally painted. In these early churches this space is very rarely arcaded, as in the majority of churches of later date;[1] and neither funds nor workmen were forthcoming to treat the wall surfaces with marble, as in S. Miniato, Florence, or with mosaics, as was customary in many parts of Italy. In the Basse Œuvre, more design is visible outside than inside. The arches of the side windows are coursed, two red tiles alternating with wide stone voussoirs; the west window has an archivolt of great delicacy,

[1] In the monastic church of Montier-en-der (c. 998) there are galleries over the aisles, and consequently triforia to the nave, but this church is an exception.

the pattern being a most unusual one, and the walls are faced with small squared stones, about 6 inches square, laid with great care. The plan of the church is Basilican; but the alternating courses of the side-window arches, the archivolt of the west window, and the outside masonry of the walls all suggest Byzantine influence.

One point worthy of mention in connection with early basilican churches in Germany is the combination of piers and columns, which has already been referred to in the first volume, as existing in such churches as S. Maria in Cosmedin, and S. Clemente, Rome (Vol. I., Figs. 112 and 114). In Münster Cathedral, and S. Michael's, Hildesheim (c. 1020), piers take the place of columns every third bay; and at Drübeck (c. 1000) and elsewhere columns and piers alternate. All these churches are timber-roofed, were built, in fact, before the reintroduction of vaulting; and the alternation of large and small supports had consequently nothing whatsoever to do with vaulting requirements. A detail of some interest in connection with these churches, and others of contemporary or slightly later date in Germany, is that the columns are generally monolithic, and, following Classic precedent, diminish in diameter from base to cap, and are entasised. Alternating piers and columns.

The plans and general ordinance of the churches mentioned above are much the same as contemporary and earlier churches in Italy, and show no signs of advance. But in addition to these there are others in both France and Germany which are of greater interest, because their plans show unmistakable evidence of the two great influences in force in the early centuries of Christianity, the ancient Roman and the somewhat later but still more inspiring Byzantine; influences which are absent in most of the churches built after the eleventh century. These examples are, in fact, connecting links between the East and the West; between the civilizations which had lost or were losing their force, and the new religious and artistic movements which, at the beginning of that century, were in their infancy. They are also especially worthy of study in that, in many cases, they contain the germs of later developments, and thus help to elucidate some points the origin of which would otherwise remain obscure. Plans due to Roman and Byzantine influence.

France and Germany were in a backward state, except during the time of Charlemagne, throughout the early centuries of the Middle Ages, when art flourished in Italy and the East; and it is only natural, therefore, that many of their early churches Roman influence.

138   A HISTORY OF ARCHITECTURAL DEVELOPMENT.

should reflect strongly the characteristic traits of the still earlier perfected work. At the beginning of the eleventh century the direct influence of the architecture of ancient Rome was by no means dead, although centuries had passed since Roman ideals dominated the civilized world. It was strongest, perhaps, in the part of France bordering on the Mediterranean, because the early colonists had introduced traditions of building there which had not been superseded by the artistic movements which effected changes in other lands. The Church of S. Pierre, Reddes (near Bédarieux), for instance, of the tenth century, is modelled on the baths of Diana, Nîmes, and like that building is covered by a barrel vault, and has attached columns lining the walls of the interior. In Germany, Roman influence crops up occasionally, and nowhere is this more marked than at Mettlach, where there is a tenth-century octagonal church. This is planned without aisles, but in the thickness of the wall are semicircular niches which recall the Pantheon, and other similarly planned Roman buildings.

Byzantine influence.   The oldest building in France showing Eastern influence is probably the Church or Baptistery of S. Jean, Poitiers, built

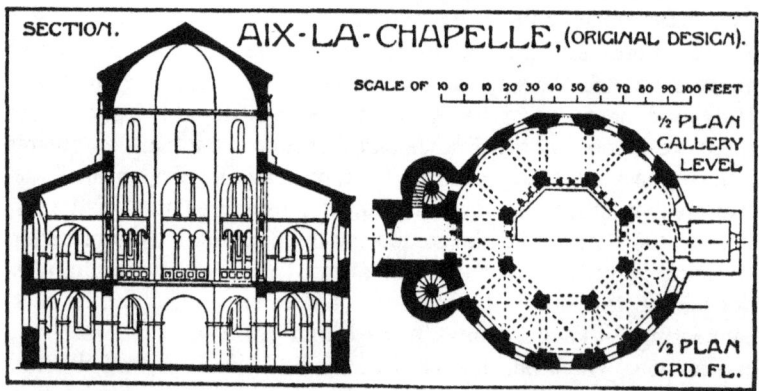

FIG. 88.

originally in the fourth century, but rebuilt and added to subsequently. It has three apses, two at the sides and one at the end. Byzantine feeling is still more marked in the church built by Charlemagne at Aix-la-Chapelle (Aachen) late in the eighth century or early in the ninth. Later additions mask somewhat the original plan. This consists of an octagon surrounded by an aisle enclosed within a multangular outer wall. On one side is a porch, flanked by turret staircases, opposite which was probably a small chancel. The likeness between the plans of this church and S. Vitale, Ravenna (Vol. I., Fig. 153), is unmistakable, although the later church lacks the columned niches between the piers surrounding the central space which give the earlier one its distinctive beauty. At Ottmarsheim, Germany, is a church similar in size and plan, although two centuries later in date than Charlemagne's church.[1] The outside wall is octagonal, not multangular, but otherwise the differences are slight. Both churches have galleries arcaded in front. More interesting than any of the above is the Church of Germigny-les-Prés (Loiret), said to have

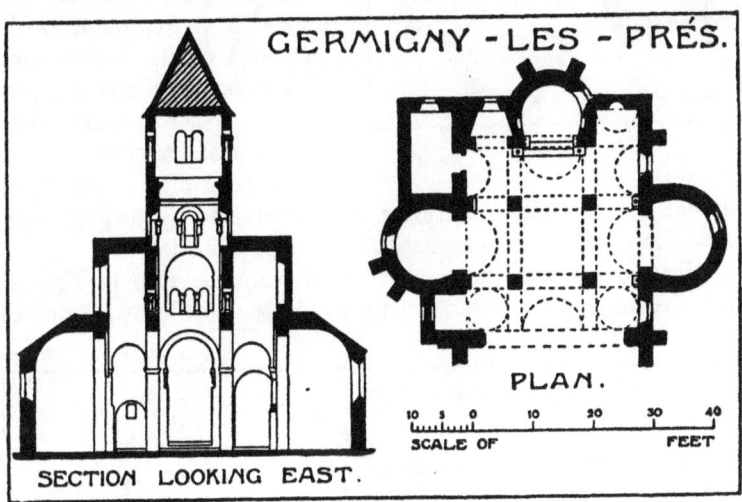

FIG. 89.

been built at the beginning of the ninth century. In plan it consists of a square, which, in orthodox Byzantine fashion, encloses a Greek cross, the cruciform portion being divided from the corners by four piers. Apses project from the sides. Above the intersection rises a moderately lofty square tower, under which, in recent restorations, has been placed a dome, although it is doubtful if one was there originally.[2] The arms of the cross are covered by barrel vaults, and the apses by semi-domes, the latter being

[1] Brescia Cathedral (Vol. I., p. 254) has a similar plan.
[2] The apses surrounding the church are shown as published by César Daly in 1849. There was possibly also a western apse, and the east end may have been triapsal.

140   A HISTORY OF ARCHITECTURAL DEVELOPMENT.

considerably lower than the main arms. In plan and general ordinance the church, save for its side apses, is like S. Theodore, Constantinople (Vol. I., Fig. 161), and numerous small churches in Greece. The building, however, to which it bears the closest resemblance is the old Church of S. Satiro, Milan (Vol. I., Fig. 168), the parent of which was probably the Church of S. Lorenzo in the same city (Vol. I., Fig. 154). Of the same type are S. Croix, Montmajour (c. 1016), and S. Martin de Londres, both in Southern France. The plan of the former is a quatrefoil, with an added porch, whilst that of the latter is similar, but instead of the western apse it has a short oblong nave. This type of plan was dropped through the succeeding centuries, but was revived by the architects of the Renaissance, who realized its great possibilities.

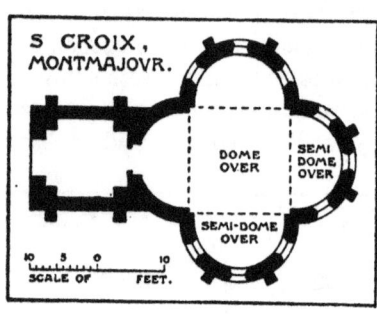

Fig. 90.

Churches with circular east ends and oblong naves.

Next in interest comes a group of churches, also in France, with circular east ends and oblong naves, the best known being S.

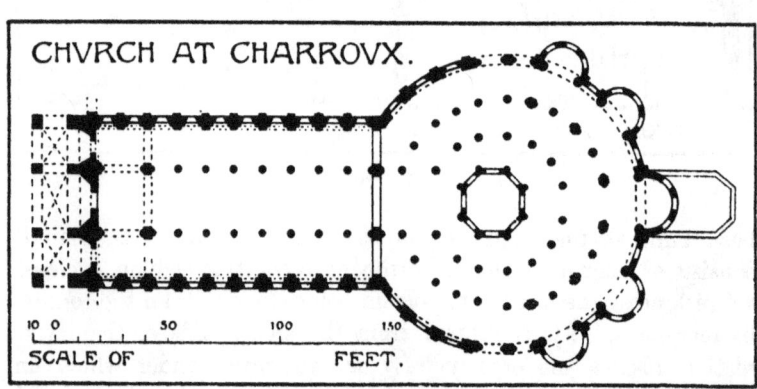

Fig. 91.

Benigne, Dijon, Charroux, near the Loire, and Neuvy S. Sepulchre. As regards the last, although the circular portion dates from c. 1045, the nave is a later addition. If one could be quite certain that the plan of Charroux, as generally presented, is the plan of

EARLY CHURCHES IN FRANCE AND GERMANY. 141

the original church, it would be one of the most interesting in existence. The central space at the east end is small, merely the width of the nave, but it is surrounded by three aisles, so that the diameter of this portion far exceeds the width of the western nave and aisles. There is more certainty regarding S. Benigne (c. 1001), although the entire western arm and the greater part of the east end have been rebuilt. Still, the crypt of the latter remains. This consists of a central circle surrounded by a couple of concentric aisles, with portions of an oblong chapel at the west end. There can be little doubt

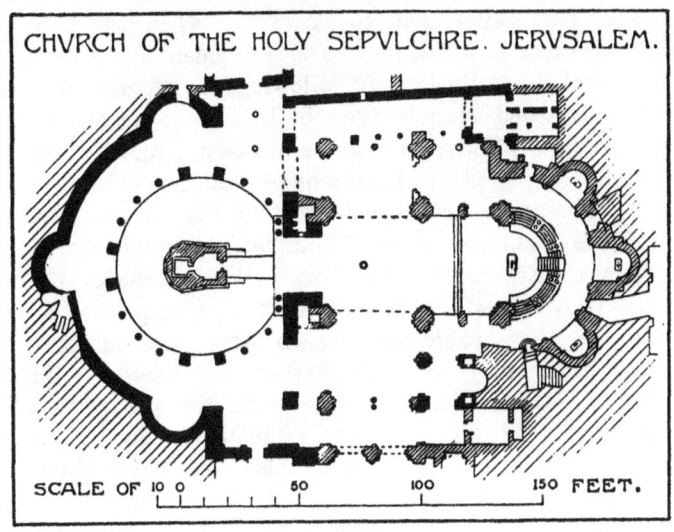

Fig. 92.

that the upper church was built on the same lines as the crypt below, and that is therefore interesting not only for itself, but as indicating the plan of the church proper.

To what extent, if any, these churches owe their plan to the Church of the Holy Sepulchre at Jerusalem is a point that may be argued. Until 1076, Christians were freely permitted to enter Jerusalem on payment of a small legal toll. In that year the city came into the hands of the Seljukian Turks (a somewhat different race from that which previously possessed it), and it was the ill-treatment of pilgrims which followed that excited the wroth of Peter the Hermit and occasioned the first crusade.

Church of the Holy Sepulchre, Jerusalem.

M. Anthyme S. Paul states [1] that between the years 990 and 1000 pilgrimages to Palestine were general, and that one Foulgues Nerra, when he died at Metz in 1040, had visited Jerusalem four times. The church as it then existed was therefore well known. But what was its plan? Constantine's church, the first to be built there, was basilican. He built it to the east of, and detached from, a great apse, about 120 feet in diameter, which he placed round the spot where he believed the tomb to be. His work was destroyed; but about 1040 his namesake, Constantine Monarchus, Emperor of the Eastern empire, built an ordinary circular church round the tomb, except that apparently only the aisle was covered, the central part being open to the sky. When the Crusaders reached Jerusalem in 1099, they at once commenced the rebuilding of the church; but, instead of following the Roman Emperor's plan of a detached church, they built their chancel on to the circular church. The result was a western circular nave—the building of Constantine Monarchus—and an oblong eastern chancel. There can be little doubt that the church as rebuilt supplied the plan for many "Templar" churches throughout Europe, such as the one at Laon, in Northern France—the nave of which is octagonal—and our own four examples at London, Northampton, Cambridge, and Little Maplestead in Essex, the last being a century or so later than the others.[2] But the churches of Dijon, Charroux, etc.—with the exception of an eastern chapel in the case of S. Benigne—show a reverse arrangement; their east ends are circular, their naves oblong. It follows, therefore, that, being built, some a century, others half a century, before the first crusade began, they cannot have been influenced by the Holy Sepulchre Church as rebuilt by the Crusaders. The builders of Charroux, Dijon, etc., devised a plan which gave them a suitable nave, and a choir so arranged that the faithful could gather round the altar. It was this desire for space at the east end which occasioned the most important of the developments which will be described in the next chapter.

[1] In his "Histoire Monumentale de la France."
[2] Although the Templars may have taken the plan from Jerusalem, it had been employed before, and probably had a Byzantine origin, as mentioned in Vol. I., pp. 255-6.

CHAPTER X.

THE DEVELOPMENT OF CHURCH PLANNING.

THE chief alterations that took place in the planning of churches during the eleventh and following centuries occurred in the eastern arm. The nave remained much the same all through the great period of church-building. At first, many churches continued to have merely a single apse or three apses side by side, either as eastern terminations to the nave and aisles, or else opening out of a transept as before described. In others, however, a more marked tendency towards greater length and increased importance of the east end is manifest. Nowhere is this more noticeable than in Burgundy, Normandy, and England, the three countries in which the greatest building activity prevailed during the last decades of the eleventh century. The great church of Cluny, in Burgundy, commenced 1089, marks the culmination of the early developments. In its plan are found not only many of the characteristic marks of later French cathedrals, the chevet, double aisles to both nave and choir, etc., but, in addition, the long eastern arm and the smaller transepts east of the great transepts, which afterwards became characteristic of many English ones. Full development was reached in both France and England about the middle of the thirteenth century; the few modifications made subsequently possess little importance. The changes in plan followed on much the same lines in all countries until about the middle of the twelfth century, irrespective of the fact that some large churches are without aisles, others are aisled throughout, whilst a few have aisles to the choir and none to the nave. After that time, considerable differences appear in the different centres, and are conclusive proof that each of the great building countries, England, France, Italy, and Germany,[1] followed its own line and worked out its own solution of the problems presented to it.

Introduction.

---

[1] Germany followed France in the thirteenth century, but afterwards was more independent.

144 A HISTORY OF ARCHITECTURAL DEVELOPMENT.

Causes for changes. The advances in planning and the modifications introduced are traceable to various causes. The most important of these are: (1) the need for additional altars, occasioned chiefly by the large increase in the number of clergy and monks; (2) the insistence on more marked separation between clergy and laity; (3) the greater interest taken by the laity in matters of religion, and their greater influence; (4) Pilgrimages; (5) Relic worship; (6) Alterations in rules relating to burial and baptism.

Change in position of altars. The increase in size of the eastern arm, although following naturally, to some extent, on the increase in size of the monasteries and corresponding increase in the number of the monks, was, in the main, due to alterations made in the placing of the altars. In the case of a large monastic church a considerable number of

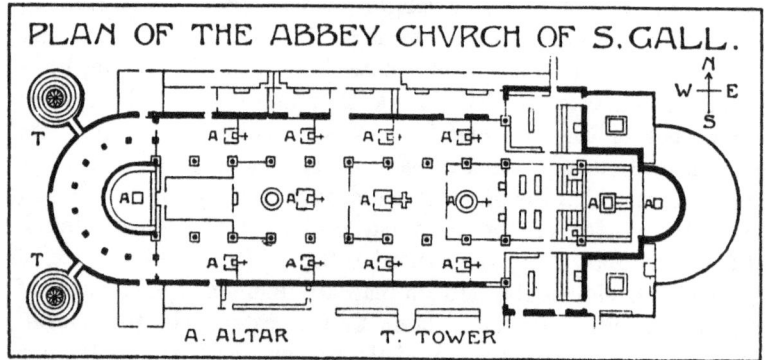

FIG. 93.

altars was essential. The one altar, or the three of the earlier, smaller church, was insufficient. Until near the end of the eleventh century, it had been the practice when more were required to place them in the nave. In the Abbey Church of S. Albans, now the Cathedral, each pier of the nave had an altar on its western face. Still stronger proof that many altars in the nave were customary is afforded by the existing plan on vellum of the church of the Monastery of S. Gall, Switzerland, built in the early days of the ninth century by, it is stated, the architect who designed Charlemagne's church at Aix-la-Chapelle. In this plan are shown, in addition to altars at the east and west ends dedicated to S. Peter and S. Paul respectively, altars down the aisles and the centre of the nave as well. These positions were satisfactory so long as the nave, in addition to the choir, was given up mainly to the monks; but the arrangement presented many difficulties if the church of the monastery was also the church of the people, in which their representative, the bishop, had his chair, as at Canterbury, Durham, Norwich, Winchester, etc., or if the church were a cathedral pure and simple, unattached to a monastery, and served by secular canons. It also required modification in the case of Cistercian monasteries, in which accommodation had to be provided for the numerous lay brethren who worked in the fields belonging to each monastery and were little more than agricultural labourers.[1] But all monasteries derived a large proportion of their income from the offerings of the faithful, this being especially the case when the relics preserved in the churches were special objects of veneration. The monks, therefore, did not desire to close their churches, and yet they desired privacy. To obtain this they removed the altars from the naves and erected them east of the crossings. The canons of the cathedrals followed suit. From this time onwards the separation of clergy and laity was complete. An altar was placed at the east end of the nave for the use of the latter, and the whole of the eastern part was screened off and reserved exclusively for the former, except on days of festival, when the entire church was thrown open to all. The present arrangement in S. Albans Cathedral is probably not unlike the original one. The choir proper extends three bays into the nave, from which it is screened. To the east of it is the high altar separated from the chapels beyond by another lofty screen. To the west of the choir proper are now another altar, and seats for the clergy and members of the choir. In Gloucester Cathedral—a monastic church which only became a cathedral at the Reformation—it is evident that the gallery round the choir was set aside for the monks alone. Portions of it formed chapels; and there are still remains of five altars there—one on the south side, two on the north, and the remaining pair over the Lady Chapel. The arrangement not only ensured the monks complete privacy, but also economized space.

In England, in most cases, the laity seem to have had access to the altars in the great transepts, but in France this is not

---

[1] At Fountains Abbey, a Cistercian monastery, the nave was for the lay brethren, and their altar was placed at its east end. The aisles of the nave were screened off for the use of the monks.

so certain. When the choir was entirely east of the crossing, as in all later cathedrals, Exeter, Salisbury, Wells, York, etc., or commenced under the crossing, as at Chichester, the transepts naturally appertained to the nave. Even when the choir extended westward of the crossing into the nave, effective separation from it and the transepts was easily obtained by means of stalls or screens. The extension westward of the choir is most marked in cathedrals to which monasteries were attached, or in abbey churches which were not cathedrals. In Westminster Abbey the choir still occupies three bays of the nave, in Norwich Cathedral two bays, in Gloucester and Winchester Cathedrals one bay.

Eastern extension. Two plans of eastern extension were followed in the latter half of the eleventh century. The earlier and simpler one con-

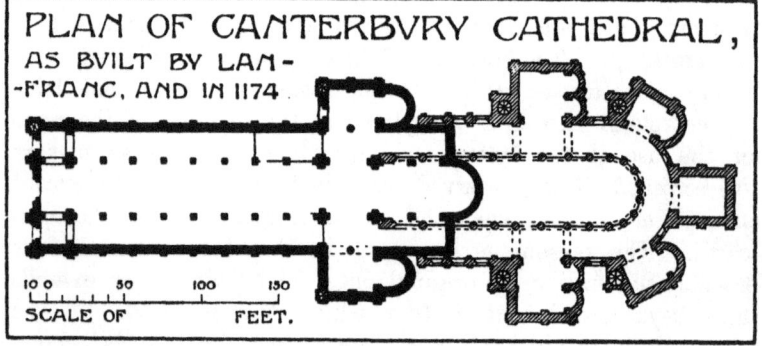

FIG. 94 (Willis).

sisted merely in lengthening the chancel by the addition of two bays, or more, between the transepts and the eastern apses. The aisles were lengthened as well, although sometimes, as in the Abbaye-aux-dames, Caen, they are completely cut off from the chancel by walls. S. Georges, Boscherville, and the church at Cérisy-la-forêt, Normandy, are typical examples of this simple elongation. In both, the aisles finish square, whilst the chancel of each has an apse. The transepts stand out beyond the aisles, and have apses or altars to the east, showing that additional altars were even then considered necessary. This was also the original plan of Canterbury Cathedral (c. 1070), and of S. Etienne, Caen (c. 1060).

THE DEVELOPMENT OF CHURCH PLANNING. 147

The chief drawback to the above plan was that circulation a the east end was difficult. The aisles formed cul-de-sacs. This was a very serious objection in churches where pilgrimages to shrines and relics were frequent, and where pilgrims came in vast numbers. The other plan, which was perhaps adopted in a few instances at the end of the tenth century, but did not become general for nearly one hundred years, solved the difficulty by providing an ambulatory behind the central apse. The apses to the aisles were swept away, and the aisles continued round the back of the high altar. It is impossible to say in which church this plan was first adopted, or even in which country it was first thought of.[1] An eastern ambulatory, with a gallery over, occurs round the Church of S. Stefano, Verona, which Cattaneo, with some hesitation, ascribes to the tenth century. In France it seems to have been introduced early in the following century; but in England not until about 1090, Gloucester Cathedral (c. 1089) being probably the first.[2] As a matter of fact, an eastern ambulatory was not so much an innovation as an adaptation. The difficulty of circulation at the east end had been overcome in S. Benigne, Dijon, and in other similar churches described in the last chapter (see Fig. 91); and all that was really done in the churches now under consideration was to substitute an oblong with semicircular end for a complete circle. The eastern ambulatory plan was especially favoured in those churches to which large crowds were attracted, through their possessing the bodies of saints and martyrs, or other valuable relics, as at S. Martin, Tours, S. Denis, near Paris, S. Sernin, Toulouse, Charroux, etc., and Canterbury Cathedral, after the murder of Thomas à Becket. The crypt of the original cathedral at Chartres, which still exists, built early in the eleventh century, has an ambulatory, which, it is almost certain, was continued above. The east end of Romsey Church (c. 1120) shows an equally suitable although slightly different plan for providing necessary circulation. This is not strictly speaking an ambulatory, but the aisles are continued east of the chancel, and open into a passage behind the high altar. The ending is thus a square one, an important detail which will be referred to later.

Eastern ambulatory.

[1] In S. Lorenzo, Milan, c. 530 (Vol. I., Fig. 154), all the apses are surrounded by aisles.

[2] Amongst English churches of the eleventh century the following had either apses or square terminations to the aisles: Canterbury, Chester, Durham, S. Albans; whilst Norwich, Bury S. Edmunds, Gloucester, had eastern ambulatories.

148 A HISTORY OF ARCHITECTURAL DEVELOPMENT.

The chevet.

The outside wall of the ambulatory in some of the earliest examples forms an unbroken semicircle, as at Morienval (Oise) and S. Saturnin, Auvergne, but in most churches apses project in

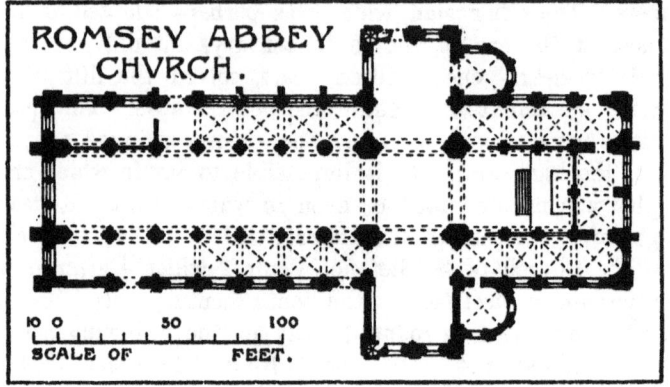

FIG. 95.

front of the curving wall and contain altars. These apsidal chapels at first were small, and, almost without exception, semicircular in plan. Between them, as a rule, were windows. In most early examples there are only three chapels, as at

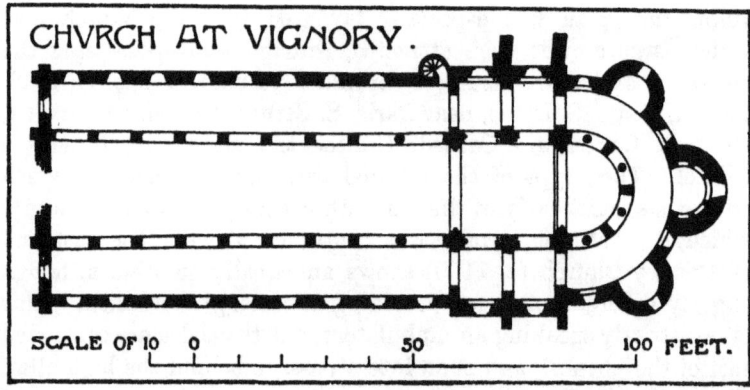

FIG. 96.

Vignory (Haute-Marne, c. 1030), although sometimes there are five, as at Cluny, S. Sernin, Toulouse (see Fig. 157), and occasionally four, as at N. D. du Port, Clermont-Ferrand. Thus was born the "chevet," the characteristic ending of nearly all

Fig. 97.—Le Mans Cathedral: East End.

[*To face* p. 149.

THE DEVELOPMENT OF CHURCH PLANNING. 149

the great churches and cathedrals of Northern France. The term is applied to any east end in which an ambulatory—sometimes consisting of one aisle only, sometimes of double aisles—is carried round the apsidal ending of a choir or presbytery, with radiating chapels projecting from it. The chevet soon lost its simple character; the chapels increased in number and in size, and, ceasing to be separated from one another, united, and formed a continuous band, sweeping round a central apse. Often they are continued down the sides as well. In Le Mans Cathedral there are as many as thirteen surrounding the choir, seven at the end, and the remainder at the sides. In Nôtre Dame, Paris, and Bourges Cathedral, the chevet is of the early simple kind; at

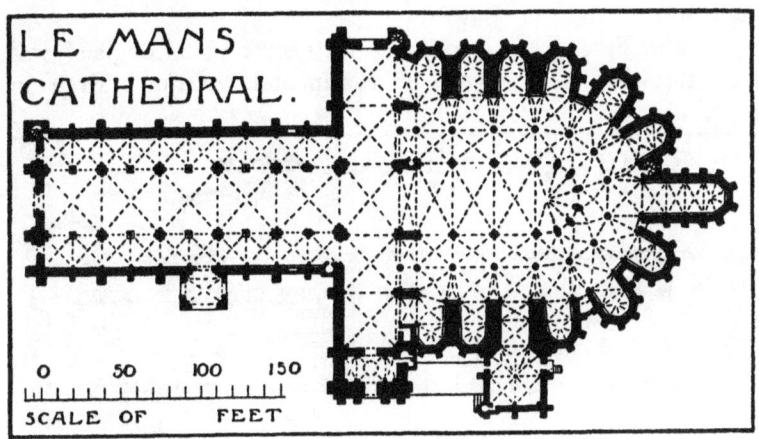

FIG. 98.

Reims (c. 1220) it is fully developed; and at Amiens, Beauvais, and Le Mans it is carried still one step further. In the last-named (c. 1230) the projection of all the chapels is considerable, and they have again become separate. Between them there are windows; probably because it was felt that, the chapels having greater projection than was customary, the windows in them would not give sufficient light to the ambulatory. The result is one of the most striking east ends in the world; and all the more striking because the whole of it can easily be seen, which is by no means always the case in French churches.

The eastern ambulatory plan was, in the fifteenth century, abandoned in many churches in France of secondary rank. In

French exceptions to

150   A HISTORY OF ARCHITECTURAL DEVELOPMENT.

<small>chevet plan.</small>
the church at Pont l'evêche, and in S. Jacques, Lisieux (c. 1500), for instance, the aisles end square, and beyond them project the chancels which have semi-octagonal or semi-hexagonal ends.

<small>The chevet in England.</small>
The chevet plan in its simple form was fairly general in English cathedrals built before the middle of the twelfth century, but after that time it disappears; the only examples of later date retaining it being the Abbey Churches of Westminster (c. 1250) and Tewkesbury. The reason for the chevet in the latter church is that it was built on the foundations of an earlier east end; and the reason for it at Westminster is that Henry III., who rebuilt the Abbey, was at heart a Frenchman, and although he could not force the workmen to build in the French fashion entirely, he could dictate the plan and general ordinance of the church.

<small>English east ends.</small>
Whilst France was perfecting its chevet plan, England was busy throwing off the yoke of continental tradition. Even in

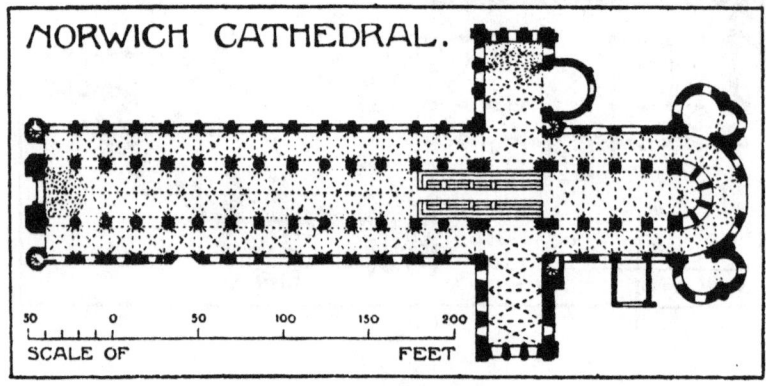

FIG. 99.

eleventh- and twelfth-century churches the eastern arm is considerably longer than in most contemporary foreign examples, showing that the desire for length existed here from quite early days. Thus the bays between the crossing and the apse number four at Norwich, Durham, and Bury St. Edmunds (c. 1089-1096), the same number as in the great church at Cluny, whilst in Canterbury Cathedral, when remodelled in 1184, this number was doubled (see Fig. 94).

This desire for length led to the adoption by later English builders of either one or other of two plans. There was not the

THE DEVELOPMENT OF CHURCH PLANNING.

same unanimity amongst them as distinguished their brethren of Northern France. In one plan, the choir, presbytery, etc., are continued the full height of the church as far as the extreme east wall, as at Ely, Lincoln, and, later, York; in the other, the high portion of the church stops short east of the high altar, and retro-choir and chapels of considerably less height are built

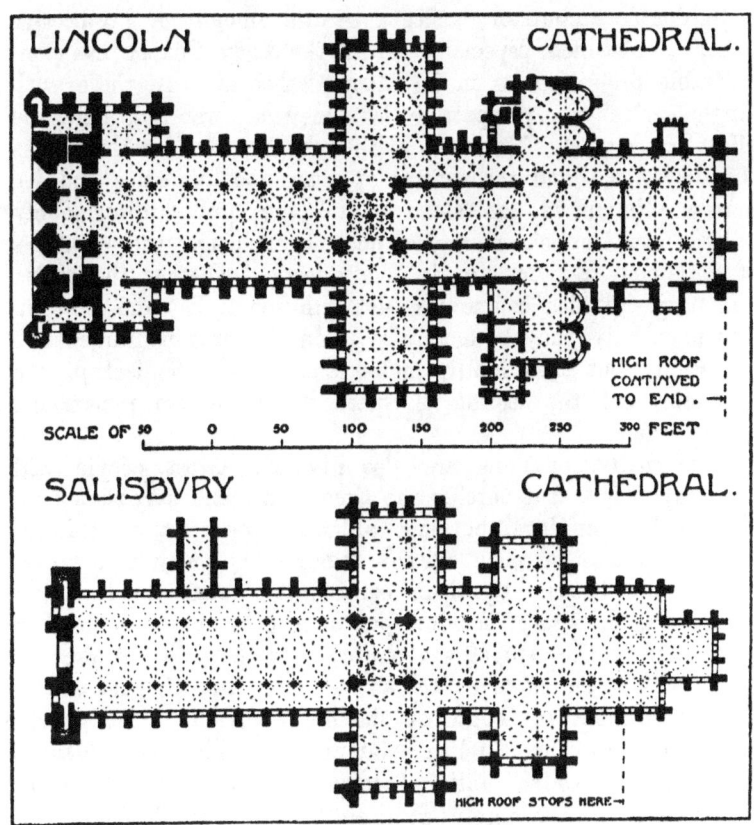

Fig. 100.

out beyond, as at Salisbury, Exeter, Chichester, Wells, S. Albans, etc. In the latter examples, below the east window of the presbytery, which starts above the roofs of the chapels beyond, are arched openings, through which delightful perspective effects are obtained. At Chester there is only one opening, at Exeter there are two openings, at Salisbury and Wells three. At

S. Albans the openings are blocked by a high stone screen, which, together with the tall reredos behind the high altar, shuts off the space in which the shrine of the Saint is placed and blocks the vista completely.

Comparison of English and French east ends.

There will always be a difference of opinion as to which of the English methods is the more satisfactory inside, and whether either is superior to the French. In French cathedrals with double ambulatory aisles a certain amount of perspective effect is obtained, especially when the Lady Chapel has considerable projection, as in Le Mans Cathedral. In those with single aisles the perspective is somewhat cramped, and the effect not so good. Moreover, in the majority of French churches the openings round the central apse are too numerous and too narrow, the piers too slender, and the arches disagreeably stilted. In English examples, charming though the result is at Salisbury, Exeter, etc., it is a question whether the better and more dignified course were not followed at Ely and Lincoln. The perspective may be more playful in the first-mentioned two cathedrals, but that hardly makes amends for the lack of the grandeur and the feeling of space which are so remarkable in the others.

Externally, opinions are also divided. Most people will probably admit that outside the French east end surpasses both the English endings, but not all. To some its restlessness is displeasing. In their opinion the simple dignity of the east end of Ely has no equal in continental work. In the plan adopted at Salisbury, the low buildings east of the high altar give scale to the rest of the church, but they do not produce so pyramidal an effect as the ambulatories and chapels abroad. The curtailment in length of the high portion of the church is no drawback in English examples in which this plan is followed, because the ratio of length to height of the main structure is always amply sufficient. Such curtailment would have been fatal abroad, where the churches are so much loftier and proportionately shorter.

The naves of continental churches are often as long as many of ours, but the eastern arms are rarely so. Between the crossing and the start of the apse there are only three bays at Reims, four at Chartres, five at Amiens, and five at Cologne, to take four of the best known of French and German cathedrals; whereas Salisbury and Exeter have seven bays from the crossing

Photo: W. A. Mansell & Co.
FIG. 101.—ELY CATHEDRAL: CHOIR AND LANTERN.

Photo: Frith & Co.
FIG. 102.—SALISBURY CATHEDRAL: CHOIR.   [*To face p.* 152.

to the return wall behind the high altar, York and Ely nine bays from the same place to the east wall, and Lincoln ten.

The greater length of English cathedrals allowed of transepts of much greater projection on either side, and in addition, of smaller transepts about halfway between the great transepts and the east end. Eastern transepts have already been mentioned as one of the features of the church at Cluny. From Burgundy they travelled to England, and appeared first at Canterbury (c. 1170), Lincoln (c. 1192), and Rochester (c. 1210), found a place in Salisbury Cathedral, when it was commenced in 1220, and at Beverley Minster a few years later. The reason for the great projection of the main transepts and for the additional transepts was simply to provide sufficient altar accommodation. The French builders needed no eastern transepts, and could be content with giving their main transepts slight projection because their chevet plan provided all they wanted. In England it was different. In Salisbury Cathedral—which may be taken as the plan regarded by English builders as the ideal one, inasmuch as practically the whole was built at one time, and after Norman influence was past—fourteen altars were possible, six in the main transepts, four in the smaller ones, two at the end of the presbytery aisles, one in the Lady Chapel, and one, the High Altar, in the presbytery; all facing west, according to the traditional English custom.

English transepts.

To what extent the people had access to the altars in the eastern chapels has already been referred to. It seems probable that the custom was not the same in all countries, nor even in cathedrals in the same country. Otherwise it is difficult to account for the fact that in many French cathedrals chapels are built out beyond the nave aisles the entire length of the western arm of the church, whilst in others there are none, as at Chartres and Reims. In cathedrals commenced before the middle of the thirteenth century these side chapels are later additions. None were built in France before 1240. The cathedrals of Laon, Paris, Amiens, Coutances, etc., were without them at first. It was not until some forty or fifty years after they were finished that the aisle walls were taken down and the chapels built out beyond, between the buttresses. At Laon Cathedral the old window-sills were cut through, and the ends still show in the walls; at Amiens Cathedral the outline of the buttresses and their set-offs are easily traceable from the chapels inside,

Side chapels.

showing where the new work joins on to the old; at Coutances Cathedral the ends of the string, which formerly ran along under the windows inside, are still visible. These side chapels, one to each bay of the nave, are separated from one another by walls, and are, so to speak, distinct shrines. The altar in each is generally placed on the east side, so as to face west, but not unfrequently it is against the outside wall, and faces north or south. At Coutances, the side walls above the altars are pierced with unglazed mullioned and traceried openings which agree in size and design with the side windows, a very good and light effect being produced. In later churches, *i.e.* in those of the fourteenth and fifteenth centuries, the side chapels are part of the original design, and were built at the same time as the rest of the church.

Side chapels in England. Chichester is the one English cathedral with side chapels lining the nave, but even these are somewhat different from those abroad. There are two on the south side, each two bays long, and three on the north, two of which are also two bays in length. All were added at the end of the thirteenth century. The chapels were divided from one another by walls, the upper portions of which were probably pierced, as at Coutances. Lincoln Cathedral has two thirteenth-century chapels at the extreme west end, one on each side, but these hardly come under the same category as the rows of chapels in French cathedrals.

Possible reasons for side chapels. Why were these side chapels not required in England, and how was it that the necessity for them arose so suddenly in France? These questions are not easy to answer. The chief reason was probably relic worship. Relics were undoubtedly prized in England from early times, but it seems certain that they were never so numerous here, and that they were not regarded as so essential as they were abroad. Or it may be that the Englishman always preferred congregational worship to the more private devotions to which side chapels lend themselves. If the exact extent were known to which the laity were admitted to the chapels of the eastern arm, in both England and France, some light might be thrown on the subject. It is known that the relations of the monastic orders and the people changed somewhat about the middle of the twelfth century, and that there was less antagonism between them; also that the power of the laity and their interest in Church matters increased considerably about the same time, but it seems difficult to connect these with the

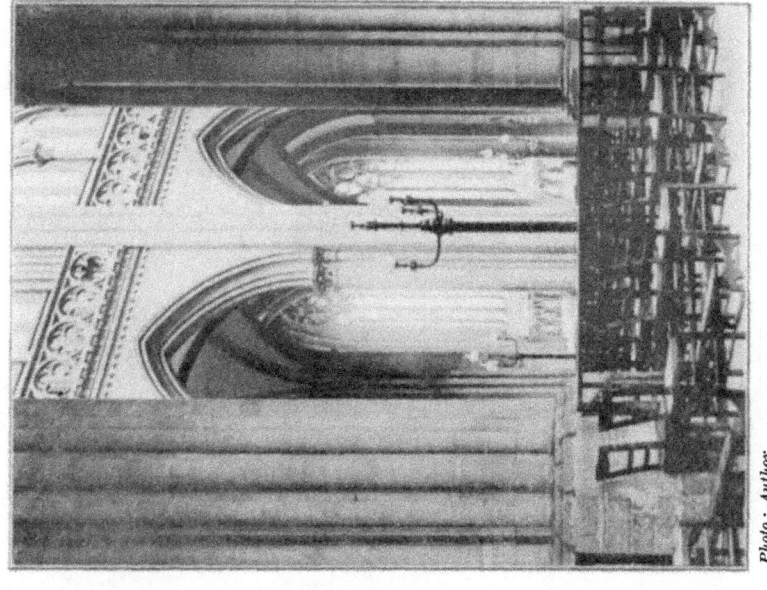

Fig. 103.—LAON CATHEDRAL: AISLE WALL CUT THROUGH FOR CHAPELS.

Fig. 104.—COUTANCES CATHEDRAL: SIDE CHAPELS.

Photo: Author.

[To face p. 154.

Photo: Salmon, Winchester.
FIG. 105.—WINCHESTER CATHEDRAL: CHANTRY CHAPEL OF BISHOP WILLIAM OF WYKEHAM.
[*To face p.* 155.

THE DEVELOPMENT OF CHURCH PLANNING. 155

remarkable increase in the number of the chapels of a church, especially as that increase took place about a century later. It may have been due to a compromise. The monks and canons may have said, "Leave to us the east end, and we will build chapels for you in the nave;" or if the people had been shut off from the east from the first they may have become strong enough to assert their rights, and demand consideration. In the absence of proof, however, this is all conjecture. A definite statement which could be proved would be welcome, because it would account for one of the differences between French and English cathedrals, which is now difficult to understand, and also for the exceptions to the French rule in France.

Although English cathedrals have not side chapels of the kind common abroad, many have chantry chapels. These, however, are different. Chantry chapels appear first early in the thirteenth century, but most of those now remaining belong to the late fourteenth or to the fifteenth century, when little else remained to be done in the way of cathedral-building. They are small chapels built either to surround tombs of bishops, abbots, etc., as at Winchester—where amongst others are the tombs of the great builders, William of Edington and William of Wykeham, bishops in succession of the See—or else at the expense of private individuals, who also left money so that masses could be chanted daily over their tombs for the repose of their souls. Chantry chapels are sometimes at the end of aisles, but in cathedrals are rarely built out beyond the main fabric.[1] There are two, however, on the south side of Lincoln choir, flanking the porch, and their small dimensions and delicate detail give scale to the mass of the cathedral behind them. They are mostly inside, and are placed under the arches between the columns separating the aisles from either nave or choir. The greatest number are at Winchester, and there are also several at Wells, Gloucester, Tewkesbury, Salisbury, etc. The custom of building these chapels continued general for some time after the Reformation. At Christ Church, Hampshire, there are three—two in the south aisle, dated respectively 1525 and 1529, and the third, the largest, in the north aisle, built by the Countess of Salisbury about the same time.

Although there is not a single instance in England of a cathedral or large monastic church being planned with double

Chantry chapels.

Double aisles.

---

[1] In parish churches they are frequently excrescences, and account largely for the irregularities in their plans.

156 A HISTORY OF ARCHITECTURAL DEVELOPMENT.

aisles—Manchester Cathedral is merely a parish church, with extra aisles added subsequently—in France there are several. Double aisles, of course, were no mediæval innovation. The three greatest early basilican churches in Rome, those dedicated to S. Peter, S. Paul, and S. John, were planned with them, because, owing to the limitations forced on the builders by lack of funds and constructive necessities, in no other way could the space necessary for large congregations be obtained. Double aisles were adopted in French cathedrals for much the same reason as brought the chevet plan into existence, namely, to provide space for pilgrimage processions, which might pass round a church without interfering with the worshippers in the central

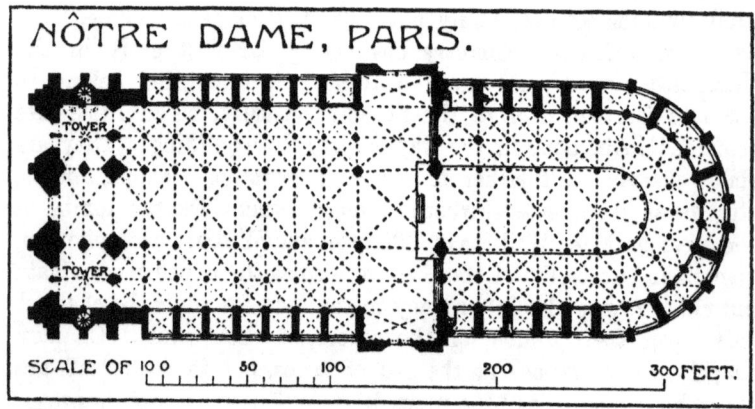

Fig. 106.

portion and in the side chapels. In some of the great French cathedrals, such as Amiens, Reims, Chartres, Le Mans, only the east end has double aisles; in others, Paris, Bourges, Troyes, etc., they flank the nave as well. Most of these churches have aisles to the transepts in addition, and these, coupled with the double aisles east and west, or east only, give that effect of spaciousness at the crossing so marked in continental churches, and especially noticeable at Amiens and Chartres. In Antwerp Cathedral additions have given the nave three aisles on each side, with unsatisfactory results. The width of the nave and aisles together in this church is practically equal to their length.

Aisleless plans.   Very different from the many aisled churches of Northern France, are the churches entirely without aisles of the South. It

THE DEVELOPMENT OF CHURCH PLANNING.

is difficult to believe that they belong to the same country, to the same style of building, and to the same period. The aisleless plan of Southern France owes its origin to Roman tradition. The Cathedral of Albi is the direct descendant of the basilica of Constantine. Both buildings have the wide, central-vaulted space, the internal buttresses taking the thrusts of the vault, and the side recesses. They differ only in the number and size of these recesses. In the basilica there are only three; in the church there are twelve, exclusive of those round the apse. The reasons for the difference are that the mediæval builders rejoiced in the reduplication of parts which the Romans, except in the Colosseum and other similarly designed buildings, did not regard as so necessary, and were afraid, perhaps, of the dangers attending the construction of great squares of vaulting a few inches only in thickness.

Albi Cathedral,[1] the church of the Jacobins at Toulouse (destroyed), and some others in the neighbourhood, prove conclusively that large churches can be built without regular aisles, and yet possess all the essentials of Gothic architecture. And yet the fetish of the aisled plan still holds the field. The majority of the clergy still clamour for it, as though the nave and aisle plan were really symbolical of the Trinity and an aid to devotions, instead of being merely a structural device for subdividing an internal space (so that it can be covered over easily, and at small expense) which was practised by the Egyptians in their Hypostyle Halls of Assembly, by the Greeks in their larger temples, and by the Romans in many of their Halls of Justice. In mediæval days the aisled plan had its circumambulatory advantages, as already stated, but for modern congregational purposes aisles of any width are an anachronism. No one can seriously maintain that columns and piers are not obstructions to the service of the present time, but in barely one modern church out of ten are they dispensed with. The problem of how to provide large unencumbered floor spaces was solved at Constantinople in Justinian's time, and in many cases by the architects of the Renaissance, because at both periods recourse was had to the Roman plan of few and large points of support. This plan can be followed as easily in the twentieth century as it was in the sixth and sixteenth centuries. No doubt its treatment presents architectural difficulties, but these difficulties have been overcome before.

[1] For plan and section, see Figs. 202 and 203.

158   A HISTORY OF ARCHITECTURAL DEVELOPMENT.

The churches of Albi, Toulouse, Perpignan, etc., are proof of this, and their example has in some cases been followed in recent times. They have, in fact, inspired some of the most successful of modern churches in England, of which may be mentioned two early examples only, Bodley and Garner's S. Augustine's, Pendlebury, and Pearson's S. Augustine's, Kilburn. In some churches of Southern France, La Trinité, Angers, for example, only the nave is aisleless, the chancel has the aisle divisions, the result being that, although the latter is still a fair width, the narrowed chancel arch and different proportions of the east end give scale and height to the church as a whole.[1]

Cistercian influence.

Until the end of the eleventh century the Benedictine order was all powerful in determining matters of church planning and ritual, but in 1098, at the very moment when the order was at its zenith, was founded a rival one, the Cistercian. The Cistercian order was started as a protest against the extravagance of both Benedictine living and Benedictine building; although the Abbey Church of Vézelay, which S. Bernard of Clairvaux, the most famous member of the order, declared in sweeping terms to be unnecessarily elaborate and over-enriched, appears plain indeed in comparison with later Gothic churches. S. Bernard, the Puritan of the Middle Ages, as he may be called, laid down stringent rules for his followers. "A church," he declared, "shall be of the greatest simplicity, and sculpture and painting shall be excluded—the glass shall be of white colour, and free from crosses and ornaments." He further stated that "no towers or belfries of wood or stone of any notable height shall be erected," and he seems to have entertained a rooted objection to triforia, as they are generally absent from Cistercian churches. Inasmuch as an apsidal eastern ending was universal in Benedictine churches, he declared for a square ending. The extremely

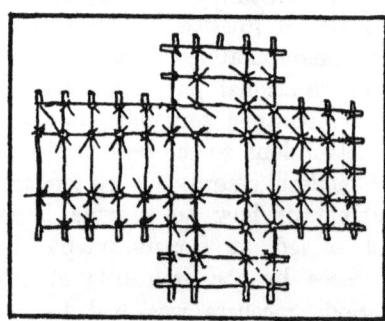

FIG. 107.—Plan from V. de Honnecourt's sketch-book.

[1] The modern church of La Trinité in the Place Blanche, Paris, has a happy combination of wide nave and narrowed chancel. The nave in this church has aisles, but they are subordinate.

interesting sketch-book, which has luckily been preserved, of Villard de Honnecourt, a thirteenth-century French architect, shows a sketch-plan of a Cistercian church. Under it the artist has written, "Vesci une glize desquarie ki fu esgardee a faire en lordene d'Cistiaux.[1]

To what extent S. Bernard's mandate influenced the development of church planning is difficult to state with certainty. The effect of it has been exaggerated by some writers. The builders of the great French cathedrals and large parish churches, in most cases certainly, paid little attention to it, and until the Renaissance upset their ideas and destroyed their traditions

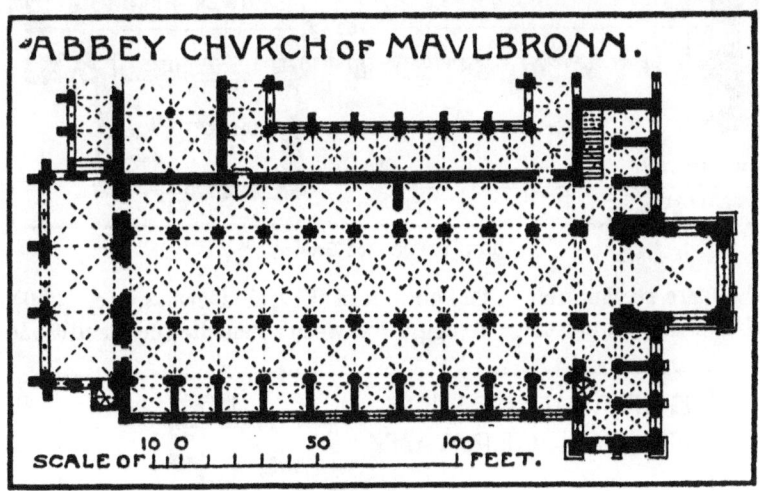

FIG. 108.

continued to develop their eastern chevet endings as already stated. But in churches built by monks of the order on the country side, on the Continent as well as in England, S. Bernard's instructions in the main were followed. The plans of Chiaravalle, near Milan, Las Huelgas, Burgos, Spain, Maulbronn, Germany, Fontenay, France, and Furness and Buildwas, England, show a remarkable uniformity. They are not, however, new plans, but reversions to an old one. They follow the early basilican plan of a transept at the extreme east end with chapels extending

[1] In modern French, "Voici une église carrée qui fut projetée pour l'ordre de Citeaux." All the sketches have been reproduced by Lassus and Darcel, with explanatory notes, in a book entitled "Album de Villard de Honnecourt," 1858.

beyond it, the only differences being that the chapels are sometimes more numerous than was thought necessary before, and

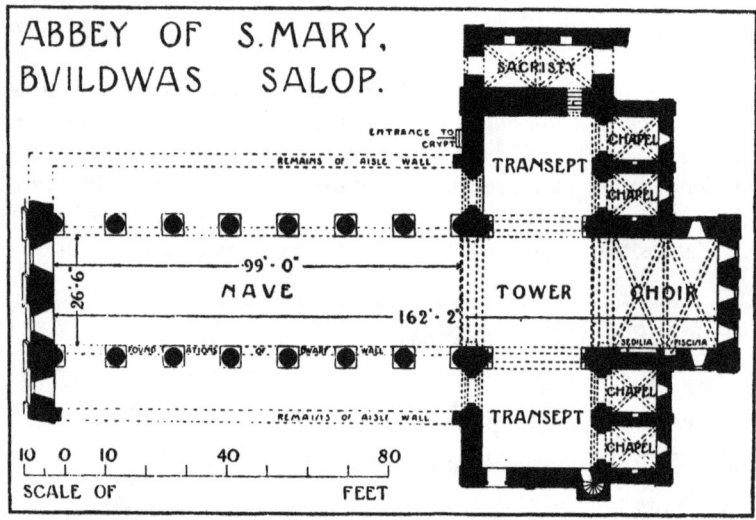

Fig. 109 (Talbot Brown).

they are rectangular. The church of Ebrach, Germany (c. 1250), shows an interesting struggle between Benedictine traditions

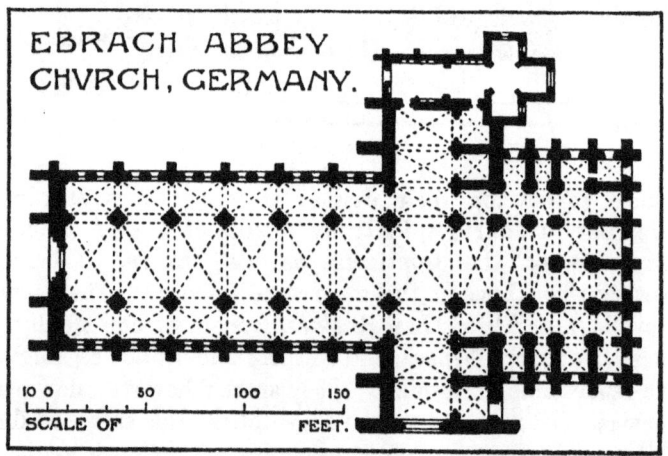

Fig. 110.

and Cistercian rules. The east end is really a chevet, but a chevet squared. To the influence of the order are due the eastern endings of Fountains Abbey Church, with its seven altars, and Durham Cathedral with its nine altars, both additions of the thirteenth century.[1] But it is a mistake to suppose that that marked feature of English cathedrals and churches, their eastern rectangularity, is due to the Cistercians. The square east end is an English tradition. It is found in pre-Norman churches at Bradford-on-Avon, Wilts, and Dover Castle; in churches in Ireland and Scotland of early date; in the eleventh-century Cathedral of Rochester; in the Abbey Churches of Romsey (see Fig. 95) and S. Cross; and in countless eleventh and early twelfth-century parish churches in England, such as Old Shoreham, Sussex, Dareth, Barfreston, and Patrixbourne, Kent, Adel, Yorkshire, etc., built long before S. Bernard became a power. All that that leader did was to revert to the simplicity of the early Christian plan which had been general in Egypt and Syria in the sixth and seventh centuries. The early square east end is not found only in Great Britain. In European countries it was never entirely abandoned during the tenth and eleventh centuries, although it was partially, owing to the power of Roman precedent. The Cathedral and S. Nicolo at Bari (see Fig. 123), the Cathedral at Trani, all three in Southern Italy, have square east ends, following Eastern custom; and many churches in France, Germany, and Belgium might be mentioned, built before the commencement of the twelfth century, of similar plan.

Two important rites of the Christian religion, baptism and burial, might, in their development, have been expected to influence considerably church planning, but they can hardly be said to have done so. In the days of the early Church the separate baptistery was a necessity, as adult baptism was general, and the unbaptized were not admitted into the Church itself. But early in the eleventh century, as infant baptism became more customary, and parish priests were permitted to baptize, fonts began to be placed in parish churches, especially in Rome. In other parts of Italy, separate baptisteries continued to be built well into the twelfth century, as at Parma, Pisa, Novara, Asti, etc. The latest example of a separate baptistery is probably at Bergamo, where, early in the fourteenth century, a little octagonal building of delightful design was placed in a small court alongside the Cathedral.[2] Outside Italy, with the possible

Baptism.

---

[1] See Fig. 177.
[2] This building has, I understand, been pulled down and rebuilt elsewhere.

exception of S. Jean, Poitiers, no building exists in Western Europe which can be stated definitely to have been built as a baptistery, and the original destination of even the Poitiers example is uncertain. For so important a rite as baptism one would have thought that special provision would have been made in churches after the transference there of the font, and that a portion of each building would have been specially set apart for it. But in no country was this done (with a few possible exceptions), probably because, as any priest could perform the rite in any church, the ceremony had lost, to some extent, its previous great importance. In English cathedrals the customary position for the font is near the western doorway, on the south side—in Winchester and Chester Cathedrals it is on the north—but its original position in every case may have been different. At Ely it occupies a good position in the south transept at the west end, and at Peterboro' it is placed in a similar position and has a bay to itself, but it is unlikely that the somewhat unusual western planning of these two cathedrals was due to baptismal requirements.[1] In parish churches the font is generally at the west end of the aisle, near the south door, and this is undoubtedly its original position as a rule, although in churches with western towers it not unfrequently occupies the space under the tower, or immediately to the east of it.

Burial. More provocative of change was the permission to bury inside churches. In the early days of Christianity the good old sanitary laws of the Romans still prevailed and bodies remained outside. But the protest against cremation, the insistence on burial on consecrated ground, the wish of the deceased or of his relatives to secure the most sacred spot, and above all, the desire to pay special honour to those who had devoted their lives to the advancement of religion, or who had lost them in its defence, brought about the change. It was strongly resisted at first. In 563 the Council of Braga gave permission for burial in churchyards "in case of necessity," but on no account within the walls of a church. This was the thin end of the wedge. A later Council at Mayence decided that "no one shall be buried in a

---

[1] In Truro Cathedral, Pearson made a feature of the baptistery, placing it at the west side of the south transept; and in some modern churches special treatment is accorded to the font and its surroundings.

church but bishops, abbots, or worthy priests, or faithful laymen,"[1] a fairly elastic and comprehensive list; and another Council, held at Meaux, left it to the bishop and presbyter to settle who should be accorded the honour. Once the custom was sanctioned it spread rapidly, and soon attained large proportions. Incidentally, it occasioned one of the most effective features of early churches, viz. the raised chancel, and also led, a few centuries later, to the little chantry chapels, already referred to, which, in England especially, add so much to the beauty of many of the cathedrals.

The early burials were in small eastern crypts, not much more than passages, as in S. Apollinare-in-Classe, Ravenna,[2] Torcello Cathedral (Vol. I., Fig. 125), and S. Ambrogio, Milan, altars being placed above the bodies. But the size of the crypt rapidly increased until, in many churches of the eleventh and twelfth centuries, it occupies the space under the whole area of the chancel, which is raised several feet above the floor of the nave. The best known of raised chancels are in S. Zeno, Verona, and S. Miniato, Florence (Figs. 116 and 117). It is impossible to overrate the fine effect produced in these two churches by this plan. In many of the earlier examples, of which the Ravenna Church may be regarded as typical, although the chancels are raised, the crypts are not visible from the naves. In the two churches of Florence and Verona, however, just mentioned, the fronts of the crypts are open and arcaded, and the vistas from the naves down into the vaulted crypts and along the length of the chancels above are amongst the most effective features to be found in mediæval church architecture. Raised chancels were contrary to the rule of the Greek Church, and consequently in those parts of Western Europe which came under its influence, notably in Southern Italy, although crypts are frequent, they are either entirely sunk, or else the nave floor is raised as well as the chancel, so that the floor throughout the church is approximately level. In Trani Cathedral, an example of the latter plan, the crypt extends over nearly the whole of its area. In more northern Europe, in Germany, France, and England, raised chancels with crypts under are far from uncommon, but the west ends of the crypts are, almost without exception, closed. That all

Raised chancels.

---

[1] A. Ashpitel, *R.I.B.A. Journal*, 1860–1861.
[2] As S. Apollinare is stated to have been finished in 549, the Council of Braga's ruling appears to have been a protest against an existing custom.

were so originally is somewhat doubtful. It is unlikely that the northern mind could not realize the beauties and appreciate the æsthetic advantages of the more southern plan; and in many cases in which no view of the crypt is now obtainable from the nave, it is possible that alterations and subsequent additions have destroyed the original design.

CHAPTER XI.

ROMANESQUE IN ITALY.

THE chaotic state of affairs throughout Italy during the eleventh and twelfth centuries was naturally reflected in the architecture of the whole country. The history of that period is a continuous account of internal troubles and external wars; of conflicts between pope and emperor; of state fighting against state; of the efforts of the Eastern emperors to retain their footing in Italy, and of the desire of the Saracens and the Normans to wrest the land from them, or from anybody else who happened to be in possession.

The Romanesque of Northern Italy, *i.e.* in and around the plains of Lombardy, had its rise in the ninth century, although little of moment that survives was built before a century or two later. The Teutonic race of Langobards, or Lombards, who were conquered by Charlemagne in 774, were unskilled in building-craft, and there is no evidence to show that their buildings possessed any of the features which afterwards were distinctive of Lombard architecture. Many existing churches which were formerly attributed to them are recognized now as belonging entirely to the eleventh or twelfth century, and, amongst the few which are older, none is earlier than the time of Charlemagne, except, of course, those built by the Emperors of Byzantium before the Lombards invaded Italy. There is always a temptation to antedate a building, especially if documentary evidence be followed, as most churches are of old foundation, and occupy sites previously built upon. This is the case in Italy more than in other countries, owing to its long history and to the vicissitudes which it has encountered.

Charlemagne's empire at the commencement of the ninth century included Northern Italy, France, the northern half of Spain, and the greater portion of Germany and Austria. At his death it crumbled to pieces; but, after a century or more of

Northern Italy.

confusion regarding the boundaries of the different kingdoms which rose from the ruins, Otto the Great consolidated the German empire, and in 951 became, through marriage, king of Northern Italy also. For the next two hundred years the German emperors were all powerful there. It follows, therefore, that most of the Romanesque churches in Lombardy were built when the country was under the rule of the Germans, and consequently owe some of their robustness to the energy and vigour of that race. The old methods of building which lingered there were not ignored, but they were gradually modified. Some of the modifications introduced were improvements, designed to meet the exigencies of ritual requirements and somewhat different construction; whilst others were simply retrograde, owing to the inferior skill of the craftsmen employed.

Central Italy.

The new feeling which, in the eleventh century, made such headway in Western Europe, and spread with such rapidity in Northern Italy, met with little success farther south. The Apennines formed an effective barrier to its introduction. Under their shelter the earlier traditions held their own. Venice also remained faithful to them, owing to its position, to its connection with the East, and to its independence. The Church of S. Mark is a proof how little it was influenced by Western developments. The papal territory was under the sway of the popes, and in Rome the basilican plan remained supreme. In Central Italy, or Tuscany, Byzantine influence in art matters was extremely strong, owing to the fact that Pisa, which for two or three centuries was the most important town in the district, like Venice, carried on a large trade with the East.[1] Florence was of little note until the destruction of Fiesole (the old Etruscan city on the heights above the town), in 1125, drew the people from the hills to the plain, and Lucca and Pistoja followed the lead of Pisa. The position in Tuscany, however, was more vulnerable, and northern methods of building were able to obtain some foothold there.

Southern Italy and Sicily.

Apulia, which embraced the greater part of Southern Italy, with Bari on the Adriatic as its capital, was from 871 until the middle of the eleventh century a Byzantine colony. Frequently

---

[1] As evidence of the close connection between the Eastern empire and Pisa, it may be mentioned that when towards the end of the eleventh century the work on Pisa cathedral was at a standstill owing to lack of funds, the Eastern emperor came to the rescue, and found the money.

harassed by the Saracens, the Eastern emperors managed to hold their own until 1040, when a new foe appeared in the shape of a band of Normans under Robert Guiscard. For about the next hundred years Apulia was ruled by Robert and his descendants.

Sicily has had a more adventurous history than any other portion of Italian territory. From the early days of the Romans and Carthaginians it was the seat of war, and later times brought it no peace. Its isolated position rendered it particularly open to attack. In 535, it came under the rule of the Eastern emperors, and remained in their possession until the advent of the Saracens, who in 827 landed and conquered the greater part of the island, although some towns held out until the end of the tenth century. The Saracens' reign over the whole island, however, was short-lived, as the Normans from Apulia, after two or three expeditions, drove them out in 1090. Civil wars with various claimants to the throne followed, and Sicily may be said to have had but brief intervals of peace until quite recently.

The architectural result of the changes and conflicts mentioned above is that there is a vast difference between the eleventh and twelfth century work of Northern Italy and that of the rest of the country. In the north the churches of that period are mostly fully developed Romanesque, and possess all the traits customarily associated with work described under that head, such as ribbed and vaulted naves, clustered piers, and triforium galleries; whereas further south, when these features do occur, they are found in conjunction with others which belong strictly to another and earlier art movement. The hyphened heading, Byzantine-Romanesque, has been coined for the work, and possesses the advantage of suggesting the main sources from which it was derived, but it does not express all. In Apulia, and especially in Sicily, the Normans and Saracens both left their mark. The churches of Tuscany differ in many important essentials from those of Apulia, and, moreover, are by no means all designed on similar lines; and Sicilian churches possess certain marked characteristics which are absent from those of the mainland. In no other country is the architecture such a mixture as in Sicily. Nearly every church shows traces of Byzantine, Romanesque, and Saracenic methods of construction and decoration, mingled together in a most fascinating manner, and mixed with detail which only the Normans could have supplied. It is better, therefore, to group all under one broad

The title "Romanesque" applied to Italian work.

heading, as, if any other plan be adopted, half a dozen different groupings would be necessary to ensure correct division.

NORTHERN ITALY.

Milan was the centre of architectural advance in Northern Italy from the ninth to the twelfth century, and it was there, and in the neighbouring towns, that Italian Romanesque was first fully developed. The most interesting churches are S. Ambrogio, Milan, S. Michele, and S. Pietro in Cielo d'oro, Pavia, and Novara Cathedral. All are vaulted throughout, have clustered piers, and, with the exception of S. Pietro, the large open triforium galleries common to twelfth-century work in all countries. The vaults are not in all cases the original ones, in fact it is open to question

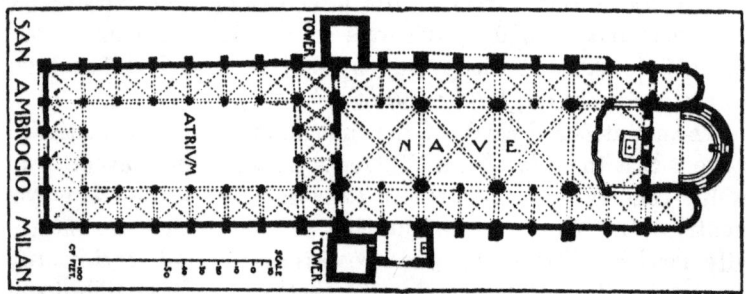

FIG. 111 (Dartein).

S. Ambrogio.

whether they are in some cases even copies of them, but there can be no doubt that these churches were designed to be vaulted.[1]

Of the above-named, S. Ambrogio is the finest, and probably also the earliest. According to Cattaneo, the east end dates from the time of Archbishop Angilbertus (824–859), the nave was rebuilt in the second half of the eleventh century, whilst the atrium and northern campanile followed at the beginning of the twelfth. The original nave of Angilbertus was of the ordinary basilican type, and the same length and width as the existing one. It had fourteen bays, whereas the present one has eight; or, if one counts by the number of vaults, only four, as each bay of vaulting covers two bays of side arcading. In basilican churches the bays are always numerous and narrow, and the columns comparatively slender. In Italian Romanesque ones a return was made to the old Roman

[1] See p. 75 for a discussion regarding the date of the S. Ambrogio vaults.

Photo: Brogi.   Fig. 112.—S. Ambrogio, Milan.

Photo: Brogi.   Fig. 113.—S. Ambrogio, Milan.

[To face p. 168.

plan of few and large piers (with smaller supports in between), which had been abandoned for some centuries, because in no other way could the vaults have been satisfactorily supported. The bays, in consequence, are few and wide. Here is the main reason for the differences in proportion and appearance between the two types of church. Each has its merits and demerits. In basilican churches, when the bays are arched, the side openings could have been wider, but the effect would not have been so good, as the scale which reduplication of parts gives would have been lost, and the continuous timber roof or ceiling would have occasioned an appearance of weakness below. In a Romanesque church, massive support for the vaults was the main essential; and although intermediate columns between the main piers possessed many advantages, unnecessary multiplication of them would only have encumbered the floor space, without adding materially to the stability of the church. In S. Ambrogio nave there are three great piers on each side, with small, unimportant piers in between.[1] The height from the floor to the crown of the diagonal ribs is over 60 feet, the crown of the transverse arches being about 10 feet less, as the vaults are domical. This is no great height considering the width, if comparison be made with Gothic churches, but it is sufficient. The proportions, in fact, are those of old Roman vaulted buildings—the basilica of Constantine, for instance, being 83 feet wide and 120 feet high—and it is doubtful if the mediæval men ever improved upon them. The piers and transverse arches are of stone, the diagonal ribs and side arches of brick, with pieces of stone inserted irregularly. These may be part of the original design, or be due to subsequent alterations.[2]

The charm of the church is due, in a large measure, to its lighting. This is ample; although standing at the west end, and looking east, hardly a window is to be seen, except those in the apse. There are a few aisle windows, but the piers hide them from most positions. The west windows are large, but they are shadowed by the gallery outside. The windows at the back of the triforium galleries give some assistance, but they are, of course, invisible

Lighting.

---

[1] There is little difference in superficial area between the columns of the destroyed nave and the piers of the existing one, notwithstanding the decrease in the number of supports, and that half of the present piers are little bigger than the original columns.

[2] The church has been extensively restored, so that the original treatment is uncertain. The third bay of vaulting from the west end has been entirely rebuilt in modern times.

170   A HISTORY OF ARCHITECTURAL DEVELOPMENT.

from the floor of the nave. The easternmost bay of the nave is brilliantly lighted by a ring of windows in the octagonal cupola above, which throws a flood of light on to the altar and its baldachino. Altogether, the effect produced by the apparent absence of windows is surprisingly good.

West front, St. Ambrogio.
The west front of S. Ambrogio differs in some respects from other contemporary churches of North Italy, inasmuch as it is preceded by a cloistered atrium, which is returned at the east end to form the narthex of the church. Over the narthex is a gallery with three large openings in front. A single gable of flat pitch spans the whole front; the descendant of the Classic pediment. The treatment is very similar to that adopted in some of the Syrian churches mentioned in Vol. I. The simple gable is typical of Lombardic churches, even when, as in S. Michele, Pavia, the roofs behind do not agree with it.

External open galleries.
The roofing of the semi-domes over apses at the east end of these churches occasioned a little bit of rational construction which led to a pretty feature outside. This is the open

APSE OF S. VINCENZO-IN-PRATO, MILAN. IXᵀᴴ CENT.

FIG. 114.

gallery under the eaves, which was afterwards adopted at west ends, round turrets, and along the sides of churches. To support the timbers of the flat-pitched roof protecting the semi-dome of an apse—for in Romanesque work this was never allowed to show outside—it was necessary to carry up the wall of the apse above the springing of the semi-dome. No great strength was required, and so this wall was pierced with openings which, simple at first, as in the apses of S. Ambrogio and S. Vincenzo-in-Prato, Milan, of the ninth century, soon became of great richness. At S.

ROMANESQUE IN ITALY. 171

Michele, the openings are grouped in pairs by narrow pilaster strips or by strong clustered pilasters. In some other examples they form a continuous gallery, the openings being separated from one another by marble shafts. Germany copied the feature from Italy, and in certain parts of France, in Auvergne, and farther south, the design is frequently met with. In Pisa and Lucca it was elaborated and duplicated to such an extent that the arcaded gallery front is the distinctive characteristic of Pisan work.

SAN MICHELE, PAVIA.

ELEVATION OF EAST END.

PLAN.

FIG. 115.

An interesting instance of the survival of Byzantine traditions is afforded by the cupola towers, either over the crossing, when the church, like S. Michele, Pavia, or Parma Cathedral, is cruciform, or over the eastern bay of the nave when there are no transepts, as in S. Ambrogio. These cupolas are, with few exceptions, octagonal, and are covered by flat-pitched roofs. They are even more common in Germany than in Northern Italy, and there are many in Southern Italy and in certain parts of France. They take the place of the Byzantine dome, and, like it, are in most cases surrounded by windows which, as in S. Ambrogio, admit a flood of light to the east end of the church.[1] The same arcaded gallery treatment as to apses is generally carried round them. They are not so striking as our English central towers, but, especially in Germany, where they often group with other towers and turrets, are very effective.

Cupolas.

[1] There are frequently domes underneath, which they cover and hide from view outside.

172   A HISTORY OF ARCHITECTURAL DEVELOPMENT.

S. Zeno, Verona.

The church of S. Zeno, Verona, built in the first half of the twelfth century, has all the characteristics of a vaulted church; sturdy clustered piers alternating with lighter columns, and, on the outside, more strongly marked buttresses than are customary in Italy, and yet apparently it was never vaulted. Transverse arches, however, were evidently thrown across the nave from each of the big piers, starting from capitals which are now halfway up the walls. One of these arches still remains towards the west end; the others were removed when the church was heightened early in the fourteenth century, and the choir remodelled. To this date belongs the present timber ceiling of the nave, a coffered barrel vault of unusual design, with tie-beams from side to side.[1] S. Zeno has no triforium; in this respect it differs from S. Ambrogio and other churches in Lombardy.

Other churches.

Farther south, at Parma, Modena, Piacenza, etc., the somewhat later churches follow sometimes Lombardic methods, sometimes Byzantine. Thus, the west front of Piacenza Cathedral has a single gable, as at S. Michele, Pavia. The cathedrals at Modena and Parma have triforia, but in both churches they are small and very different in appearance from the spacious galleries of S. Ambrogio. Both churches also have clerestory windows. The Cathedral at Novara has a fine atrium in front of the west end. It is a thousand pities that this most effective addition to the approach to a church was discarded in later mediæval days, and has not been revived in modern times. All architects are agreed as to the necessity for designing the approaches to and surroundings of a house, and what is necessary for a house is still more appropriate for a church. It is a blot on the Gothic shield that the dignified tradition left by the Romans, and handed down by the early Christian builders, was ignored. The ritual reason for an atrium may no longer exist; the æsthetic advantage of it is as great and as pressing as ever.

Porches.

A feature in all northern churches in Italy, and in a few southern ones as well, is the projecting porch. Such porches are sometimes two storeys high, as in the Cathedrals of Verona and Piacenza, but are more often of one storey only, as at S. Zeno, Verona (Fig. 71). They are vaulted, and possess, as a rule, two peculiarities. One is that the vault is carried on detached columns, standing well away from the wall, which could not

[1] The following churches have similar roofs: S. Fermo Maggiore, in the same city, S. Stefano, Venice, and the Cathedral of Aquileja, not far from Trieste.

Photo: Alinari.   FIG. 116.—S. ZENO, VERONA.

Photo: Brogi.   FIG. 117.—S. MINIATO, FLORENCE.

[*To face p.* 172.

possibly stand if it were not for the iron tie above them, which prevents the vault from spreading; and the second is that the columns rest on the backs of animals. Whence came the latter device is difficult to say. In ancient Assyrian work, executed centuries before, pilasters against a wall often start from lions' backs in a similar way; but if any connection ever existed between these and the much later Western work, the links have been lost. The more likely hypothesis is that the idea originated north of the Alps—perhaps in columns of wood—where the love for the grotesque was strong, as the early carvings show. In Southern Italy, windows are sometimes treated in a similar manner. At the sill level of the east window of Bari Cathedral, for instance, carved elephants boldly project and carry shafts which support a rich archivolt. On the south transept of the same building there are two windows with somewhat similar corbels, and in other churches of Bari, Trani, etc., further instances are to be found.

TUSCANY.

In Central Italy greater variety in design is noticeable than in Lombardy, because no one influence was paramount. In Rome, old traditions still held the field, and there is little difference between the churches built in the eleventh and twelfth centuries and those of the ninth and tenth. In Pisa, Florence, Lucca, Pistoja, etc., the plans also remained basilican, but more traces of Byzantine feeling are visible. In addition, the virility of the northern Romanesque was such that it could not be confined entirely within its boundaries. Even close to Pisa there is one church, S. Pietro-a-Grado, the outside of which is purely northern in design, whilst the plan shows no trace of northern influence, and old materials are freely used inside. Much the same may also be said of the two churches, S. Pietro and S. Maria, at Toscanella, near Viterbo, about fifty miles north of Rome.[1]

In S. Miniato, Florence (c. 1013), built on a hill above the town, the three influences, Basilican, Byzantine and, to a less extent, northern Romanesque meet. In many respects it is an ordinary basilican church, except that its crypt is larger, and its chancel more raised than in earlier examples. Old columns

S. Miniato, Florence.

---

[1] Toscanella was an independent town of some importance, and it showed its independence in its architecture by ignoring, to some extent, the work immediately to the north and south of it.

and capitals—some of the latter much too small for the columns below—are extensively used; over the nave and aisles are open timber roofs; and in its general plan, construction, and proportions, there is little to distinguish it from the earlier churches in Rome. It was never intended to be vaulted; in fact, it could not be, and

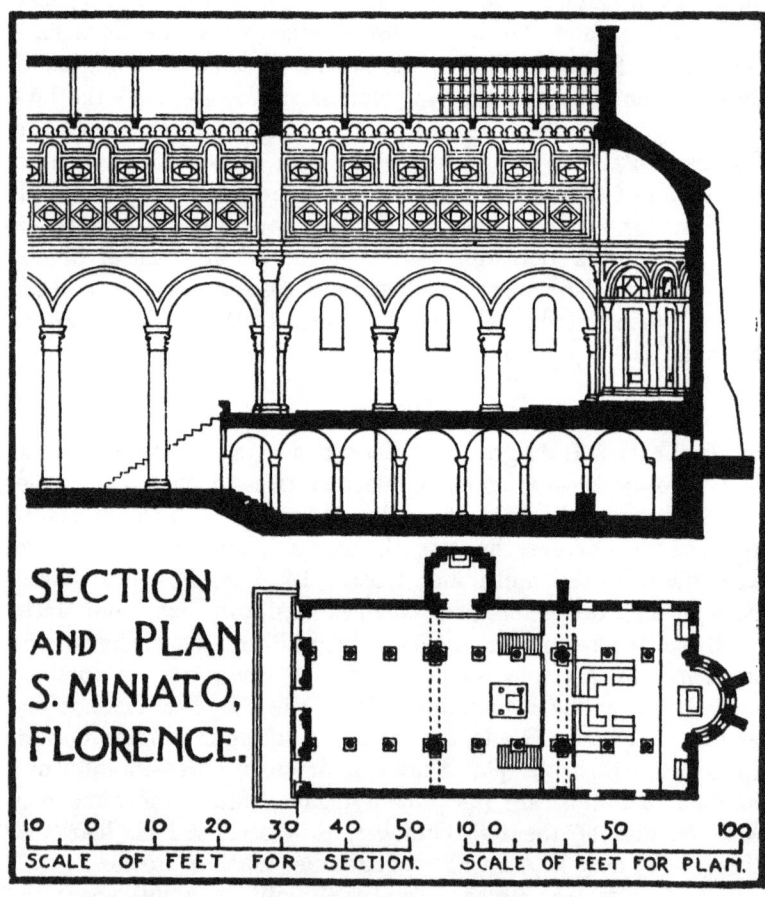

Fig. 118.

every part of the design proclaims that fact. But—and herein lies the main difference between this church and ordinary basilican churches—transverse arches span both nave and aisles and divide the upper part of the church longitudinally into three divisions, as though there were vaults between. The nave and aisle ceilings are, in consequence, not continuous as in the earlier examples. To carry these transverse arches, piers are introduced every third bay. These are not plain rectangular ones, like those in S. Clemente, Rome, etc., but are quatrefoil in section. One quarter of each on the nave side is carried up above the crown of the arches, forming a half-round pilaster, to support the main transverse arches, whilst from the quarters in the aisles spring the side transverse arches, starting from the same springing line as the arches of the arcades.

Byzantine influence in Tuscany is shown mainly in the decoration of churches. The Tuscan architect declined the constructional mixture of brick and marble, which produces such excellent effects in many churches in Northern Italy, and employed marble only. Sometimes he used it in alternating bands of light and dark—a method first used at Pisa, and afterwards carried to extremes in the later cathedrals of Siena and Orvieto—or else {Byzantine influence.}

FIG. 119.

he covered his carcase walling with thin veneers of different-coloured marbles, arranged in simple geometrical patterns. The absence of triforium galleries—Pisa Cathedral is the only important church in which they occur—afforded excellent opportunities for the latter treatment inside, which, as at S. Miniato, Florence (Fig. 117), for instance, were not neglected. In addition, circles, triangles, and lozenges, formed of marble tesseræ (sometimes of glass mosaic) were inserted in the plain marble facing outside; notably in the tympana of arches, between windows, etc., giving pleasant variety, and producing jewel-like effects. Hardly a church in Pisa, Pistoja, and Lucca, has not some of this work, which was also a favourite with the builders further south, as the west front of Troja shows.

But the most marked features of Tuscan churches outside are the arcadings and open galleries. The whole of the ground storey is generally arcaded, the arches springing from pilasters of slight {Galleries.}

projection or from shafts of marble touching the walls. The arcading is carried across doorways, but emphasis is generally given to these by raising the arches above them. This is the rule in the churches of Pistoja, and was also adopted in the west front of Troja. The open galleries above, at Pisa and Lucca, often consist of three or four tiers across a west front, and sometimes along the sides of a church as well. They are seldom divided into bays by pilasters, as in Lombardy, but are continuous. The result is somewhat flat and monotonous in consequence, notwithstanding the fine effects of light and shade produced by the arched heads and slender detached shafts. It was, perhaps, as a corrective

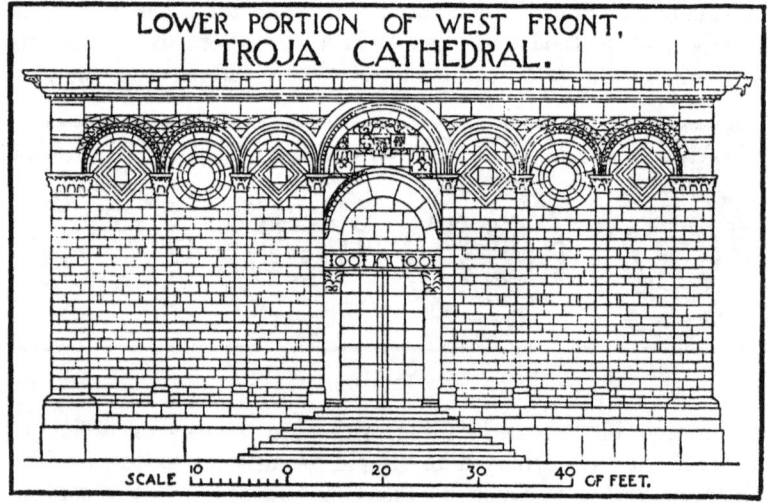

Fig. 120.

to monotony that in the west front of Pisa Cathedral the architect did not place the bays of the arcading and galleries central with one another. The nineteen openings of the lowest gallery come irregularly over the seven bays of the ground floor arcade, and in the two top galleries eight openings are placed above nine in the gallery below (see Vol. I., Fig. 179). A somewhat similar arrangement occurs along the side of the Church of S. Giovanni, Pistoja. This is an instance of the arcaded method of design carried to extremes, which is only relieved from absolute monotonous ugliness by the fact that the arches of the topmost storey do not centre with those below. The windows of Pisa

Cathedral show also how unnecessary exact centering was considered by the Pisan architects. The clerestory windows are placed in alternate bays of the external arcading, but this arcade bears little relation to the internal divisions of the church. The same may be said of the aisle windows, which come sometimes behind columns and sometimes between them. It was left for later architects to discover, with doubtful results, that everything in a church must be arranged symmetrically.

One of the most delightful architectural pictures in the world Pisa. is that formed by the cathedral, baptistery, leaning-tower, and

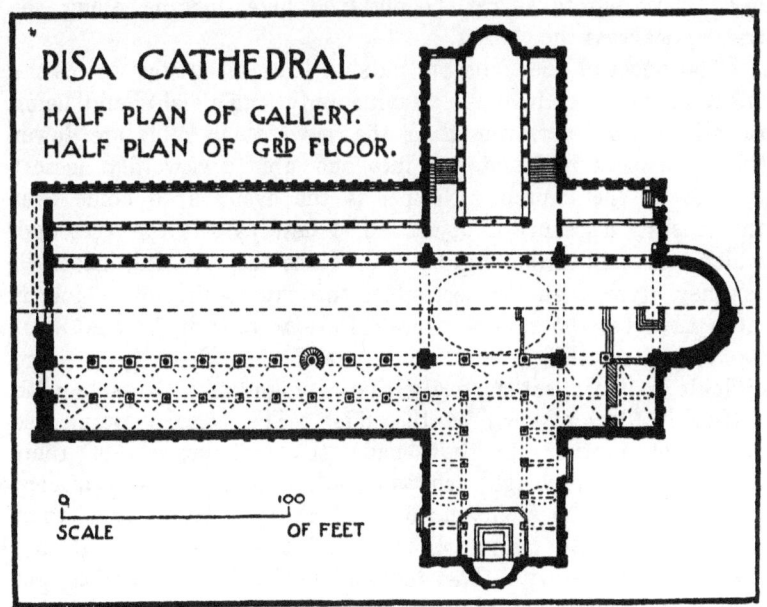

Fig. 121.

campo santo at Pisa. The effect these buildings produce is not owing so much to their intrinsic beauty, since each has many faults, as to the way in which they group and harmonize with one another.

The cathedral was commenced in 1063 and consecrated in 1118. It consists of nave and choir, both with double aisles, and wide, projecting transepts with single aisles and an apse at the end of each. The aisles throughout are vaulted, the rest of the church being covered by timber roofs. Over the aisles is a triforium which forms a high, wide gallery round the church.

One peculiarity inside is that the transepts are cut off from the crossing by similar arcading to that of the nave, and by the triforium galleries above, which are carried across their ends. This plan shows that not only were transepts an innovation little understood at Pisa when the church was built, but also the desire of the architect to adhere to the basilican plan of continuous arcades.[1] The result is excellent; there is no feeling of weakness, such as is often apparent in mediæval churches when the arches at the crossing are far higher than those at either side; and in few churches in Europe are there such fine perspective effects as can be obtained here, looking along the transepts across the church.

Exterior: Pisa Cathedral. The effect of the transepts outside is as unsatisfactory as the effect inside is the reverse. Having only single aisles, and being in all respects narrower than the nave, their roofs are lower than the nave roof, and cut into and abut awkwardly against the rest of the church. Neither is the oval-shaped dome over the crossing a beautiful object. The best part is the west end, which has considerable dignity. Its lines are truthful, inasmuch as they agree with the section of the church behind, which is more than can be said for most Italian western façades. But its virtue in this respect is a drawback. Nothing is more difficult to treat satisfactorily than a high central gable with half-gables lower down at the sides. The Greeks were wise in not attempting it; they made the ambulatories of their temples the full height, so as to allow of a single pediment at each end. The architects of S. Ambrogio, Milan, and other churches in North Italy, followed the same plan, although not always so truthfully. The builders of basilican churches got over the difficulty by masking the aisles by a narthex; and the later mediæval ones by the introduction of western towers, or by screens as at Wells and Lincoln. Western towers, however, are rare in Tuscany, in fact, throughout Italy, and very few churches in Pisa and the neighbourhood do not follow the example of the Cathedral.

Refinements. Along the flanks of Pisa Cathedral the lines of the string-courses, etc., are not straight, but rise and fall so uniformly that it is difficult to believe these curves are unintentional.[2] In

---

[1] The idea may possibly have been taken from S. Demetrius, Salonica (Vol. I., Fig. 130), where a somewhat similar plan is followed.

[2] Measurements showing these curves are given in Cresy and Taylor's

other churches in Italy, and notably in Tuscany, other curves have been recorded by Mr. Goodyear. Many of these there can be little doubt are due to settlements, earthquakes, thrusts of arches and vaults, or to alterations made from time to time which have disturbed the equilibrium of the building. The fact that indifferent construction has, in some cases, forced piers out of the perpendicular, or careless setting out has led to walls being not in straight alignment, makes the proving of intentional inclinations, either outwards or inwards, very difficult. Some of the simpler curve-and-line phenomena, such as the diminution and entasis of columns, the entasis of spires, the "batter" of towers and buttresses, are refinements admitted by every one. They are directly traceable to Classic traditions, preserved and handed down by Byzantine and Italian workmen from the Greeks and Romans; and they were retained because the artistic sense of the mediæval builder realized their value in correcting optical illusions. The north transepts of S. Fermo Maggiore, Verona, has brick pilasters at the angles which are carried up above the gable as square pinnacles. These pilasters are $4\frac{1}{2}$ inches wider at the bottom than at the top, the diminution in width being gradual, and the sides slightly curved. About halfway up are small closers.[1]

The desire to improve the internal perspective of a church by such devices as narrowing either one or both ends, dropping the height of a vault, decreasing gradually the width of the bays of an arcade, etc., were practised undoubtedly by both Byzantine and mediæval builders, although not universally by either. These devices are not confined to any one country. In Pisa Cathedral the easternmost arch at the crossing is some feet lower than the western one. In the beautiful little early Gothic church of Montreal, Burgundy, the transverse arches of the nave are stilted, but the chancel arch is not stilted, and consequently the chancel vault is 3 or 4 feet lower than the nave vault.

As regards the curves in plan of outside walls and the curves inside of walls and piers there is much room for scepticism as to whether they were in many cases intentional. That some outside walls curved, and curved uniformly, is undoubted. Poitiers Cathedral is an example. The walls here not only curve, but

"Monuments of Pisa," published 1829, and by Mr. Goodyear in *The Architectural Record* (New York) of January, 1898.

[1] I noted this diminution and rough entasis when at Verona in 1896.

the church is narrower at the two ends than in the middle. The logic of the curves in piers, described by Mr. Goodyear, is not always clear. Some piers curve outwards, others inwards. If the curves are intentional, the builders cannot have been all of one mind; if unintentional, they can be accounted for in many ways. In the Romanesque work of Italy and Southern France they can reasonably be expected as definite refinements introduced by the designers. In those countries old traditions may easily have survived; but to believe in such intentional refinements in the later Gothic work elsewhere requires more proof than has yet been forthcoming. The subject is of considerable importance, but space does not permit of its being argued here.[1]

APULIA.

The churches in Apulia, and Southern Italy generally, have suffered terribly from neglect, from ill-judged restorations, and especially from unfortunate additions and alterations made in a particularly rococo manner in the sixteenth and seventeenth centuries. Notwithstanding this, they deserve more attention from the student than they generally receive. Their fittings will compare in beauty and interest with those of Rome and Florence; the pulpits in the Cathedrals of Sessa and Ravello, with their inlays of glass mosaic, being especially noticeable. No part of Italy is so rich in bronze doors. This branch of industry, which was doubtless reintroduced here by the Byzantines, seems to have been practised by the local men to a considerable extent. The finest doors are in the Cathedrals of Troja, Trani, and Ravello; those in the two last-named being the work of Barisanus of Trani, and were executed about 1180. They are of solid cast bronze, after the old Roman and Byzantine method, and are very different from the S. Zeno, Verona, ones, in which bronze plates and moulded and pierced bronze rails and stiles are nailed to doors of wood. The carving is generally far superior to that in other parts of Italy, owing to the district having been for so many years under Byzantine rule. In most cases it is extremely delicate and refined; but occasionally it is quite the reverse, although the design is much the same, and may have been by Norman carvers,

---

[1] The above was written before Mr. Goodyear held his exhibition in Edinburgh in 1906. At the moment of going to press, his reply to Mr. Bilson appears in the November number of the *R.I.B.A. Journal*. Readers are referred to this for arguments in support of his theory regarding the curves in Gothic churches.

who copied with a heavy fist the lighter fingers of Greek artificers. This is most marked in a frieze round the top of the octagon cupola which covers the square at the crossing in Bari Cathedral. Byzantine influence is also conspicuous in the substitution of flush bands of glass mosaic for moulded dripstones over windows. Over each semicircular-headed window of the crypt in the east end of S. Nicolo, Bari, is a concentric band of glass mosaic, flush with the stonework, instead of the usual projecting hood-moulding, with squares of the same material let in above. The jewel-like effect is very telling, and all the more pleasing since it comes as a surprise. The pierced marble window-slabs of Bari Cathedral are amongst the latest of their type, and there are many others in most of the churches of Bari and Trani, those of S. Gregorio, alongside S. Nicolo, being especially numerous and beautiful.

Fig. 122.

The churches on the Adriatic, or eastern, side are, as a rule, larger than those on the western, or Neapolitan, side. The most important of the former are the Cathedrals of Trani and Bari (c. 1100), S. Nicolo, Bari, commenced 1087, and the Cathedrals of Molfetta, Canosa, and Troja, the last being built soon after the town was founded by the Greek prefect Bugianus, in 1017.

Examples.

S. Nicolo is the most characteristic. The west end is severely plain; the east end a straight wall which masks the towers at the angles and the apse in the centre. The transept, as at Trani, is continuous from north to south. One peculiarity in the church is that the columns of the three western bays of the nave are coupled, the inner columns carrying transverse arches, which reach as high as the string-course below the triforium. These columns, although old, are manifest additions, but it is somewhat difficult to say why they and the arches were added. The most reasonable hypothesis is that they were inserted to strengthen the side walls, which are of good height.[1]

S. Nicolo, Bari.

---

[1] In Trani Cathedral the columns are also coupled, but there are no transverse arches to the nave. The outer columns carry the aisle vault.

182 A HISTORY OF ARCHITECTURAL DEVELOPMENT.

Outside arcading.

The best feature is the arcading of the aisle walls outside. The arches do not spring from pilaster strips or from slender shafts, as in Tuscany, but from wide buttresses projecting about 8 feet.[1] In Trani and Bari Cathedrals there is similar arcading, although the projection is a few feet less. The boldness of these buttresses is all the more curious because a very little break is all

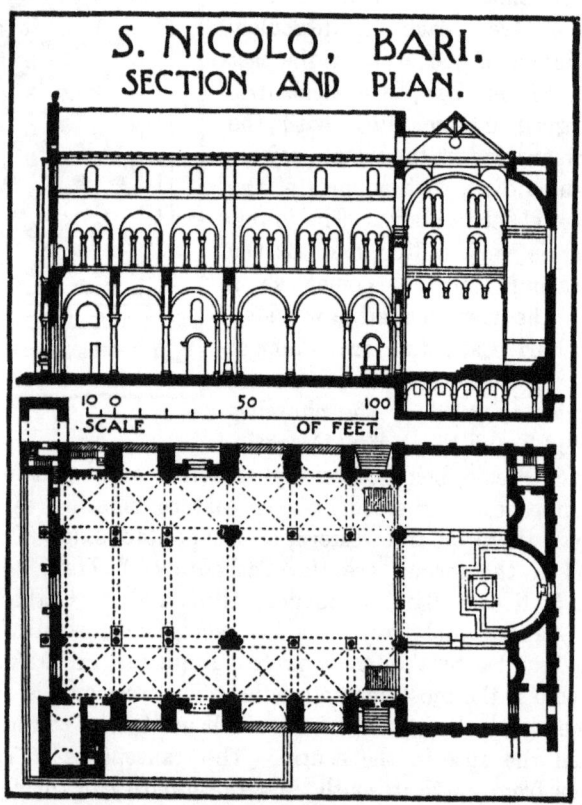

FIG. 123.

that is necessary to ensure a deep shadow in the South. There are similar arcades, but of less projection, along the aisle walls of the Cathedral of Issoire, Auvergne (see Fig. 153), and round the

[1] In S. Nicolo, the aisle walls have been brought forward to the face of the buttresses to provide side chapels inside, but these are evidently additions, and no attempt has been made to bond the new work with the old. In Trani Cathedral the buttresses still show their full projection, and the arcade extends from west to east in an unbroken sequence of many bays.

upper part of the chancel of S. Philibert, Tournus, Burgundy, but none in other parts of Italy. They cannot be due to Norman influence, because although contemporary churches in Normandy and England have buttresses of considerable width, these only project a few inches, and the space between them is never arched. That the buttresses of Bari and Trani were not regarded as mere ornaments—no Italian ever did regard a buttress as an ornament, he conceals it whenever he can—and as proof that their statical value was well understood, it may be pointed out that along the transept walls, against which no vaults exercise thrusts, there are no buttresses, only pilasters of slight projection to carry the arches.[1] Above the outside arcading at Bari and Trani was evidently originally an open gallery, as in Pisan work. In S. Nicolo the gallery exists, but the openings are now walled up. In Trani Cathedral the gallery has been entirely swept away.

In nearly all the churches in and about Bari, the extrados of an arch is rarely concentric with the intrados. The latter is generally semicircular; the former approaches closely to horse-shoe form, the voussoirs being longer at the top than at the sides. This method of construction (a sound one it must be admitted) is not confined to any one part of Italy, although it is more general in the centre and south than in the north.[2] The true horseshoe arch is more frequent in buildings round Naples than on the eastern side, showing that Saracenic influence was stronger there. It occurs over windows and doorways in the churches of Caserta Vecchia, Benevento, etc. *Arches.*

Scattered about Southern Italy are several churches which differ from those already described, inasmuch as they are domed. The Cathedral at Canosa has five domes—two over the nave, one over each transept, and one above the crossing. In plan it is therefore similar to many Eastern churches. The Cathedral at Molfetta, and the Church of S. Maria Immaculata, Trani, have three domes each, the central one being the highest. The aisles have quadrant vaults. At Trani, the central dome appears outside as a low octagonal tower, covered by a roof, whilst the side domes *Domed churches.*

---

[1] In the Byzantine church of Daphni, near Athens, each transept has projecting buttresses, and the space between them is arched. It is not unlikely that Bari and Issoire took the idea from Greece.

[2] Neither is it confined to any one period. The pointed arches of later mediæval work are frequently built in the same way, and in the buildings of the Renaissance a pointed extrados and a semicircular intrados are common.

are completely hidden. The reason for domes in these and other churches of similar design was probably that the workmen, being

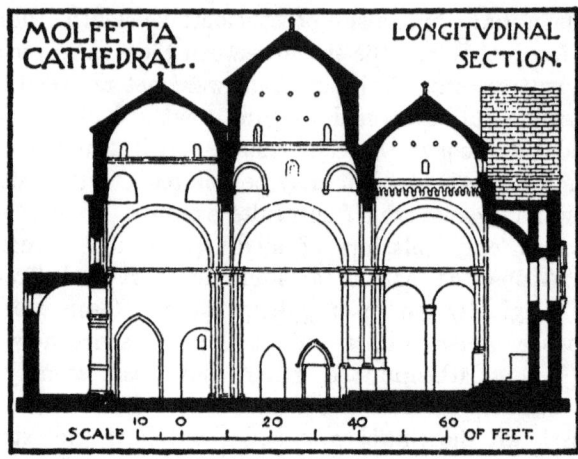

Fig. 124.

Greeks, knew how to construct them, whereas the ribbed vault had not yet penetrated so far south.

Sicily.

The influence of the Saracens accounts largely for the distinctive peculiarities of Sicilian churches, although their construction is, in the main, due to Byzantine Greeks. In addition, the Norman element, which is often manifest, forms a link of interest to Englishmen.

Various influences. It is interesting to note how these influences react on one another. Thus, although the dome is a Byzantine feature, the stilted form used in Sicily comes from farther east than Constantinople; and although the lofty marble dadoes that line the walls in many churches recall Byzantine methods of decoration, much of the detail introduced into them is Saracenic. The mosaics that often cover the domes and upper parts of walls are unmistakably Byzantine; but these are found side by side with stalactite-vaulted ceilings, which only Saracenic workmen could have made. The ceiling over the Cappella Palatina, Palermo (c. 1132), and the whole of the interesting porch, or open-sided entrance hall, in the Palace of La Zisa, Palermo (c. 1160), with

Photo: Alinari.

Fig. 125.—Cloisters, Monreale Cathedral.

Photo: Alinari.

Fig. 126.—Monreale Cathedral.

[*To face p.* 184.

its fountain and stalactite vaults, are the most marked examples of Saracenic work in the island. The crestings or battlements which crown some of the buildings outside may, with equal certainty, be ascribed to the Saracens. They present forms unknown in both mediæval and Byzantine churches. The jambs of doorways and windows are often a curious mixture of Greek, Saracenic, and Romanesque detail. Their mouldings are very shallow; and pilasters, carved with acanthus leaves and other running patterns of Greek origin, are more common than shafts. The members of the arches are of correspondingly slight projection, and zigzags, lozenges, and other enrichments generally associated with Norman work, are frequently carved side by side with more classic detail. These, however, are as likely as not to be due to the Saracens, from whom the Normans borrowed—not necessarily from Sicily, but from Palestine—much of their ornamentation. Other arches and jambs have the heavy "billet" ornament—each billet a separate stone—which is characteristic of many of the churches in Cairo.[1]

An interesting instance of conflict between Norman and Saracenic ideas is afforded in the cloisters of Monreale Cathedral. The arches are moulded in true northern fashion, with a somewhat rough semicircular member as an inner order, and are stilted and pointed. The shafts supporting the arches are extremely delicate coupled shafts, each alternate pair being inlaid with coloured mosaic, while the intermediate shafts are plain. All the capitals are exceptionally well carved, and the variety in design is most remarkable. A single oblong abacus covers each pair of capitals, but is nothing like wide enough to support the inner order of the arches above, which consequently overhangs. This shows conclusively that two sets of workmen were employed; one set designed the arches, the other the shafts and capitals, and no one made any attempt to bring the work of the two into relation with each other.

Cloisters, Monreale Cathedral.

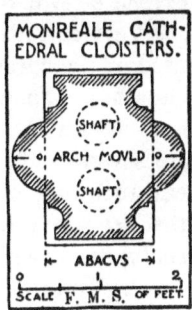

Fig. 127.

All the arches of Sicilian churches are pointed. The pointed arch was undoubtedly used in Sicily long before it came into

Pointed arches.

---

[1] Good examples of this at Palermo are in the Cathedral, and round the lower windows in the tower of the church of La Martorana.

general use in more western countries; but it does not follow that there is any connection between this fact and the introduction of the pointed arch elsewhere. Although the Normans conquered Sicily in 1090, they had something else to do for the next thirty or forty years than bother themselves about the shape of arches, or, in fact, about building at all. No work of theirs was finished before 1130; Cefalû Cathedral was commenced in 1132, and Palermo and Monreale Cathedrals not until 1170 and 1174 respectively. There were undoubtedly plenty of native pointed arches on the island when the Normans landed, and these would have familiarized them with the form; but adventurers—for so the Normans were—intent on conquest, would be less likely to observe architectural detail than pilgrims to holy shrines eager to note everything they saw. In Palestine, pointed arches were more numerous than in Sicily; and if the pointed arch were an importation, which is doubtful, it more likely came from there than from farther west.

Stilted arches. Most of the arches besides being pointed are stilted, like most early ones in France, especially in the south. The Saracens always stilted their arches, whether semicircular, horseshoe, or pointed, and the form used in Sicily is certainly due to their influence, although it is possible that their influence did not extend elsewhere.

Detached shafts. Very curious is the way in which stumpy, detached shafts are used at the corners of apses and other recesses inside most Sicilian churches. They are set back in reveals, and not only add colour and interest to the design, but also help to give scale. There are several such at the east end of Monreale Cathedral and in the entrance hall of La Zisa, Palermo. In S. Cataldo (see Fig. 129) the reveals remain in which they were placed, although the shafts have been removed.

Inlays. A favourite method of decoration on outside walls, which remained popular for centuries in Sicily for both domestic and ecclesiastical work, is a kind of inlay in which the stone is cut away and lava or black composition inserted. The lava sometimes forms the background to a pattern, sometimes the pattern itself. The outside of the Cathedral of Monreale is particularly rich in work of this description, and in Palermo Cathedral the walls of the porch, sacristy, and other portions of the building are covered with diaper patterns cut in the stone, but so slightly sunk as to be little more than incised. These lines were originally filled with black composition which has almost entirely disappeared; the result being that, except in a strong light, the patterns are hardly visible.

The Cathedral of Monreale, near Palermo, has by far the most striking interior of any Sicilian church. Its magnificent perspective is largely due to the way in which the eye is carried upwards towards the east end to the grandly designed mosaic head and shoulders of Christ which fill the semi-dome of the apse. The arch at the east end of the nave—which, by-the-bye, is not stilted—springs from about the level of the crown of the arches of the nave arcade, but the arch and vault east of the crossing, and the semi-dome beyond, are much higher. The different springing-

Monreale Cathedral.

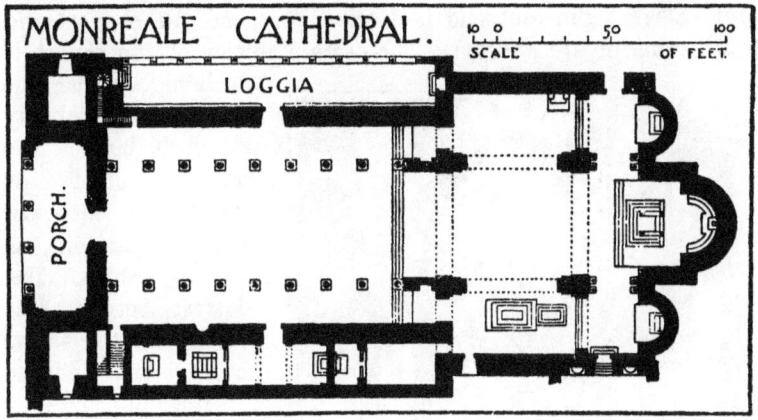

FIG. 128.

lines are marked by simple abaci covered with mosaics. The choir vault and semi-dome over the apse, like all the arches in the church, are pointed. The roofs over the nave, crossing, and transepts are timber, and the effect would certainly have been finer if there had been a dome at the crossing with vaults to north and south, like the one to the east. The capitals of the nave columns are finely carved, although their appearance is somewhat spoilt by the heavy cushion dosserets above covered with mosaics. Counterchanging is freely employed in the mosaic decoration on the walls, soffits of arches, jambs of windows, etc. The figures are always either white or many colours on a background of gold, but wherever conventional patterns are used, as in the window jambs and arches, the patterns are in gold and the ground

188 *A HISTORY OF ARCHITECTURAL DEVELOPMENT.*

in colour. The panelled marble dado, 23 feet high, round the aisle walls, has its rails and cresting in coloured glass mosaics.

The outside of the church is very striking on all sides. On the south side are the cloisters; at the west end is a porch, sandwiched between the two western towers, which stand almost clear of the church; on the north side a loggia, an almost unique position for one; and at the east end are stately apses decorated with intersecting arches (all of which are pointed), the upper tiers being carried on detached marble shafts.

Cefalû Cathedral.

In the Cathedral of Cefalû, Romanesque feeling is more apparent than at Palermo or Monreale, although it is the earliest church of the three. The arches of the nave are of two orders; moulded square abaci take the place of the mosaic dosserets of Monreale; at the east end is a triforium; and the chancel and south transept are vaulted. The eastern portion of the church is much higher than the nave, and probably was built later. The walling outside is stuccoed, evidently the original treatment, as it is of rubble. The contrast between the stucco and the ashlar buttresses, windows, arcading, etc., is very striking, and may be recommended to those who have cleared the plaster off outside walls of churches in England and called it restoration. At the west end the plan is the same as at Monreale. Between the two projecting towers is a porch, and in front is a fine open court, surrounded by a wall, which recalls pleasantly the atrium of earlier churches.

FIG. 129.

Churches.

In addition to the three cathedrals already mentioned, there

Photo: Alinari.
FIG. 130.—CEFALÛ CATHEDRAL: EAST END.

Photo: Author.
FIG. 131.—S. GIOVANNI DEGLI EREMETI, PALERMO.

[*To face p.* 188.

are a number of small churches throughout the island worthy of study. The most noticeable are in Palermo, and include the Cappella Palatina, in the Castle, and the churches of S. Giovanni degli Eremeti, La Martorana, and S. Cataldo. All were built by command of the Norman kings, but as the workmen employed were either Saracens or Byzantine Greeks, Northern characteristics are hardly perceptible. They are more thoroughly Eastern than the cathedrals, and most of them are domed. S. Cataldo (c. 1161), although shorn of its mosaics, is the most interesting, chiefly because in its present state its construction can easily be studied. The plan is nearly a square—but the two steps across prevent this from being too apparent—and is divided by columns in the same way as the smaller churches of Greece, etc. (Vol. I., Fig. 174). The aisle apses at the east end are formed in the thickness of the wall, but the central apse shows outside. The three squares of the nave are covered by domes rising from octagonal drums, carried on squinch arches. The drums are circular in plan outside and there is no break between them and the domes, so that the latter have the bulbous appearance of Cairene ones. The oblong divisions of the aisles have intersecting vaults, without ribs, beautifully built with courses parallel to the ridges. The main difference outside between this church and similarly planned Greek ones is that there are no transepts. The aisles are one height and are nearly as high as the nave, excluding, of course, the central domes.

CHAPTER XII.

ROMANESQUE IN GERMANY.

Introduction. The wealth of Germany in early Romanesque churches has been referred to in a previous chapter, and until the middle of the twelfth century the Germans well held their own with other nations in the importance, beauty, and originality in design of their buildings. After that they made little advance. They were handicapped by their own creations. They could not shake themselves loose from the shackles of the style which, if they had not originated, they had undoubtedly done a great deal to foster. The extent to which the workmen had lost the faculty of design, and spirit of independence so essential for artistic advance, is shown in the church at Andernach, built at the beginning of the thirteenth century. It is a remarkably fine example of architecture, big in scale and well proportioned, but considering the hundred years or more which separate it from other equally fine churches in the country it is evidence of the stagnation which unfortunately had set in. Other churches of about contemporary date show a similar retention of forms and proportions which had long been abandoned elsewhere. An undue craving for novelty and change is no doubt a curse, and one that has done more harm to architecture than to any other art; but the legitimate desire to improve on what had been done before, which animated the French and English builders at the end of the twelfth century, was a laudable ambition. When in the middle of the following century the Germans awoke to the necessity for change, they had sunk too deeply into the rut of tradition to be able to extricate themselves unaided. They therefore turned to France, and in the fine churches of the north found models which they imitated with more or less success. But there is little that is characteristically their own in their thirteenth and fourteenth-century work. The fame of German church architecture rests mainly on the early efforts of the eleventh century, and on the fine buildings of the following one.

At the beginning, the Germans, like all other nations, owed much to Italy, but their dependence on that country was, from the first, coupled with a boldness and strength and sense of fine scale and simplicity in design largely their own. They used ornament sparingly, but what little they used is good. The forms of their capitals and the designs of their carvings are based on Byzantine work, but have a distinct character; less refined, no doubt, than the work further south, but more in keeping with the solid construction of their buildings.

One of the most characteristic traits in German churches is the double apsidal ending; one apse being at the east end, the other at the west. Double apses were by no means unknown in earlier churches elsewhere, but in many cases they are due, as in the church in the Valpolicella district near Verona,[1] to the change in the orientation of churches, which resulted in the building of a new apse for the altar at the east end, and the retention of the original chancel apse at the west end to serve as porch or as baptistery. Some early Christian churches in the East were built in the first instance with double apses, but the plan of these was probably due to special ritual requirements which can hardly have existed in Germany many centuries later.[2] The generally accepted reason given for the two apses in that country is that the eastern apse was for the abbot, or prior, and monks, the western one for the bishop and the people. Each is stated to have had its own choir. If this reason is the correct one the arrangement architecturally was a far finer one than that general elsewhere, which placed the people's altar at the east end of the nave and accorded it no specially treated surroundings. It was, moreover, a return to the ancient custom, altered in the fifth century, which allowed the priest to face the east without obliging him to turn his back on the altar. Whatever the reason for it, it is a tribute to the artistic power of the early German builders—perhaps, also, to the freedom of the people from monkish rule.

Double apses.

In some churches, it is true, there is no western apse—Speier Cathedral is the largest exception to the general rule—but in most examples the apse at the west end is equal in size and importance to that at the east. In Mainz Cathedral the western

[1] See Cattaneo's "Architecture in Italy," Fig. 30.
[2] In the plan preserved in the Monastery of S. Gall, double apses are shown (see Fig. 93).

192   A HISTORY OF ARCHITECTURAL DEVELOPMENT.

arm is far larger than the eastern. It was built (c. 1200) about one hundred years later than the rest of the church, and although this may account partly for its extent, its size and beauty are also proof of the determination of the laity in the thirteenth century that their altar and their representative should have noble surroundings.[1]

There is never more than one apse at the west end, although not unfrequently there are three side by side at the east end, as at Laach Abbey Church. These provided space for the additional altars required by the monks, and further accommodation could be obtained in the crypts, which, although by no means universal,

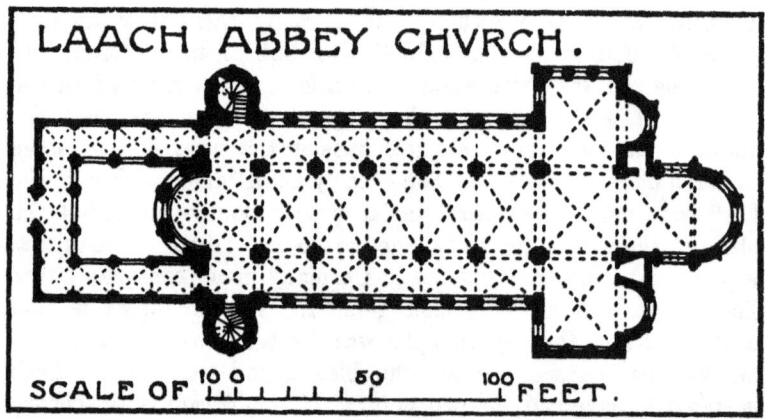

Fig. 182.

are not uncommon under the eastern choirs, as at Mainz Cathedral.

Transepts.

The crossing in front of each central apse, west as well as east, is generally covered by an octagon tower, or cupola, carried on squinch arches, which rises above the roof, and on either side of it, in most churches, are transepts. These are invariably of slight projection, if they project at all. There is more compactness about the plans of German churches as a whole than is generally found elsewhere. The main result outside is that there is little to show which is the west end and which is the east. Each end has its apse, its pair of transepts, as a rule, and its cupola; whilst the unbroken line of the roof over the nave forms a connection. Considerable ingenuity is displayed in varying

[1] The western altar is the one now used for service.

the designs, so that of no one church can it be said that the east and west ends are alike. And yet, notwithstanding the striking effects which are frequently produced, a feeling of dissatisfaction is not altogether unnatural. One misses the marked differences in treatment between west and east fronts which are so fascinating in many of the churches of other countries.

The most effective feature of the German church externally is generally its skyline. This is owing to the fine balance which the two large cupolas give to the central main roof, and to the subordinate towers or turrets which are appendages to nearly all the large churches. The Germans understood thoroughly the art of grouping these to the best advantage, and of placing them so that they should assist, and not conflict with, the larger features. There are generally two turrets at each end. In some

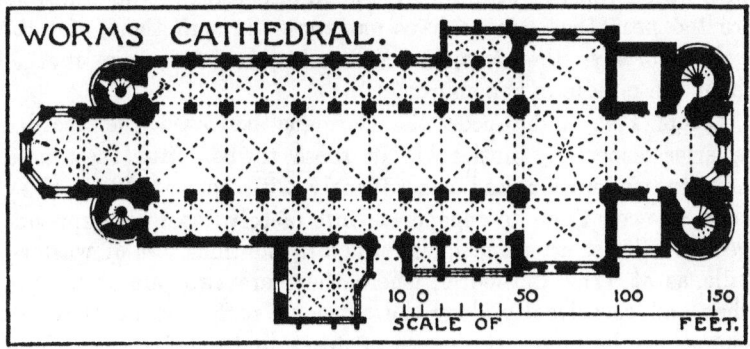

Fig. 183.

cases they stand out in bold projection from the transepts, as in Mainz Cathedral and the Church of S. Michael, Hildesheim; in others they flank the apses, as in the Cathedrals of Speier, Worms, and Bonn. In other countries circular towers are rare; in Germany they were common in all the early centuries of church building. In the parchment plan preserved in the monastery of S. Gall, two such towers are shown at the west end (Fig. 93). They appear as though they were detached, but this may be merely a defect in draughtsmanship.[1]

One result of the double apse plan is that, as a rule, the lateral entrances to a church are at the sides, and not at the west end.

---

[1] Some of the Ravenna towers are detached, but they are in different positions. The tower of S. Apollinare Nuovo is somewhat similarly placed, but this is attached to the south-west angle of the aisle wall.

There are exceptions, of course, when there is no western apse, as at Speier Cathedral, and in some cases also, as at Trier, Mainz, and Laach, there are doorways at the west end opening into the aisles. But the central western doorway is rare, not only in Germany, but also in churches in Switzerland built under German influence. It often finds no place even when there is no western apse, as in Zurich Cathedral. By its omission the Germans deliberately lost an opportunity for architectural display, and also for fine scenic effect. A central west doorway affords an excuse for the exercise of the architects' and the sculptors' skill, and at the same time provides the only truly dignified entrance to a church. It might have been thought that the Germans would have transferred their energies to the lateral entrances, but, with a few exceptions, these, so far as can be judged from the original ones which remain, were small and unimportant. The transepts are too near the ends to have entrances through them, and the main doorways therefore, in most examples, face one another about the middle of the church.

Open galleries.   From Pisa and Lucca the Germans borrowed the arcaded galleries, especially noticeable in those towns. But they used them in moderation, and consequently with better effect. They never allowed them to degenerate into merely decorative appendages. Galleries are sometimes formed in the thickness of western walls, as at Trier Cathedral, where there are two, one above the other, and occasionally along the sides, as at Speier, but they are generally only under the eaves of apses and cupolas. In these positions they are especially effective, and are, moreover, particularly appropriate for reasons already given (see p. 170).

Pilasters, etc.   The walls outside are, with the exception of the galleries, treated very simply and with great severity. The thin pilaster strips, and arched, corbelled string-courses of Lombardy are general, especially round the smaller towers and turrets; but otherwise there is little attempt at decoration. In this respect there is much greater resemblance to the architecture of Northern Italy than is found in the Romanesque work of any other country. In S. Philibert, Tournus, it is true, the design is much the same as at Mainz, Speier, etc., which is accounted for by the fact that Burgundy belonged to the German Empire in the eleventh century; but elsewhere in France and in England the pilasters are generally of different proportions, more structural and less merely decorative, and the string-courses of another character.

Fig. 134.—Worms Cathedral: East End.

The east end of Worms Cathedral, with its octagonal tower behind, shows well the circular turrets, the galleries under eaves, and the pilaster treatment just mentioned. Moreover, it is a striking example of the desire of the Germans to obtain variety in the ends of their bi-apsidal churches. The square outside encloses a semicircular apse, and the whole east end is most happily grouped. *Worms Cathedral.*

In many large churches of the twelfth century the aisles only are vaulted—and not always those—the naves being covered by timber roofs. When vaulting was first employed for naves is somewhat uncertain. The three largest of the Rhenish Romanesque churches, Speier, Mainz, and Worms, may have been intended to be vaulted from the first, but if so the probability is that the vaults were simple intersecting ones, without diagonal ribs. The nave vaults of Mainz and Worms are now ribbed, the ribs being moulded, and the transverse arches plain. In all three churches the vaults are very domical. The aisle vaults of Mainz Cathedral have no ribs, only transverse arches. This, coupled with the fact that on the nave side there are no projections from which either diagonal or wall ribs can spring, seems proof that the nave vault of this church is a later addition. The transverse arches are slightly pointed, an additional reason for doubting that the vault is the original one. In Worms Cathedral diagonal ribs may have been intended from the first, as the piers are large, and there are projections. These, however, are not conclusive proof of this, as there are similar ones at Speier, where the vaults, which date from the middle of the twelfth century, have no ribs. *Vaulting.*

In nearly all the churches, late as well as early, the fine plan of one big bay of nave vaulting equalling two bays of aisle vaulting is followed. The early builders preferred this plan because of the fine effect which it produces, and not because they wished all bays square. They wanted their vaults to be big and to look big, and they relied on the subdivision of the arcade at the sides to give scale and to emphasize the result they were striving for. Most of the vaults are quadripartite, but in some cases where the vaulting is a subsequent addition, as in S. Maria, Cologne, the sexpartite plan is adopted. The vaults of this description in the Church of the Apostles, in the same town, are more satisfactory than is customary. None of the bays in either naves or aisles of the three large representative churches mentioned above is exactly square—those of Mainz Cathedral, in fact, are distinctly oblong.

Absence of triforium.

The grand simplicity inside of the three great Rhenish churches is one of their chief beauties. There are no triforia; in fact, the

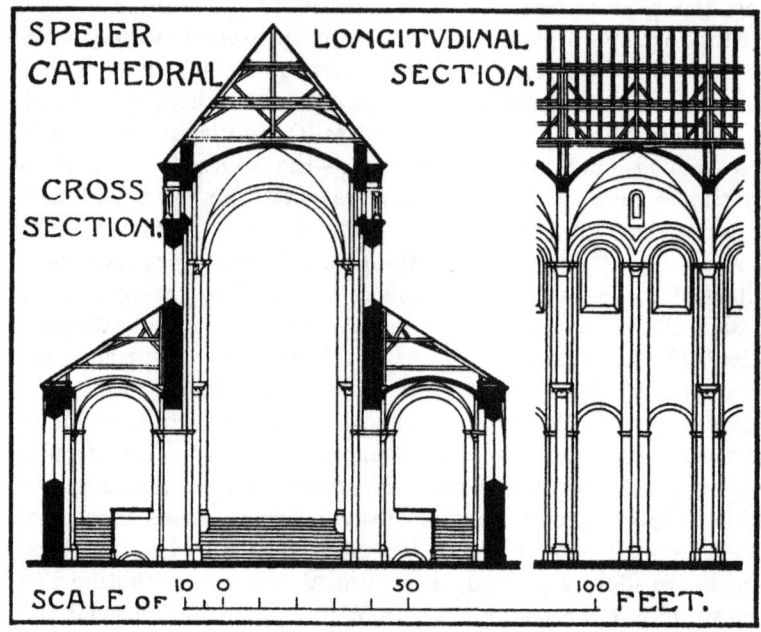

Fig. 185.

general absence of galleries from the majority of German churches—an early exception is at Gernrode (c. 1000)—suggests that, what-

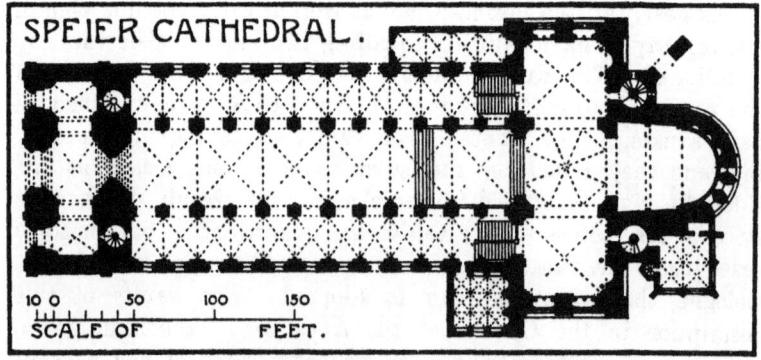

Fig. 186.

ever may have been the case elsewhere, there was no use for them in Germany. Desire not to increase the internal height

Fig. 137.—Worms Cathedral, looking West.

may have had something to do with their omission. The nave of Speier Cathedral is about 46 feet wide and 108 feet high. This is the tallest of the three. In Mainz Cathedral the width is the same, but the vault is some 20 feet lower. In Auvergne, as already mentioned, they introduced triforia, but did without upper windows. In the churches now under consideration they adopted the opposite plan. Opinions, doubtless, will always be divided as to which is the better, but the builders in both Germany and Auvergne showed their good sense in not attempting to have both features. Arcade, triforium, clerestory, is no doubt a natural and proper division in a church of French loftiness, but in the earlier work, in which a more modest height sufficed, it means the cramping of either the top storey or the bottom one. In the large cathedrals of Switzerland, Bâle, Zurich, and Lausanne, which, however, are more Lombardic than Teutonic, there are triforia, but the arcade suffers in all cases.[1]

The Germans, although content with a moderate height inside, were by no means averse to the effect which height gives. This is shown in the treatment of the nave arcades of Speier, Worms, and Mainz Cathedrals. There was evidently a strong desire to obtain verticality by continuing the piers above the springing of the arches. In all three churches the piers are alternately large and small, the latter being perfectly plain rectangular ones, with attached shafts to carry the transverse arches on the aisle side only. In Speier Cathedral there is a similar shaft on the nave side as well. The design in the three churches varies slightly. At Speier and on the south side of Worms Cathedral,[2] the face of the pier is carried up straight to the springing of the clerestory windows, arches being then turned from one pier to the next. The only break is the abacus moulding from which start the arches below, which are set back a few inches. In Mainz Cathedral the piers are not carried up so high, and the arcade really consists of two arches one above the other, the lower arch being set back, and the upper arch coming underneath the clerestory windows.[3] The

Arcades.

---

[1] In the thirteenth-century churches of Limburg-on-the-Lahn, Andernach, etc., galleries are also introduced—in the former there is an upper triforium as well—but in these churches the influence of Northern France was beginning to make itself felt.

[2] The view is looking west.

[3] In Jedburgh Abbey Church is a somewhat similar arrangement, but there are columns instead of piers, and the treatment is more architectural, although the British example is on a smaller scale (see Fig. 223).

effect in all is exceedingly fine. It may be urged that it is somewhat bare. Those who feel that may have the consolation of knowing that the plain surfaces offer magnificent opportunities for decoration, and that probably they were painted originally. Those who are satisfied with fine, simple architectural lines and do not crave for ornament will be content with the churches as they are.

Western façades. The western façades of some of the churches which are not biapsidal suffer from the fact that the central west doorway is omitted. This gives a meaningless appearance to the whole elevation, as it lacks an important feature on which the eye can rest. In nearly all the later churches, however, and in some of the earlier, the omission is rectified. But if the churches lack a western doorway, they are seldom without western towers. Speier Cathedral is almost the only large church without a western apse in which they are omitted. In smaller churches without them the western wall often has no gable, but is carried up above the ridge of the roof behind and is straight at the top. S. Castor, Coblenz, is one of the best known churches with western towers without the apse in between, but its front suffers from the fact that the towers are too close together. The nave behind is of considerable width, and there is therefore no excuse for cramping. As it is the towers are partially behind the nave, with the result that the aisles with their roofs project beyond them with unsatisfactory results. This fault was remedied in the later churches of Andernach and Limburg-on-the-Lahn. Laach Abbey Church (c. 1112), besides being a remarkably good example of straightforward honest building, has one distinctive feature which is always welcome—a western atrium (see Fig. 132). This helps to make its entrance front one of the most effective in Germany, as the apse, central tower, and side transepts, with their circular turrets at the ends, rise above the low roof over the cloisters round the court, the cloisters adding scale to the church behind.

Trier. Trier Cathedral is noted for being a remodelling of an old Roman building, and for having the biggest vaults of any Romanesque church in Germany. The original building was a square, enclosing a cross (as in Byzantine churches), the arms of which were probably the same height as the vault over the centre. This accounts for the unequal spacing of the bays, a peculiarity which was happily followed in the western part of the church when that was built about the middle of the eleventh century. The

Roman building was not pulled down, and in the walls of the existing church are brick voussoirs of the old arches and the capitals of four pilasters which may have belonged to the great piers at the angles of the central square. The large bays are about 53 feet square. When the vaults were built is somewhat uncertain, but probably not before the end of the twelfth century, or the beginning of the thirteenth. The vaulting is slightly domical; the transverse arches dividing the large bays from the narrow ones are pointed and of considerable width, and the diagonal ribs are, by comparison, exceedingly thin. The vaults resemble so closely those of S. Pierre, Saumur (see Fig. 164), and the Churches of Poitiers, etc., that it is not unlikely aid was obtained from Southern France,

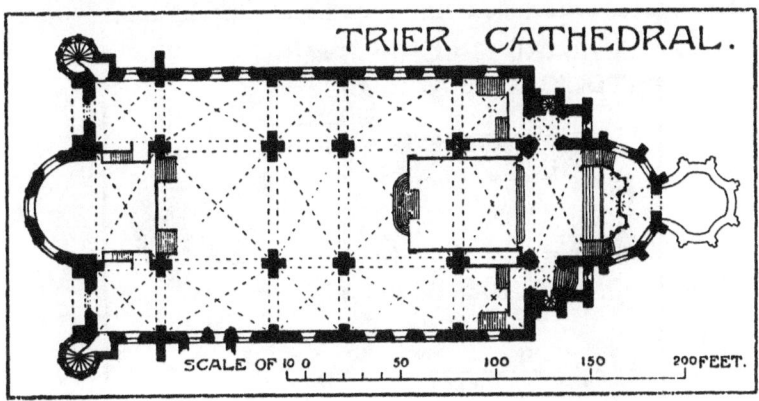

FIG. 138.

where the workmen had already had considerable experience in the building of vaults of similar size. The vaults of the transepts, to the north and south of the eastern square, are the same height as those of the nave, the other side vaults being lower. The church thus retains its cruciform plan, although both the western and eastern arms have been lengthened. Altogether, whether viewed from the east or the west end, the interior is one of the most striking in Europe.

The number of churches with apsidal endings to transepts as well as to choirs is unusually large in Germany. At Cologne alone there are three—S. Maria in Capitolio, S. Martin, and the Apostles Church. S. Quirin, Neuss, and Bonn Cathedral are two other examples, but in the case of the latter a long chancel has been added, which destroys the original effect at the crossing. *Tri-apsidal east end.*

None of the above has aisles round its apses except S. Maria, and consequently this church is by far the most interesting of all. Mention has in previous pages been made of other churches elsewhere of similar plan, and their possible derivation from S. Lorenzo, Milan, and other Byzantine churches, has been referred to. The nave of S. Maria has to some extent lost its original character, as the vaulting is an addition, but the eastern portion is much the same as it was when built some time in the eleventh century, except that the decoration is new. It occupies the site of an older church, the foundations of which may have influenced its plan. The transept arms are covered by barrel vaults, the apses by semidomes, and the crossing by a low dome carried

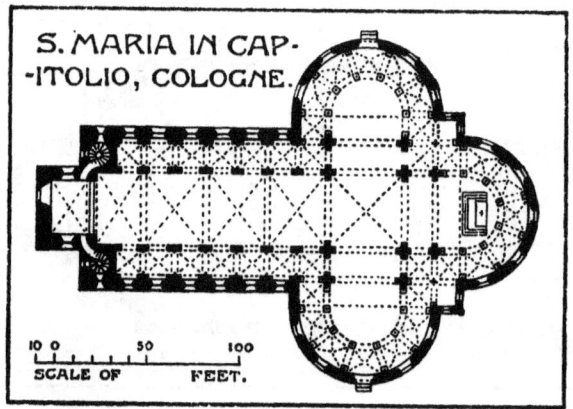

Fig. 189.

on true pendentives. Tapering columns with cushion capitals surround the apses and separate them from the aisles. To the little square chapels to the north and south, beyond where the aisles of transepts and chancel meet, much of the fine perspective effects at the east end are due. The whole of the eastern part is raised a trifle above the nave, and under the chancel is a well-lighted crypt, approached now by steps down from the two transepts. There is nothing that calls for special mention in the exteriors of these churches except the tower over the crossing of S. Martin's. That is about 40 feet square, without the octagonal turrets which come one at each corner and add greatly to its apparent width.

Tournai Cathedral.

Perhaps the finest cathedral in Europe in which the triapsal

Fig. 140.

plan was adopted is at Tournai, in Belgium. The original chancel apse has been destroyed, and the choir belongs to a later date than the rest of the church, but the transepts remain practically unaltered. The effects inside are very fine, but finer still is the result produced outside by the central tower with its lofty spire, and the four towers, also with spires, which flank the northern and southern apses.

CHAPTER XIII.

ROMANESQUE IN SOUTHERN FRANCE.

THE churches of the eleventh and twelfth centuries in France exhibit almost as much variety as contemporary ones in Italy, notwithstanding that the influences which caused the differences in the latter country hardly existed in the former. The Saracens had been driven out of France long before the churches now under consideration were commenced, and although here and there a detail may suggest a Saracenic origin, the resemblance, in most cases, is probably accidental. Byzantine influence is more marked, but most of it was indirect, and was due to tradition more than to the employment of foreign workmen. The Eastern emperors had no footing in France, and to what extent, if any, Byzantine craftsmen entered the country is a debatable question.

In the first half of the eleventh century, before the native builders found their feet, the Eastern plan, no doubt, was frequently followed, as many of the earlier churches show, but as the wealth and influence of the great Benedictine monasteries increased, and the people manifested more interest in religion, the reliance on foreign models decreased. The fine domed churches of Aquitaine are to some extent an exception, but only one, S. Front, Périgueux, is unmistakably Byzantine in plan. This is undoubtedly a copy of S. Mark's, Venice. The characteristics of the other domed churches may in part be due to Greek or Venetian colonies in the neighbourhood,[1] or to the merchants of like origin who traded in those parts, but they are more likely the result of local traditions of building which had lain more or less dormant during the dark ages. Of Classic influence there are unmistakable traces, especially in Southern France. In the North, the remains of work of the ancients were few and unimportant; in the South, Greek

---

[1] Sharpe, in his "Domed Churches of La Charente," states that there was a large colony of Venetians and Greeks at Limoges.

buildings, as well as Roman ones, were plentiful. The monuments of Classic art still existing there are probably but a hundredth part of what were standing in the days when the church-building movement was at its zenith. Eight hundred years ago these exercised enormous influence. The detail of the South is almost entirely based on Roman models. It is true that some of the capitals are of the "corbel" type first used in the East (see Vol. I., Fig. 149), and that the diaper of different coloured stones—so marked in the volcanic Puy de Dome district, and existent also in all countries—had its origin in Eastern architecture; but most of the capitals are free renderings of the Roman Corinthian, and diaper work occurs in many of the earlier churches in France, such as S. Jean, Poitiers, S. Généroux, etc., and had become a vernacular trait long before the twelfth century. The fluted pilaster, so prevalent in Burgundy and Provence, is not Byzantine—in fact, it is seldom, if ever, used in Byzantine architecture. It is a Roman feature preserved in Southern France, owing to the numerous remains there of Classic art and the conservative instincts of the people. To the same causes are due many Corinthian capitals which might belong to the second century A.D.; mouldings of a delicacy unknown in contemporary work in Northern France, England, or Germany; and the carvings on the mouldings, the eggs and darts, acanthus leaves and guilloches, and fret patterns, differing but slightly from those executed by Roman workmen in the later days of the empire, which had descended straight from Rome without Eastern modifications.

But the abundance of ancient remains in the South only partially accounts for the differences between the churches of Northern and Southern France. The people of the South were of a different race from the people of the North. The language they spoke was different. Moreover, the King of France, in early days, could claim complete control over but a small portion of what is now France. Burgundy, at the beginning of the eleventh century, was part of the German Empire; the dukes of Normandy and Brittany were to all intents and purposes their own masters; in both South and North were other dukes and counts who practically ruled as they pleased their large domains. They acknowledged the king at Paris as their suzerain, but suzerainty in feudal days was a very doubtful quantity. In the latter half of the twelfth century more than half of France belonged to, or was dependent on, the King of England; and although the beginning of the thirteenth century saw a vast extension of the French king's territory and influence, a large portion of the country still remained semi-independent. No wonder, therefore, that, apart from differences of race and language, apart, too, from the presence or absence of Classic remains, the South differed from the North, and that in the South especially there is a variety in contemporary examples greater even than that to be found in Italy.

An analysis of the Romanesque churches in Southern France shows that, although there are weighty points of difference between them, in some respects there is agreement. For instance, the aisleless plan of church was used throughout to an extent unknown elsewhere. It becomes rarer as one proceeds northwards, towards the Loire, but the two most important churches in Angers, the Cathedral and La Trinité, are of this type. Small churches without aisles are common to all countries, but in Southern France many large churches—churches with a span of from 50 to 60 feet—consist of nave alone. Some of these are covered by intersecting vaults; others by barrel vaults; a group are domed. The three methods of covering were employed irrespective of whether a church was aisled or not. The barrel vault is found everywhere, in large churches as well as in small; on the Loire, in the far South, and especially in Burgundy and Auvergne. The ribbed intersecting vault did not penetrate into the southernmost parts until the twelfth century was nearly over, but on and about the Loire are some of the finest early examples of it in France. An irregular line drawn from Tours to Bordeaux passes through the country possessing the most notable of domed churches, but this method of covering was not confined to this one district. No satisfactory hard-and-fast division can, in consequence of so many exceptions, be made dividing the churches of Southern France into vaulted or domed, into aisled or non-aisled. As, however, the covering, in these examples, presents more characteristic treatment than the plan, it is followed in preference to the other in this chapter.

Analysis.

Périgueux may be taken as the centre of the domed churches of France. In this town there are two, S. Etienne, built in part about 1050, and the great five-domed Church of S. Front, which, excepting portions of an earlier church which form a kind of narthex at the west end, was rebuilt after a fire in 1120.

Domed churches.

206 *A HISTORY OF ARCHITECTURAL DEVELOPMENT.*

The dome covering the original square bay of S. Etienne, like most of the domes of the district, is carried on true pendentives.

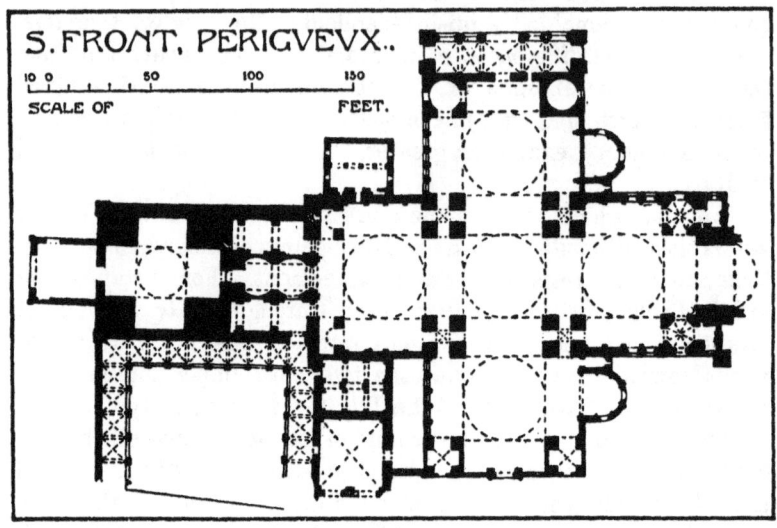

Fig. 141.

The arches under it are slightly pointed, but otherwise it is thoroughly Byzantine in its plan and construction. The simi-

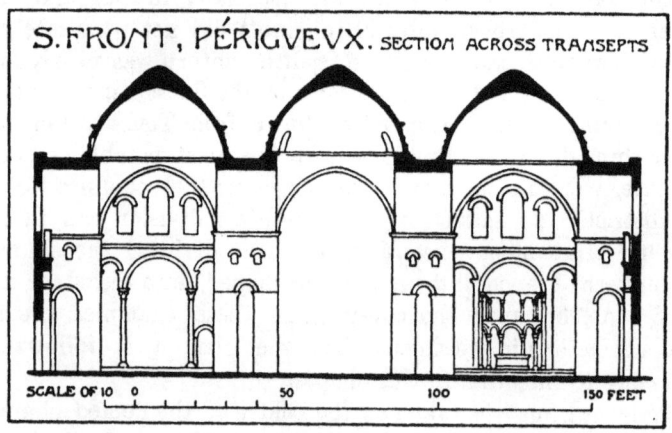

Fig. 142.

larity between S. Front and S. Mark's, Venice (see Vol. I., Fig. 164), as regards plan, construction, and dimensions cannot be accidental. S. Mark's is a copy of the Church of the Apostles at Constantinople, pulled down by the Turks in the fifteenth century, and it is therefore possible, although extremely unlikely, that the architects of S. Front may have gone farther east than Venice for their inspiration. The rebuilding of S. Mark's was begun in 1063, and by the end of the eleventh century the fame of its plan, novel to Western eyes, had spread far and wide. Why the plan was adopted in this one church at Périgueux, and not in other domed churches of the district, is impossible to say. No records exist of Byzantine architects or workmen having been employed upon it; and the influence of the Venetian traders, who no doubt sang the praises of their church wherever they went, can hardly in itself have been sufficiently strong to account for the adoption of a plan essentially Eastern. The only reasonable supposition is that as the dome was already recognized in the district as the natural covering for a church, the suggestion of a plan which would give an opportunity for five domes was eagerly adopted.

The domes of S. Front, like those of S. Mark's, come one over each arm and one over the crossing. All are carried on pointed transverse and longitudinal arches, which spring from heavy square piers, pierced with narrow semicircular headed openings. There is a certain clumsiness about the way in which the domes start from the pendentives which suggests that the builders were not thoroughly at home with the construction they had adopted. The domes are set back behind the face of the pendentives. In other churches of the district, mostly a few years earlier in date, Angoulême, Fontevrault, etc., they spring naturally from the face of the pendentives as in Greek churches.[1] S. Front lacks the arcading between the big piers which (as already stated in Vol. I., p. 244) helps to give scale to S. Mark's, and partly owing to this omission, and partly to the absence of mural decoration, it does not look so large as its prototype. One refinement of the Eastern church is also wanting. All the domes of S. Front are the same diameter, about 40 feet, and there are no detached shafts against the piers, as in the transepts and choir of S. Mark's, to diminish the span at these places, to form pleasant breaks in both wall and vault, and to vary the size of the domes. This in itself suggests the absence of a Byzantine architect; for no one who had

S. Front, Périgueux.

---

[1] In S. Etienne, Périgueux, and Cahors Cathedral (c. 1100) the domes start as in S. Front.

worked on S. Mark's could have failed to notice the fine effect the breaks produce, or would have omitted them in any subsequent church for the design of which he was responsible. The lighting of S. Front is mainly from the side walls, and one misses the rings of windows in the domes which add so much to the charm of S. Mark's. There are a few windows in the domes, but they are very small.[1]

Aisleless domed churches. S. Front can hardly be said to be without aisles, although they are merely the width of the great piers supporting the domes, and are in no way cut off from the rest of the church. Most of the other large domed churches in the neighbourhood must be termed aisleless, notwithstanding that there are inside buttresses of sufficient projection to allow in most cases of strong longitudinal arches from west to east. These buttresses take the thrusts of the transverse arches, which together with the longitudinal ones support the domes (with the assistance of the pendentives), as in churches of Eastern plan.

Angoulême Cathedral. In some of the smaller churches such as Mouthiers, Berneuil, etc., only the square near the centre of each church is domed, the nave and chancel being covered by barrel vaults. In all the larger ones, however, Angoulême, Fontevrault, Châtres, Solignac, Souillac, etc., the naves, which, exclusive of the bay at the crossing, are from two to four bays long, are domed. The Cathedral of Angoulême (c. 1101–1119) may be taken as the typical example. In plan it is a Latin cross. The transepts

FIG. 143.—Church at Souillac.

---

[1] The church has practically been rebuilt in modern times, and much of its interest has gone in consequence. For particulars of the alterations made in the so-called restoration, see Mr. R. Phené Spiers, "Architecture: East and West," article on S. Front of Périgueux, etc.

have considerable projection, as the squares ending them (over which are towers) are separated from the crossing by a bay on each side

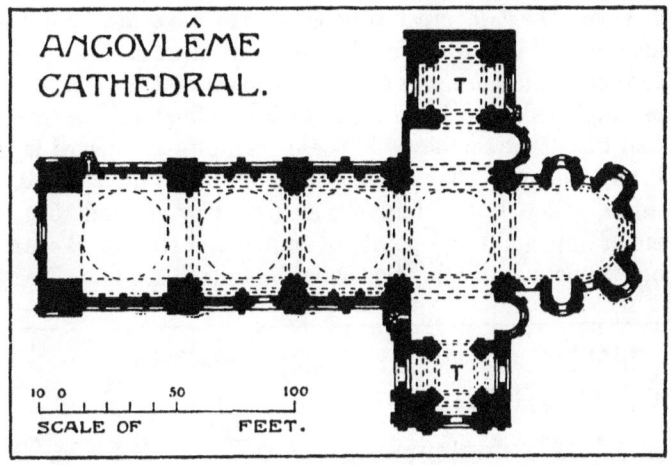

Fig. 144.

which finishes with an apse. The apses round the chancel are somewhat unusually placed, the arrangement being similar to that in Issoire Cathedral, Auvergne, except that there is no ambulatory aisle. The whole of the church, with the exception of the chancel and narrow transept bays, which are barrel vaulted, is domed, but only the dome over the crossing shows from the outside, the nave domes being hidden by the covering timber roof. In the last fact lies one of the main differences between Angoulême Cathedral and other churches of similar plan, and Périgueux Cathedral. In S. Front all the domes show; and this gives it that Eastern look which the others lack. The covering timber roof also prevents any

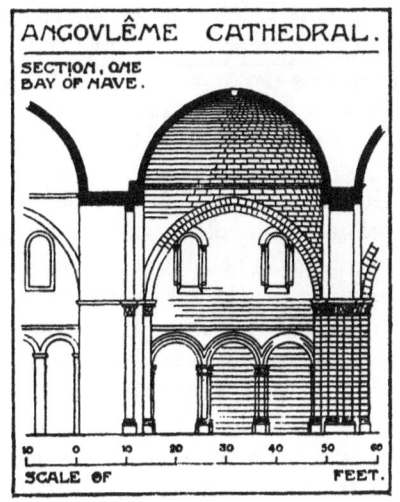

Fig. 145.

possibility of windows in the domes, which, however, does not much matter in an aisleless plan because plenty of light can be obtained from the sides. In Cahors Cathedral, however, the domes which cover the two great squares of the nave are both visible outside, and are carried on moderately high drums.

The above churches prove beyond a doubt that the aisleless plan can be employed on a large scale with excellent effects both outside and in. That the naves in these examples are domed is, so to speak, an accident. They could just as well be vaulted, like Angers Cathedral, which has a similar plan (see Figs. 47 and 162). The scheme of few and large points of support is the old Roman one, and one cannot help feeling that it is superior to the more Northern

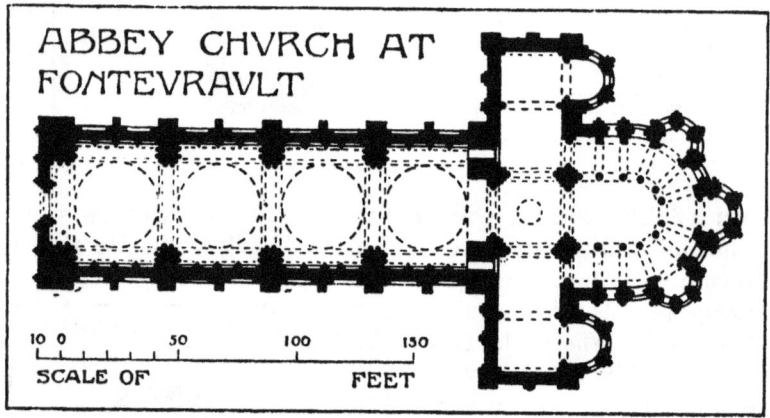

Fig. 146.

Gothic plan of multiplicity of piers. The want of columns between the piers, which give scale in Roman and Byzantine buildings, is not felt so much because their place is taken by the arcading on the side walls, which produces much the same result. In width, Angoulême Cathedral is about 53 feet between the walls and 37 feet between the piers. One of the objections to the aisleless plan is the danger of the chancel being unnecessarily wide. At Angoulême this is avoided by narrowing it, so that it is only a trifle wider than the space between the piers. At Fontevrault the arrangement is a still happier one. The square at the crossing is much narrower than the nave, and is separated from it by an arch of fair proportions with narrow openings on either side. Eastwards is an apsidal-ended chancel, round which is an ambulatory out of which open chapels. The result is a complete eastern chevet joined on to an aisleless nave, any effect of

S. HILAIRE, POITIERS.

Fig. 147.

incongruity, either outside or inside, being avoided by the projecting transepts.

Domed aisled churches. Of the many domed churches with aisles only two need be mentioned, Le Puy Cathedral (Auvergne) and S. Hilaire, Poitiers, because these, besides being remarkably fine churches, illustrate two different methods of carrying domes without employing true pendentives. In S. Hilaire the domes are irregular octagons in plan, and the corners of the squares below are merely covered by rough squinch arches like those over the crossing in S. Ambrogio, Milan. This is also the usual method adopted in the many churches in Italy, Germany, and France which have domes over the crossings only, the naves being either barrel-vaulted or groined. In Le Puy Cathedral, in many of the bays, a more graceful method is adopted. The domes are well raised, and in the corners below, starting from the string-course which runs round each bay above the level of the top of the transverse arches, are niches covered by semidomes. The outer angles of the niches are enriched by shafts, and corresponding shafts flank the corners under the centre of each semidome. It is the pseudo-pendentive plan already noticed when dealing with the later churches of Greece (see Vol. I., Fig. 143), with the addition of shafts which improve greatly the design.[1]

S. Ours, Loches. A church that marks the conflict between the predilection of the Southerners for a rounded dome and the preference of the Northerners for a steep-pitched roof is S. Ours, Loches, to the south of Tours. The nave of two square bays is similar in plan to the domed churches farther south, such as Cahors Cathedral, and to the rib-vaulted, aisleless churches a little to the north, of which those at Angers are the most remarkable. It seems probable that, when the church was first planned, either vaults or domes were intended. But neither form was built. Each square of the nave is covered by a stone pyramidal spire, which is octagonal in plan inside and out. There is no inner ceiling or shell; the corbelling for each octagon is treated decoratively, and it and the stonework above are visible from inside. The pair of spires are sandwiched between two towers, each of which has also a spire. The sky-line is a most striking one, and the combination of four spires, and otherwise no roof, is absolutely unique.

Barrel-vaulted churches. Probably the most interesting of barrel-vaulted churches in

---

[1] A somewhat similar design comes under the dome over the crossing of S. Philibert, Tournus, but the shafts there are differently spaced.

Photo: Author.

FIG. 148.—LE PUY CATHEDRAL: DOME OVER ONE BAY OF NAVE.

[*To face p.* 212.

France, of the first half of the eleventh century, is S. Philibert, Tournus, the nave and narthex of which were finished about 1019, the choir being a century later. The reason for the large narthex is referred to later (see pp. 222-3). The main point of interest to consider now is the vaulting of the church. In the nave, instead of rectangular piers or stumpy columns, as in most contemporary

Fig. 149.

churches, there are fine, lofty, cylindrical columns, built with many small stones to each course. Their diameter is greater than the thickness of the wall above, and from the segments projecting beyond the wall on one side spring transverse arches across the aisle, whilst on the other side the segments are carried up above the crown of the longitudinal arches to carry transverse arches across the nave. Much the same arrangement exists in the church at Carcassonne.[1] The chief peculiarity of S. Philibert, however, which differentiates it from all other barrel-vaulted churches, is that the nave transverse arches support barrel vaults which run transversely from north to south. The advantages of the plan are many. Each vault forms an abutment to the vault

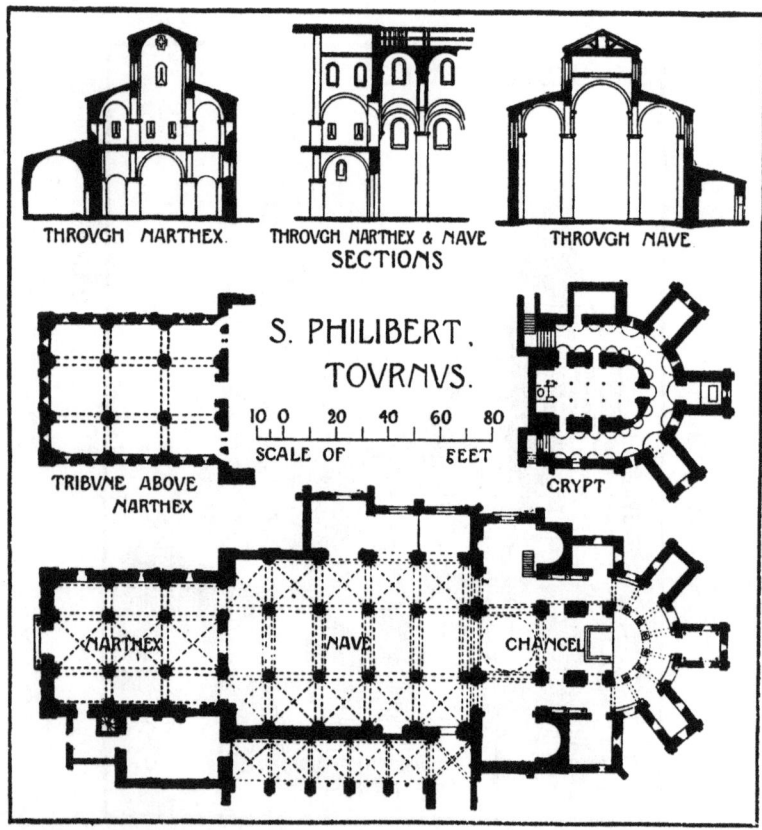

Fig. 150.

on either side of it, and it is only at the east and west ends that precautions have to be taken to resist the thrusts. At the west end of this church there was no difficulty, as the narthex is two storeys in height. What the method of resistance at the east end

---

[1] See Fig. 151. The same plan, elaborated, is followed in the later Gothic cathedrals in France, which, with few exceptions, have supports considerably thicker than the walls they carry (see Fig. 19, Reims).

was originally is uncertain, as the transepts and choir are additions of the early twelfth century. At the crossing now is a dome, over which is a tall tower, the solidity and weight of which are more than sufficient to counteract any thrusts at this point. In the lower storey of the narthex, the central portion is vaulted with intersecting vaults, but the aisles are covered by barrel vaults which run from north to south like those of the nave, and like those in the old basilica of Constantine, Rome. The central part of the upper narthex is roofed with a barrel vault running east and west, and the aisles by continuous quadrant vaults. It is a little curious that the method of vaulting adopted in the nave of S. Philibert was not more generally followed elsewhere, before the craze for great height set in. It provides perfect lighting, as the high side windows are almost invisible to any one standing in the nave, and it also produces proportions which must delight all except those whose one idea in a church is height. The barrel vaults hardly show, unless one deliberately stands under a bay and looks up. The same method was adopted in a few later examples, but only over aisles, not over naves. Over the side galleries of Nôtre Dame, Paris, were originally barrel vaults running north and south, but these were swept away during alterations made some fifty years after the church was first built. In England we have similar examples over the aisles of Fountains Abbey, Yorkshire (c. 1150), and although the vaults are now destroyed, their haunches remain, and the original design is clear. There are no earlier examples in Europe than at Tournus, but as this mode of vaulting appears to have been a not uncommon one in Persia, it is possible that the idea came from the East. In the Tag Eïvan, which is ascribed by M. Dieulafoy to the sixth century, barrel vaults, carried on very wide transverse arches, run north and south. The proportionate width of the transverse arches in the Tag to the spaces between them is much the same as in domed buildings, and it would be interesting to know why the typical Eastern covering was in this and other similar buildings abandoned for the vault. Other barrel-vaulted churches can be grouped under three heads. In the first, the churches have lofty side arcades supporting nave barrel vaults, which are generally pointed. They have no triforia or clerestories. Some have aisles, others merely deep recesses separated from one another by internal buttresses. Of the aisled type, S. Nazaire, Carcassonne, with its aisles covered by semi-circular barrel vaults, is amongst the earliest (c. 1096). The abbey church of Fontfroide and S. Trophime, Arles, are similar, but the aisles of both churches have quadrant vaults, and S. Trophime has small clerestory windows under the nave vault. The Cathedrals of Avignon and Orange, the abbey church of Montmajour, and N. D. de Nantilly, Saumur, amongst others, have no aisles, but the side recesses are covered by semicircular barrel vaults. Their scale is very fine. The Montmajour Church is 43 feet across, Orange Cathedral 45 feet, in both cases exclusive of the side recesses, which in the latter church add over another 20 feet to the width. Churches under the second head, mostly in Auvergne, have large triforium galleries over the aisles, but no clerestories; whilst those of the third have the three customary divisions, and belong mainly to Burgundy.

S. NAZAIRE, CARCASSONNE.

Fig. 151.

Auvergne. There is probably no district in Europe in which the churches bear so close a resemblance to one another as in the old province of Auvergne.[1] All might well have been designed by the same architect and built by one set of workmen. The most important are N. D. du Port, Clermont-Ferrand (c. 1080) (probably the earliest), the churches of Chamalières, Orcival, Polignac, S. Nectaire, the last, although small, being one of the most perfect, and the Cathedrals of Issoire and Brioude, built in the first half of the twelfth century. Many of their characteristics they share

[1] The Cathedral of Le Puy is an exception, but then it is the southernmost of all, and seems to have been built under other influences.

with churches of similar construction outside the province, such as S. Sernin, Toulouse, S. Etienne, Nevers, and the abbey church at Conques, but others are distinctively their own. In plan, they are all aisled, have thoroughly developed eastern chevets— that of Chamalières has been altered inside—and, as a rule, projecting transepts on the east side of which are apsidal chapels. The chevets are remarkably well arranged, and their effect outside

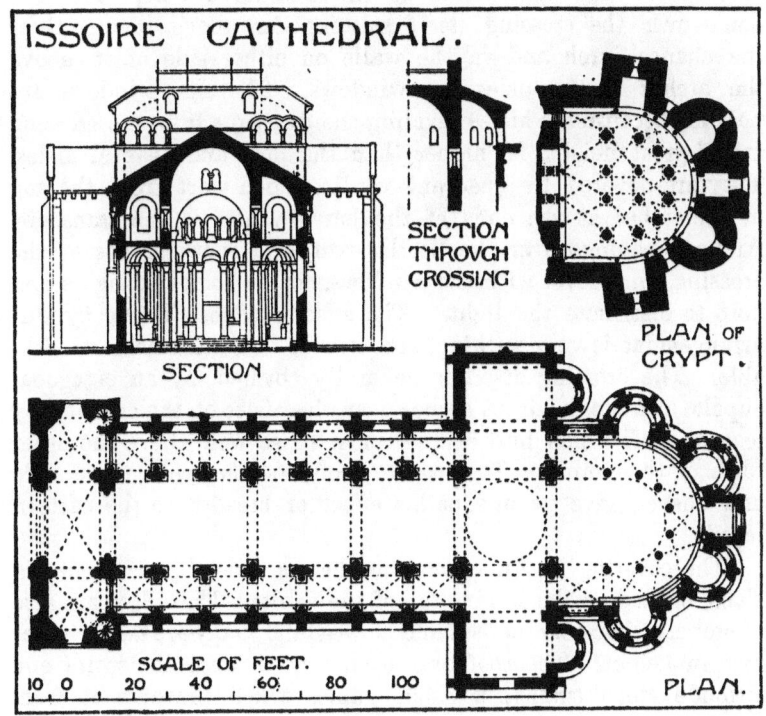

Fig. 152.

is in all cases most striking. At S. Nectaire there are three apses, at Clermont-Ferrand four, at Brioude and Issoire five, but at the last-named the central apse is a square one squeezed in between two semicircular ones. The naves are covered by semicircular barrel vaults, with transverse arches at somewhat irregular intervals, and the aisles by intersecting vaults with, as a rule, transverse arches but no ribs.[1] Over the aisles are spacious

[1] In the church of Polignac, near Le Puy, the aisles are barrel-vaulted as well as the nave.

galleries ceiled by quadrant vaults which take the thrusts of the central vaults. There are no clerestory windows,[1] but the churches are perfectly lit. The windows in the aisles are large, and a certain amount of light filters through the triforia openings from the small windows in the outside walls. The crossing and aisles alongside are as well lighted as the crossing of S. Ambrogio, Milan, but by a different method, and one that is peculiar to Auvergne. The four arches at the crossing are kept low, the dome over the crossing itself starting far above them. Over the chancel arch and in the walls on either side of it, above the arches of the aisles, are windows. The side windows are possible because the aisles dividing the transepts from the crossing are of great height, far higher than the nave and chancel aisles. They are covered by quadrant vaults, which start from the top of the arches at the ends of the barrel vaults of the transepts. Arched openings over the north, west, and south arches at the crossing, on a level with the windows, act as borrowed lights and help to distribute the light. The effect produced inside by this arrangement is very striking, and outside it is still more remarkable. The crossing itself is generally covered by an octagonal cupola, and the quadrant arches over the aisles of the crossing by lean-to roofs which butt against it, and rise well above the other roofs of the church. The lean-to roofs, together with the cupola and chevet, give an unequalled effect of breadth to the eastern façade.

Outside detail. The covering in Auvergne churches is generally stone, in big slabs, bedded on the sloping top of the vaults. The ridges are also of stone, elaborately pierced and carved, and many are two or three feet in height. The roof over each eastern apse at Issoire and Brioude stops against a small gable, which prevents it from cutting unpleasantly into the ambulatory roof. At the apex of each gable is carved a Greek cross. These crosses, the elaborate ridges, the delicately carved capitals of the many shafts round the apses—those of Chamalières are perhaps the best—and, above all, the diaper inlay of lava and red or white volcanic stone[2] in the gables and round the upper part of the apses are all so reminiscent

---

[1] In the church of S. Etienne, Nevers, which belongs architecturally to the province, although it is some distance north of it, there are clerestory windows, which come down unpleasantly close upon the arches over the triforia openings, and would have been better omitted.

[2] The richest diaper work in Auvergne is in the Cathedral of Le Puy (the centre of a volcanic district), especially in the cloisters attached to the church.

Photo: Author.

FIG. 153.—ISSOIRE CATHEDRAL: EAST FRONT.

Photo: Author.

FIG. 154.—ISSOIRE CATHEDRAL: APSES AT EAST END.

[*To face p.* 218.

Photo: Author.

FIG. 155.—ISSOIRE CATHEDRAL, LOOKING EAST.

[*To face p.* 219.

of Byzantine work that one cannot help suspecting that either the designers must have been Greek by birth, or else that they had been trained in an Eastern school. The arched recesses outside along the aisle walls of Issoire Cathedral are so similar to those at Bari and Trani as to suggest also a connection between, or like descent for, the builders of Auvergne and those of Southern Italy.

One curious trait found in many of the churches, generally inside, is the trefoil or cinquefoil arch, horseshoed at the springing. One hesitates to ascribe this to Saracenic influence, but it is difficult to account for the feature in any other way, unless, like the arched recesses, it filtered through from Southern Italy.[1] In Issoire Cathedral all the openings in the triforium on the north side have trefoil heads, except in one bay, where they are semicircular; whilst on the south side the very reverse is the case, all the heads are semicircular except in the one bay facing that in which the heads are of that form.

Trefoil arches.

Fig. 156.

Other churches of similar plan and construction outside Auvergne are S. Sernin, Toulouse (c. 1090), its Spanish sister, S. Iago, Compostella, the Abbey Church of Conques, S. Isidoro, Leon, Spain, etc. They differ mainly from the others in not having the central arrangement described above, and in the greater importance of their transepts. The similarity between the Spanish examples and those on the other side of the Pyrenees is easily accounted for. No churches of any size were built in Spain until Toledo was recaptured from the Moors in 1085, and the Spaniards, having no school of building of their own, naturally sought architects and workmen from Southern France. The

Barrel-vaulted churches farther south.

---

[1] Street, in his "Gothic Architecture in Spain," shows a sketch of an extensively foliated arch inside S. Isidoro, Leon, Spain, which must have been suggested by some Moorish example, but the Saracenic occupation of the country of course lasted later in Spain than in Auvergne.

church at Conques is in some respects finer than S. Sernin, although not so large. It is barrel-vaulted throughout, except at the crossing. This is covered by an octagonal lantern, with a window on each of its sides, which throws a flood of light into the church. Its chevet has a fine appearance outside, but it lacks the decorative additions which give such distinction to the chevets of Issoire and Brioude.

S. Sernin, Toulouse.

S. Sernin is the largest of barrel-vaulted churches in France (excepting the Abbey Church of Cluny, now practically destroyed). The nave is narrow, being less than 30 feet wide, but then it has double aisles, which make the total internal width

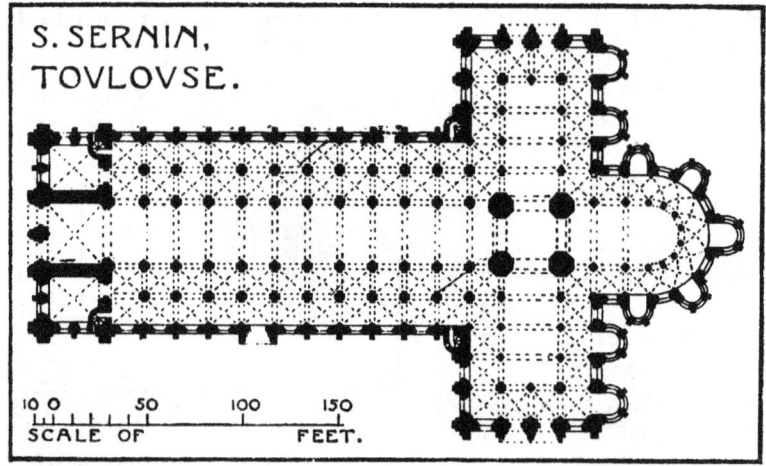

FIG. 157.

of the western arm not far short of 100 feet. The transepts have single aisles on both sides, and aisles at the ends as well, like the Cathedral of Winchester. The crossing was probably originally covered by a low octagonal lantern tower or cupola, as at Conques, but at a later period the present telescopic tower, with spire over, was added, which necessitated strengthening the piers below it. The effect outside is striking, but hardly compensates for the damage done to the interior by the narrowing of the openings at the crossing.

Burgundy.

Burgundy was a large province, and its vicissitudes, coupled with its extent, account for the variety of design in its churches. Belonging to the German empire in the eleventh century, it did not become an integral part of France until some centuries

Fig. 158.—Vézelay Abbey Church, looking East.

later, and for many years the Dukes of Burgundy were the equals of kings. But the real rulers of the duchy were the monks. The abbots of Cluny, Citeaux, and Vézelay kept almost royal state. Their energies were unbounded, especially in the direction of church building. To them is mainly due the superiority of Burgundian churches at the end of the eleventh century and commencement of the twelfth, but to their conservatism must also be attributed the failure to take advantage of the developments which later took place elsewhere.

From Sens in the north, to Autun and Tournus in the south, through the hilly district in the centre, known anciently as Le

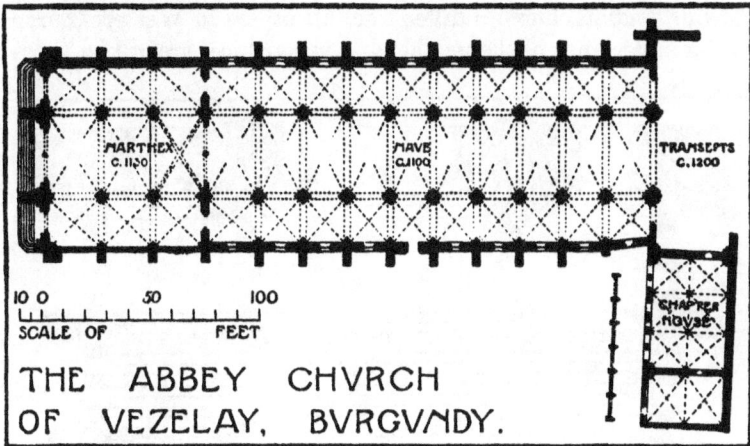

Fig. 159.

Morvan, which boasts Vézelay, Saulieu, Semur, Avallon, are many churches of the early twelfth century of great interest and considerable variety. The majority of these are barrel-vaulted; the principal exception being the fine Abbey Church at Vézelay, which has the intersecting vault throughout.[1] Here, in 1146, the French king, at the bidding of S. Bernard, announced the second crusade; and from here, in 1190, our own Richard I., and Philip Augustus of France started for the Holy Land.

The nave of Vézelay was consecrated in 1104. Its ten bays are oblong, and the transverse arches and wall ribs are semicircular; all being stilted, the latter especially so. There are no diagonal ribs to either nave or aisles. Contemporary aisle

Vézelay.

[1] Except in the choir, which is later work.

222   A HISTORY OF ARCHITECTURAL DEVELOPMENT.

vaults are common enough, but there are few nave vaults of this date, and particularly few oblong ones. The narthex of three bays was built 1128-1132, and there the vaults have pointed arches, but no diagonal ribs, except in the eastern bay.[1] The absence of diagonal ribs is one of the peculiarities of Burgundian intersecting vaults. Their omission at Vézelay is natural, as the church is early in date, but their absence from much later vaults in the duchy is proof of the conservative spirit which reigned there. The church of Pontaubert, near Vézelay, built, it is stated, by the Templars towards the end of the twelfth century, is one instance out of many. It is vaulted throughout, and, although the central bays are over 17 feet square, there are no diagonal ribs.

Narthex.   Burgundian churches differ from all others in Western Europe in the importance of the narthex. The narthices are of two types:

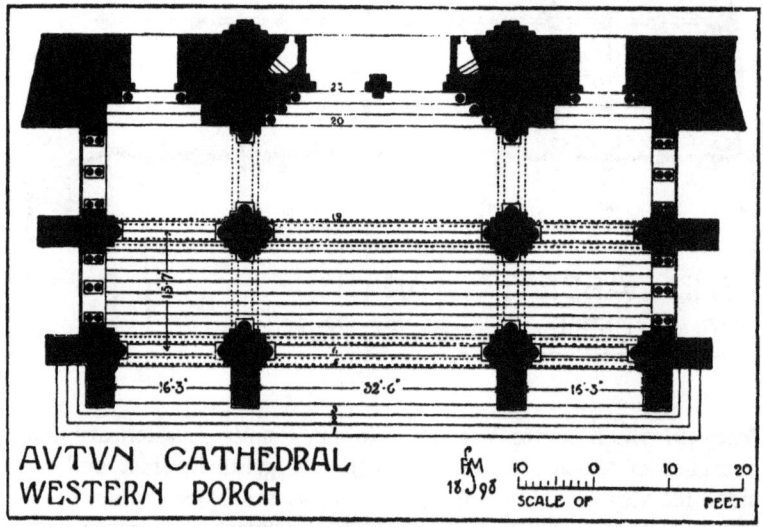

Fig. 160.

open porches, as at Autun, Paray-le-monial, Beaune, Semur, N. D. de Dijon, etc.; enclosed, forming ante-churches, as at Tournus, Vézelay, and Cluny (see Figs. 150 and 159). Of the former, Autun (c. 1160) is by far the finest. The central bay in front is exactly double the width of each side bay, and the porch is two bays deep. Much of the effect it produces is doubtless due to the striking beauty of the sculpture in the tympanum over the great central

---

[1] Viollet-le-Duc says that these ribs are additions.

doorway (see Fig. 83), but, in addition, its proportions and dimensions are truly noble. The reason for these striking additions to the west ends of Burgundian churches is not quite clear. The narthex in the Eastern church, and in early churches in Italy, was for those who could not, by the laws of the Church, be admitted into the Church proper, but the regulations regarding admission in the Western church were different. The institution of infant baptism and the abandonment of adult baptism had destroyed the probationer class, and the rules against the entry into churches of evil-doers were not so strict as in earlier days. Other reasons must therefore be sought; and these may be found in the large number of pilgrims who, on days of high festival, flocked from afar, and in the need that existed for having some spot under shelter where they could be marshalled. It hardly seems likely that even the enclosed ones actually housed the pilgrims, they were too small for that, but it is quite possible that they were used for this purpose when other sources failed, or in special cases. The enclosed narthex is generally attached to churches belonging exclusively to a monastic order; probably because the monks guarded zealously the right of entry into their churches. The open narthex is more commonly found in cathedral churches into which the people had the prescriptive right to enter. Whatever were the reasons for the narthex, they ceased to exist after the thirteenth century. The open porches of French and English cathedrals are very different from the great western additions of either Vézelay or Autun, and are merely architectural features.

S. Philibert, Tournus, the earliest of Burgundian barrel-vaulted churches, has already been described. The other barrel-vaulted churches of the duchy are totally different in design, and are mostly one hundred years or more later in date. The first to be built was the great church at Cluny, which was begun in 1089, the nave being finished about 1130, and the narthex some fifty years later. Its total length, including the narthex, was 580 feet, which is about 50 feet longer than Winchester Cathedral. The peculiarities of its plan, the double aisles, double transepts, and eastern chevet have already been mentioned. The greater part of the church has disappeared. The Cathedral of Autun, consecrated in 1132, is a copy of it on a smaller scale, and from it one is able to realize perfectly the design of the parent church. All the principal arches and the barrel vault of the nave are pointed, as was the case at Cluny, and the arches are stilted, as

Barrel-vaulted churches.

was general in all Southern examples. The vault is divided into bays by a transverse arch over each pier. The aisles are covered by intersecting vaults without diagonal ribs. The fluted piers,

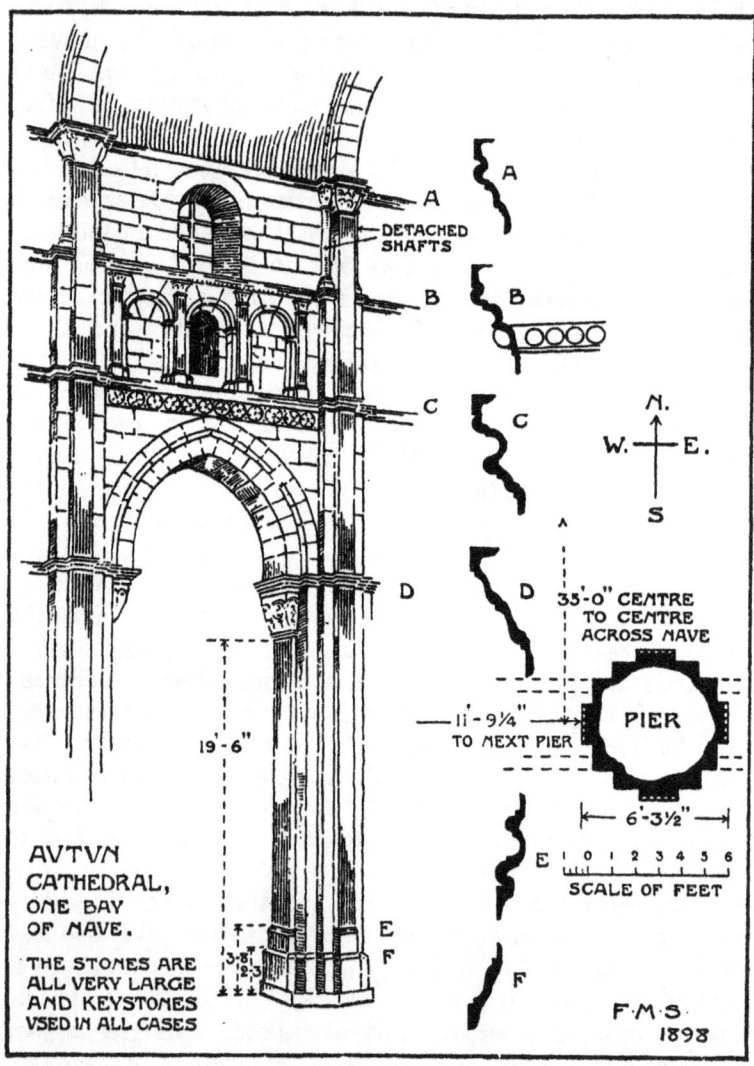

Fig. 161.

or rather piers with fluted pilasters on their face, the carving and design of the capitals, the use of large stones and of keystones in the arches, pointed as well as semicircular, the delicate contours of many of the mouldings, the design of the triforium, with its fluted pilasters and semicircular-headed arcading, all proclaim the strong influence exercised by the old Roman remains in the town, and contrast curiously with the pointed arches and vault.[1] The Cathedrals of Paray-le-monial and Beaune are practically identical in design with Autun. Beaune Cathedral has the same detached shafts immediately under the vault; nearly the same arrangement of triforium and clerestory; the same fluted pilasters as vaulting shafts; the only difference of any importance being that the arches of the arcade spring from three-quarter columns instead of from fluted pilasters.

The main differences between the churches of Burgundy and those of Auvergne, apart from the shape of the arches, are that the former have clerestory windows and the latter none; and that in the Burgundian church the triforium is unimportant and the openings in it small, as it is essentially a blind storey, whereas in Auvergne it is of considerable importance. The work in Burgundy is a step in advance of the other, fine though that is, notwithstanding its reliance on old detail. One thought occurs to one in studying it, and that is, how curiously extremes often meet; how transitional work produces much the same effect at the end of a movement as at the commencement. At Autun, Beaune, etc., the new order is beginning to take the place of the old; in many of the early Renaissance churches in France— S. Eustache, Paris, S. Michel, Dijon, for example—the new order, grown old, is being in its turn supplanted by a revival of what in the twelfth century was a disappearing tradition. Autun Cathedral and S. Eustache are wonderfully alike in many respects, notwithstanding that during the four hundred years that separate them, one of the greatest of all architectural styles had budded, blossomed, and withered.

The fame of the great churches of Northern France, commenced in the first half of the thirteenth century, has somewhat prevented full justice being done to the slightly earlier vaulted churches bordering on the Loire. Everything has been judged by Amiens; and because these churches have not its great height and daring construction they have been counted as inferior by the student of architecture.[2] And yet they have points in their favour, especially when judged by modern requirements, which the other lacks.

Rib-vaulted churches.

---

[1] The two gateways at Autun are amongst the most interesting of Roman ones.
[2] As well complain because the dachshund has not the greyhound's length of leg.

226   A HISTORY OF ARCHITECTURAL DEVELOPMENT.

They are of moderate height, and yet do not look low. They are sensibly planned and sensibly lighted, although in the latter respects, they cannot compare æsthetically with the type of church of which S. Ambrogio, Milan, and Issoire Cathedral are examples. They belong in plan and general proportions to the same class as the domed aisleless churches already described, the main difference being that they have ribbed intersecting vaults instead of domes. The most interesting are the Cathedral and La Trinité, Angers, S. Pierre de la Couture, Le Mans (all c. 1150), S. Pierre, Saumur, and S. Radegonde, Poitiers (c. 1170). All these have aisleless naves. Angers Cathedral has transepts, which are

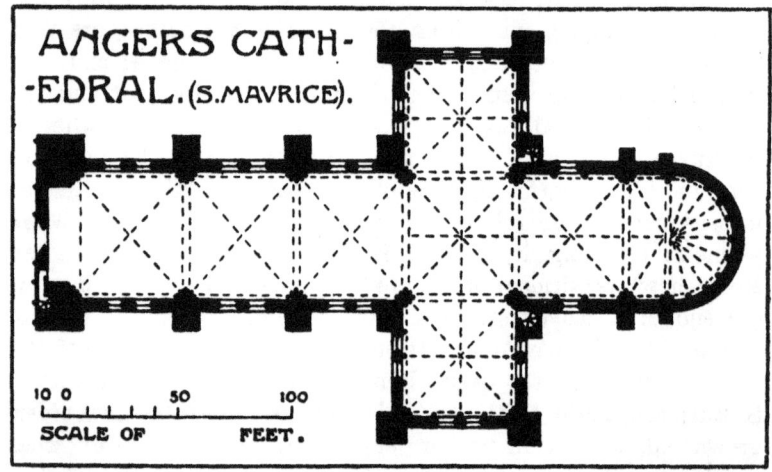

Fig. 162.

additions, whilst the chancels of La Trinité, S. Radegonde, and S. Pierre are earlier than their naves, and date from the eleventh century.

Angers Cathedral.

The nave of Angers Cathedral, owing to its fine scale and simplicity of design, is exceedingly striking. The vault is very domical, like all the early vaults in France, and the transverse arches, diagonal ribs, and the longitudinal arches against the side walls are strong and bold. Each bay of vaulting is nearly square, the span being over 50 feet, and the height from floor to apex about 80 feet. These are no mean dimensions. Of course abutment was easy. There were no aisles over which the thrusts had to be transmitted, and the supports could be any size the architect chose to make them; in fact, the whole of the continuous wall could indirectly be utilized. The difficulties to be surmounted were therefore far less than in the later vaults, carried on thin piers and stiffened by flying buttresses. And yet their accomplishment in the middle of the twelfth century was a wonderful achievement. The men who designed Angers Cathedral and other similar churches, S. Pierre de la Couture, Le Mans, La Trinité, Laval (another church of the same type), must have had a trace of Roman greatness in their composition, and a keen distaste for everything mean and petty (see Fig. 47).

Along the side walls of Angers Cathedral (and the two other churches just mentioned) are big, pointed arches, one to each bay, which produce a much better effect than the smaller arcading in the later transepts and choir, which is similar to that in S. Pierre, Saumur (see Fig. 164). Over the arches, partly carried by them and partly corbelled out, is a gallery, which runs round the church below the pairs of semicircular-headed windows.[1] It is a pity that the transepts were ever added; they detract from, rather than add to, the effect inside. The faults in the church are that the chancel is the same width as the nave, and that there is no break between the two. The pleasant feeling of mystery, the sensation that there may be a surprise in store, and the finer perspective effects which a chancel arch gives are in consequence lacking.

La Trinité, Angers, is superior to the cathedral in this respect. The openings on each side of the chancel arch are mere slits, and

La Trinité, Angers.

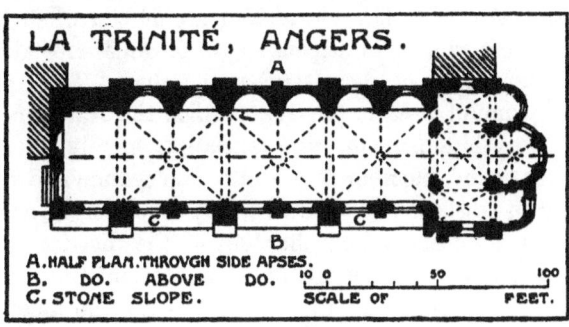

Fig. 168.

might have been treated more architecturally, but they are right in idea, as three openings look better than a single one. The vault

[1] In the Le Mans church the windows are somewhat smaller, and over each pair a circular light has been subsequently pierced, but the circles are no improvement.

is sexpartite, clumsily built, and some 10 feet narrower than the Cathedral one. There is very little difference, however, in the width of the two churches inside, if recesses are measured, as on each side of La Trinité are semicircular apses, or chapels, in the thickness of the lower part of the wall. The upper part is set back outside, and above the slope over the semi-domes of the apses are strongly projecting buttresses, to take the thrusts of the main arches and ribs, and smaller ones for those of the intermediate transverse arches.[1]

S. Pierre, Saumur.

There is no great disparity in size between S. Pierre, Saumur, and S. Radegonde, Poitiers, and the Angers churches, but there is a marked difference in detail. This is most noticeable in the vaulting. The transverse arches are still bold and sturdy, but the diagonal ribs are of the most slender description. Strong transverse arches are a structural and æsthetic necessity when the vaulting is domical, and they possess also the great advantage of emphasizing the bays of the vault. It is extremely doubtful if the later builders, in their pride of craftsmanship, made any improvement when they reduced these arches to much the same size as the other ribs. Many a vault, both English and French, of the thirteenth and fourteenth centuries looks flat and monotonous, owing to the absence of strongly marked divisions. Moreover, the effect of length is lost. The eye wanders over the vault without really noting its extent. It is the transverse arches that make barrel vaults so impressive; and possibly it was a knowledge of this that led the Burgundian architects, when building their intersecting vaults, to dispense with diagonal ribs altogether, more than ignorance of their structural value. They preferred that nothing should weaken the effect which the transverse arches produce. The thin diagonal rib, consisting merely of a single three-quarter round member, found in S. Radegonde and S. Pierre, is not confined to these two churches, but occurs in nearly all the contemporary domical-vaulted churches of the district. Another local peculiarity is the ridge rib, of same section and size as the diagonals. The presence of this feature is all the more curious because ridge ribs were seldom employed in other parts of France —never in early work—and the English vaults in which they appear are some fifty years later in date.[2] The vaults over the

[1] La Trinité has been so extensively "restored" that it is practically ruined inside.

[2] Similar ridge ribs occur in the Cathedral of Trier, Germany.

Fig. 164.

230　*A HISTORY OF ARCHITECTURAL DEVELOPMENT.*

chancel of the Church of S. Serge, Angers, are probably the most domical in existence, and their shape is the more remarkable as they were not built until the thirteenth century.

Existing chancels saved both S. Radegonde and S. Pierre from the mistake made in the Cathedral at Angers, and each has its chancel arch. In the former church, this is flanked by narrow openings which are better managed than in La Trinité, Angers. For many reasons these two churches are more worthy of careful study than others which have a far greater reputation.

West fronts.

The west fronts of Romanesque churches throughout France are, as a rule, no richer than any other parts. In many cases there is a pair of towers, but these emphasize, rather than modify, the general plainness. At S. Etienne, Caen,[1] the design is simplicity itself; between the towers two tiers of three round-headed lights come over a doorway which could not well be plainer. At the Abbaye-aux-Dames, Caen, more attempt is made at ornament, but the work is later, and the design of the rest of the church is somewhat less austere. The Cathedral of Angoulême has a front of exceptional merit, and the west end of N. D. la Grande, Poitiers, is covered with carving and sculpture. But similar enriched west ends are rare. The towers, when they occur, seldom project more than a foot or so, and there are no examples having the bold projection which gives such distinction to the fronts of Monreale and Cefalû Cathedrals, Sicily. The original west front of Rouen Cathedral had apparently three arched recesses, somewhat similar to those of Lincoln Cathedral; but the design is difficult to determine, as much of the earlier work is hidden by later additions. In Burgundy the west ends are more elaborate than elsewhere in France. A great deal of the richness against which S. Bernard thundered is found in the entrance doorways. At Avallon there are three which, for beauty of execution, are hard to beat. At Charlieu the carving over the doorways is not only exceedingly fine, but it is full of a truly remarkable classic feeling and delicacy. The open porches of the Duchy have already been referred to. In Southern France there are many fine western porches of earlier date than these. The most notable are at S. Gilles, and at S. Trophime, Arles. But these are more the result of special effects of sculptors, probably imported for the purpose, than of the designers of the churches. In concentrating their

[1] For Normandy churches, see Chapter XV.

Fig. 165.—Le Puy Cathedral: West Front.

Photo: Author.

Fig. 166.—S. Michel de l'Aiguille, Le Puy.

[To face p. 230.

efforts on one part, and not frittering them over a larger area, these artists showed sound judgment. The exceeding plainness of the surrounding walls of both churches acts as a foil to and emphasizes the richness of the porches. The church at S. Gilles boasts three doorways side by side, and the design is more ambitious than that of S. Trophime.

The most remarkable west end in Auvergne is that of Le Puy Cathedral. The church owes its imposing appearance to the commanding position it occupies on a steep slope near the top of a hill, and to this is due the unique arrangement of its western façade. The triple entrance porch, which occupies the entire width of the church, does not stand in front of the nave, but is *underneath* it. The approach to it is by a straight, wide staircase of many flights (each flight of about twelve steps), which continues under the porch, and then turning to right and left, leads on one side to the cloisters, on the other direct to the church above. The result is one of the most striking entrances in Europe. The peculiarities of the interior have already been referred to in this chapter.[1]

[1] Le Puy possesses other original buildings; not the least, although the smallest, of which is S. Michel de l'Aiguille, perched on top of a lofty needle of rock which rises abruptly from the plain. In plan it follows the outline of the summit, and is like a snail-shell.

CHAPTER XIV.

EARLY ROMANESQUE IN ENGLAND.

Introduction.
THE early work in England, executed some time before the Norman Conquest, which commonly goes by the name of Anglo-Saxon, is an offshoot of the great Romanesque style quite as much as the later Norman is. The examples of it are neither numerous nor, in an architectural sense, important, but are nevertheless exceedingly interesting, owing, in many cases, to certain traits they possess which are absent in later churches. Some were built before the eleventh century, others in the sixty odd years before William I. landed, and a few in the decade or two following. Two examples belonging to the last period are the churches of S. Mary and S. Peter, Lincoln, which are built at the foot of the hill on which stands the cathedral. No examples in England above ground can boast any great antiquity. None are contemporary with the old basilicas of Rome and Ravenna, or the great church at Constantinople. Christians some of the Britons were in the days of the Roman occupation, but when Rome, attacked on all sides, recalled her legions in 411–418, the country fell into the hands of the Saxons, the people returned to paganism, and any churches which may have been built were destroyed. The foundations of the church in the Roman city of Silchester, Hants, show that it consisted of nave, aisles, transepts, and narthex, and that at the end of the nave was an apse. In Ireland, Christianity continued after the Romans left England, and, moreover, flourished exceedingly.[1] In the sixth century the Irish church was second to none, and the fame of its teachers extended over the greater part of North-Western Europe. S. Columba converted Northern Scotland, S. Columban settled in Burgundy, and when driven from there passed with S. Gall and other monks into Switzerland. The number of churches abroad dedicated to S. Columba, S. Chad, and S. Gall,

[1] Whether the Irish Church owed its origin to Rome or to farther East is a debatable point which can be left to ecclesiologists.

etc., and the numerous old Irish manuscripts which have been discovered in Switzerland, Germany, etc., show how widespread was its influence. The second conversion of England to Christianity dates from the mission which Gregory the Great, Bishop of Rome, sent to this country in 596. In the following year, Augustine, Mellitus, Paulinus, and some forty other monks of the Benedictine order landed in the Isle of Thanet. Their success was immediate. In a few years the whole of England was once more Christian. The Roman monks and their adherents early came into collision with the followers of S. Columba. The great point of difference between them, the keeping of Easter, was settled in their favour by King Oswy of Northumbria, at the Synod held at Whitby in 664, and after that the power of the Church of Rome increased, and that of Ireland declined. Christianity, however, was not to prevail unmolested in this country for long, as towards the end of the eighth century the Danes commenced the series of raids which culminated in the submission of the Saxons to Sweyn in 1013. His son, Canute, received baptism, and then church building recommenced. The old Saxon chronicles state that the Danes "everywhere plundered and burnt as their custom is," and the last foray of Sweyn's seems to have been unusually sweeping in this respect. Not many churches escaped the fire, and of those that were fortunate, a number were pulled down fifty years or so later by the Normans in order to be rebuilt on a larger scale and in more sumptuous fashion.

Whilst some Saxon churches were of stone, the greater number were built of wood, and were consequently easily fired. Only one church remains in England to give an idea of what these timber churches were like. That is at Greenstead, in Essex. The outside walls are low and are built of halved trunks of oak trees placed vertically side by side, the rounded half being outside, with fillets of wood inside to cover the cracks. Without asserting that any of the original timbers remain—although possibly nearly all the existing ones are original—the church may be taken as a fair example of Saxon method of building. Another method was doubtless logs or balks laid horizontally, the ends of the logs crossing one another at the corners, in the same way that chalêts, barns, etc., are built in Switzerland, and in other countries where wood is plentiful, at the present day. *Timber churches.*

Owing more to the ravages of Sweyn and his predecessors than to time, one cannot expect to find many entire churches in this *Existing churches.*

country earlier in date than the beginning of the eleventh century, and possibly there is not one. The crypts at Hexham and Ripon are undoubtedly older and probably date from 671–678. The greater part of Escomb Church, Durham, is also apparently about contemporary with these. Portions of S. Martin's, Canterbury, may well be older still, but the church has been much altered. The difficulty in determining dates is complicated by the fact that windows and doorways have sometimes been re-used in later walls, and that in some walls, which are evidently early, all the openings are later insertions. Roman bricks in bands, and herringbone coursing, whether in brick or stone, prove nothing, as both were used after the Conquest quite as much as before. There was more church building in the seventh and eighth centuries than in either of the two following ones, and an attempt is made by archæologists to differentiate between eighth-century detail and detail of the tenth. Their arguments are not always entirely convincing and are too minute to be discussed here. Satisfactory reasons can be advanced why some churches cannot be earlier than the eleventh, but as regards an anterior date, much is conjecture and proof is difficult.

Bradford-on-Avon. The most complete early church in England is S. Lawrence, Bradford-on-Avon, Wilts, but there are no distinctive features by which its date can be fixed. In plan it consists of a nave and chancel with a large porch on the north side, and there are indications that a similar porch also existed on the south. The opening between nave and chancel is only 3 feet 6 inches wide. Its exterior is more architecturally treated than any other example, and the walls are faced with ashlar throughout. The upper part is arcaded, the arches being carried on short pilaster strips, many of which are roughly fluted. The arches and pilasters are not built independently of the walling in between, but are formed merely by cutting away the face of the latter to a depth of about 2 inches. The masonry is very good, and this suggests that the church belongs more likely to the first half of

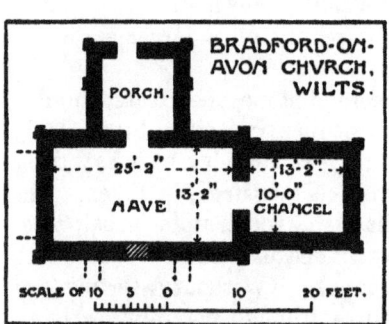

Fig. 167.

Photo: E. K. Prideaux.

FIG. 168.—BRADFORD-ON-AVON CHURCH: EAST END.

[*To face p.* 234.

the eleventh century than to the end of the seventh, the period which some would like to give to it. Its design, so unusual in England, may have been suggested by an illuminated missal or a carved ivory, as on both arcading was a favourite motif; or it may have been the work of foreigners. In any case the original inspiration is clear. The sixth-century churches of Ravenna, such as S. Apollinare in Classe (Vol. I., Fig. 117), are decorated with similar arcading in brick, and these form the connecting links by which this treatment of walls can be traced back to Imperial Rome.

There is much more certainty regarding the dates of towers which are ornamented with long, thin pilasters and rough cornices, or string-courses, as at Earls Barton, Barnack, Burton-on-Humber, etc. These cannot possibly be earlier than the tenth century, and more likely belong to the first half of the eleventh. Their central position at the west end is English; but their design is Lombardic, and came either from there direct or through Germany or Burgundy. The majority of tenth-century towers in Lombardy—there are not many—are exceedingly plain. The earliest example, which is also the richest, is that of S. Satiro, Milan, which, according to Cattaneo, was built in 879. The pilaster and string-course method of ornamentation found on it did not become general in Lombardy, Germany, and portions of France until one hundred years later. It is absolutely impossible that the examples of it in England can be earlier than the examples in those countries; and the towers mentioned, and portions of walling in which similar

Pilaster treatment.

Fig. 169.

features occur, are more likely to belong to the time of Canute, or his successors in the eleventh century, than to have been built in the tenth. The richest is at Earls Barton. There are pilasters of slight projection at the angles, and in between are rounded pilasters similar to those on the face of the north tower of S. Ambrogio, Milan, built 1129. This treatment has, of course, nothing whatsoever to do with joinery construction. It is in no sense an imitation of it. It is masonry construction; and is especially valuable when, as in the majority of English examples, it frames in walls of rough rubble, possessing little bond, which need strengthening at intervals.

"Long and short."

A halo of mystery has been thrown over the so-called "Long and short" bonding found in so many Anglo-Saxon churches. This, whether at angles or on the face of a wall, has been regarded as precious, and as peculiar to this country. As a matter of fact, in many countries and at most periods, from Italy in the days of the Roman empire downwards, the people formed their quoins in this way whenever the stone of the district was such that it split up naturally into small rubble, with occasional bigger stones which could be used as stiffeners without squaring or chiselling. In Sussex and other parts such rubble and stones come out of small quarries daily now. All over Normandy similar long and short bonding is found in garden walls and walls of outbuildings, whereever, in fact, the work is rough. There, as a rule, the short stones go through the thickness of a wall, the long ones only halfway; pilasters not on an angle having two long stones, one behind the other. It is ordinary common-sense rough building, and is general where workmen are unskilled, or when the work is not of sufficient importance to justify the expense of labour on the stone. Surrounding the precincts of the Abbeys of Jumièges and S. Georges de Boscherville; at Caen, and in the country round; at Chartres and elsewhere, are many such walls. The objection to this method of building is that the long stones are not generally on their natural bed, but that does not seem to have had a bad effect in Anglo-Saxon work. Long and short bonding has one virtue, it differentiates Saxon work from Norman, and is therefore some guide to the date of a building. But that is merely because the Normans were better masons, and had learnt at Caen to quarry bigger stones and to cut and square them.[1]

[1] Saxon masonry is sometimes excellent, as at S. Lawrence, Bradford, and King Odda's Chapel, Deerhurst, already mentioned, but the latter was built, as the

Photo : Author.

Fig. 170.—Wall between Caen and Falaise.

[*To face p.* 236.

The pilaster strips on Sompting Church, are 9 inches wide, and project about 2 inches. The bonding stones are from 3½ inches to 6 inches high, and the vertical stones from 1 foot 6 inches to 2 feet 9 inches high, the last being the height of the bottom stone. The actual stones composing the pilasters are rather more than 9 inches wide, but portions are cut back to the face of the walling, and their ragged edges now show. These were originally hidden by the stucco which covered everything except the straight-sided projecting strips.

The brief historical sketch on a previous page shows that in the seventh and eighth centuries there were rival churches in England. This is of some importance, because it bears on one of the most interesting features of English church architecture—the square east end. In Vol. I. it was pointed out that although square east ends are common enough in Egypt, Syria, etc., all early churches in Rome had one or more eastern apses; and in preceding and subsequent chapters of this volume the preference shown during the Middle Ages by all continental nations for an apsidal ending is proved conclusively. This preference never extended to England, except during the century following the Norman Conquest; and the reason why it did not may be sought for in the first place in the early churches of Ireland. These follow the plan of the buildings in which the Christian primitives held their services. Like them they consist of two rooms (except the oratories, which are merely single cells), the larger one for the congregation, the smaller one for the altar and clergy. Both are rectangular; no early church in Ireland has an apse. There is no need to speculate as to whether the Celts thought out this plan for themselves, it required no great effort of the imagination to do so, or had it suggested to them by others; the only point of importance to us is that these Irish examples show that the customary ending for a British church at the east was square. Existing pre-Norman churches with square east ends in England are double the number of contemporary ones with apses. Apses were probably reintroduced by S. Augustine—the earlier Roman church at Silchester had an apse,—and his church at Canterbury on the site of the present cathedral is stated to have had two apses, one at the east end, the other at the west. It was only natural that he and his followers should advocate the plan customary in Rome,

Square east end.

dedication stone shows, " in the fourteenth year of the reign of Edward, King of the English," *i.e.* in 1056, when the intercourse with the Normans was very close.

238   A HISTORY OF ARCHITECTURAL DEVELOPMENT.

and if more of the churches built by them remained it would probably be found that all had the apsidal ending. After their death, however, the people returned in most cases to the traditional British form. Amongst existing churches the following have square east ends: Bradford-on-Avon, Wilts; Wittering, Northants; Escomb, Durham; Dover Castle, Kent; Breamore, Hants; whilst Worth, Sussex; Brixworth, Northants; and one or two others have apses. Some of these apses, like Byzantine ones, are multangular outside and semicircular inside. At both Brixworth and Wing, Bucks, the outer face is seven-sided. Below the apse of the latter is a small five-sided crypt surrounded by an ambulatory. At Worth the outer and inner faces are concentric.

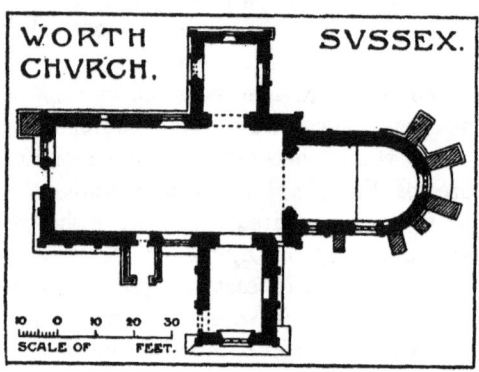

Fig. 171.

General plan. The majority of churches have only nave and chancel, whilst some have a western tower in addition. The latter has already been mentioned as an early English tradition. The churches of Worth and Dover have transepts, which are narrower than the nave in each case. Churches with aisles were not uncommon, although few retain their original ones, Wing being perhaps the only example. Augustine's large church at Canterbury had aisles, and existing side arches in the nave walls of Brixworth show that this church was also aisled.

Proportions. One peculiarity about most of the examples under consideration is that their naves are exceedingly lofty and narrow, proportions which exist also in Irish churches. In Deerhurst Church the nave is 38 feet long, 21 feet wide, and 38 feet high to the wall plate; the chancel being of the same width and height with a length of 20 feet. The dimensions of the Bradford-on-Avon Church are: length of nave 25 feet 2 inches, of chancel 13 feet 2 inches; width of nave 13 feet 2 inches, of chancel 10 feet; height of nave to wall plate 25 feet 3 inches, of chancel 18 feet. The nave of King Odda's Chapel, Deerhurst, is 16 feet wide, the chancel 11 feet wide, the height of each being only 17 feet. In the three largest Saxon churches in England, Brixworth, Worth, and Dover, the height, although considerable, cannot compare proportionately with that of either Bradford or Deerhurst, but there is one peculiarity about them worth noting: the nave of each is 60 feet long. The total internal length of Brixworth (excluding the tower) is 117 feet, of Worth 95 feet, of Dover 120 feet. The nave and chancel of Brixworth and the nave of Worth are 30 feet wide, the chancel of the latter being 21 feet wide. Dover has a nave 27 feet wide, and a chancel 18 feet 6 inches wide. These are all very fair dimensions—Westminster Abbey is only 35 feet wide—and although all three examples probably date from the eleventh century, it shows that large churches were built before the Conquest. Moreover, they look large, Dover especially. There is a bigness and simplicity about the chancel arch and arches to the transepts in that church which are particularly telling. The arches are unmoulded and of two orders; the inner order being nearly the whole width of the wall, whilst the outer order has a projection of only 2 or 3 inches. The resemblance between these arches and early ones in Lombardy of two orders—those of S. Ambrogio, Milan, for instance—is very great.

Saxon windows were probably not glazed, or, if glazed, the glass was fixed in wooden frames. In many cases the openings were filled by pierced stone slabs, such as have already been described when dealing with Byzantine work, and Romanesque churches in South Italy. At Barnack Church, Northants, there are two especially good examples, the pattern being of the interlacing character which was such a favourite with Byzantine craftsmen. The windows themselves are sometimes semicircular headed, sometimes triangular headed, the latter being a common form with the Romans, as the Baths of Caracalla and other buildings testify. The jambs in some cases are splayed on both sides, but more often are quite straight. When two or more lights are side by side, they are divided from one another by shafts in the centre of the wall. The capitals generally are of the corbel type already described as common to Byzantine and Romanesque work (see Vol. I., Fig. 149), and have slight projection at the sides,

Windows.

Fig. 172.

but considerable projection in front and at the back in order to reach from the outside to the inside face of the wall. This form remained the customary one in Italy, Germany, Southern France, and Switzerland through the eleventh and twelfth centuries, but the Normans abandoned it and generally placed their shafts near the outside face and carried their inside face independently of them. For that reason the presence of such capitals in England is a fairly certain sign that the work is pre-Norman, but cannot be absolutely relied upon. The two light side windows in the nave walls of Worth Church are particularly valuable examples, because Saxon windows in such positions are rare. Their jambs are straight, and so are the jambs of the tower windows of Sompting Church, Sussex. Most Saxon windows are in towers, in the belfry stage; those in the Earls Barton tower having five lights. The shafts dividing the lights were generally turned in a lathe, and well turned too. They are considerably entasised and are numerously banded. The Worth ones are an exception, they being roughly worked by hand.

Anglo-Saxon work—Romanesque.

Mention has frequently been made in this chapter of the resemblance between pre-Norman work in England and contemporary or earlier work abroad. All early churches in this country, whether built by the followers of S. Augustine, by the Saxons before the Danes arrived, by the Danes after their conversion, or by Edward the Confessor, are offshoots of Roman tradition, or belong to the great school of Romanesque building which prevailed throughout Europe during the early centuries of the Middle Ages. That they possess some characteristics not generally found elsewhere does not make them any the less Romanesque. Other countries have other characteristic traits of their own. Whether the feeling came direct from Italy, or filtered through Germany and Burgundy, is immaterial. Those countries were certainly nearer to England, but the germ first appeared in Italy, and maturity had not been reached anywhere when the English churches were built. The connection between Rome and this country was fairly close in the days of Alfred the Great, and later under Canute. Both kings paid pilgrimages to Rome, and even if they did not bring back workmen with them, they must have returned with ideas. Foreign craftsmen are stated to have been imported to assist in the building of some churches, Monkwearmouth amongst others. Who these workmen were is somewhat uncertain, as the term Franks applied to them might mean

Germans, Burgundians, or French. In Italy, in the eighth and ninth centuries, a large number of carvers were Byzantine Greeks, and it is possible, but not probable, that some of these men found their way to this country. The world was surprising small in those days notwithstanding the difficulties of travel. A design itself proves little regarding the nationality of the worker of it, because many designs which in their origin are characteristically Byzantine—the interlacing one which appears in the window slabs of Barnack Church, for instance—had been adopted by Italian, German, and French workmen, and had become almost universal everywhere. The skill shown in the execution of a design is a surer guide, and the roughness of English work suggests a local carver. In connection with that, brief reference may be made to the many so-called Runic crosses in Great Britain. That the patterns on these can have been originated in the north seems impossible. The claim for great antiquity formerly put forward for these crosses has been abandoned by most authorities, who place them mainly between the eighth century and the tenth. But almost identical patterns were common in Byzantine work of the sixth, as numerous carvings at Constantinople, Ravenna, and Venice testify. There is no suggestion from any one that Runic crosses were carved by foreigners, but it may be suggested that they were copied from carved ivory crosses which might easily have been brought to this country in considerable numbers. Some of the figure sculpture of the South of France is probably founded on carvings in ivory executed by Byzantine workers. These men were far more proficient in the carving of beautiful patterns than they were in representing the figure, and examples of their skill in this respect travelled far and wide. There are very few important old churches in Switzerland and Southern France, for instance, which do not possess some specimens of their art, and in Italy, of course, examples are still more numerous. The carving on the jambs of the west doorway of Monkwearmouth Church is Byzantine in feeling, although it is rough. Only one church in England may be stated to possess a feature which is Teutonic, that is Sompting Church, Sussex. Its tower finishes with four gables, from the top of which starts a spire of shingles. This feature is certainly not Italian, and may well be derived from Germany, where there are many similar towers and spires of all periods (see Fig. 77).

CHAPTER XV.

ROMANESQUE IN ENGLAND AND NORMANDY.

Introduction.
FOR nearly a hundred years after the battle of Hastings the architecture of England and Normandy proceeded on identical lines. The movement began in Normandy, and sixteen years before Hastings, Edward the Confessor, with the aid of Norman craftsmen, had commenced his Abbey at Westminster.

There can be little doubt that the Normans obtained their inspiration originally from Lombardy; but they soon introduced special traits which differentiate their work from contemporary buildings in Italy, Germany, and other parts of France. They certainly did not bring the germ of their architecture with them from the North; and they can hardly have obtained it from the neighbouring royal domain of France, which in the first half of the eleventh century had, to a great extent, lost the pre-eminent position in the arts which it enjoyed in the time of Charlemagne. The nationality of the two prelates who exercised such influence over William I. and his successor, supplies the clue to its origin. Both were Italians; Lanfranc came from Pavia, Anselm was a native of Aosta.

Normandy.
The earliest existing church in Normandy with architectural pretensions is probably that of the Abbey of Jumièges (c. 1050), and its ruins show that it was also one of the largest. Columns and clustered piers alternate, and although the nave was only covered by a timber roof, the aisles and galleries over were vaulted. Next come the two finest of the Caen churches, S. Etienne, or L'Abbaye-aux-Hommes, commenced 1066, and La Trinité, or L'Abbaye-aux-Dames, which, according to M. Enlart, was built between 1062 and 1066. The dates of the other early churches in Normandy are not known with any certainty. Bayeux Cathedral was consecrated in 1077, but a fire, some thirty years later, left little of the original building. The Abbey Church of S. Georges de Boscherville, one of the finest in the country, and the Abbey Church of Lessay, the design of which inside resembles

Photo: Author.

FIG. 173.—JUMIÈGES ABBEY CHURCH, FROM THE SOUTH.

[*To face p.* 242.

somewhat La Trinité, Caen, date from about 1100. Other churches at Cérisy-la-forêt, Ouistreham, the port for Caen, Bernières-sur-mer, etc., were probably built during the last five and twenty years of the eleventh century, or in the first quarter of the following one. One of the most interesting of Norman churches is S. Nicolas, Caen, commenced 1083. The apse at the end of the chancel is covered by a very steep pitched roof of stone which rises high above the existing roof behind, and the apses on the east side of the transepts are covered in a similar fashion. The roofs of the two latter have a much better appearance than the central one, as they stop against the transept walls under the eaves course. At the intersection rises a low tower, gabled on the east and west ends—an excellent way of ending a tower when funds do not permit of its being carried high. At the west end of the church is a narthex porch of three arches—an unusual feature in Norman work.

Interesting though the above-named churches are, they cannot, with the exception of Jumièges Church and S. Etienne, Caen, compare in size with the cathedrals and great monastic churches built in England during the last thirty years of the eleventh century and the following two decades. The extent of the list is astounding. Until the outburst of building in France a hundred years later, no country at any period could boast so many important churches in course of erection at one time. Little seems to have been attempted before 1070. The Conqueror and his nobles were otherwise engaged, and the priests had to accustom themselves to new surroundings, choose their sites, and make the necessary preliminary arrangements. But when once building operations began, there was little further delay. The following list contains the names of most of the large cathedrals and churches, and the approximate dates when they were commenced; the letter B. signifies that the church was a monastic one of the Benedictine Order; the letters S.C., a cathedral served by secular canons; and A.C., a church belonging to the Order of Austin Canons, which had been founded in 1061 :—

England.

1070-1080.—Hereford, S.C.; Canterbury, B.; Lincoln, S.C. Rochester, B.; S. Albans, B.; Winchester, B.; and York, S.C. (practically no remains above ground).

1080-1890.—S. Paul's, London, S.C. (practically no remains); Ely, B.; Gloucester, B.; Malvern, B.; Tewkesbury, B.; Worcester, B.; Pershore, B.; St. David's (Wales), S.C.

1090–1100.—Bury St. Edmunds, B.; Chester, B.; Chichester, S.C.; Christ Church, Hampshire, S.C. (and later A.C.); Durham, B.; Norwich, B.

1100–1110.—Sherborne, B.; Southwell, S.C.; Carlisle, A.C.; Bangor, S.C.

1110–1120.—Peterboro', B; Waltham, A.C.; Romsey, B. (Nuns); Exeter, S.C.; Llandaff (Wales), S.C.; Kelso (Scotland), B.

Southwell and Waltham, although served by canons, were not Sees, but of the monastery churches of the Benedictine Order named above the following were also cathedrals in Norman times: Canterbury, Durham, Winchester, Ely, Norwich, Rochester, and Worcester; Carlisle became a cathedral soon after the church was built; and to the list should be added Old Sarum, the original site of Salisbury.[1]

England and Germany seem to have been the only two countries in Romanesque times in which a bishop's chair was placed in a Benedictine monastic church. In such cases the bishop was little more than a nominal head, all administrative power being in the hands of a Prior and Chapter. So many bishops in early days were "half priests, half warriors," were engaged in political intrigue, or in public duties for the good of the country, that they were often absentees from their churches for long periods. The fact of a church being merely a monastic one, or a cathedral ruled either by secular canons or lay monks, seems to have made no difference whatsoever in the plan. Peterboro' was only an abbey church, Ely an abbey church that was also a cathedral, whilst Chichester and Hereford had no monasteries attached to them; and yet the only difference that can be noted is that the two last have slightly shorter naves than the others. Even this is no real distinction, as the nave of Rochester—a cathedral served by Benedictine monks—is even shorter. Gloucester, a monks' church, pure and simple, has some features which are absent from the others (see p. 145); but it stands almost alone in this respect.

The Norman nobility and priesthood.

The above list is no mean record of fifty years' building, and it is far from complete. To it must be added the hundreds of parish churches which from Sussex to Northumberland, from Cornwall to Kent, were built either on new sites or in place of

[1] Other Benedictine monastic churches, such as Chester, Gloucester, Peterboro', etc., did not become cathedrals until the Reformation.

those which were deemed unworthy. The Norman Conquest did something more than substitute one race of rulers for another. It introduced throughout the country new religious ideals, a new intellectual standard. The strict monasticism of the Benedictine Order had, it is true, been introduced into England a few years before; but it had only found favour in London and one or two other centres. Now it was carried all over the country. Many of the Norman nobles had spent some time in the University of Paris, then the chief centre of intellectual activity in Western Europe; Thomas à Becket was educated there later. The Saxons, both priests and people, were far behind the priests and people of France. The Normans may have been rough and rude, as judged by modern standards, but they were polished as compared with the greater number of the English thanes and nobles.

The majority of French cathedrals were built after plan development had practically ceased, and consequently, even when altered later, each conveys the impression of having been begun and finished with very little break. Not so with English cathedrals, especially with the ones given in the previous list. Owing to various causes, there are few amongst those mentioned in which the whole development of English mediæval architecture from Romanesque to Tudor cannot be traced. The necessity for a longer choir led to the destruction of the apses of Canterbury, S. Albans, Ely, S. Etienne, Caen, etc. In no cathedral in England does the Norman east end remain exactly as it was when built; even Norwich, otherwise complete in plan, has lost the central chapel of its chevet. Peterboro' retains the apse to its choir, but eastwards is an addition of later date. The Durham apse had to make way for the Chapel of the Nine Altars. The alterations to western arms and transepts have not been so extensive as to eastern. The craze for vaulting, however, has changed the appearance of many a nave, notwithstanding that the arcades, triforia, and clerestories remain much as they were built. In the naves of Ely and Peterboro', and in the transepts of Winchester, wooden ceilings remain; elsewhere, at Gloucester, Tewkesbury, Norwich, etc., they have been replaced by stone vaults. Structural defects sometimes entailed wholesale rebuildings, as at Ely Cathedral, where the central tower fell, bringing down with it the neighbouring bays. Fire, which played such havoc all through the Middle Ages, also did as much damage in England as in France; although why it should have

English Romanesque churches seldom unaltered.

been so frequent and fatal in vaulted churches is difficult to understand. At Chichester Cathedral, after the fire in 1186, the three-quarter attached shafts in the angles of the piers were replaced by more slender detached ones; the cushion capitals disappeared, lighter ones being substituted, and mouldings were worked on the wall face of the arches on the nave side in order to tone down their severity. The disgust which the heavy proportions of Romanesque evidently aroused in the later builders, and their desire to have their churches up-to-date, led to much fine work being entirely remodelled. At Gloucester, the monks, unable to bear the cost of pulling down and rebuilding entirely their choir, faced the whole with delicate pierced stone panelling. From their stalls all they could see was modern; from the aisles and triforia alone were the solid piers and sturdy old arches visible. At Winchester, Bishop William of Wykeham, either more blessed with this world's goods or else a bolder spirit, carved the Romanesque piers on the south side of the nave into the forms that pleased him better; and on the north side, finding the other method too slow or too expensive, removed the facing stones of the piers, leaving only the cores which he recased. He swept away the triforium, raised and altered the shape of the arches of the main arcades, inserted new windows in the clerestory, and over the whole of the central area built an elaborate ribbed vault (see Figs. 105 and 219). As he paced up and down the church, provided he did not allow his eyes to glance to right or left as he passed the transepts—where the old work remained in all its native vigour—he might congratulate himself that he was in a brand new church. At Exeter much the same thing had been done some fifty years or so before, but in a still more drastic fashion; and at S. Albans, on two separate occasions, with an interval between them of nearly a hundred years, determined attacks were made on the old work.

Length of naves. One of the most marked peculiarities of English Romanesque churches is the long nave. The nave of Norwich Cathedral has fourteen bays; the Cathedrals of Ely and S. Albans have each thirteen; Peterboro' has eleven, and Winchester, which now has twelve, originally had the same number as Norwich. In the west of England, at Gloucester, Hereford, and Tewkesbury, and also at Rochester and Chichester, the naves are shorter. On the Continent, with the exception of the great Basilican churches in Rome, S. Peter's, S. Paul's, etc., there are very few churches which can compare in length of nave with English examples. S. Sernin, Toulouse, is one. It has fourteen bays, including the two between the towers at the west end. The church at Vézelay has only ten bays, and even at Cluny there were only eleven; excluding in each case the narthex, which formed practically a separate church. At Caen, the Abbaye-aux-Hommes has nine bays, the same as Gloucester Cathedral, and the Nuns' church has one more. The nave of Durham Cathedral is comparatively short, only eight bays, but that is partly accounted for by the rapid fall in the ground at the west end, which rendered further extension in that direction impossible (see Figs. 177 and 182).

The eastern arms are short in comparison with the western, but they are longer than in contemporary churches abroad. From the first the tendency to lengthen this part of the church, so marked in later English examples, is evident. Norwich Cathedral has four bays between the crossing and the apse, and that was the original number at S. Albans and Ely. Gloucester and Chichester only had three bays; but, then, their naves are shorter. Durham has four bays, a number that makes the choir more proportionate to the nave. S. Etienne, Caen, had only two bays to the east, apart from the apse; and that is the number at S. Georges de Boscherville, S. Sernin, Toulouse, etc., notwithstanding the great length of nave of the latter. In any comparison of the proportionate number of bays in the eastern and western arms, it should be remembered that in Romanesque churches the seats for the choir were placed partially or entirely in the nave. In Norwich and S. Albans Cathedrals and Westminster Abbey they still occupy three bays of it. East of the crossing there was little except the high altar, and the eastern arm could consequently be short. At Norwich, Gloucester, and Worcester it finished with a chevet; and this was also apparently the plan at Durham. Canterbury Cathedral, as built by Lanfranc, ended in one apse; Peterboro' and, probably, Chester in three apses. The Nuns' church at Romsey has a square east end; and this traditional Anglo-Saxon ending was also followed at Hereford and Rochester. At S. Etienne, Caen, the original choir ended with an apse, but the aisles finished square. *Eastern arm.*

All English Romanesque cathedrals are cruciform in plan; the transepts in most of them having the considerable projection which afterwards became so marked a feature of English work. In Normandy, as a rule, they are equally strongly marked; the *Transepts.*

248   A HISTORY OF ARCHITECTURAL DEVELOPMENT.

arms north, east, and south of the crossing being equal, as at S. Georges de Boscherville. The transepts of Ely and Winchester Cathedrals have aisles on both west and east sides, and the aisle passage is returned along the north and south ends of the latter, and the same was probably also done originally in the former. The transepts of Durham Cathedral have no western aisles, whilst those of Norwich and Gloucester Cathedrals have no aisles at all. In the two last, however, a large apse opens directly out of each transept on its east side. This was the customary plan in most Romanesque churches, each apse forming a chapel with its own altar. The two churches at Caen have, or had, similar apses; and the same may be said of most of the contemporary churches in both Northern and Southern France.

Internal divisions.   In all large churches built by the Normans, whether in England or Normandy, the division of the nave wall into arcade, triforium, and clerestory is universal. But there is by no means equal agreement regarding the height to be allotted to each. In the Cathedrals of Norwich and Winchester (as originally built) all three divisions are approximately equal. Ely is much the same, except that its clerestory is somewhat low. In Durham Cathedral and in the naves of Tewkesbury and Gloucester, the arcade storey is by far the highest of the three. In the choir of Gloucester, on the other hand, the arcade is low, the triforium lofty, the proportions being much the same as those of Norwich. The following table gives the approximate heights of the internal divisions in four typical examples, and their total heights:—

	Floor to string below triforium.	Triforium to string below clerestory.	Clerestory to apex of vault or wall plate.[1]	Total height.
	′ ″	′ ″	′ ″	′ ″
Norwich Cathedral	25 0	24 0	24 0[2]	73 0
Peterboro' Cathedral . . .	32 0	23 9	20 0	75 9
Gloucester ,, (nave)	39 6	9 6	18 6[2]	67 6
Durham ,, . . .	40 11	17 10	12 11[2]	71 8

Norwich and Durham were commenced in the same decade, were both Benedictine cathedrals, are about equal in height; but their heights are very differently divided. These two churches show that there was absolutely no rule of relative

[1] In churches now vaulted the apex of the vault is about on a line with the original wall plates.
[2] Vaulted.

Photo: Author.
FIG. 174.—S. ETIENNE, CAEN: TRIFORIUM.

Photo: Author.
FIG. 175.—OUISTREHAM CHURCH.

[*To face p.* 249.

proportions for the internal divisions of Romanesque churches. Of the two principal churches at Caen, S. Etienne resembles Peterboro' in its proportions; whilst La Trinité is more like the nave of Gloucester, the height of the triforium being even less than in the English church. Durham has the finest proportions of all. Its lowest storey considerably exceeds in height the two upper ones together, and yet does not swamp them entirely, as happens at Gloucester. Its total height is not great, but it is sufficient; the verticality of the great piers counteracting their massiveness and also the bulk of the intermediate columns, and allowing it to tell.

Fig. 176.

The design of the triforium is as varied as its height. In Norwich Cathedral, Waltham Abbey Church, S. Etienne, Caen, etc., each bay consists of a single arched opening, about the same width as the opening below. The most usual design, however, is a pair of openings enclosed under a single arch, as at Winchester (originally), Ely, Peterboro', Chichester (Fig. 79), etc. The stonework of the tympana under the enclosing arches has often chevrons, triangles, and other patterns roughly chiselled or axed on its face, as at Christ Church, etc. Sometimes there are three or more openings, as at Jumièges (Normandy) and Malmesbury Abbeys. At La Trinité, Caen, the triforium is not pierced at all. In this church, and in all those with open triforia as well, a passage-

Triforium design.

250 A HISTORY OF ARCHITECTURAL DEVELOPMENT.

way round the church is provided in the thickness of the upper walls, immediately below the clerestory windows. The design of the clerestory is nearly always the same. On the inside face is a lofty arched opening (central with the window on the outside face) which is flanked by two small openings, each divided from the middle one by a shaft. The effect is far more dignified than that produced by an upper triforium, which cuts off the clerestory from the main triforium and produces another division, as in the somewhat later French churches of Laon and Noyon.

Naves of English cathedrals. In the naves of Ely, Peterboro', and Durham, English Romanesque architecture can be seen in perfection. The naves of Tewkesbury Abbey and Gloucester Cathedral are also fine, but spoilt by later vaults. Very different from the two last

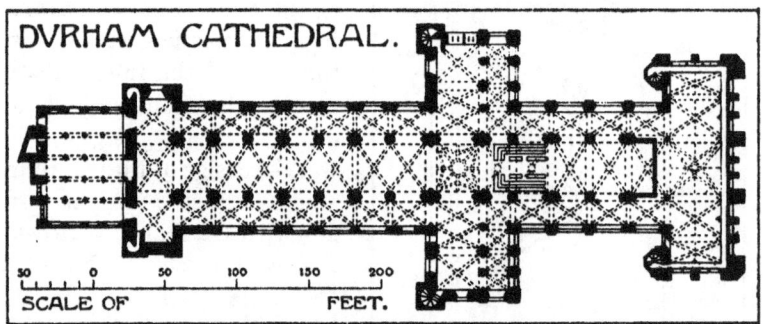

FIG. 177.

is their neighbour, Hereford Cathedral. At Tewkesbury and Gloucester the columns are possibly too high, and the capitals and arches exceedingly plain. At Hereford the columns are certainly too low, the capitals very elaborate, and the arches unusually rich. The naves of Ely and Peterboro' are surprisingly alike. In both churches the shafts that support the ends of the tie beams of the roof start from the floor, and are incorporated in the piers. At Ely, all the piers are similar in bulk, but are different in section; and the alternation of the two forms is one of the reasons—and not the least—why the nave of this church ranks amongst the most striking in England.

Durham Cathedral vaults. Durham differs from all other English Romanesque cathedrals, in that its nave vault is approximately the same date as the rest of the church. The church was commenced in 1093 by

Photo: Salmon.

FIG. 178.—WINCHESTER CATHEDRAL: TRANSEPT.

FIG. 179.—DURHAM CATHEDRAL.   [*To face p.* 250.

Bishop Carileph, who, according to Mr. C. C. Hodges,[1] "had been an exile in Normandy for three years, and there can be no doubt that his design was inspired by what he had seen in progress in that country." If this is so, the inspiration was merely an incentive to better things, for Durham Cathedral far surpasses all Romanesque work in Normandy. The great piers that alternate with the cylindrical columns suggest S. Ambrogio, Milan, rather than any church in Northern France. When Bishop Flamard was appointed in 1099, the eastern arm was finished, and considerable progress had been made with the western. That the aisles were already vaulted with ribbed vaults seems certain; although it is doubtful if any other portion of the church was intended to be covered in like manner. In the transepts, some shafts, which start from the triforium level and run up to the apex of the present vault, suggest that there was no intention of vaulting this part at all. The alternation of large and small supports is not positive proof that vaulting was to be carried throughout. In S. Zeno, Verona, and in many early churches in Germany, there is similar alternation, but no suggestion of any vaults to the naves. Whether Carileph wished to vault his nave or not, his successor, Bishop Flamard, according to Mr. Hodges, had no such desire. He proposed a flat ceiling, broken by strong transverse arches over the great piers, as in S. Miniato, Florence, S. Zeno, Verona, etc. The existing transverse arches, which are pointed, may possibly be his.[2] If so, the reason why they are nearly the width of the three shafts below is plain,[3] and so are the peculiarities in the existing vaulting to be next described. At Flamard's death, in 1128, the present nave vault was immediately commenced, and to the credit of his successor must be placed the building of one of the earliest ribbed vaults of wide span with pointed arches in Europe. Mr Bilson has proved conclusively that this dates from 1128-1133. The most curious point about the Durham nave vault is the awkward way in which the diagonal ribs start from corbel heads, and not from the side vaulting shafts, as might have been expected. If the transverse arches were built before the vaults were commenced, this is

[1] *The Builder*, Cathedral Series.
[2] The four great arches at the crossing, which support the central tower, and the transverse arches of the transept vaults, are semicircular, and probably the work of Carileph.
[3] In Autun Cathedral, Burgundy (see Fig. 161), the transverse arches under the barrel vault of the nave are as wide as the pilasters and side shafts below.

accounted for. There is a head each side of the capitals of the main piers, and a pair of heads under one abacus over each column, from which the two diagonal ribs which meet here spring. There is no transverse arch above this point. The clerestory windows are not exactly central with the vault compartments. A fact which gives some colour to the theory that Carileph intended to vault his nave, is that if the vault had been a sexpartite one—a form commonly adopted in Normandy in early work—and if the diagonals had started from above the side shafts of the main piers, and had been bisected by an intermediate transverse arch above each column, the windows would have centred exactly. Against this, it may be pointed out that each bay of vaulting between the great piers (especially the second and third bays west of the crossing) are much longer than their width, and the span of the diagonal ribs would consequently have been excessive. The vault of the choir is undoubtedly of later date than the substructure. The fifth bay, which occupies the space of the old apse, was built when the chapel of the nine altars was added in the middle of the thirteenth century, and its vault is of this date. The vaults of the other four bays are a trifle earlier, but they probably also belong to the same century.

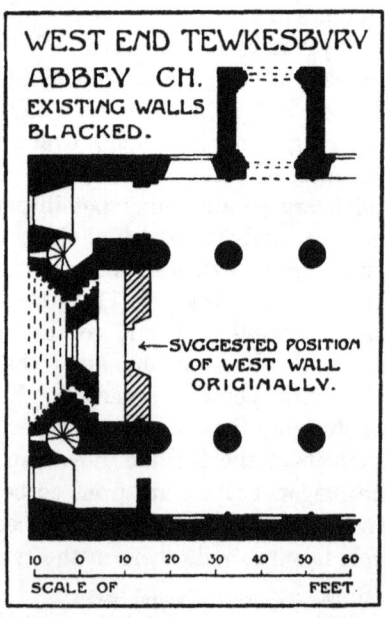

Fig. 180.

West fronts.

The west fronts of Romanesque cathedrals in England have suffered as severely as their eastern arms. Durham Cathedral retains its two towers, but the Galilee porch, added towards the end of the twelfth century, has obliterated its original entrances. The addition is no drawback; on the contrary, its lowness gives scale to the front and to the towers which rise behind it, and its foundations carried down the slope of the hill help to give height. Tewkesbury Abbey has the finest Romanesque portal

Photo: Bedford.
FIG. 181.—TEWKESBURY ABBEY CHURCH.

Photo: J. Valentine & Co.
FIG. 182.—DURHAM CATHEDRAL.   [*To face p.* 252.

in England. On each side are six attached shafts, and the remains of a seventh. These are carried up to support a semicircular arch of many orders which rises higher even than the transverse arches inside at the crossing. Below the arch is now a wall, in which is inserted a window of late date,[1] but it is by no means improbable that originally the wall was farther back, and that the archway was but the entrance to a recessed porch. The responds inside at the end of the nave arcades are unusually deep, so there would have been room for an outer porch. Lincoln Cathedral has three western porches, and although the central one has been raised the original design is clear. The porches at Lincoln, and the Tewkesbury one, if it may be admitted as such, are the forerunners of the fine later example at Peterborough.

[1] The window is dated 1686, but, except that its detail is curious, it is a very fair copy of fifteenth-century work.

CHAPTER XVI.

THE CATHEDRALS OF NORTHERN FRANCE, 1120–1500.

Intro-
duction.

THE revival in Church building in Central and Northern France commenced about the end of the first quarter of the twelfth century, at the moment when the great outburst in England initiated by the Norman kings was on the wane. The country immediately surrounding Paris and to the North and East of it—the only part which then admitted directly the French king's rule—was at that time slowly emerging from a period of great depression, which was not finally dissipated until the accession of Louis le Jeune in 1137. The commencement of this king's reign marks a new era in France—political, social and architectural. The power of the French king rapidly increased; the strength of the semi-independent rulers of Flanders, Aquitaine, Anjou, etc., slowly but sensibly diminished. The land became peaceful, and peace brought prosperity. The farmers could till their fields without a constant fear, almost a certainty, that bands of marauders would render their labour vain. The trade of the dwellers in towns advanced rapidly, and these men soon became strong enough to assert their rights, which had been in abeyance for so long, and to claim privileges of charter, which they had not previously enjoyed. Moreover, the people both in town and country began to interest themselves in matters of religion to a far greater extent and in a more thoughtful manner than they had done before. The authority of the bishop, the people's representative, became more widely acknowledged, in fact the bishops regained to a great extent, if not entirely, the power they had possessed in the days before Charlemagne and before the ascendancy of the Monasteries. The monastic orders were still strong, in fact were multiplying rapidly in number, but that the Benedictine order was no longer sole and supreme, was in itself a source of weakness. It is not too much to say that the revolt of S. Bernard at the end of the eleventh century marks the commencement of the gradual decline of monkish rule. This, however, was not so much the cause of that decline as the growing intelligence of the people; although dissension and secession are weakening to any body. Until then, the attitude of most laymen towards the Church was either one of absolute dependence on monkish guidance, or else of opposition to that guidance. Before the middle of the twelfth century was reached both feelings had undergone considerable modification. On the one hand, religion was becoming more and more a matter understanded of the people; and on the other, the sagacity of the monks had shown them that the best way to disarm opposition was to work in harmony with others for the advancement and good of the Church. Thus, in the building of the Abbey Church of S. Denis, near Paris, in 1140, the people banded themselves together to raise the money required, acting in concert with the Abbé Suger, the man who, amongst his contemporaries, did more than any other to advance church architecture in France in the twelfth century.

The fervour with which all men threw themselves into the task of building the great cathedrals of Northern France is a proof both of the prosperity of the country and of the better understanding which existed between all classes of the community. A large percentage of the revenues of sees were devoted to the work; the canons helped with their share; the nobles and rich burgesses gave large sums; and the people contributed what they could, sometimes their chattels, sometimes their money, or else their time and strength to transport the materials required. M. Enlart says that the columns for the church of S. Denis were dragged there from the quarries of Pontoise (some fourteen miles distant) by the faithful themselves harnessed to the carts.[1] At Laon oxen were necessary to drag the stones up the steep hill to the site, and the services rendered by these animals are commemorated in their stone effigies which to this day look down from the niches in the towers of the cathedral. Large sums were also realized by the display of relics, which were carried about the country to stimulate the generosity of the faithful. The requests for funds were, in some cases, by no means confined solely to the diocese in which the cathedral was being built. M. Anthyme Saint Paul[2] recounts how in the rebuilding of Laon Cathedral in the twelfth century, begging expeditions were made one year throughout the whole of

[1] " Manuel d'Archéologie Francaise."
[2] " Histoire monumentale de la France."

Northern France, and in the next that they penetrated even as far as England.

Architects.

One fact in particular illustrates the altered conditions under which the great French cathedrals of the twelfth and thirteenth centuries were built. The artists responsible for their design were in most cases laymen. Until the middle of the twelfth century the monks themselves had been the architects. They had designed, superintended the erection of, and in most cases found the money for the large churches. The monasteries were at that time the centre of intellectual, artistic life. In the schools attached to the larger and more important ones were trained priests and laymen alike. The men thus trained either worked on the church and buildings of the monastery in which they had learned their craft, or, if found worthy, were sent by the monks to superintend building operations for them in other countries, sometimes in far distant lands. Thus Villard de Honnecourt went to Hungary for this purpose. Gradually the teaching of apprentices in purely technical matters passed from the monks to the lay master masons, as it was natural that when the bishops, chapters, and people took the building of cathedrals into their own hands they should prefer laymen as their head workers. Many of these had received in the monastic schools the best education the times could provide, and were as well read as the majority of clerics and nobles. They probably took good care that the general education of their apprentices was as sound as their own. Some of these master masons were attached to cathedrals; some to towns; whilst others took service with high nobles or with the king.[1] That they were skilled craftsmen is undoubted, capable of executing themselves all work required; they had served their apprenticeship, and that in the middle ages meant that they had mastered the technicalities of their trade. But it does not follow that when they reached the proud position of master mason they continued to work with their hands as they had done when younger. They had higher work to do. They

---

[1] M. Enlart, in his Manuel, gives amongst his list of Gothic churches in France, the names of many of the men who in turn superintended the work in different cathedrals. Some are commemorated in the French fashion, which is so excellent, in the names of streets. Thus at Amiens, facing the south transept of the cathedral, is the Rue Robert de Luzarches, and at Reims, on the north side of the cathedral, the Rue Robert de Coucy, who, however, can hardly have been the first master mason of the cathedral, as the rebuilding commenced about 1211, and he died exactly a hundred years later.

dictated the plan and general ordinance—the first essentials without which no building can be carried out satisfactorily—drawing them on parchment or paper sufficiently well to make their meaning clear to the workmen under them. The modern architectural draughtsman may smile a superior smile at the execution of some of these drawings, but they served their purpose. That so few of them have been preserved is owing to the fact that they were regarded merely as a means to an end, as all architectural drawings should be, and when the end was accomplished, their utility ceased.[1] The full size details of mouldings were drawn on the spot, probably on boards,—much in the same way as the full-size heads of traceried windows, for instance, are set out now—either entirely by the master himself or else were merely corrected by him. Whether the men who did work of this description should be termed architects, or masons, or masters of the work, is an academic question which hardly requires discussion, except that the term "mason" is confusing, inasmuch as it conveys a totally wrong idea of the position these men occupied. The laymen who, in France in the thirteenth century, took the place of the monks of the previous centuries were men of substance, held in high repute by their patrons and townsfolk, and artists in the true sense of the word. De Honnecourt's sketch-book shows that he was interested in more than the plan and fabric of a building, and that in his travels he sketched and studied architectural accessories as well. The post of master mason to a town or to a cathedral was a high and responsible one, and descended in some cases from father to son, as at Amiens Cathedral, where, after R. de Luzarches, Renaut de Cormont succeeded his father, Thomas; or, as at Strassburg, where Erwin von Steinbach's two sons continued the work he had commenced. The spirit of the age was such that there was no fear of the workers in different crafts being out of harmony. The mason had confidence that the painter would not want to apply his colour and gilding on the wrong mouldings, and that the glass stainer would not try and ignore the design of the window. By the beginning of the thirteenth century there was absolute sympathy between all branches; and to this sympathy is largely owing the beauty and completeness of the mediæval cathedral.

[1] Villard de Honnecourt's sketch-book has already been mentioned. M. Enlart mentions, amongst others, twenty-two drawings at Strassburg. In Spain are preserved many others, although most of these are later in date.

To the infusion, so to speak, of secular blood in the twelfth century, is due in a great measure the enormous strides made in France in architectural construction and design between 1150 and 1220. The monk-designer was by no means a recluse, living a life of seclusion within the cloister walls; but his training had saturated him with traditional methods which he found difficult to discard. This, as already stated, is especially noticeable in Burgundy, the stronghold of the monastic orders in Western Europe. The lay-designer, on the other hand, although he might have served his time in the same school, was outside monastic life, and mixed freely with all sorts and conditions of men. The result was inevitable. Gradually old ideals gave place to new. The traditional methods of ornamentation—methods based on old Classic or Byzantine design—were supplanted by fresh ones. Tradition was treated reverently—as it must be if good art is to result—but nature and not tradition became the governing factor for ornament and figure sculpture. Owing to this the differences between the carvings executed at the beginning of the twelfth century and those of fifty years later, are even greater than the structural changes which took place during the same period. There was a slack tide towards the middle of the century when ebb and flow conflicted, but this did not last long. By 1160 throughout the greater part of France proper and Normandy the transition was complete, and for the next 300 years or more there was no looking back.

Priority for France.

There can be no doubt, and it is best to admit this quite frankly, that by the end of the twelfth century French architectural art was considerably in advance of our own, as well as of that of all other countries in Europe. The work in England and Normandy had been done a hundred years before, and with us the necessity for new cathedrals no longer existed. When the awakening came in Central France, the magnificent monuments of Romanesque art we possessed helped at first more to retard than to advance architectural progress in our country. The fact that the workers in the Isle de France had lagged behind in the eleventh century was no drawback to the builders there of the twelfth. They had nearly everything before them and little behind them. Their existing traditions were hardly their own, but belonged rightly to the surrounding districts of Burgundy, Normandy, and the South. In consequence they clung lightly, and were easily

Photo: Author.

Fig. 183.—S. Pierre, Lisieux: Nave.

Photo: Author.

Fig. 184.—Noyon Cathedral: Nave.

[*To face p.* 258.

thrown off. The result was a progress unparalleled for rapidity in architectural history.

Most French writers claim that the birth of Gothic—and by Gothic is understood pointed arches, ribbed vaulting, and flying buttresses, combined with a new system of mouldings and a fresh feeling in carvings—took place in the Isle de France, and from there spread outside. To some extent they are right, but not entirely. Properly speaking, Gothic art had no birth. What is called the birth of Gothic was but the coming of age of Romanesque; and that the celebration of this majority took place solely in one particular part of France is open to question. There is so little difference in date between the early examples scattered about the country that it is permissible to conclude that the movement was a far wider one than the above contention allows. Otherwise it could not have risen to maturity so soon over so large an area. *The rise of Gothic architecture.*

It is unnecessary to do more than mention by name the churches built between 1120 and 1140 in which the germ of Gothic is apparent; such as S. Etienne, Beauvais; the narthex of Vézelay Abbey Church (Burgundy); the Cathedral of Evreux (Normandy) rebuilt, according to M. Enlart, immediately after a fire in 1119; and not much need be said about those built in great part between 1140 and 1160 in which development is more advanced, in some cases almost complete. The best known amongst these latter are S. Denis, near Paris (1140-1144), which, though it retains the semicircular arch over its lower windows, and traces of Romanesque feeling in its carving, is a Gothic church; and the nave of Lisieux Cathedral (Normandy), Gothic of pure early type. 1141-1182 are the dates given to the latter by M. Enlart. If the first is the correct one, then priority for Normandy over the Isle de France could easily be claimed, as the work is far more advanced than any elsewhere of similar date. The probability, however, is that little was done before about 1160, but even taking 1160-1180 as the date it proves that architectural design was quite as far advanced in Normandy at the beginning of the second half of the twelfth century as in any other part of France. Other early Gothic churches are Angers Cathedral (1150-1156, see Fig. 47), although it is not the Gothic of the North, inasmuch as it has no aisles, and consequently no triforia or flying buttresses; Sens Cathedral, Burgundy, commenced 1140, doubly interesting to Englishmen, *Early buildings.*

as William, the master mason of Canterbury, came from there; and Noyon Cathedral (c. 1150), with its apsidal ends to the transepts, the first church in France to show evidence of a strong desire for lightness in all parts. The plan of Noyon was no doubt inspired to some extent by the fine church at Tournai, Belgium (see p. 202), the transepts of which are similar. The piers are alternately large and small, the arches of the arcades and triforia are pointed, but elsewhere pointed and semicircular arches are used indiscriminately. The triforia are large open galleries, as at Laon and Paris, with arcading in the wall above, as in the former church. Pairs of semicircular headed lights to each bay form the clerestory. The church is now vaulted with quadripartite vaults added after a fire in 1293, but the original vaulting was sexpartite. On the whole the design inside is too small in scale, has not the breadth of later examples, and the desire for lightness is carried too far.[1]

The south transept of Soissons Cathedral (c. 1170) also ends with an apse, and is built on the same scale as extends throughout the whole of Noyon Cathedral. It is, however, far superior in plan to the transepts of Noyon, as the apse is surrounded by an ambulatory aisle—the Noyon transepts have no aisles—out of the east side of which opens an unusually large chapel. The rest of Soissons Cathedral was luckily carried out on a far bigger scale than the transept, and presents one of the finest examples in France of simple, robust building, spoilt now, alas! by staring mortar joints.

Nave, Le Mans Cathedral. The nave of Le Mans Cathedral is a striking example of how a Romanesque unvaulted nave of ten bays, with arcades of semicircular arches supported by columns, was converted about 1153 into a Gothic nave vaulted throughout with rib-vaulting, without taking down the nave arches. The arches were originally of two orders, unmoulded, the outer order having a projection of only a few inches.[2] The lower order of each bay was removed, and

---

[1] The most interesting portion of the church to my mind is the choir, with its fittings, which date from Louis XIV.'s time. The plan of these is very dignified. The high altar stands under the crossing, not quite in the middle, but slightly in front of the eastern piers. The stalls of the same period start one bay back, and extend along two bays each side and in front of the apse. An iron grille of eighteenth-century workmanship surrounds the choir, and there are also many fine screens of the same date in front of the chapels lining the nave.

[2] The easternmost bay on both sides remains unaltered, as far as the arches are concerned, so the original design is easily seen.

Photo: Author.

FIG. 185.—SOISSONS CATHEDRAL: SOUTH TRANSEPT.

Photo: Author.

FIG. 186.—LE MANS CATHEDRAL: NAVE.

[*To face p.* 260.

underneath the upper one was built a pointed arch (one half of which is concentric with the original arch), which, being narrower than the other, allowed room for the great clustered piers, the outer members of which are carried up to the vaulting to support the massive transverse arches and the diagonal and wall ribs of the vault. As an example of adaptation it is a monument to the clever ingenuity of the mediæval builders (for plan see Fig. 98).

The above-mentioned churches do not, with the exception of S. Pierre, Lisieux, display fully those characteristics of early French Gothic which are so marked in the group next to be considered. The alternation of large and small piers at Le Mans, and Noyon, for instance, belongs to an earlier school. Between 1160 and 1200 the plain cylindrical column—sturdy, but never heavy, as in our Romanesque work—was general; and this was often employed even when it had to support as many as five independent vaulting-shafts, as at Laon,[1] Lisieux, and Paris, in addition to the arches of the arcade. This afterwards gave way to the column with attached shafts, already referred to (see Fig. 19), as at Chartres, Reims, etc., but the proportions and appearance of the columns were very little changed by the addition of the shafts. A point worth remembering in connection with French Gothic is that very few changes of any moment were introduced between 1200 and 1350, except in window design. The walls, it is true, were made thinner; windows were divided into a greater number of lights—a window of two lights is the general rule in early work; the main vaulting-shafts were carried down to the floor, as in Romanesque churches, and once again formed part of the piers; but very little alteration was made in the mouldings until towards the end of the fourteenth century, and the vaulting, as already stated in a previous chapter, retained its simple quadripartite form for a couple of centuries or more. There are differences in the carving of capitals, etc., but they are slight as compared with those which took place in English work during the corresponding period. In resting content with what he had done the Frenchman showed not only sound common sense, but good taste as well. He knew when he had got a good thing and, in the main, he stuck to it. He modified here, lightened there—after 1250 in his delight in technical skill he often went too far in this respect—but until France went to

The great early churches.

---

[1] Some of the columns at Laon have detached shafts in front of them, which help to carry the vaulting-shafts, but not all.

pieces after the battle of Crecy, in 1347, he kept his art free from trivial novelties. Owing to this in a great measure there is a completeness and uniformity about French cathedrals which seldom exist in those of other countries. The French builder of course had not to contend with the disadvantages his English brother laboured under, at least not to the same extent, of having to enlarge churches built one or more centuries before; but apart from this, a wholesome conservatism prevented the glaring differences which are sometimes so marked in England.[1] When fire played havoc with a new church, as it frequently did, its ravages were repaired without introducing marked changes in design. Thus, at Amiens Cathedral, there is little difference between the original work of c. 1220, and the reconstruction after the fire in 1257. Window tracery is practically the only detail in which changes of any importance were introduced. Even in this, when complete development was once reached, which may be said to date from the building of La Sainte Chapelle, Paris (c. 1240), few modifications followed until after the end of the fourteenth century, when the Hundred Years' War had sapped the vigour of French art.

Best period of French art.

The reigns of Philip Augustus (1180-1223) and Louis IX., known as Saint Louis (1226-1270), form the glorious period of church building in Northern France. During these two reigns most of the famous cathedrals were in course of erection. To Philip's reign belong mainly Laon Cathedral, commenced 1160; Nôtre Dame, Paris, commenced 1163: the work in both churches continuing to the middle of the thirteenth century; Chartres Cathedral, the major rebuilding of which dates from 1194; Rouen Cathedral, chiefly 1202-1220; Troyes, with its fine choir of the early thirteenth century; Mantes Cathedral, not far from Paris, and evidently inspired by the capital; and Reims Cathedral, rebuilt after a fire in 1211.

The great achievement of Louis' reign is Amiens Cathedral. Commenced in 1220, and completed in 1257, the greater part was burnt in the following year, the rebuilding lasting until 1288. Other contemporary famous cathedrals are Bourges, which belongs chiefly to the middle of the thirteenth century, although some

[1] Take S. Albans Cathedral, for instance. It was no doubt impossible to harmonize the later work on the south side of the nave with the earlier work on the north; but the thirteenth and fourteenth-century portions need not have been so different.

portions are earlier and others later; Tours, to which the same remark applies; the choir of Le Mans, 1217-1254, the chevet of which is externally the most striking in France, partly from its forest of forked buttresses, flying buttresses, and pinnacles, and partly from its fine position at the end of a large market-square, above which it towers; and Beauvais, that memento of a soaring ambition which came to grief. The cathedral was commenced soon after Amiens, with the notion of surpassing it in all respects. The choir alone was finished in 1272, but twelve years later the vaults fell in and wrecked the church. The work of reconstruction was not accomplished until 1347, the piers being doubled and other portions strengthened, and later the transepts were added.[1] The time had gone by for great efforts in church building, and a nave was never attempted. The added piers in the choir must, on the whole, be counted a gain; as the great width of most of the original bays and the slenderness of the piers must have caused an appearance of weakness, in addition to being weak. If the builders, after the catastrophe, had continued the outer member of the original arch so that it enclosed two narrow arches (as at Boxgrove Priory, Sussex) the effect would have been excellent. The collapse, in the hands of an able man, might have proved a blessing, but the builders seem to have lost their heads under the magnitude of the disaster. The new intermediate piers are the same depth, from north to south, as the old ones, but they are considerably narrower.

Corresponding with the above cathedrals are others in the neighbouring provinces, many of which are little inferior to the great examples mentioned. In Normandy are Coutances (c. 1251-1274), famous for its side chapels, divided from one another by walls pierced above with traceried openings similar to the windows alongside them; Sées (c. 1270), the distinguishing mark of which is the slender detached shaft which starts from the floor, in front of each cylindrical column, and reaches to the vault, passing in front of a beautiful little cusped niche. The effect of these shafts is most striking, and very unusual, if not unique. On the boundary of Normandy and Brittany is Dol

<small>Cathedrals outside the Isle de France.</small>

---

[1] The transept vaults are dated 1577 and 1578, and 1575 is the date on some of the bays of the choir vaulting. The vaulting throughout the church is sexpartite, owing to the added piers. The vaulting in the aisles is especially curious, as each intermediate transverse arch consists really of a ridge rib supported by an arch, the stonework between being pierced.

264   A HISTORY OF ARCHITECTURAL DEVELOPMENT.

Cathedral, with a fine choir, 1231–1265. In Burgundy, the work proceeded at Sens Cathedral towards the end of Louis' reign; and at Auxerre the choir was built 1215–1234, the nave belonging to the next century and the west front being left unfinished. At Dijon is one of the most remarkable churches of second rank of this period, Nôtre Dame de Dijon, which was built about 1240. It appears earlier, as it has all the characteristics of the work of Philip's reign, but Burgundy was conservative and to some extent cut off from the movement taking place farther north. It is a model of early thirteenth-century French methods and, although the work is somewhat frigid inside, few larger churches can beat its fine proportions. Vézelay choir is much earlier (c. 1180), but contrast with the Romanesque nave makes it look later than the date given.[1]

Sites of cathedrals.

One fault sometimes found with French cathedrals is that they seldom, if ever, stand clear. They are surrounded by streets, hemmed in by houses; and one sometimes longs for the cool green sward and the quiet of an English cathedral close. At the same time their positions emphasize the connection between the Church and the people. The cathedral was their work; they wished it in their midst, where they could see it without let or hindrance, enter it without encroaching on property not their own; and so, as at Amiens especially, it towers above all surrounding buildings, and from a distance stands out a great black mass, a landmark to the dwellers in the country round, a beacon to town folk when returning home. Owing to their surroundings it is difficult, as a rule, to obtain a good view of any cathedral except from a distance. Most of the east ends are enclosed, and visible only from private gardens—often those of the bishop or archbishop—and the approaches to the west fronts, or to the fine transept entrances, are often poor in the extreme. The Gothic builder, unfortunately, did not appreciate what the Roman architect knew instinctively; that the approaches to a building are quite as important as the design of the building itself. In some of the Romanesque and slightly later monastic churches and cathedrals in France, there was, no doubt, originally something of the nature of an atrium or forecourt to the west. At Chartres, Sens, Paris, Caen (in front of S. Etienne), and elsewhere are large open spaces opposite the main entrances; but in the majority of cases, either

[1] Most of the dates are taken from M. Enlart's "Manuel d'Archéologie Francaise."

land was too valuable to be devoted to such a purpose, or else the builders were indifferent to everything except the church itself. The east end of Le Mans Cathedral stands free, as already stated; and at Bourges a magnificent view is obtainable of the cathedral, with its long, unbroken roof-line, from the formally planned gardens to the south-east. This view is one of the finest architectural ones in France. At Auxerre is another fine view of an east end, although a more distant one as it is from the opposite bank of a river. The cathedral, raised on its double crypt, towers above the old bishop's palace, the grounds of which slope down to the river-side. The lower portions of the church are hidden, but the clerestory windows and buttresses stand out well.

An analysis of the plans of leading French cathedrals shows proportions very different from those which, as will be shown later, appertain to English ones. French cathedrals, on the whole, are considerably wider; their height is far greater; and although there is not such great difference in the actual length of the examples in the two countries, French cathedrals, owing to their width and height, appear much shorter. Their proportionate length to width, including both side and end chapels, is approximately as follows, the width being taken as the unit:— *Proportions.*

Name of cathedral.	To width of western arm.	To width of eastern arm.
Paris	2·8	2·8
Chartres	3·77	2·8
Reims	4·55	3·03
Bourges	2·31	2·31
Amiens	2·95	2·9

Their superficial area and cubic contents are far in excess of ours. The average width of the churches named in the Appendix table, exclusive of side chapels, is 111 feet, as against 82 in the English cathedrals mentioned.

The real differences between the transverse dimensions of the churches of the two countries lie in the fact that so many of the great churches in France have double aisles, sometimes to both nave and choir, sometimes to choir alone, whilst beyond the aisles are frequently chapels. Nôtre Dame, Paris, has a total width of 149 feet, Bourges Cathedral 16 feet more, in both cases the side chapels being included (see Fig. 106). The best-known churches *Double aisles.*

with double aisles all round, including the chevet, are the two just mentioned. Troyes has double aisles to nave and choir, but only a single aisle divides the chapels of the chevet from the apsidal termination of the choir. The east ends of Amiens and Reims are similar to Troyes, but the naves have only single aisles, although at Amiens there are chapels beyond, which is not the case at Reims. Chartres, Le Mans, and Coutances, have likewise only single aisles at the west end, but beyond the transepts they widen out into double aisles which are continued all round the east end

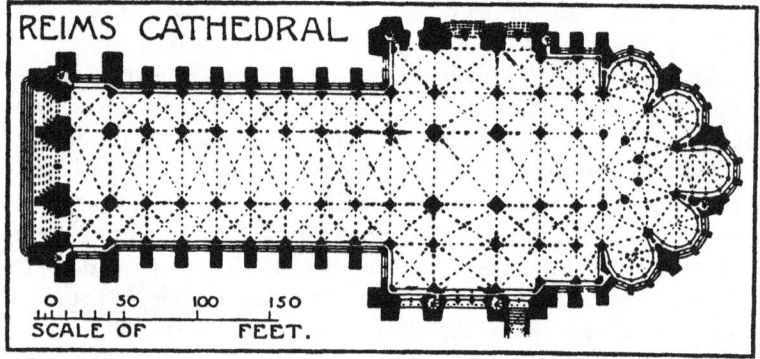

FIG. 187.

with radiating chapels in addition. The chapels in Le Mans are continued down the sides as well, making thirteen in all (see Fig. 98).[1]

INTERIORS.

Internal results of plan.
The main results of the French plan of doubling the aisles and adding chapels are, in the first place, that the effects obtained by looking across the churches from north to south, either straight or diagonally, are, as a rule, far finer than the vistas from end to end; and, in the second, the great spaciousness of the central part surrounding the crossing. The latter is partly due to the fact that the transepts in nearly all the principal examples have an aisle on both sides. The transepts themselves have very slight projection, far less than in England, but this so far from

[1] The vaulting of the choir of Le Mans is much higher than that of the nave; and by hipping back the nave roof, it has been possible to insert a window in the west wall of the crossing above the nave vault, which produces a particularly good effect inside from the east.

THE CATHEDRALS OF NORTHERN FRANCE. 267

detracting from the effect mentioned, in reality adds to it. Amiens Cathedral is the most remarkable in this respect. The appearance inside is that of a great square of flooring broken in places by a few columns; the nave—which is unusually short by comparison with the rest of the building—and the chevet appearing but as adjuncts. The effect of spaciousness is no doubt helped by the great height of the church, but it is mainly due to the plan.

The chevet, as before mentioned, forms the ending to most of the great cathedrals of France, the exceptions being chiefly in the South. Although few will deny that externally the chevet surpasses in effect the result obtained by the two characteristic

Chevet.

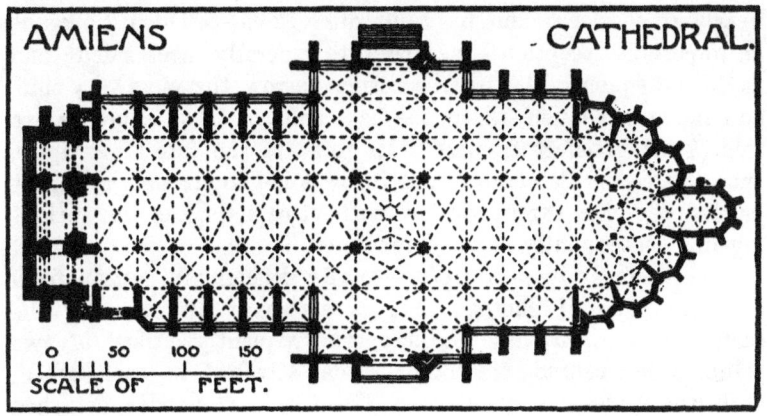

FIG. 188.

English methods described on p. 151, it is very doubtful if the gain outside is sufficient compensation for the cramping effect it often produces inside. In order that all supports in the chevet shall radiate from one centre, the bays round the end of the choir are too numerous (especially in those churches in which double aisles surround the apses) and too narrow; the piers, as a rule, too slender, and the arches, in many cases, disagreeably stilted in order that they shall be the same height as the other arches of the choir. In most churches with only a single aisle behind the choir apse, such as Reims and Rouen Cathedrals, there are only five bays. At Amiens it is difficult to say whether the apse should be termed one of five or seven bays, as its centre is on a line with the middle of a bay, and not on a line with a pier. This modification of the usual plan is followed at Chartres and Le Mans, and

268   A HISTORY OF ARCHITECTURAL DEVELOPMENT.

was all the more necessary, as the apse of each is surrounded by double aisles. In the Cathedrals of Bourges and Paris there are again only five bays to the apse of each, although both churches have double eastern ambulatories. At Bourges the spaces between the columns dividing the ambulatories from each other are unusually wide; at Paris a more ingenious plan is followed. The columns between the aisles are doubled in number, there being nine, to four round the apse. Some of the columns of the back row come central (on the radiating lines) with the columns in front, and the others are placed in between. The vaulting of the aisles is naturally affected by this duplication of supports, and the severies are all triangular in plan instead of being quadrangular. In nearly all the large churches built after 1250—S. Ouen, Rouen, is an important exception—the apses are generally seven-sided; and as, in consequence, the bays are very narrow, the piers very thin, and the arches much stilted, the east ends of these churches are their least satisfactory part. In some of the latest examples, such as Orleans Cathedral, the stilting is not so strongly apparent because the piers throughout are without capitals, and the springing-line consequently is not emphasized.

Apse piers.   The piers of apses are often totally different in section from the side piers of choirs. This is especially the case in the early chevets. In these the supports frequently consist of two columns one behind the other, often attached to each other; with sometimes, as at Bayeux Cathedral, a slender detached shaft nestling between them on each side. The object in changing the plan of the piers was to give as much width as possible to the openings, and at the same time not diminish unduly the strength of the supports (see Fig. 19).

Choirs of Chartres and Paris.   The success of the choirs of Chartres and Paris Cathedrals is largely due to the fact that in these two churches the faults in apse planning, apparent in others, have been avoided. Chartres, it is true, has more bays at the east end than some churches, but its choir is the widest in Northern France, and so the bays are of fair width (Fig. 194). Moreover, all the arches of the main arcades throughout the church are stilted, and the little extra stilting of the apse arches is hardly apparent. At Paris, the bays of the apse are only a trifle narrower than those at the sides, and all the piers surrounding the choir are of the same size. These facts, coupled with the fine perspective effects east of the apse, due to the number and

FIG. 189.—NÔTRE DAME, PARIS.

[*To face p.* 268.

spacing of the columns between the ambulatories, help largely in making the Paris choir the finest in France.

The most important exception in Northern France to the chevet plan is Laon Cathedral. The original choir consisted of six bays (or three double bays, as the vault is sexpartite) and ended with a chevet. About the year 1200 the chevet was removed and four bays added to the east, making the choir ten bays long and the end square.[1] The square ending is more likely due to English influence than to the preaching of S. Bernard, as Cistercian choirs are invariably short, and the length of the choir of Laon is characteristically English, and unusually long for France. Other English features in the Cathedral are the considerable projection of the transepts, and the presence of the dog-tooth ornament. The latter feature cannot be claimed as an exclusively English one, as it is present in Le Mans Cathedral and in a few other French churches outside Normandy, but it was not used as an ornament in France to anything like the same extent as it was in England. With these exceptions Laon Cathedral is as characteristically French as Salisbury Cathedral is English. *Square east end, Laon.*

In the cathedrals of Paris, Laon, Sens, Bourges, etc., which are sexpartite-vaulted, the flying buttresses which transmit the thrusts of the intermediate transverse arches only, are made as strong as those which transmit the thrusts of the main transverse arches and diagonal ribs as well. M. Corroyer, in his "Architecture Gothique en France," terms this illogical. To a certain extent it is; but æsthetically there can be no doubt that the arrangement he objects to is right. Laon, Bourges, and Paris would lose considerably in external effect if half their flying buttresses were omitted or made much lighter. Structurally, there must be buttresses; and considering that the function of a flying buttress is to support the high nave wall, quite as much as to transmit thrusts, M. Corroyer's objection seems uncalled for. In the sexpartite-vaulted church of La Trinité, Angers, the side buttresses are alternately large and small, but then there are no aisles, and consequently no flying buttresses, and the walls are of no great height (see Fig. 163). *Buttresses to sexpartite vaults.*

Laon and Paris are the only two of the great Cathedrals—and *Triforia.*

---

[1] The later work is easily distinguished from the earlier by the different carving on the oversailing course under the top parapet of the easternmost four bays outside, and inside by the carving on the capitals.

to them may be added Noyon Cathedral, and the south transept of Soissons—which have the fine open triforia, vaulted like the aisles, which are so frequent in the earlier Romanesque work of England, Normandy, and Italy. At Paris the upper triforium,

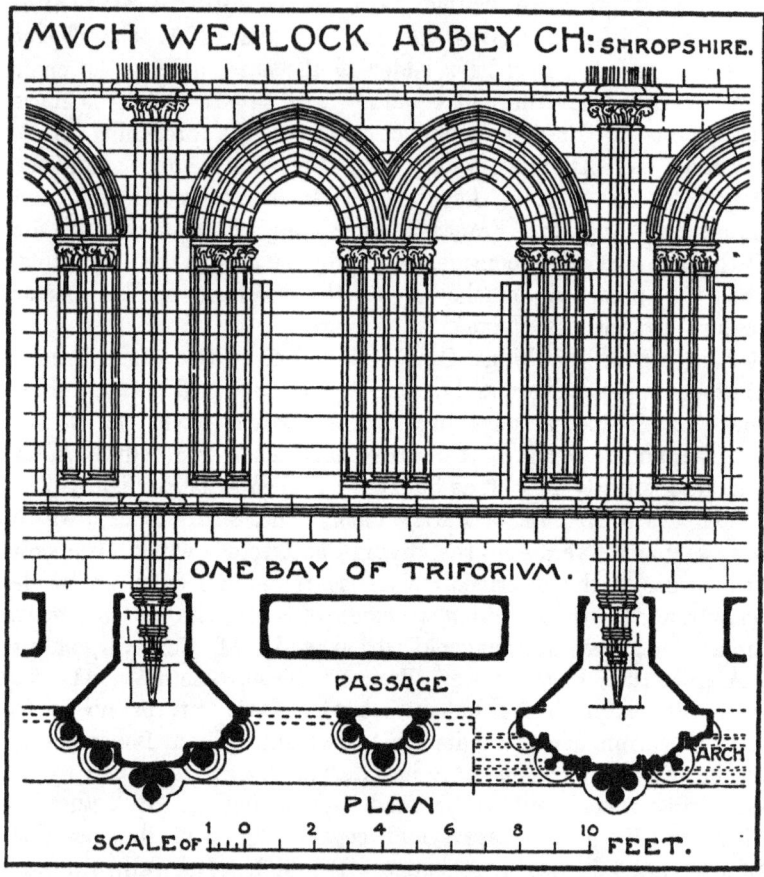

Fig. 190 (G. Langshaw).

present at Laon and Noyon, is wisely omitted, and the extra amount of plain wall space thus obtained is an undoubted gain.[1]

---

[1] Nôtre Dame, Paris, as originally designed, had an upper triforium. The lower one was covered by pointed barrel vaults, at right angles to the nave, like those formerly over the aisles in Fountains Abbey Church. In the transepts and in the easternmost bay of the nave, between the main triforium and the clerestory windows, are pierced circles divided by bars. In the transepts these circles are glazed, and over each is a very wide single light. This was the original design of the church before it was altered at the beginning of the thirteenth century.

Photo: Author.

FIG. 191.—S. PIERRE, CHARTRES.

[*To face p.* 271.

THE CATHEDRALS OF NORTHERN FRANCE. 271

In most of the large French churches of c. 1180-1250, Chartres, Reims, Amiens, etc., the triforia are absolutely closed by a wall behind the arcading in front; and this remained the usual design until the craze for lightness and for glass opened them out in another sense, and occasioned the glazed triforium. The reason for the wall at the back at Chartres, Reims, etc., was partly that the builders feared for the stability of their churches, as their vaults, in each succeeding example, rose higher and higher; and partly that they felt the advantage of a blind storey, to divide the open arcades from the nearly equally open clerestories. The semi-open triforium of England, as at Salisbury, Lincoln, etc., is rare in France. To pierce and glaze the wall behind the arcading of what had hitherto been a blind storey, did not mean much actual weakening of a church, as the ashlar mullions on the outside face are, as a rule, strong and fairly numerous; but the sense of security given by the wall disappeared. In the choirs of the Cathedrals of Metz, Amiens, Beauvais, etc., in the churches of S. Ouen, Rouen, and S. Pierre, Chartres, etc., the triple division of arcade, triforium, and clerestory is retained, but glass practically reaches from the top of the main arcades to the summit of the vaults.

Glazed triforia.

Before the triforia could be glazed it was necessary to get rid of the lean-to roofs behind them over the aisles, which would have blocked all light. Lead flats were sometimes substituted for these, or else high-pitched roofs of double slope with a gutter on each side, that against the nave wall being at about the same level as the floor of the triforium. Often each bay of the aisle has its separate high-pitched roof, hipped on all sides, as at S. Ouen, Rouen. These numerous roofs add a certain picturesqueness to many a late French church, but it is a question if this is not dearly bought by the loss in dignity which results.

In all mediæval work, and not merely in France, the tendency, as development proceeded, was steadily in the direction of increasing the height of the main arcade and of the clerestory, and of diminishing that of the space between them. In the choir of Le Mans the triforium is omitted entirely, and the clerestory windows start from the top of the arcade. The following table illustrates the development, and at the same time emphasizes the loftiness, at all periods, of the ground storey of French cathedrals. In English ones this storey is considerably lower; even after allowance is made for their less total height.

Name of cathedral.	Height from floor to string-course under triforium.	Height between string-courses above and below triforium.	Height from string-course under windows to apex of vault.
	Feet.	Feet.	Feet.
Paris	37·0	33·0	40·0
Chartres	50·0	16·0	48·0
Amiens	70·0	22·0	48·0
Beauvais	74·0	20·0	60·0
Bourges	70·0	19·0	36·0
Le Mans, choir . .	70·0	40·0	

Westminster Abbey has practically the same proportions as Amiens, namely, one half the height to the arcade, and the remaining half, one-third to the triforium and two-thirds to the clerestory; but no other French example follows exactly this division. In a few cathedrals built towards the close of Gothic art in France, Flour, in the south of Auvergne, for instance, and in a great many large contemporary town churches, such as S. Aignan, Orleans, S. Pierre, Auxerre, etc., there is considerable space between the arches and the windows above, where the triforium generally comes, but it is neither pierced nor arcaded. The expanse of plain wall surface is a great gain. From the first the French builders had a fondness for plain walling which they never entirely lost, even in their days of huge windows. They realized its advantage as a foil to surrounding moulded work. The space between the top of the main arcade and the string under the triforium is considerable at Laon, Paris, Chartres, Amiens, etc., and is left quite plain. In the nave of Amiens the plain wall surface is especially valuable, as it lends emphasis to the richly-carved string-course above it. In the four cathedrals mentioned, and also in Reims Cathedral and in other churches, there are no hood moulds over the arcades, such as are almost universal in England—a wise omission, as they are unnecessary in a church faced with ashlar inside, and they take up space which is better left plain.

Bourges Cathedral.
Bourges Cathedral requires special description, as its section is unique. The church has double aisles. Over the main arcade throughout are triforium and clerestory. Arcade, triforium, and clerestory, all of good size, also come between the inner and outer aisles on both sides. The three combined are the same height as the arches alone of the nave, which measure nearly 70 feet—the height of the nave of many an English cathedral. This design has no parallel in France or in any other

FIG. 192.

country.[1] The choir of Beauvais is the nearest approach to it, but in this church the corresponding triforium and clerestory are mean. In Le Mans and Coutances Cathedrals there is the same triple arrangement between the inner and outer aisles surrounding the choirs, but in neither church has the choir itself a triforium. In the nave of Rouen Cathedral the arches between the aisles and the chapels beyond them are as high as the main arcade and the triforium combined, but then the nave arches are low. The interior

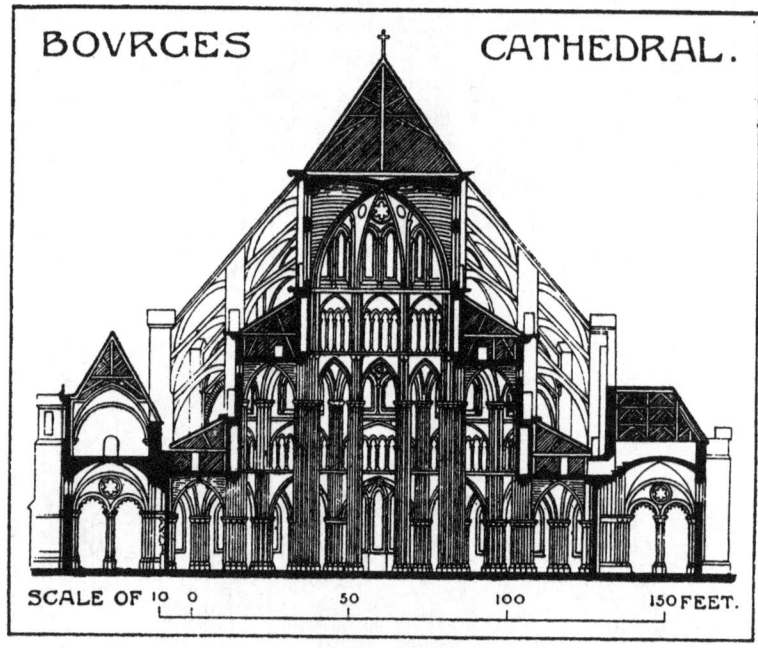

Fig. 193.

of Bourges stands alone; and although it may not equal in beauty the sturdier work of Paris, Chartres, and Reims, it produces an effect of great height, and appears far taller than Amiens Cathedral which really exceeds it by nearly 20 feet. The outside of the Cathedral also presents some unusual features. There are no transepts whatsoever, a distinct advantage, as the church is less than 400 feet long and is 165 feet wide, and the roof runs

---

[1] In some of the large double-aisled cathedrals in Italy, such as Milan, there is the same gradation of nave and aisles, but not the same three divisions (see Fig. 242).

unbroken from east to west.[1] Over the chapels of the chevet are steep-pitched stone roofs, similar to those over the apses of the eleventh-century church of S. Nicolas, Caen. At the west end are five magnificent double doorways, affording direct access to the nave and the four aisles.

Of the different cathedrals in France, Reims is probably the best built. Street eulogizes the construction as perfect, and says that there is not a crack in the building. This is partly because there has been no tampering with it. The aisle walls have not been cut away to form chapels, as at Laon, Paris, Amiens, etc.,[2] and the fine aisle windows are still framed, as they should be, by projecting buttresses. The main columns are sturdy but not heavy; the shafts of the triforium (12 inches in diameter) are a trifle stouter than in other churches; the buttresses are substantially weighted on top by well-designed canopied niches, each containing a figure; and throughout there is a feeling of well-balanced strength which is often absent from churches of more massive proportions. The walls of the nave are carried high above the vaulting—the space between the tie-beam of the timber roof and the extrados of the vault below is about 10 feet—and the added weight gives stability. But the main reason why the church has stood so well is the absence of false bearings. There is very little balancing of upper walls over next to nothing, as is the case at Amiens and Beauvais. At Beauvais false bearings and excessive height brought destruction. At Reims the builders played no pranks (see Fig. 62).

Stability of French churches.

Exteriors.

The results of the proportions already detailed and of the peculiarities of the planning are shown as unmistakably in the exteriors as in the interiors. The great height of the majority of French cathedrals rendered a central tower, in most cases, an impossibility. Its accomplishment would have been a *tour-de-force* from which even the builders of the Isle de France shrank, greatly though they delighted in overcoming structural difficulties. There is one at Laon, but the dimensions of the cathedral as

Towers.

---

[1] In Southern France transepts are frequently omitted, and it was probably the influence of the South which suggested the plan adopted at Bourges. Bourges is about 150 miles due south of Paris.

[2] The old stone seat against the aisle wall still runs round the greater part of the church.

276   A HISTORY OF ARCHITECTURAL DEVELOPMENT.

regards both width and height are more modest than in most other examples. In Normandy central towers are common, and nothing can exceed the beauty of the one at Coutances. Elsewhere in France, in Gothic times, they left them severely alone; substituting for them, in many cases, a *flèche* of wood and lead at the intersection of the roofs—a poor substitute for the square tower, or tower and spire, of so many an English cathedral. At Amiens the top of the flèche is 422 feet from the ground, some 20 feet higher than the top of the stone spire which rises above the well-proportioned and comparatively high central tower of Salisbury. Another result of the height of French churches is that the western towers are often dwarfed by the roof. At Amiens the ridge actually rises higher than the parapets of the towers.

Transept towers and entrances.   That the Frenchmen had no objection to towers is shown by the fact that seven were commenced at Laon Cathedral, a central

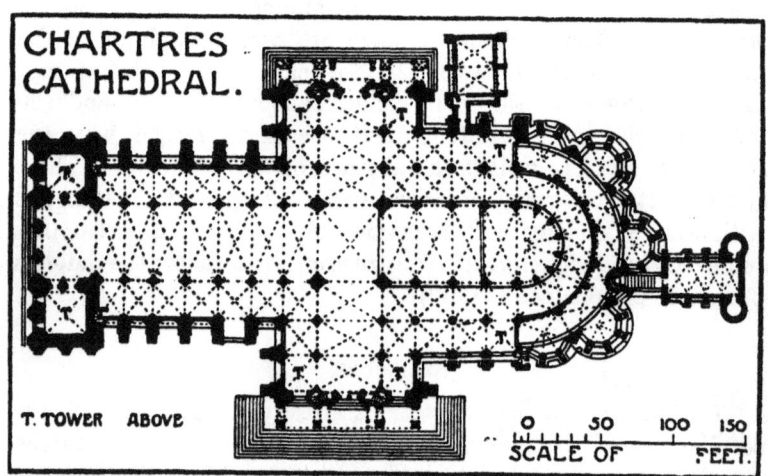

Fig. 194.

tower, two west-end ones, and two to each transept. At Chartres eight were actually intended, there being no central tower, but two additional ones are placed, one on each side, over the outer aisles of the choir, just before the chevet begins. Rouen, like Laon, has, or was intended to have, seven. Reims has six, two at the west end and two flanking each transept. Transept towers, on a big scale, occur first in the Romanesque part of Tournai Cathedral, Belgium (c. 1120), where their lower portions are

Fig. 195.—Amiens Cathedral. [To face p. 276.

hidden by the aisles of the semicircular transept apses which
stand in front. In France the whole tower, as a rule, shows. The
reason for these towers in French cathedrals is the natural
objection, which all architects must feel, to the display in elevation
of the ugly sectional outline of a church which has a high central
part with lower side aisles. The Frenchmen saw no reason why
this outline should appear any more at the sides than at the west
end. For it must be remembered that transepts in France have
an importance almost equal to a west front itself. Their doorways are often as fine as those of the main entrance. At
Chartres the porches in front of the transepts, with their wealth
of glorious sculpture, are far more important than the western
entrances. At Sens, Beauvais, Rouen, Reims, Abbeville, etc.,
almost everywhere in fact, the north and south doorways, with
their large windows over, are amongst the richest portions of each
church.[1] The towers of the transepts of Reims and Rouen
Cathedrals are alike in design. All are unfinished, being carried
no higher than the springing of the gable. In each tower the
upper storey is very open, and is pierced on three sides by two
very long unglazed lights. At Laon the west towers of the north
and south transepts and the central lantern are complete, and,
owing especially to the position of the cathedral, form a striking
group. In towns, however, in which the church occupies a more
cramped position than Laon Cathedral does, it is a question
whether the multiplication of towers was of any advantage, except,
perhaps, from a distance. It is certainly difficult to understand
the reason for the two eastern towers of Chartres. At Coutances
Cathedral there are two small ones in similar positions, but then
they are little more than large pinnacled buttresses, and the transepts, moreover, have no flanking towers. The builders of Nôtre
Dame, Paris, were the first to abandon towers at the transepts,
and their example was followed at Amiens and in subsequent
cathedrals. It was probably felt in most cases that they were
not necessities, and in addition there was the unlikelihood that
they would ever be finished. So many western towers in France
were left incomplete until the fifteenth century—some were not
finished until the Renaissance had obtained a footing in the following one; Tours Cathedral is an instance—that the desire of the

---

[1] At Reims the north transept only has doorways. Over the westernmost one
of the three is incorporated some interesting carved work from the original cathedral
which was burnt down in 1211.

278   A HISTORY OF ARCHITECTURAL DEVELOPMENT.

builders to concentrate their energies on work the completion of which they might possibly see, may be the sole reason for the disappearance of towers from the transepts.[1]

Eastern transepts.

Eastern transepts, as at Salisbury, Beverley, Lincoln, etc., were impossible in French cathedrals. They would have curtailed too much the apparent length, which already was too short. For the same reason the builders were careful not to give too much projection to the main transepts, which sometimes, as at Paris, are practically flush with the side chapels of the ground storey, although, of course, owing to the sectional outline of the church, they stand clear above.

West fronts.

The earliest west front to which the term Gothic can be applied is that of Chartres Cathedral (c. 1145). Here is found the ordinance which, slightly modified from time to time, appertains to all French cathedral façades. Two western towers may be said to be the universal rule;[2] portals are generally three in number, Bourges Cathedral being an exception with five; over the central doorway comes a huge rose window; immediately above it, as at Laon (c. 1180) and Reims (1211–1311), or with windows in between, as at Chartres. At Paris (1208–1235) the rose window is separated from the doorway below by a band of figures which is continued across the towers the whole width of the front. At Amiens (c. 1260), owing to the great height, more division was necessary. Between the three portals and the central rose window and windows alongside it, is a row of windows (see Fig. 208), and above that a band of figures similar to the one at Paris. Above the rose window at Chartres is a straight band of arcading, the spaces being filled with figures, which forms a parapet. Behind this, set back some feet, rises the gable terminating the nave. The crowning horizontal line is a characteristic of all churches of the thirteenth and fourteenth centuries in France in both western façades and transepts. The gable was never allowed to come to the front until towards the fifteenth century, although a portion of it sometimes shows behind the straight line, as at Chartres. At Laon it is hidden entirely at the west end. At Nôtre Dame, Paris, the nave roof and gable

---

[1] On the west side of each main transept of Canterbury Cathedral is a small Romanesque tower, but the pair form the only attempt made in England in this direction, and that not a very important one.

[2] In some abbey churches of late date there are no western towers, as at Vendôme, or only one, as at S. Riquier, near Abbeville.

Photo: *Neurdein.*
Fig. 196.—Laon Cathedral.

Fig. 197.—Nôtre Dame, Paris: West Front.

[*To face p.* 278.

are set back on a line with the eastern face of the towers, and are practically invisible, allowing the arcading above the band of figures to be pierced, and at the same time giving an importance to the side towers which they would not otherwise possess. This arcading is continued straight across the towers, and projects a trifle in front of them, thus producing a lighter effect than if it had been set back against the walls, and preventing too strong a contrast between the open centre and semi-closed sides. At Laon the arcading in the centre is a trifle higher than at the sides. At Reims the crowning arcade becomes a series of niches filled with figures, and over each niche is a canopy with a pediment on top. The result is spikey, and far inferior to the simplicity of the earlier work; the general effect being by no means enhanced by the struggles, so to speak, of the gable behind to get to the front. At Amiens the designers wisely placed their figures below the rose window and not above it, as the upper part of the centre of the front cannot be seen unless one goes on the housetops. This consists of a gallery, with some pierced panelling above, behind which rises the gable. Even in so late an example as Orleans Cathedral the straight line is retained, the gable not showing at all. In Tours Cathedral it is more in evidence, but this was not finished before the end of the fifteenth century.

From the above it will be seen that horizontal lines are far more marked in western façades than in any other part of a church. Vertical lines are still strong—the churches could hardly be Gothic if they were not—but there is not the same insistence on verticality to the exclusion of everything else that is so noticeable in the interiors. At Amiens, it is true, the carved string-course under the triforium marks a stronger horizontal line than is generally found inside Gothic churches, either in England or France, R. de Luzarches and the De Cormonts probably feeling that the great height was sufficient to stand it. In the church of Nôtre Dame de Dijon, the horizontal lines on the western façade are especially prominent. The entire front is carried up above the roof, and finishes square. The horizontality of the design, however, is not so much due to this as to three carved bands of boldly projecting animals, which stand out from the wall, framing in, and dividing from each other, two bands of arcading. These animals are in many respects even more remarkable than the animals and devils that look down from the parapet of Nôtre Dame, Paris.

The great portals of France far exceed in magnificence the Doorways.

doorways of English cathedrals. Great similarity runs through them all. The detail varies, and the later examples are richer than the earlier ones, but in the main there are few differences. The doorways themselves are generally double, and are always spanned by lintels. Over the lintels is a tympanum framed in by an arch of many orders, which forms the head of the portal. The jambs of the portal, or porch as it may be called if the doorways are much recessed, the support between the doorways, and each order of the arch, are filled with figures under canopies which form a bewildering array of sculpture of the highest order. The tympanum also has figure sculpture, generally arranged in bands.[1] In the sculptured tympana and carved concentric orders of the porches the Gothic builders were only developing the idea introduced in Romanesque times. There is no difference in principle between early and late designs in this respect. By their multiplication of the arch orders, however, and by their greater skill as sculptors, the French craftsmen of the thirteenth century advanced far beyond their predecessors. At Chartres their superiority is especially marked in the sculpture and carvings literally covering the projecting porches of the north and south transepts. No other country can boast such Gothic doorways as France, although in Spain an early example at Santiago de Compostella is probably finer than any French Romanesque one.[2] In Spain also and in Germany there are some late doorways of the fifteenth and sixteenth centuries which, if excess of richness were a desideratum, might compare with French ones.

Wide west fronts. The west fronts of Bourges and Rouen Cathedrals deserve a special word because of their width. In nearly all other churches the towers come at the end of the aisles. Even in Nôtre Dame, Paris, a church with double aisles, the space between the towers is only the width of the nave. Each of the side towers is as wide as the two side aisles, which, under the tower, have no dividing column and become a single square. At Bourges, however, the towers start from beyond the inner aisles, and project considerably beyond the outer ones; even beyond the side chapels.

---

[1] At Reims the sculpture of the three tympana was removed, probably in the fifteenth century, and windows inserted. From the inside the effect is not so bad; outside it is deplorable. About the same time the simplicity of the gables over the three porches was destroyed by the addition of groups of figures, standing on clouds; and in the case of the central one, surmounted by gimcrack tabernacle work.

[2] A full-size cast of this doorway is in the Victoria and Albert Museum, South Kensington.

Hence the possibility of the five doorways, each a double one, already referred to. In Rouen Cathedral, which has only single aisles, although there are chapels beyond, the towers start outside the aisles altogether. A west front of unusual width is the result, which, before it was altered in the fifteenth century and "restored" in the last century, must have been very striking.

The main characteristics of the great churches of France have been outlined in this chapter; a similar treatment is accorded to their smaller brethren in England later. French cathedrals, owing to their height, double aisles, side chapels, and the resulting complicated arrangement of buttress, flying buttress, and pinnacle— familiar to all acquainted with French architecture—produce in some a feeling of unrest which displeases them. In the chevet the culmination is reached. "An arch never sleeps," says the Arab proverb; and throughout a French cathedral, at the east end especially, one has always the sense of movement; the feeling that stone is always grinding against stone; that the whole, although a triumph of beautifully balanced counteracting forces, cannot possess that stability which a lasting monument should have. It is but fancy. The French cathedrals have lasted as long as ours, and are in as good a state of preservation as ours; in many cases in a better. English cathedrals are quieter; more soothing; less daring; more peaceful. Flying buttresses are often lacking altogether. Pinnacles are few, and dimensions modest. The English church is suitable to its close; the French church in harmony with the turmoil that often surrounds it. Each is best in its own place, and no one can truthfully say that the churches of one country are right, and that those of the other are wrong.

Summary.

With the building of La Sainte Chapelle, Paris (1240–1248), French Gothic architecture enters on its second stage. But there is no radical change to chronicle, save in the tracery of the window heads, and no specific difference that can be stated in terms between the churches of the succeeding hundred years and those of the previous century. But there are differences nevertheless. The virility of Chartres and Reims was passing away. The work was already somewhat wirey and hard. The builders, fortified by experience, were becoming technically bolder. Plain wall surfaces, both outside and inside, were disappearing as though by magic. The enlarged windows left no room for them, and the glazed triforium had destroyed what before

Later work.

had been a strengthening band, both in appearance and in actuality, between arcade and clerestory. The piercing and panelling of flying buttresses, which commenced about this time, destroyed further the vigour of the churches outside, although adding to their richness. All structural supports and adjuncts grew smaller. Soon little was left inside except the piers, arches, and vaults; and outside, the buttresses, flying buttresses, and window-frames. The result was well summed up by the late G. F. Bodley, in a lecture at the Royal Academy, in the phrase, "late French cathedrals are all vigour and glass."

S. Ouen, Rouen.

The most striking church of the middle period of French art is S. Ouen, Rouen, commenced 1318, by l'Abbé Marc d'Argent. The choir and transepts were finished at his death in 1339, but certain portions, the central lantern, for instance, were not completed until the beginning of the sixteenth century. Its internal height is practically the same as that of Westminster Abbey, although the width of its nave is a few feet less. In total width the Rouen church is the larger, as its aisles are wide, as in many other late examples. The detail of Marc d'Argent's portion of the church is very pure, and not unlike the slightly earlier work at York Cathedral. The nave is more flamboyant, but shows more restraint than is customary in late work.

English influence on fourteenth-century churches.

Many of the fourteenth-century churches in certain parts of France show traces of English influence. This is especially marked in the Southern and Western districts, which at that time were either under the direct rule of the English kings, or in close communication with England. At Figeac, for instance, the clerestory windows in the Church of S. Sauveur are strangely like contemporary ones in this country. The feeling is the same in many of the Brittany churches—at Guingamp, Quimper, Tréguier, etc. The size and shape of the windows, the lines of their tracery, and the sections of the mouldings are all more in accordance with English dimensions, proportions, and forms than with French ones. England had learnt from France towards the end of the twelfth century; a hundred and fifty years later, when France was in a parlous state, her kings weak, and her lands devastated, England was able to teach in her turn. Her influence did not extend throughout the whole of the country. To the east and north of Paris there is little trace of it; the churches there are unmistakably descended from the great French cathedrals of the thirteenth century; but in the west, in the towns mentioned above, and in others, are several examples which owe many of their features to English architecture.

Fig. 198.

French archæologists use the term "flamboyant" for their architecture of the fifteenth century, and the word expresses it well; not merely because the tracery of the windows forms flowing lines, but because throughout all the buildings of the period there is a light-heartedness which no other term would convey the effect of

Flamboyant.

so well. Contemporary work in England is equally well expressed by the term "perpendicular," not only because the heads of windows are filled with vertical bars, and the wall surfaces panelled with upright panels, but because the architecture, in its main lines, is stiff and angular. The work in France expresses the *joie de vivre*, inherent in the nation, which found expression after the triumph of the French in freeing the country from the English; and English work shows evidence of the gloom which settled over the country after the Black Death and War of the Roses, which was not dissipated until the Tudors came to the throne.

The first sign of flamboyant feeling, according to M. Enlart, is seen in one of the chapels of Amiens Cathedral, built 1373, but it was not until some fifty or sixty years later that it appeared in full force. S. Maclou, Rouen (1437–1450), is the most delightful existing example of it. The west front expresses in overwhelming fashion the *joie de vivre* already referred to. It is to earlier work what the reel is to the minuet; a burst of jollity which the purist in Architecture may shake his finger at, but none the less a tangible and vivid expression of the feeling of relief and delight which the delivery of the country from war and anarchy had produced. At Alençon is a somewhat similar porch at the west end of the cathedral, but it lacks the abandon which is so marked in S. Maclou. Throughout Normandy are many other fine churches of the fifteenth century, such as S. Vulfran, Abbeville, unfinished, but nevertheless most impressive; the churches at Caudebec, Dieppe, and elsewhere. The two churches which display the richness of this period more extravagantly perhaps than any others are Nôtre Dame de l'Epine, near Chalons-sur-Marne, and the Abbey Church of Vendôme, near the Loire. The west fronts of both are striking; that of the former especially so, with its two towers crowned by spires which recall somewhat the north-west spire of Chartres Cathedral.

The last word. A considerable amount of church building was done after the sixteenth century had commenced—far more than in England where Protestant ideas took root earlier—and much of this is a mixture of Gothic and Renaissance detail which is often far from unpleasant. In the doorways of many churches, Beauvais Cathedral and at Abbeville, for instance, rich fifteenth-century Gothic masonry frames in Renaissance woodwork, which is by no

Fig. 199.—S. Maclou, Rouen.

[*To face p.* 284.

means out of keeping with its earlier surroundings. In travelling through France one is frequently astonished at the dates given to churches in which Gothic feeling is still paramount, although the detail shows that its reign was nearly over. S. Pierre, Auxerre, is a striking church, and yet it is stated to have been rebuilt entirely in the seventeenth century. S. Nicolas, Coutances, the nave of which belongs to the sixteenth century, the choir and transepts to the following one, is quite a remarkable example of imitation thirteenth-century work. The detail is by no means bad, although it betrays its date in places. The traditional methods of mediæval building are followed religiously, and the church is vaulted with ribbed vaulting, whilst under the tower the corbelling has been copied from that over the crossing in the cathedral. S. Pierre, Coutances, is earlier (c. 1500). Of the same date is S. Jacques, Lisieux, a far finer church, with the simple quadripartite vault which the French clung to until the end, enriched with most effective painting dated 1552. These late churches, and others which might be mentioned, show how traditions were handed on unadulterated across the barrier of the century, and that many years after Gothic was counted as dead it survived in the churches of France.

CHAPTER XVII.

GOTHIC ARCHITECTURE IN SOUTHERN FRANCE.

THE Romanesque monuments of Southern France are so full of originality and beauty, that no wonder they influenced to a considerable extent the churches of the thirteenth and fourteenth centuries of the district. All are founded on old Roman traditions, which were still powerful when the latter were built. Wherever the Roman settled he left behind him a legacy of grand scale. His love for large parts and for as few supports as possible, his preference for open, unencumbered floor spaces, and above all his dislike for active demonstration of the means by which his buildings stood, are as evident in the mediæval churches of Southern France as they are in the buildings of Imperial Rome. The result is that the main characteristics of the Southern church plan are wide naves, square bays (with some exceptions), internal buttresses, and a complete absence of flying buttresses. No cathedral in Northern France has the span of either Angers Cathedral (56 feet) or Albi Cathedral (60 feet). Not even in sexpartite-vaulted churches of the North do any double bays equal in size the single, square quadripartite-vaulted bays at Angers.[1] In detail the Southern churches may not differ much from the Northern; in plan and general ordinance they belong to a totally different school.

Types of Southern churches.

Most Southern churches can be grouped under three heads—

(1) Churches without either aisles or side chapels, such as Angers Cathedral (see Fig. 162).

(2) Churches without aisles, but with chapels at the sides between internal buttresses of considerable projection, as Albi Cathedral.

(3) Churches with aisles, the aisles being nearly as high as the central nave. The section was a common one in Romanesque

[1] The sexpartite bays of Nôtre Dame, Paris, are each about 45 feet by 35 feet.

GOTHIC ARCHITECTURE IN SOUTHERN FRANCE. 287

churches of the South, such as S. Nazaire, Carcassonne, and the later Gothic churches of this type are their direct descendants.

Poitiers Cathedral (c. 1160) is certainly the most remarkable of those under the third head, and it is probably also the earliest

Poitiers Cathedral.

Fig. 200.

of the Gothic examples. In it, and in other similar churches, there are neither triforia nor clerestories. The lighting is entirely from the aisles and from the west and east ends. Owing to the great height of the aisles, and the absence of side windows in the nave walls, the aisle windows are considerably larger and of greater importance than in the Northern type of church. Poitiers

Cathedral has no chevet; its east end is square, although in the thickness of the wall are three apses, as in the early churches of Syria, Egypt, and Rome. The transepts are mere chapels, and of little importance. The church is narrower at the east end than at the west, both in total width and in the width of its nave. The vault diminishes in height towards the east end, not so much owing to the decrease in width, as because its springing-line over the three bays forming the choir is the same as the springing-line of the side arches, whereas in the nave it starts from a considerably higher level. In the church at Pontaubert, Burgundy, the chancel arch and vault to the east are dropped in a similar way, the springing-line of the vault of the apse at the end of the chancel being lower still. In the church of Montreal, also in Burgundy, the gradation in height is obtained in a still more subtle fashion. The transverse arches of the nave are stilted; those of the chancel are not, the result being that the vault of the latter is a few feet lower that the nave vault. In all three churches the differences in height are not noticeable; the only place in each where they are apparent at all is above the chancel arch, as there a small portion of wall shows below the nave vault. The above-mentioned devices, and others which are generally met with in countries where old classic traditions still lingered, are not only legitimate, but are deserving of all praise. They are evidence of the care and thought which the builders devoted to their work; and when unobtrusive, as in the examples described, are well worth the attention of modern architects.

La Chaise Dieu. A connecting link between Poitiers and Albi Cathedrals is the Church of La Chaise Dieu, Auvergne (c. 1344), although chronologically it is later than either. It is one of the best examples of a monastic church in France. The nave only consists of three bays, whereas the choir has seven. The stalls, one hundred and forty-six in number, return at the west end and separate the monks' part from the people's. The nave and choir are about 50 feet wide. At the sides are aisles, which continue round the church, except at the east end, where they stop against the five radiating chapels which open directly out of the choir. These chapels are unapproachable from either the nave or aisles; they belong exclusively to the choir. The church is like Poitiers Cathedral in having neither triforia nor clerestories: it differs from it mainly in the narrowness of its aisles, which, although lofty, are little more than ambulatories.

Fig. 201.—Albi Cathedral.

[*To face p.* 289.

The cathedral at Albi (c. 1282) and the numerous churches in Toulouse form a group in which can be studied the essential differences between Northern and Southern ideals. Almost all are built of red brick. Even the jambs of windows and the buttress set-offs are generally brick, although the mullions and tracery are stone. Nearly all are aisleless, but the naves and choirs of most are surrounded by chapels, built between the strong internal buttresses which carry the thrusts of the vaults. At the west end of Albi Cathedral a square tower, with great circular buttresses at the angles, takes up the whole width of the front, and there is no western doorway. This alone marks a difference between

Albi Cathedral.

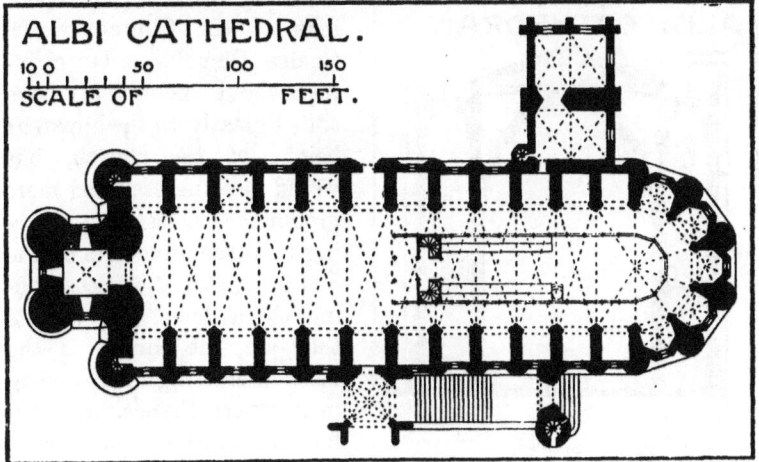

Fig. 202.

Northern and Southern work. A Northern builder would no more have dispensed with his western doorway than he would with his vault. There are no transepts. The only entrances are lateral, the main one on the south side consisting of a fine fifteenth-century stone porch, near the middle of the church, which is approached by a flight of steps, at the bottom of which is a gateway nearly as elaborate as the porch itself. The buttresses outside are segmental and have very slight projection. They, like the walls, are built with the long, thin bricks of the South, with wide mortar joints. The appearance inside is somewhat disappointing after the towering height of the outside, helped as it is by the lines of the buttresses and the unusually lofty proportions of the windows. A hundred feet is no mean height for a vault;

but when that vault has a span of quite 60 feet, its springing-line is no higher from the floor than the nave is wide. The effect would probably have been better if the length had in some way been broken. Nothing of consequence marks the division between nave and choir. The choir is merely a portion of the east end screened off by a stone screen, so as to allow of free passage to the chapels at the sides and end. Over the chapels which surround the church are galleries, the vaults of which are as high as the main vault. The galleries, like the aisles below, are divided into distinct bays by walls, and one misses, in consequence, the perspective effects which are given by the lofty side openings of the Church of La Chaise Dieu. Similar openings would undoubtedly have added greatly to the apparent height of the church, but would have necessitated more pronounced external buttressing than the architects of the South desired. Notwithstanding these defects, if defects they are, the church is the most interesting and inspiring in Southern France. Its plan for congregational purposes is far superior to the triple division plan almost universal for large churches in Northern Gothic. The Cathedral of Perpignan, commenced about the same time as Albi, has a similar plan and like dimensions, although its height is a trifle less. The main differences between the two churches are that there are no galleries over the chapels at Perpignan, and that over the arched openings to the chapels, which are much higher than at Albi, are uncusped circular windows, one to each bay. Clerestory windows of this simple type are common in Italy and Spain, and probably found their way to Perpignan over the Pyrenees.

FIG. 208.

Toulouse.   The Church of the Jacobins, Toulouse (c. 1300), is one of the most striking in a town full of churches of unusual plan and noble proportions. Most were built by either the Dominicans or the Franciscans, who exerted themselves so unenviably in the

GOTHIC ARCHITECTURE IN SOUTHERN FRANCE. 291

thirteenth century in the extermination of the religious sect known as the Albigenses. The Church of the Jacobins differs from the others in that, as is frequently the case in churches built

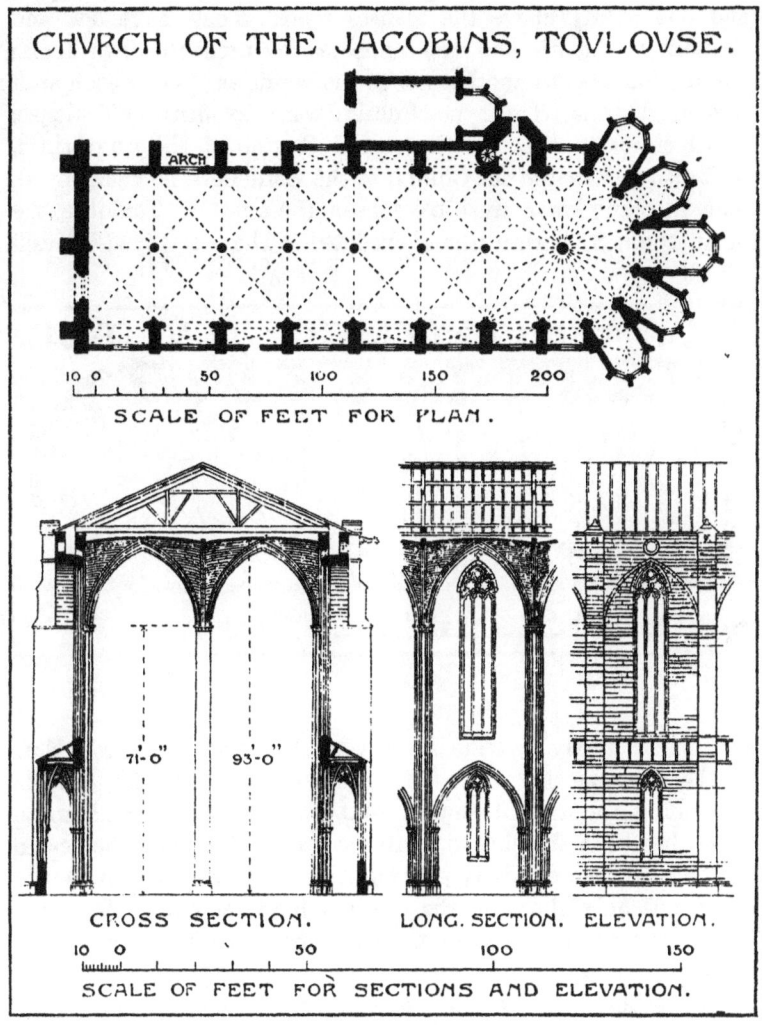

Fig. 204.

by the Dominican order, it has double naves of equal height divided from each other by lofty cylindrical columns which reach from the floor to the springing of the vault, and help to make the church appear far more lofty than the single-span Cathedral of Albi, although in reality it is nearly 10 feet lower. Along the sides are low chapels without galleries over them. Outside, the buttresses, which are internal for the height of the side chapels, stand out boldly above the lean-to roofs. They have few and unimportant set-offs, and are connected by arches thrown across from one buttress to another above the windows. Over each arch is a pierced circle. This type of design was a favourite in Toulouse. It still exists in the partially-ruined Church of the Augustines, and it also occurred in the Church of the Cordeliers, now destroyed, which in many ways must have been the finest in Toulouse, the Romanesque S. Sernin alone excepted. The destroyed church

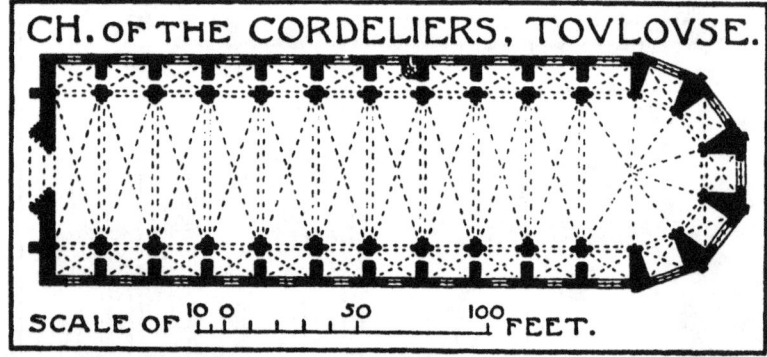

Fig. 205.

had a nave nearly as wide as that of Albi Cathedral, with low chapels opening out of it on either side. Over the chapels surrounding the apsidal ending were other chapels, carried up to the full height of the church, so that round the east end the design followed still more closely that of Albi. Of the Church of the Augustines only three of the original bays remain. These are 21 feet from centre to centre, the width from north to south being 60 feet.

Altogether there are few towns in France which can compare with Toulouse in churches the plans of which are so suitable for large congregations. They are proof that the Gothic of the North, with its nave and aisles, its flying buttresses and its inside divisions of nave walls, is not the only Gothic worthy of study. The fame of Chartres, Reims, Paris, and Amiens has eclipsed the

Southern work; but when one comes to practical considerations, to dealing with the plan and ordinance best suited to modern requirements, it is a question whether it is not far better to shut one's eyes resolutely to the glamour of the Northern churches, and to open them freely to the many good points which the Southern ones possess.

CHAPTER XVIII.

GOTHIC ARCHITECTURE IN ENGLAND.

Introduction.
THE middle of the twelfth century marks the commencement of a new era in English church building. From it dates the rise of a national feeling which in less than half a century led to the freeing of English art from continental tradition, and to its development on lines different from those which were being pursued elsewhere. Nearly a century had passed since England had come under foreign rule. During that time great changes had naturally taken place in the relations between the two races, between the conquered and the conquerors. The old conditions, under which a hard-and-fast line was drawn between Normans and English, had to a great extent changed, especially amongst the dwellers in towns. The Norman traders who followed the Conqueror to England had at first lived apart in their own quarter, alongside that occupied by the original inhabitants but separate from it. Gradually the barriers were broken down. The descendants of William's followers had no longer need for them. England was the country of their birth; and by the intermarriage of their forebears many were half of English blood. A more powerful reason for fusion was the identity of interests between all burghers, no matter what their descent. Union between the two races was necessary in order to obtain freedom for their cities, security for themselves, and to repel more easily the aggressions of the barons, the extortions of the king.

The marriage of Henry I. with Matilda, an English Princess, helped, to a great extent, to reconcile the English to foreign rule. It bore fruit when Henry's elder brother Robert, Duke of Normandy, claimed the English throne. The sympathies of the Norman barons in England were largely with Robert, and the army that followed Henry to Normandy and won the battle of Tenchebray was composed mainly of English yeomen. With the accession of Henry II., the grandson of Matilda, through the marriage of Geoffrey of Anjou with the daughter of the first

Henry, one more step was taken towards breaking down the barriers of race. Besides being King of England, Henry II. was the master of Anjou, by descent, of Normandy, which his father had conquered, and of Aquitaine, through his marriage. He therefore owned practically half France as well as this country. His accession meant that the crown passed to one whose Norman strain was equalled by his English, and who, in addition, was half Angevine.

No wonder the accession of Henry II. brought together the dwellers in England. The king was as much a foreigner to the Normans as to the English, and just as much a fellow-countryman of both. At the same time it was long before there were any changes in the Court and in the Church. The barons and prelates remained Norman, with the addition of a few Angevines. No bishop or abbot was English. Wulfstan of Worcester was the only surviving bishop of English blood when William the Conqueror died, and no Englishman was appointed to a see until the thirteenth century. But a break had been made in the Norman succession, and the break brought about a change. It came gradually. The Benedictine monks still controlled all the great monastic churches in England and still looked to Normandy, or to Burgundy the cradle of their order, for guidance in architectural matters. Until the end of the twelfth century, as conservative here as their brethren were abroad, they continued to build on the old lines, as at Ely and Peterboro'. It might have been thought that the union of England, Anjou, Aquitaine, etc., under one ruler would have led to the importation of Southern methods of building into this country. But such was not the case. Although the inhabitants of the above countries were in a sense fellow-countrymen, Angevine characteristics— the aisleless plan for large churches, domical vaults and heavy transverse arches—found no echo in English work. *Angevine influence.*

To the activity of the Cistercians, foreigners as they were, must be attributed in part the break with Norman traditions. In the first quarter of the twelfth century they flocked to England, bringing with them the maxims of their order and their ideals of church building. Their first settlement was at Waverley, near Farnham. That the square east end was an innovation of theirs has already been denied (see pp. 161 and 237), although their advocacy of it probably helped to make it more general. Neither can they be said with any certainty to have introduced the pointed *Cistercian activity.*

arch into England, although it is quite possible they did so. No church of theirs with pointed arches is so early as the nave vaults of Durham Cathedral, and as this was a Benedictine church it is unlikely that they had any say in its building.

Transitional work.

What is commonly called Transitional work in England covers approximately the latter half of the twelfth century. In it there is an increasing lightness of all parts, a mingling of pointed and semicircular arches—the former being used for main arcades and for vaulting, the latter for heads of windows and other small openings—and a change in mouldings and ornamentation. The work is transitional in a double sense; it not only marks the transition from Romanesque to Gothic, but it expresses also the change that was taking place in England in the relations of the people towards the barons, the barons towards the king, on which the seal was set by the Magna Charta of 1215. The period was by no means one of stagnation; but advance was only partial. There was no longer the same building activity as prevailed during the previous century. Whilst contemporary French art was advancing by leaps and bounds, English art was but carefully feeling its way. For this the quarrels of Henry with the church and barons, the restless ambition of Richard, which emptied the exchequer, and the double dealing of John with both the Pope and his own people, are mainly responsible.

French influence.

Although French Gothic art of the latter half of the twelfth century was considerably in advance of contemporary work in England, there are very few examples in this country which can be classed as direct evidence of French influence. Indirectly there may be many, as the English builders cannot have been ignorant of the great strides their art was making across the channel. The choir of Canterbury (c. 1175–1178) is universally admitted to be the work of William of Sens, a Burgundian, and to be continental in design. The mouldings of the arches, the carving of the capitals, the shape of their abaci, the starting of the vaulting shafts from above the capitals, and the sexpartite character of the vault recall Laon, Paris, and Lisieux. The coupled columns of the eastern apse are similar to those in Sens Cathedral, and in the apses of some of the large Normandy churches. In the choir of Ripon Cathedral (c. 1170) the vaulting shafts start as at Canterbury, and the quadripartite vaulting of the aisles is more domical than is usual in English work. The retro-choir of Chichester Cathedral (c. 1186) is, in some of its

GOTHIC ARCHITECTURE IN ENGLAND. 297

details, similar to Canterbury, although built after the death of William of Sens. The foreign influence traceable in Chichester may be due to its proximity to the coast of Normandy, it being the nearest English cathedral to that country. But these examples are few on which to base the assumption that English Gothic was derived from the French. It developed mainly out of its own Romanesque. There are other contemporary churches in England which show little trace of French Gothic influence and some which show none at all, proving that the Englishman, slowly but steadily, was finding a way for himself.

Amongst the earliest examples in England in which the pointed arch occurs in arcades are the abbey churches of Malmes- *Transitional examples.*

FOUNTAINS ABBEY CHVRCH SHEWING AISLE VAVLT RESTORED

FIG. 206.

bury (c. 1145), Buildwas (c. 1148), and Fountains (c. 1150). The first was Benedictine, the other two Cistercian. At Buildwas the design is frankly Romanesque; the substitution of the pointed arch for the semicircular being the only modification. The same may be said of Malmesbury nave, except that the pointed form is also used in the vaulting of the aisles. At Fountains the aisles are vaulted by pointed barrel vaults running from north to south, each bay being carried on semicircular transverse arches in similar fashion to the nave vaults of S. Philibert, Tournus. The two bays at the west end of the nave of Worcester Cathedral (c. 1160–1180) show a lighter and more advanced treatment, although the work is still impregnated with Romanesque feeling. The piers have detached shafts in the angles instead of the attached ones which had hitherto been customary. In the abbey church of Much Wenlock, Shropshire (see Figs. 25 and 190), ascribed by Mr. Prior to c. 1180, a great advance is noticeable; in fact, if the above date is correct little improvement was made for the next twenty or thirty years.

Connecting links. The connecting links between the Transitional work of the second half of the twelfth century and the fully developed Gothic of the following one are to be seen best in the two cathedrals of Wells and Lincoln. In these can be traced the steps by which the later work emerged from the earlier by a natural development, unassisted, or only assisted indirectly, by contemporary work on the continent. Mr. Prior gives the date of the nave of Wells Cathedral as 1170. It may have been commenced then, but it seems unlikely that much was done beyond foundations before the end of the century. The little ruined chapel of Glastonbury Abbey close by was begun after a fire in 1184. Notwithstanding its delicacy and refinement it is still essentially Romanesque in its ornamentation, without a trace of the later feeling conspicuous at Wells, excepting the pointed arches of its vault. Allowing for possible jealousies between the monks of Glastonbury and the canons of Wells, it is inconceivable that the work of the cathedral, if it had been at all advanced, should have exercised no influence on a building only a few miles off; a building, moreover, which for richness of detail has no contemporary equal. The piers of Wells are square with added attached shafts. The main difference between them and Romanesque ones is that the shafts are clusters of three instead of single shafts. It is quite possible that in 1170 the earlier form may have been contemplated, but as the work proceeded the section was changed.[1] The Wells

[1] In the nave of Chichester Cathedral, the semicircular shaft on the face of each pier was carved into a cluster of three when the rebuilding took place after the fire in 1186.

piers are certainly an advance on earlier English forms, and they are, moreover, quite different from continental ones. The square abaci of the capitals show the lingering of Romanesque traditions, and are not suggested by the square abaci of France. The nave of Wells is thoroughly English; and the only question is whether it should be assigned to 1170 or to some thirty years later. The triforium storey consists of very narrow pointed headed openings, which form a continuous band of arcading, there being no vaulting shafts above the piers to divide them into bays. The existing stumpy vaulting shafts start above the arches of the triforium, and appear as after-thoughts. It is quite possible that at first there was no intention of vaulting the nave at all. The work throughout is very simple, and is as sturdy as that of Reims

Fig. 207.

Cathedral. Detached shafts are conspicuous by their absence, and although one misses the differences in colour which are so striking in Salisbury Cathedral and Worcester retro-choir, it is question if the sense of dignity and repose which the nave of Wells possesses is not ample compensation.

The eastern transepts and the choir of four bays of Lincoln Cathedral, the work of Bishop Hugh, were commenced in 1192, and early in the next century a start was made with the great transepts (Fig. 100). The designer was De Noyer (or De Noyers), but whether he was an Englishman or some one brought by S. Hugh from his native town, Avallon, in Burgundy, is a matter of dispute. The introduction of eastern transepts suggests the great church at Cluny; and the double apses to the east of each may also be regarded as a somewhat foreign plan. These, however, are quite as likely due to the bishop as to his architect.

The great transepts and the aisles of the smaller transepts have sexpartite vaulting, and the vaulting shafts of the former start French fashion from the top of the capitals of the piers. Otherwise, outside inspiration is lacking. The vaulting of the choir shows an irregularity in the plan of the ribs which no Frenchman would have dreamt of attempting. It can hardly be considered satisfactory, but may be regarded as an early attempt to reduce the size of the compartments of each bay; a desire which animated all English builders throughout the following centuries, and led to the developments in vaulting peculiar to England which have already been described (see Fig. 52). A feature in S. Hugh's work is the double arcading which runs under the windows round the aisle walls. Trefoil arches supported on shafts stand in front of pointed arches against the wall, the arches crossing one another. The idea was doubtless taken from the intersecting semicircular arcades so common in all Romanesque work, but only in England was it developed in this manner.[1] In the Galilee porch of Ely is a particularly good example of somewhat similar design.

Fully developed Gothic. By the beginning of the thirteenth century English Gothic had fairly found its feet, and was capable of walking alone. With the one exception of Westminster Abbey, and that only as regards its plan and proportions, there is no church built subsequently which can truthfully be said to owe its plan, its ordinance, or its detail to French influence. Window tracery was certainly more developed in the middle of the century in France than it was in England; La Sainte Chapelle, Paris, is earlier than either Westminster Abbey or the Presbytery of Lincoln Cathedral. But the designs of English window heads executed towards the end of the century are very different from contemporary French ones, and early in the following century our masons in their turn gave a lead to the French by the substitution of flowing lines for purely geometric forms.

Normandy French. The beginning of the thirteenth century saw the severance of England and Normandy. Château Gaillard, which had been built by Richard I., a few years before, surrendered to Philip Augustus in 1204, and the whole duchy passed to the French crown. Intercourse between the people of the two countries

---

[1] Lincoln Cathedral ranges over the whole gamut of Gothic, from the Romanesque of the entrance doorways to the fifteenth-century chapels flanking the south porch of the presbytery, which give such scale to the great mass of the cathedral rising behind them.

Fig. 208.—Amiens Cathedral. [*To face p.* 300.

ceased, except on occasions when it was otherwise than friendly. Notwithstanding this, it is interesting to note that for many years architectural development proceeded on much the same lines in some respects in both countries. Constantly in Normandy, especially in its western half, one comes across detail of the thirteenth century, as at Bayeux (c. 1230), Coutances (c. 1220), etc., almost exactly the same as is to be found in England. In the dismantled church of the Abbaye d'Ardennes, near Caen, this similarity is especially marked. Detached shafts, circular capitals and mouldings of alternating deep hollows and bold round members are almost as general there as here. The masons of the two countries had been trained in the same school, and they continued to work on much the same lines and with similar stone. In plan, Normandy churches of the thirteenth century are very different from our churches. The Normans employed the chevet at Lisieux before the separation came, and this plan they did not abandon until late in the fifteenth century, and then only partially. In other respects—side chapels to nave aisles, for instance—they also followed the Isle de France. As time went on and generation succeeded generation the masons' work changed, and the later mouldings in Normandy bear little resemblance to our fifteenth-century ones.

1200–1250.

Comparison has so frequently been made between Salisbury and Amiens that the present choice of these two cathedrals for this purpose may suggest a lack of imagination. But no others can so well and forcibly bring home the fact that English and French methods of design were proceeding on totally different lines when these two churches were building.[1] They are brothers, but as unlike each other as brothers often are who come of a common stock. Salisbury was commenced by Bishop Poore in 1220 and was finished some forty years later, with the exception of the cloisters (1263–1284), which show the hold tracery had then obtained over the masons, and the central tower and spire, the

Salisbury and Amiens.

---

[1] For plans of these two churches see Figs. 100 and 188. In one respect comparison is unfortunate, as Amiens is the largest of French cathedrals, and the highest except Beauvais, while Salisbury is exceeded in height by York Cathedral and Westminster Abbey, in length by no fewer than nine cathedrals (including old S. Paul's)—Winchester being nearly one hundred feet longer—and in width by six; but the comparison is not so much made as regards size, but as regards design.

greater part of which belongs to the fourteenth century. Amiens was begun in the same year, and although finished earlier had to be partially rebuilt, owing to a fire, as already stated. In the rebuilding, alterations were made in the original design, especially in the clerestory windows, and it is not, therefore, so complete an example of consecutive building as the English church. The choice of Salisbury Cathedral as the chief example of work of the first half of the century possesses this great advantage, that the church was built on a new site, and the builders consequently were not hampered by having to consider old foundations or existing remains. Both plan and general ordinance may therefore be taken as representing the ideals of the English builders of the day. The most noteworthy points about the plan are its absolute symmetry and its rectangularity (see Fig. 100). So much is said about the irregularity of Gothic work, that it is as well to emphasize the fact that when not tied down and restricted by existing surroundings, the mediæval builders adopted plans as symmetrical as any to be found in ancient Rome. The only features which have not their counterparts are the north porch, and the cloisters and chapter house to the south. Salisbury has a nave of ten bays west of the crossing, and a choir and presbytery of seven bays to the east of it, beyond which is a Lady Chapel of four bays, all ending square. The great transepts project three bays beyond the aisles, the smaller transepts two bays. On the east side of both pairs of transepts is an aisle divided into chapels. There are single aisles to nave and choir and no side chapels. Amiens has a nave of seven bays and a choir of four, or five including the apse. Beyond is the semicircular chevet with its radiating chapels. The eastern arm has double aisles, the nave single aisles, beyond which are chapels, and the transepts have an aisle on both sides. The transepts project only one bay beyond the outer choir aisles, and that bay on each side is much narrower than any other in the church (see Fig. 188). There are no eastern transepts. The internal width of Salisbury is 78 feet, exactly half of which is the width of the nave from centre to centre of the piers, the aisles dividing the remaining half. The western arm of Amiens is 103 feet wide, exclusive of chapels, and is divided in the same way. The eastern one is about 155 feet wide, nearly double that of Salisbury. On the other hand, the measurement of Salisbury across the transepts from north to south is 204 feet, which is some 5 feet wider than in the great French church. In total length

Fig. 209.—Salisbury Cathedral.

[*To face p.* 302.

Salisbury also has a slight advantage. From the west wall to the arcade at the back of the high altar—the high portion of the church—is 377 feet, the total length being 450 feet. Amiens, measured from a similar position, is 373 feet to the apse terminating the choir, and 449 feet to the east wall of the Lady Chapel. The total eastern arm in each church is a trifle longer than the western, but as the full height is not maintained for the whole length in either, externally the western arm appears to be longer in both. The differences in proportion become still

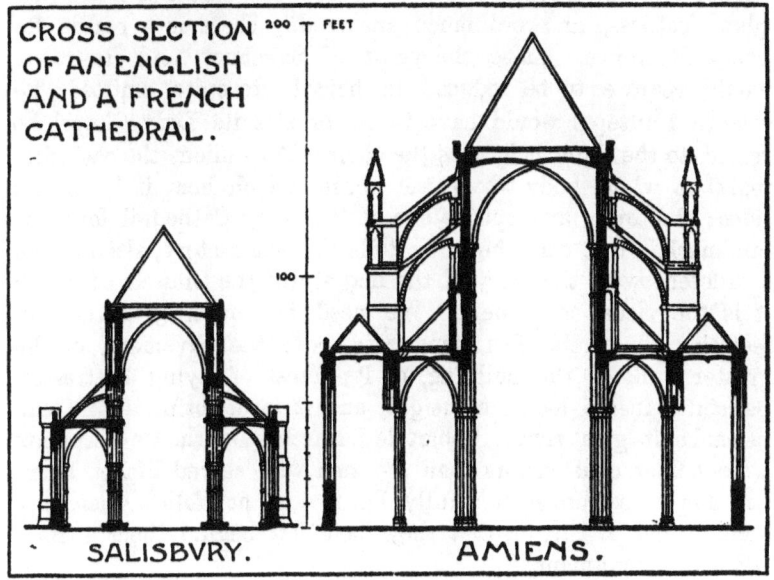

FIG. 210.

more marked when the heights are considered. Amiens, the second highest church in France, is 140 feet high from floor to apex of vault; Salisbury, the third highest in England, is only 84 feet.

The above is sufficient to show how, whilst breadth and height were the aims of the French builders, the English, modest in these respects, relied more on length. The latter could, in consequence, afford to give their main transepts considerable projection and to add eastern transepts. They could carry a stone tower and spire above the crossing, a far more effective feature than the wood and lead flêche of Amiens, although the latter does rise some

20 feet higher than the former. A tower and spire to the latter church, even if possible, would have been a mistake.[1] It would have detracted from rather than added dignity to the outside. No one studying the plan, appearance, and main ordinance of these two churches can doubt for a minute that the ideals advanced on one side of the channel were not those striven for on the other. If it be asked which are right and which wrong, there is only one answer. In art there are no rules, no laws, no absolute right or wrong. Each building is a law to itself and to itself alone. Each should be studied separately; its defects and beauties noted; its plan, features, and ordinance analyzed. There is a reason for every difference. Raise the vault of Salisbury, and its tower would require to be reduced in height, its spire omitted; its eastern transepts would have to go, or else its Lady Chapel be raised to the same height as the choir. At Amiens the cathedral rears its whole body above the houses which hem it in on all sides; the tower and spire alone of Salisbury Cathedral form the landmark. But each building tells the same story, although in a different way, the story of the majesty of the Church, of which it is the visual monument. We need feel no envy of the 140 feet that the vault of Amiens rises above the pavement, of the greater bulk of the building, of its forest of flying buttresses. Salisbury inside looks its height, and it is doubtful if that can be said of its great rival. Robert de Luzarches and the De Cormonts were bolder constructors than the men who served Bishop Poore and his successors so faithfully, but it does not follow that they were bigger artists, or that they have left behind them a more beautiful monument.

West fronts.
The west fronts of English Cathedrals are weak, and Salisbury is no exception to the general rule. In fact, it is one of the least satisfactory, especially when seen sideways. There are no western towers, and a horizontal parapet connects the gable with angle turrets which are poor substitutes for them. At Lincoln, horizontality is still more marked, as on each side of the central gable is a screen which extends far beyond the western towers, which rise behind it, and finishes with turrets similar to those at Salisbury. The two most famous thirteenth-century fronts are Peterboro' with its triple porches, the central one, curiously enough, narrower than the side ones, and Wells (c. 1220). More has

[1] At Beauvais an attempt was made in the sixteenth century at a crowning feature over the crossing, more a dome than a spire, but with dire results.

Photo: Frith & Co.

FIG. 211.—WELLS CATHEDRAL: WEST FRONT.

Photo: Frith & Co.

FIG. 212.—SALISBURY CATHEDRAL, FROM NORTH-EAST.

[*To face p.* 304.

probably been written about the west front of Wells Cathedral than about any part of any other building, mainly because of the beauty of its sculpture, which extends round the towers at the angles as well as along the entire front. The west front is unusually wide for an English Cathedral, because the towers stand entirely beyond the aisle walls, and do not terminate the aisles, the usual custom both in England and abroad. Nothing can be finer in design than the lower part, notwithstanding the insignificance of the doorways. For the smallness of the doorways leading to the aisles there is every excuse; in fact, they are better small, because they give scale—as the small doorway does in the north side of the nave of Westminster Abbey; but the main portal might with advantage have been twice the size, and yet have been none too big. The difference in relative size and importance of French and English entrances is an interesting point of difference in the work of the two countries. Climate can hardly account for it; and Wells is a proof that it was not want of skill on the part of English sculptors which led them to dispense with the many figures in the jambs and the multitude of canopied figures in the arched heads which are so characteristic of French work. Other countries copied the doorways of France, England did not.

The east end of Salisbury spreads itself out over much ground with buildings lower than the bulk of the cathedral behind. Not so Ely Cathedral, which is, perhaps, the finest example of work of the first half of the thirteenth century in England. There the choir and presbytery (c. 1235) are continued their full height to the east wall. In these two cathedrals, therefore, the two methods of eastern ending can be studied (see also pp. 151 and 152). The large window in the gable of Ely Cathedral lights only the roof above the vaulting, and consequently does not show at all inside. At the east end of Lincoln the window which occupies a similar position is even larger. In many of the Yorkshire churches, Selby Abbey, for instance, the top windows are also of considerable size. They add greatly to the external effect, but otherwise are not of much use, as much smaller windows would have given all the light necessary. Additions which were made towards the end of the first half of the century at Durham Cathedral and Fountains Abbey Church show that neither the Benedictine monks of the former nor the Cistercian monks of the latter were desirous of imitating the chevet plan which was general on the continent. At

East ends.

306 A HISTORY OF ARCHITECTURAL DEVELOPMENT.

Durham the Chapel of the Nine Altars (1242-1280) (see Fig. 177), and at Fountains a similar chapel for seven altars, form transepts at the extreme east end, stretching beyond the aisles on either side. In both cases the resemblance in plan to the eastern transepts of some of the large basilican churches in Rome is marked, except that there are no apsidal projections to the eastward in either church similar to those in the earlier basilicas. Cistercian influence is probably responsible, to some extent, for the form these additions took, notwithstanding that Durham Cathedral belonged to the monks of the rival order. The Durham chapel forms a magnificent vaulted hall about 35 feet wide, 127 feet long, and 80 feet high. Its floor is dropped some 6 feet below the choir floor, which accounts for its height being greater than that of the rest of the church. At Fountains the addition is even larger, about 36 feet wide by 132 feet long, but its length is broken by two piers, continuous with those of the choir, which rise to a great height and support arches immediately under the vault. Its effect as a great hall is therefore somewhat impaired, but on the whole the introduction of piers is an improvement.

Other examples. The south transept of York Cathedral (c. 1230) is another contemporary example, and equally fine is the north transept (c. 1250), in which the "Five Sisters" window shows the determination of the English builder to adhere to the tall lancet lights as long as possible, and his disinclination to spoil what he regarded as right proportions by the insertion of traceried heads. Besides its metropolitan church, Yorkshire supplies other interesting work of the period in the ruins of its abbey churches—some Cistercian, as Jervaulx, Rivaulx, etc., commenced towards the end of the twelfth century, and others Benedictine, as Whitby, built early in the following one. The greater portion of Hexham Abbey Church, Northumberland, is also contemporary.

Early English. Between 1180 and 1250 is comprised what is commonly known as Early English. It is the Doric of Gothic architecture. At no other period do the designs show such strength, freshness, simplicity and refinement. There is a stateliness and quiet dignity about everything built between these years which had not been reached before and was never equalled afterwards. The work may not have the vivacity and little fascinations—architectural chiffons —of that of fifty years later, but it possesses other and sounder qualities. Moreover, it is thoroughly English. The steps by which it was evolved are so unmistakable, and can be traced so

Photo: W. A. Mansell & Co.

FIG. 213.—ELY CATHEDRAL: EAST END.

[To face p. 306.

easily, that any student of architecture who knows it, and also preceding work in England and contemporary work in France, can see that its growth was a natural one from local examples, and that it owed little to outside influence. There are no breaks or sudden changes such as would have been perceptible if it had been an importation from outside. Its counterpart, it is true, is sometimes to be met with in Normandy; but in other parts of France the churches show other qualities, not less beautiful and often more advanced, but none the less quite different.

1250–1300.

Two examples, Westminster Abbey and the Angel choir of Lincoln Cathedral, will suffice to demonstrate the characteristics of the architecture of the second half of the century, and wherein it differs from the work of the first half.

Henry III., who is responsible for the rebuilding of Edward the Confessor's Abbey Church at Westminster (c. 1245–1256), took a keen interest in architecture, but he was so much under the thumb of foreigners that his church at Westminster naturally possesses some of the characteristics found mainly in the art of France. That he invariably spoke French is not of much moment, because that tongue was for another century at least the language of the court.[1] The chevet plan of the eastern arm and the main proportions throughout the church point to the employment of a French architect to make the design. The size of the windows (in the clerestory (c. 1253) the lights are each 4 feet wide), the number of flying buttresses (Westminster is the only church in England which has double tiers), and the relative width of wall to column (see comparison with Salisbury, Fig. 17) are also evidence of continental influence. But if the designer was a Frenchman, the masons employed were English. The use of Purbeck marble, the detached shafts round the columns and the moulded bands, the rounded abacus and the detail of capitals, bases, arches, etc., the design of the triforium and wall arcading, the absence of any stilting of the window heads in order to get larger circles above

Westminster Abbey.

---

[1] Until the Great Plague of 1349 all teaching in the better class schools and all pleadings in the law courts were in French. John Richard Green, in his "Short History of the English People," records that in 1362 an order was issued that English was to be used in law cases because "the French tongue is much unknown," and he adds that after 1385 French was abandoned entirely in English Grammar Schools.

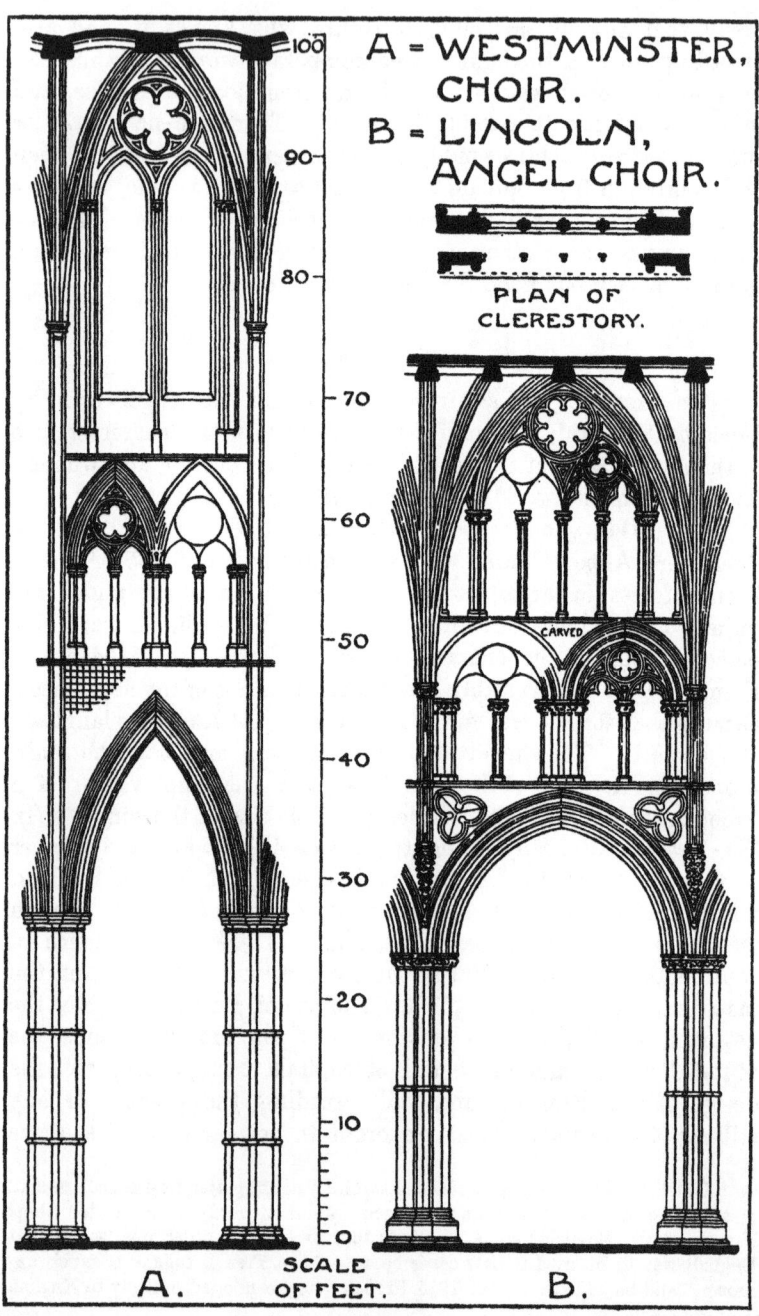

Fig. 214.

the lights, and the diaper-work on the walls, all belong to this country. By the middle of the thirteenth century the English masons had established a tradition, and although willing to adopt features which they felt would be improvements, they were by no means willing to sacrifice others which were to their liking. Westminster Abbey undoubtedly exercised some influence on work immediately following it, although not to any great extent. The clerestory windows of Hereford Cathedral (c. 1260) strongly resemble those in the outer wall of the triforium at Westminster, and the latter may also have suggested the spherical triangles, filled with cusped circles, which form the clerestory windows in Lichfield nave (c. 1275).

The Angel choir or presbytery of Lincoln (c. 1256) follows close on Westminster. Tracery had been tentatively introduced in the triforium arcades of both the transepts (c. 1210) and the nave (c. 1230), but the design of the windows of the presbytery shows a marked improvement on these, and also on the windows at Westminster. If the builders of the extension learnt anything from the latter, they mastered their lesson so thoroughly that they were able to advance far beyond it. They probably knew little or nothing about the other church. Certainly two contemporary examples more unlike it would be difficult to find. At Lincoln the problem was how to improve on the design of the rest of the church and yet make the new work in harmony with the old. The bays of the Angel choir are perhaps the most beautifully proportioned of any in England, and they are as unlike the bays of Westminster as could well be imagined. Each bay in the latter church is 17 feet 6 inches wide from centre to centre of the columns, and the height from the floor to the apex of the arch is about 42 feet. At Lincoln the corresponding dimensions are 23 feet 2 inches by 33 feet 6 inches. The triforium in both examples consists of four openings, grouped in pairs, but the greater width of the bays in the cathedral makes the proportions altogether different. The Westminster triforium is lighted by windows on the outside wall, but Lincoln triforium is dark behind. Triforia in English cathedrals of the thirteenth century and first half of the fourteenth, as a rule, are more important than in contemporary churches abroad. They are not vaulted, as in early French churches, but are covered by lean-to timber roofs, which finish under the clerestory windows. In some cases these roofs are of flat pitch, and the walls of the aisles are raised high above

Angel choir, Lincoln.

their vaults so as to allow of windows above the aisle windows. In the western arm of the Cathedral of Worcester (which is late fourteenth-century work) pairs of windows to each bay light the triforium. The plan is in many respects superior to that in which the roofs are of steeper pitch, and the aisle walls in consequence no higher than the aisles themselves. The extra height given to the side walls is a great gain to the outside; the roofs over the galleries are entirely concealed by parapets; the triforia are well lighted, and a certain amount of subdued light finds its way into the church through its middle storey. At Westminster, the clerestory windows are each of two lights, uncusped, with a foliated circle above; at Lincoln they are each four lights, with three circles above. Moreover, in the cathedral a pierced screen of similar but richer design is repeated on the inside face of the wall behind each window. The vaulting at Lincoln starts unusually low, some feet below the clerestory string-course; that at Westminster starts many feet above it, an exceptional position for England, but common in France. The general effect would probably have been better at Lincoln if the vault had been raised, but its apex was fixed by the earlier vault alongside it.

Churches of the Fourteenth and Fifteenth Centuries.

Introduction. With the thirteenth century departed much of the virility which distinguishes the first phases of Gothic art in England. Much good work continued to be done, work far more elaborate than anything which had been attempted before, but lacking the rare charm and simple directness of that which preceded it. For this, social changes and national calamities are largely responsible, although in all art movements a period of advance is invariably followed by a gradual decline, just as daylight breaks, expands, and then wanes. The preaching of Wyclif and the consequent agitation of the Lollards caused dissension and weakness in the Church. A series of years of famine was followed by the Black Death in 1349, a scourge which, it is estimated, destroyed more than one-half of the population. It affected all classes. The farmers were unable to till the land and gather the crops for want of labour; prices rose considerably because of the amount of land thrown out of cultivation, and all workers, whilst having to pay a far higher price for the necessities of life, were forbidden by law to demand a higher wage than that which had been customary before the pestilence came. The effects of the Black Death would not have been so disastrous, and recovery would have been more rapid but for the continuous wars abroad, and the constant demands on the people's purse which their prosecution entailed. The unrest throughout the land was exemplified by the peasant revolt of 1381. Early in the fifteenth century the victory of Henry V. at Agincourt brought glory to the king, but little profit to the people. The latter part of the century witnessed the War of the Roses, but this had not the paralyzing effect on commerce and trade that civil war generally entails, as it was a Barons' struggle in which the people took little part. No century, hardly any decade, in the Middle Ages passed without insurrections or wars, and those of the fourteenth and fifteenth centuries damaged architecture far less than the Black Death. The extent of cathedral and abbey church building was less than in the previous centuries, because early activity had left little to be done in that direction. But there was by no means stagnation in ecclesiastical centres; only their energy took another form. The number and size of parish churches increased to an extraordinary extent. No king interested himself strongly in church architecture after Henry III., but many bishops, such as William of Edington and William Wykeham, both of Winchester, were as keen on having their churches beautiful and up to date as any of their predecessors. The clergy, outside those of high position, were poor, and the monastic orders indifferent, but another race of donors was springing up. Increase in trade had brought great wealth to the merchants and others of the middle class, and many were willing to spend it royally. The rich burgesses had no doubt subscribed freely in the past, but not to the same extent as their descendants did in the fifteenth century. At Lavenham, Suffolk, the greater part of the cost of the church was defrayed by a wealthy clothier named Spring, and evidence of secular generosity, as well as anxiety for the welfare of their souls, is shown in the chantry chapels erected in many of our churches and cathedrals at the expense of laymen. The fourteenth century is perhaps more noteworthy for its castellated architecture than for its ecclesiastical. No cathedral was commenced after the thirteenth century, and none illustrates the characteristics of either fourteenth or fifteenth century Gothic so thoroughly as Salisbury and Lincoln do those of the first and second halves respectively of the previous one. But although none was begun, such extensive remodelling was carried out at

312   A HISTORY OF ARCHITECTURAL DEVELOPMENT.

Exeter in the fourteenth, and at York and Winchester in the same and the following century, as almost to amount to entire rebuildings.

<small>Absence of conservatism.</small>

Up to the end of the thirteenth century a certain amount of respect for earlier efforts is noticeable in additions, and a desire to harmonize new work with old; but in much subsequent building a total disregard of what existed becomes apparent, and a determination to obliterate it at all costs. Thus, at Gloucester (c. 1340-1350), the monks, unable to afford to take down bodily and rebuild the sturdy walls and piers of their predecessors, nevertheless went to great expense to conceal them with a veneer. They did take down the eastern apse, and beyond it built a magnificent east window, cleverly planned with slightly canted sides to rest on the walls of the old ambulatory. A more conservative spirit was shown in the naves of Worcester Cathedral and Westminster Abbey. In the former a most creditable attempt was made to follow the very beautiful earlier work of the retro-choir. The bays on the north side were built first c. 1320), and are better than those on the south side, which followed some fifty years later. On both sides the capitals have circular abaci—an unusual form at this period—and, like those of the presbytery, are of Purbeck marble. The design of the triforium of the eastern arm is also repeated in the western, with some modifications, the most important being the omission of the Purbeck marble shafts which are such a feature in the earlier work. In the nave of Westminster Abbey, commenced 1350, but not finished until some seventy years later, absolute harmony with the choir was obtained, although differences in detail are apparent to those who look for them. The columns are surrounded by attached shafts, not detached ones as in the eastern arm, and the capitals and bases are octagonal in plan and not circular. The bands which bind the shafts to the columns in the earlier work are retained, and their presence may be forgiven, as, although no longer needed, they help to produce a uniformity of design throughout, which few large churches in England built at different times present.

<small>Exeter Cathedral.</small>

Exeter Cathedral may be taken as a fairly complete and representative example of fourteenth-century work, although its foundations and portions of its superstructure belong to the earlier church which was built at the same time as the Norman towers which still stand over the transepts. Owing to the lateral position of these, the piers at the crossing are no larger than those of the nave and choir, and consequently there is no break in the arcade. It is this, coupled with the continuous vault, that makes the church appear too low, and not so much its actual want of height (see table, p. 376). Its lowness would be far more marked if it were not for the screen and organ which luckily stand at the entrance to the choir—by far the most dignified position for an organ—thus giving scale, and at the same time providing a break in the length where one is most needed. The proportions noticeable inside are still more remarkable outside, especially at the west end, and at the east where the Salisbury plan of a low retro-choir and Lady Chapel is followed. The design of the west front shows a determination to sacrifice height to breadth which is never met with in Gothic churches abroad. The battlemented parapet of the

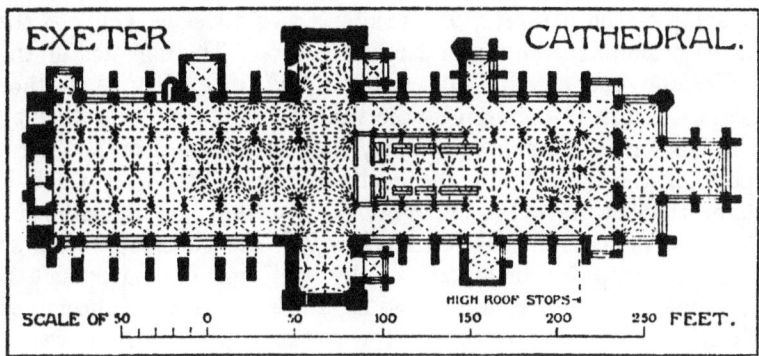

FIG. 215.

main roof is continued horizontally across the front, the gable standing back some feet behind it. It is also returned on the rake down the sides, masking the aisles, with not a very happy result. The front would doubtless have looked better if it had not been for the porch, added in the fifteenth century, which extends across the full width and forms another horizontal division. The builders of Exeter were consistent throughout. In all the windows the lights are unusually short for the traceried heads above them. In the west window the great decorated circle reaches from the springing of the window arch almost to the apex, whilst the tracery of the lights starts well below the springing-line.

Contemporary with Exeter Cathedral are the nave of York (c. 1300–1338), the choir, etc., of Lichfield (c. 1330), and the presbytery and Lady Chapel of Wells (c. 1326–1363). All three show

Omission of triforium.

a disposition towards a dual rather than a triple division of the side walls, but only in Lichfield choir is the triforium absolutely abandoned.[1] At Wells there is no string-course above the arcade, a network of panelling filling the spandrils between the arches and reaching to the sills of the clerestory windows. The effect, although rich, is hardly satisfactory. At York the triforium is recessed, and the mullions of the clerestory windows, which are near the inside face of the wall, are continued down to the string above the main arcade to form its divisions. In Lichfield choir the design is somewhat similar, but the effect more marked, as the window is set near the outside face. The passage way above the arcade is retained, and is, moreover, protected by a pierced parapet, but the panelled wall behind it is flush with the windows above, the jambs of which run down to the top of the parapet. The result is two divisions, and not the three hitherto customary in large churches. The omission of the triforium undoubtedly adds height, and verticality is further emphasized in this church by the vaulting shafts, which, following the custom in Romanesque days, start from the floor and form part of the piers.[2] In the choir of York Cathedral, which is later than the nave, the triple division survives, and the triforium has a string-course above and below it. The clerestory windows are flush with the inner face of the wall, and on the outside is a pierced screen. Similar screens are by no means uncommon in fifteenth-century Gothic.[3] The earlier English custom was to have a screen on the inside, as in Lincoln Angel Choir, the windows being placed near the outside face, and this was also sometimes done in late work, as in Melrose Abbey Church, Scotland, and in the great east window of York. The design of the triforium of York choir is much the same as in French cathedrals with glazed triforia, except that the wall behind, although pierced, is not glazed.

[1] In parish churches and in many abbey churches of fair size, such as Boxgrove, Sussex (c. 1235), Pershore, Worcestershire (c. 1230), there is no triforium gallery. The change recorded in cathedral ordinance is, therefore, only an adoption of what had hitherto been general in smaller churches.

[2] At York the vaulting shafts also start from the floor, but alas! save for the tas-de-charge, which is stone, the vault is only of wood. Judging by the size of the flying buttresses outside, which are broken away, no other material would be possible. They are absurdly small as compared with those of Amiens, for instance, which has a vault of the same width.

[3] In the choir of the Cathedral of Sées, Normandy, the clerestory windows have screens on the outside (c. 1330), but the design was not a favourite one with French architects as a rule.

Photo: *J. Valentine & Co.*

FIG. 216.—YORK CATHEDRAL.

[*To face p.* 314.

Photo: Dr. A. G. C. Gwyer.

FIG. 217.—ELY CATHEDRAL: INTERIOR OF LANTERN.

[To face p. 315.

Glazed triforia on the French model, with glass on the outside face and pierced arcading inside, were never popular in England.[1]

The unique feature of the fourteenth century is the lantern of Ely Cathedral. In 1322 the old Norman tower at the crossing fell, bringing down with it the neighbouring bays of the choir, which at that time extended west of it into the nave. To have rebuilt the tower would have necessitated new foundations, and Alan of Walsingham, the sacrist of the cathedral, was probably afraid that the fate that befell the old one might be in store for a new. He, or some one employed by him, therefore hit on the happy idea of covering the ruined area by an octagonal lantern the full width of the church. This necessitated strengthening eight of the existing piers, a less difficult feat than building four new ones. The lantern of Ely measures about 68 feet from north to south, and about 65 feet from east to west. The canted sides are shorter than the cardinal ones, and each is pierced by a large traceried window. Light, in addition, comes from the lantern proper above the wood vault. This lantern is also of wood, covered with lead, and although stated by some to be a temporary makeshift it seems difficult to believe that any more solid superstructure can ever have been intended, or that stone was ever contemplated for the vaulting below. Timber vaults in imitation of stone ones were not uncommon in English churches after the middle of the thirteenth century. At York the octagonal chapter house (c. 1300), which unlike other chapter houses in England has no central column, is vaulted in wood. Its width is only 45 feet, and if the York builders hesitated to build a vault of stone over it, how much greater must have been the disinclination of the Ely ones to use that material at a far greater height over a much wider span. *Ely lantern.*

The choir of York (c. 1380–1405) and the naves of Canterbury (c. 1379–1400) and Winchester (c. 1371–1460) form the connecting links between the fourteenth and fifteenth centuries. The fashion started at Gloucester in the middle of the fourteenth century, of perpendicular panel design for both windows and walls, was adopted generally, although in some cases more thoroughly than in others. At Canterbury the window tracery has vertical lines, but there is very little panelling on the walls. At Winchester, on the other hand, the west front is covered with it. This method of ornamentation reached its climax in Henry VII.'s *Fifteenth century.*

---

[1] I cannot remember a single instance in which they form part of the original design, although in some churches the triforia have been glazed later.

Fig. 218.—Winchester Cathedral, as originally designed.

Fig. 219.—Winchester Cathedral, as altered by William of Wykeham.

Chapel, Westminster, where no plain surfaces are left anywhere, either inside or out. In the remodelling of the nave of Winchester by William of Wykeham (bishop 1367–1404), a great improvement was effected in the internal proportions. In the old Norman church the three divisions of arcade, triforium, and clerestory were approximately equal in height. The bishop raised his piers to the level of the floor of the triforium, abolished the triforium itself, whilst retaining a passage gallery higher up, and panelled the wall at the sides of and below the clerestory windows. The arches of the main arcade he made four-centred, but they are not so flat as later ones of similar shape, and consequently do not look weak. Over the arches runs a boldly carved and moulded string-course which forms a strong division between the upper and lower storeys.

The latter half of the fifteenth century saw the beginning of the end of Gothic art in England. But what an end, what a blaze of glory for a finish! English Gothic did not flicker and linger and drag out an inglorious life; but still full of strength and vigour it laid itself down with majesty and pomp, with all the trappings of carving, sculpture, and colour, and surrounded by a richness and wealth of ornament such as never had been known before or has been equalled since. Between 1450 and 1520 some of the most remarkable of English ecclesiastical buildings were built. Little was done to cathedrals, except to finish a tower, as at Canterbury, or to add chantry chapels, outside, as at Lincoln Cathedral, inside, between the columns, as at Winchester. Bath Abbey Church (c. 1500–1539) is the only large monastic church commenced after the middle of the fifteenth century, but extensive alterations were made to Malvern Priory Church (1450–1486) and to the Abbey Church of Sherborne (1436–1504), where the nave piers and arches are richly panelled, and the vault a fan one.

But in place of cathedral and abbey church are a number of chapels, royal and collegiate, which if inferior in size to the earlier churches, surpass them in richness. The most famous are King's College Chapel, Cambridge (1446–1461), the fan vault not being finished until early in the sixteenth century. S. George's, Windsor (1481–1537), Eton College Chapel (contemporary with King's, Cambridge), and Henry VII.'s Chapel, Westminster, finished by his successor a few years after his death. The metal screen surrounding his tomb is almost the last word in really fine English mediæval craftsmanship. The Italian sculptors were

Chapels.

318 *A HISTORY OF ARCHITECTURAL DEVELOPMENT.*

knocking at the door, and the tomb itself is the work of Torregiano, the best known of the first batch of foreigners who came to our shores.

Henry VII.'s chapel, with its side chapels, is almost a church

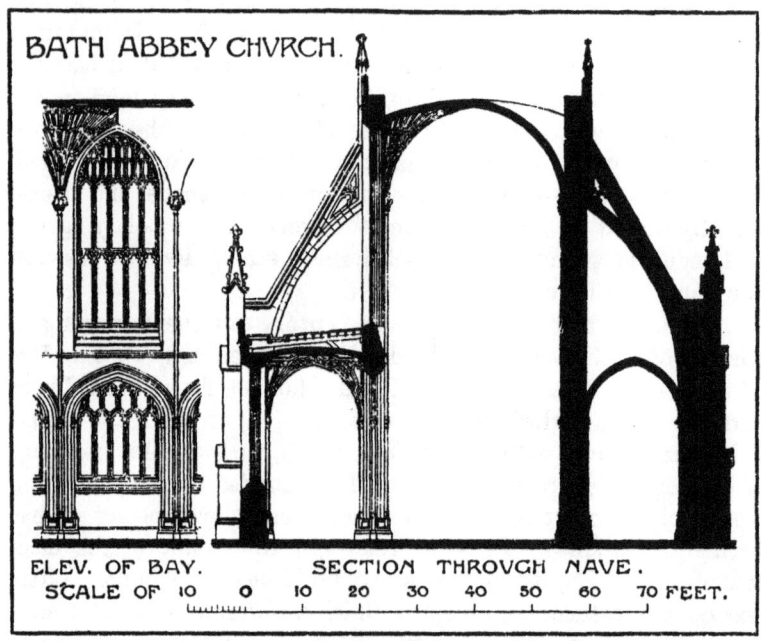

Fig. 220.

in itself, and the same may be said of the Royal Chapel at Windsor. King's College Chapel is a chapel pure and simple, as although it has low aisles, which form side chapels, these are cut off from the main body. The latter forms a magnificent hall, 45 feet wide, 284 feet long, and 81 feet high, vaulted with one of the most successful fan vaults in England, because it is one of the simplest. Unlike most vaulted buildings, the windows do not reach to the apex of the vault, their heads being little higher than its springing, and the spaces over them are filled with sunk panelling. The chapel might have been barrel vaulted, with but little alteration in external design, and if the treatment of the vault had been similar to that over the little chapel of Abbotsbury, Dorset, an effect perhaps finer than that now produced might have resulted.

The end. Little did the workmen who built and gloried in these sumptuous chapels dream that in a decade or two an art revolution would take place in England, and that the methods and ideals they believed in and followed would be counted as barbarous. The revolution had already taken place in Italy, but it is doubtful if Brunelleschi's triumph at Florence had reached their ears, and even if it had, it was probably merely regarded as "just foreign nonsense." The Pope at Rome was planning S. Peter's when the vault of King's College was nearing completion, and although the wood stalls below the latter show that a few years later the old order was giving place to new, there is no trace of foreign innovations in the masonry of the chapel. Mediæval art was dead and buried before the sixteenth century was a quarter over, but its spirit still walked abroad. As late as the middle of the following

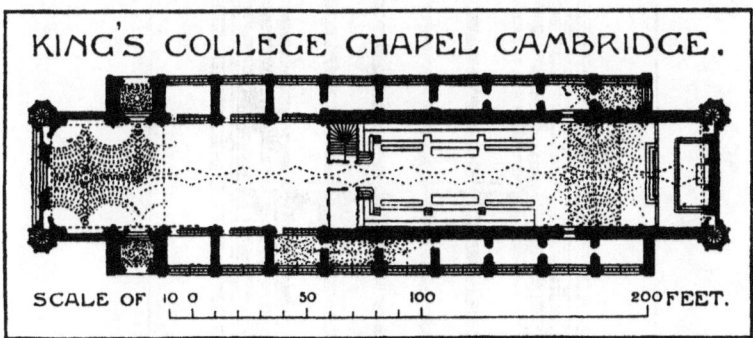

FIG. 221.

century, the papist leanings of Archbishop Laud caused the church of S. John the Baptist, Leeds, to be built in a manner which, externally, at least, recalls the work of two hundred years before. Many seventeenth-century dates on porches, over windows, etc., show that when alterations and additions were needed, an attempt was made to harmonize the new work with the old. Small buildings, such as the chapel of the Whitgift Almshouses at Croydon, the end window of which is dated 1597, still had Gothic detail, and not such bad Gothic either. At conservative Oxford, the old traditions held the field longer than in any other town—the college of Christ Church being a notable instance—and in outlying country districts the people continued to build their cottages, farmhouses, and small manor houses in much the same way as their forefathers had done, and with but little difference in detail. In fact, the Gothic spirit lingered in England until, strange irony of fate, it

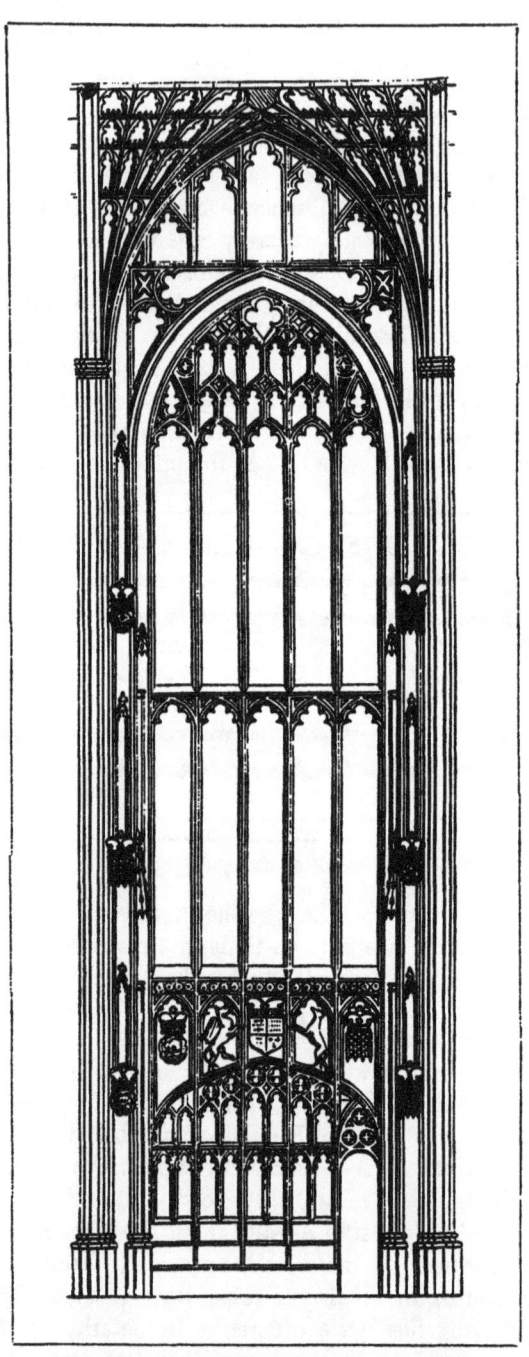

FIG. 222.— King's College Chapel, Cambridge.

was destroyed by the movement in favour of a Gothic revival. An insistence on the letter of the style then cut the threads of a tradition which had descended from father to son for generations, and the Gothic and Greek revivals between them destroyed the last vestiges of vernacular art.

Scotland.

Brief mention only can be made of mediæval church work in Scotland, although it possesses many examples, some intact and more in ruins, of great interest. The Irish church, which was so powerful there in the sixth century and in the one following, had sunk almost into oblivion before the eleventh was reached, and consequently exercised no influence on later work. The Romanesque of Normandy did not reach the country until after the end of the eleventh century, and it continued later than in England, so Scotland can hardly be said to have assisted architectural development to any extent at either the Romanesque or the early Gothic period. There was considerable building activity during the thirteenth century—activity often occasioned by English misdeeds—but in the fourteenth there was a lull. During these two centuries Scottish architecture proceeded on much the same lines as in England, although often little mannerisms show the independence of the country and its workmen. In the fifteenth century, the close friendship between France and Scotland, a friendship which extended for another hundred years or more, led to the introduction of a few French traits apparent in some of the late work.

The paucity of examples remaining intact in the southern part of the country is mainly due to the numerous forays of the English kings. Near the border hardly a single abbey was not sacked at least once, some more often, and many were never rebuilt. The four principal abbey churches of the Lowlands— Kelso, Jedburgh, Dryburgh, and Melrose—are ruins. But they are none the less interesting because of that. In fact, their present state enhances their value to a student of architecture, because they afford him a peep behind the scenes and an opportunity of studying construction which, in a building roofed in and intact, is generally hidden. The four churches mentioned are excellent examples of different periods, and in them architectural progression can be as well studied as in any group in England equally close together, except, perhaps, the famous one in the west which includes the churches of Tewkesbury, Gloucester, Hereford, Malvern, Wells, and Bath.

Kelso.

Kelso Abbey is the earliest. It was founded in 1128. All the arches are semicircular, except those supporting the remains of the tower, which are later in date and pointed. The chief peculiarity of the church is the exceeding shortness of the nave. This, like each of the transepts, consists merely of a single square. The monks evidently saw no reason why they should provide for the religious wants of the people, but were by no means niggardly in providing for their own. They made amends for the shortness of the nave by the length of the choir.

Jedburgh and Dryburgh.

Jedburgh Abbey Church is architecturally the most interesting on the Scottish border, although it has not the glamour which has been cast over Melrose. The two westernmost bays of the choir and the west wall of the nave are the oldest portions (c. 1150). The design of these choir bays is similar to that in some of the bays of Romsey Abbey Church. A lofty cylindrical column rises from the ground to the springing of the arches above the triforium, the arches of the main arcade cutting into its side. The nave of the church is an exceedingly fine example of simple sturdy work of the last decade or two of the twelfth century, rendered all the more attractive by being in ruins. The remains of Dryburgh Abbey are of different dates, but the most interesting portions belong to the latter half of the thirteenth century. The builders were evidently of two minds regarding the triforium of the church. They did not wish to follow the Cistercian example and omit it altogether, and yet they were anxious not to cramp the dimensions of their top and bottom storeys by giving it too much space. The only openings in it are foliated circles, enclosed by arched heads and moulded jambs, one circle to each bay.

Melrose.

Melrose suffered more perhaps than any other abbey from English incursions, and the last, in the sixteenth century, proved fatal to it. The greater part of what is now standing belongs to a rebuilding after 1385, and to additions made in the fifteenth century. The plan of the church is somewhat curious for so late a date, but is probably accounted for by the fact that the monks had neither time nor money to spend in sinking new foundations, and so in their rebuildings did not extend beyond the old. The arm east of the crossing consists merely of two

FIG. 223.—JEDBURGH ABBEY CHURCH: CHOIR.

Photo: G. W. Wilson.

FIG. 224.—JEDBURGH ABBEY CHURCH: NAVE.   [*To face p.* 322.

aisled bays, and one square additional bay without aisles. The choir aisles really project only one bay beyond the transepts as each of the latter has an aisle on its east side. The result of the shortness of the eastern part of the church is that the choir extended three bays into the nave, as in Romanesque churches in England and Normandy. The whole of the south aisle of the nave is lined by chapels. This French trait in planning, which is never met with in English churches, is evidence of the strong sympathy existing between France and Scotland. There is also a suspicion of French influence in the tracery of some of the windows, but most of these follow the perpendicular treatment of contemporary English ones. The web of the vaulting in the side chapels is built with parallel courses, and it speaks well for the skill of the masons, and is also an argument against the necessity for vaulting ribs, that whilst many of the ribs have fallen the web remains standing.

Glasgow Cathedral is the most important mediæval church in Scotland. It is especially famous for its crypt, or under church, which extends over the whole of the eastern arm of the church proper, and has no equal in England, probably none in Europe. The rapid fall of the ground towards the east afforded the opportunity for this unusual feature. The high portion of the choir above stops short of the extreme end, and behind the high altar are two aisles, side by side, divided from one another by columns. These are low, being little higher than the side aisles of the choir, and although they stand up well outside, owing to being raised above the crypt, they have not inside the dignity and distinction which the lofty eastern transepts of Durham Cathedral and Fountains Abbey Church possess.

Glasgow Cathedral.

CHAPTER XIX.

GOTHIC ARCHITECTURE IN GERMANY, BELGIUM AND HOLLAND.

Introduction. So long as the Hohenstaufen dynasty ruled over Germany, the builders clung to the traditions of their forefathers, and, heedless of the changes taking place in the architecture of other countries, continued to build churches, as at Bamberg, Bacharach, Naumburg, etc., practically identical with those of a hundred years before. In the Cathedral of Limburg-on-the-Lahn (c. 1210–1240) the influence of the French Cathedrals of Laon and Noyon is seen in the internal proportions, double triforia, etc., but externally the design shows little trace of the new movement. When the abovementioned dynasty came to an end in 1254, the crown was made elective, and direct heredity became more an obstacle to succession than a help. Constant wars followed between rival claimants and their supporters, and the country, for a long period, was split up into what were virtually a number of separate kingdoms, the larger cities also claiming an independence which they had not possessed before. The Hohenstaufen rulers had spent so much time in their Italian domains, that they had individually done little to advance architecture in their native country, but under them their dominion was at least united, and one style of architecture was general, although it was a somewhat obsolete one. Such was not the case during the long period that followed. In France and England, Romanesque architecture passed into Gothic by a natural and gradual process of evolution. It was different in Germany, especially in the centre and the south. The problem of transforming the heavy Romanesque art into something lighter and more graceful had been solved in France before the Teuton builders dreamt of attempting it. Original effort on their part was therefore unnecessary. In addition, the confusion in government which reigned in Germany during the thirteenth century and in the following one, made a national development an impossibility. No wonder, therefore, when the need for change became apparent on the Rhine, that the builders turned for help to the country whose art occupied the most commanding position in the civilized world. It is a thousand pities that they did so. Their forefathers had carried Romanesque architecture so far, and had produced such exceedingly fine work, that if the old instinct had not been dead, a school of Gothic, more robust and less adventurous than that of France, might have arisen in the old empire worthy to rank with that more to the west. Even if the Germans had been content to take the Cathedral of Chartres, or of Reims, as their model, instead of Amiens, the sudden transition would not have been so great. But Amiens loomed tall on the horizon, in more senses than one; its fame had spread all over Western Christendom; it was the last word that had been spoken; and so the good men of Cologne threw to the winds their old traditions, and German architecture started afresh on entirely different lines. Cologne Cathedral was not quite the first church to be built in the French fashion, but, owing to its size and importance, it exercised an influence on subsequent work which no number of smaller examples could have done.

One of the earliest and at the same time most perfect of fully-developed Gothic churches in Germany is the Liebfrauenkirche at Trier (c. 1240). Built on the foundations of a circular building, by a clever disposition of side chapels, it appears cruciform externally, and yet preserves approximately the plan of the older building. The plan of the chapels at both ends is the same as at the east end of the Church of S. Yved, Braisne, near Soissons (France), consecrated 1216, which has an oblong nave. The church at Xanten, Germany (c. 1210) has a similarly planned east end. It is not a chevet, inasmuch as there is no ambulatory, but the chapels radiate, and the perspective effects are exceedingly good. The Liebfrauenkirche has no triforium, the columns are lofty (35 feet high), and the internal proportions throughout are excellent. This church is merely one of many which prove the wisdom of the German builders in so frequently omitting the middle storey. The main arms are 30 feet wide and the vault over 80 feet high, very respectable dimensions.

Liebfrauenkirche, Trier.

The foundation stone of Cologne Cathedral was laid in 1248, the only part of the church commenced being the eastern arm. Even in that the work progressed but slowly, and the choir was not ready for consecration until 1322. The transepts and nave

Cologne Cathedral.

were then proceeded with, but funds failed, and, when half finished, they were covered over for service and left. The unfinished portions soon fell into decay, and it was not until the last century that the church was completed. The eastern arm is therefore the only part that belongs properly to the Middle Ages. The original design for the rest existed and was followed, but the mediæval builders cannot be blamed for its present unsatisfactory appearance. The

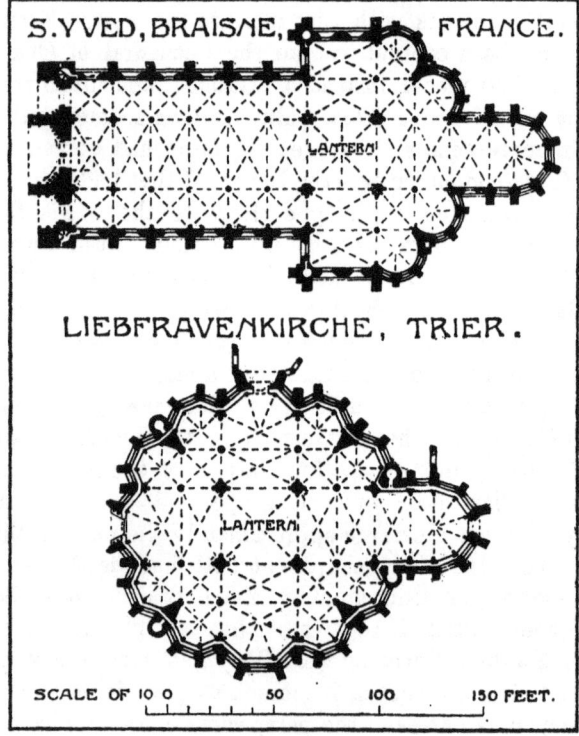

Fig. 225.

eastern arm is almost an exact replica of Amiens Cathedral. The dimensions are the same, and the design of the aisle windows of the chevet is practically identical. The plainness of the lower storey acts as a pleasant foil to the later and richer work above. Apart from the florid character of the latter, little fault can be found with the east end. It is reminiscent of Amiens and Reims, and its great width and height, its broken outline, and elaborate panelled and crocketted buttresses, produce an extremely imposing

GOTHIC ARCHITECTURE IN GERMANY, BELGIUM, ETC.

effect. The western arm is practically the same length as at Amiens; but it has double aisles instead of single, the gigantic western towers occupy two of its bays on each side, their buttresses projecting in all directions, and each transept has one more bay than in the other church. The result outside of these alterations to the French plan is deplorable. The nave, from most points of view, is swallowed up; only three whole bays stand clear between the aisles of the transepts and the towers (as the end bays east and west are cut into by buttresses), and the towers are so large, so

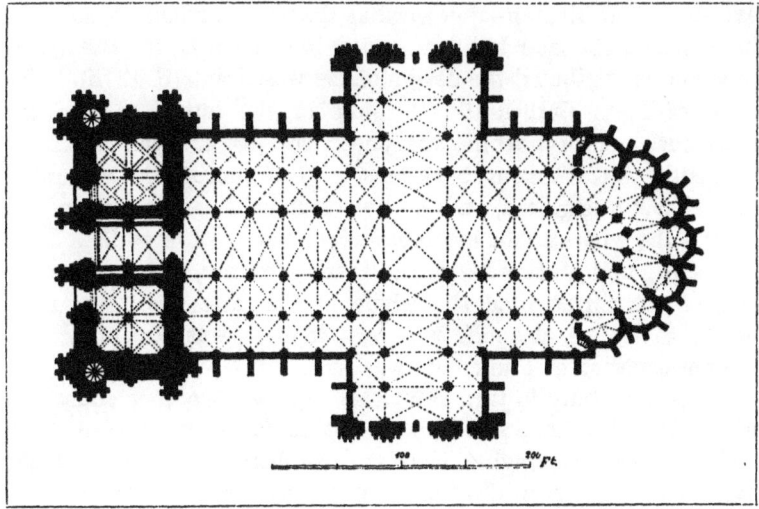

FIG. 226.—Cologne Cathedral.

close together, and spread out so much that, except when immediately facing them, they appear to touch. At Nôtre Dame, Paris, the western towers also occupy two bays, but the full width of the nave is retained between them, and their buttresses are not allowed to straggle as at Cologne.[1] The interior is more satisfactory than the outside, because, notwithstanding that the vault rises 150 feet from the floor, and that the double aisles of the nave detract somewhat from its apparent length, the tower-bays count in the length, the break at the crossing is not marked, and

---

[1] Cologne shows that the Frenchmen, in keeping the towers of Amiens Cathedral comparatively low, were not so wrong after all. It is better that the nave should dwarf the towers than that the towers should completely destroy the nave.

328 *A HISTORY OF ARCHITECTURAL DEVELOPMENT.*

the church as a whole appears long enough. The clerestory windows are of great size, and together with the triforium, which is glazed, take up more than half of the height. The outer aisles are the same height as the inner ones (63 feet), which is unnecessarily high for the outer aisles and not sufficient for the inner. If the gradation of Bourges Cathedral had been followed, the extra 25 feet in height of Cologne might have produced still finer proportions than in the French church.

Other French plans.

Strassburg and Metz are, after Cologne, the most important of German churches designed on French lines. In the former, the extremely fine Romanesque work at the east end had no sobering influence on the later builders, certainly none on E. von Steinbach, to whom is attributed the design of the west front (c. 1275). The nave of Metz Cathedral was built in the latter part of the fourteenth century, whilst the choir was not finished until the sixteenth. It is amongst the most airy of continental examples. The triforium is glazed, and the huge four-light clerestory windows occupy the whole of the available upper part of the walls. Both Strassburg and Metz were on the French frontier, and the western arm of the former and the whole of the latter architecturally belong to France, although the work in both was executed after the finest period of French art was past.

Typical German plans.

It is a pleasure to turn from these to two types of church in which French influence, if apparent at all, is in entire subjection, and the work thoroughly German. In both types most of the churches are of brick. Even the piers, mullions and tracery-bars of windows, and string-courses are of this material, which accounts to some extent for the differences between them and the German churches with French prototypes, just described. The churches of the first type follow the customary ordinance of a high nave and lower side-aisles, whilst those of the second have their nave and aisles equal, or approximately equal in height. The majority of the examples of both classes are in Northern Germany, where the power of the Hanseatic League in the fourteenth century gave an importance to towns and an independence to their inhabitants far greater than existed in either France or England.

First type.

The earliest and most important of churches of the first type is the Marienkirche, Lübeck (c. 1275). There is no dependence on French models here. The sturdy brick flying buttresses are very different from the more ornate and lighter contemporary stone ones elsewhere, and are even more effective. The church was

GOTHIC ARCHITECTURE IN GERMANY, BELGIUM, ETC. 329

built by the townsfolk for themselves, and the plan is as simple as the general ordinance. There is no triforium, and

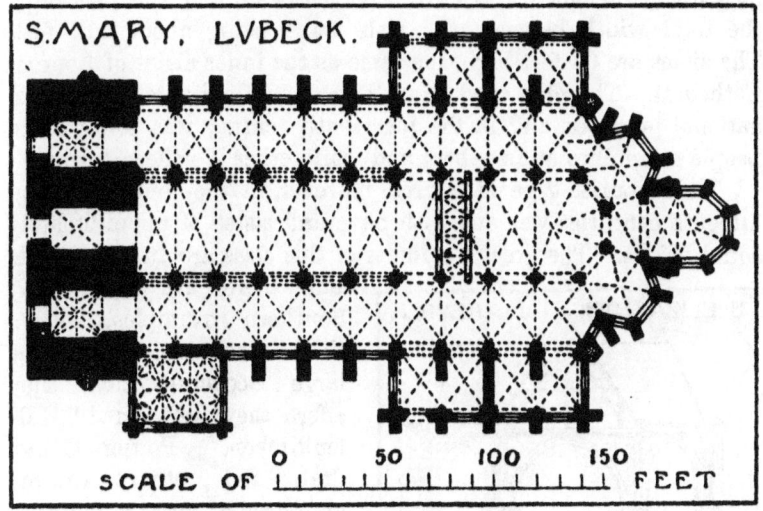

Fig. 227.

the lofty clerestory windows are carried down to the string-course

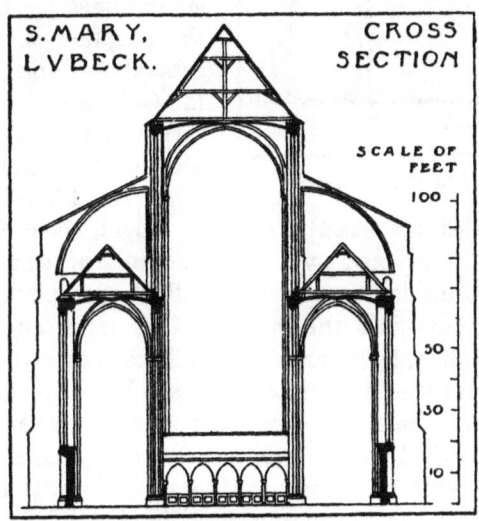

Fig. 228.

above the arcade, the aisle roof each side being a double-pitched one to allow of this. The church is worthy to rank in size with

Hallen-kirchen.

the first-class cathedrals of Northern France, except that it is short. Still, as there are no transepts, and no break in the vault, the length is sufficient. The nave is 41 feet wide and 125 feet high, the total width between the aisle walls being about 112 feet. The aisles are 67 feet high, the same as the inner aisles of Bourges Cathedral. The plan of S. Mary's was found suitable for congregational purposes, and in the fourteenth century was followed in people's churches at Lüneberg and many other Northern towns.

The favourite type of church, however, in the fourteenth and fifteenth centuries was one with nave and aisles of approximately equal height. The greater number of this class are in the North, but there are also many Southern examples. From their spaciousness and the large accommodation they afford they are termed "Hallenkirchen." Poitiers Cathedral, and other vaulted churches of less importance in Southern France, had earlier been built on somewhat similar lines, but nowhere was the adoption of this plan so general for large churches as in Germany. One of the earliest and best-known examples is S. Elizabeth, Marburg (c. 1235-1283). The nave and aisles are exactly equal in height, about 68 feet, the central vault is covered by a high-pitched roof, whilst each bay of the aisles has its own roof of still steeper pitch, hipped in front, which cuts into the main roof at right angles. In its method of roofing, however, it differs from most other examples of the Hallenkirchen type, in which a single roof spans both nave and aisles. In some churches, such as S. Severus, Erfurt, and S. James, Lübeck, there are double aisles, and yet one roof suffices to cover the whole. Vienna Cathedral, S. Peter's, Lübeck, etc., also differ from the Marburg church in that in each the aisles are somewhat lower than the nave, the vault of the latter starting about on a level with the apex of the side vaults. All these churches are perforce lighted from the aisles, although small

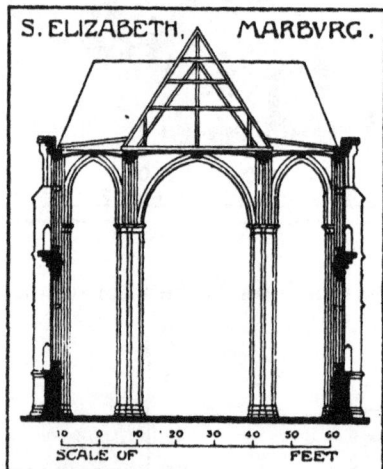

FIG. 229.

GOTHIC ARCHITECTURE IN GERMANY, BELGIUM, ETC. 331

clerestories might have been managed at Vienna and Lübeck, if it had not been for the single roof.

In fourteenth and fifteenth-century churches which have clerestories and lean-to roofs over the aisles, there are seldom triforia, notwithstanding that the space between the arcades inside and the windows above is considerable. This is especially marked at Ulm Cathedral (c. 1377). This church has an exceedingly lofty nave, nearly 140 feet high, and as the aisles are 50 feet

Absence of triforia.

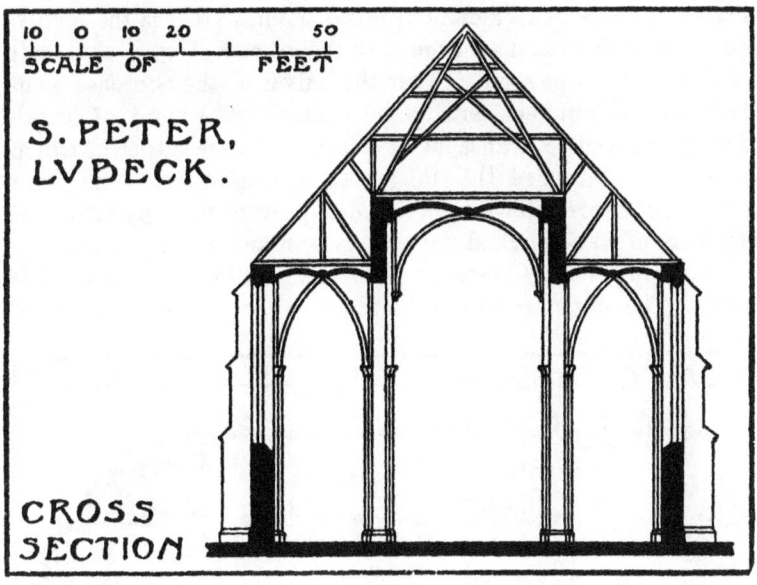

FIG. 230.

wide,[1] and the lean-to roofs over them unusually steep, there is a space of about 40 feet each side, between the top of the arcade and the window-sills, which is unbroken, except by the vaulting shafts which split it up into bays. The German builders were ever averse to the middle storey, and much may be said for their dislike of it—a dislike which the later builders of other countries evidently shared. They omitted it generally in their Romanesque churches, in their later churches of S. Mary, Lübeck, type, and therefore may be said to have been consistent throughout. But 40 feet of plain wall is sufficient to crush in appearance any

[1] At the beginning of the sixteenth century the aisles were each divided into two by columns, so the church has now double aisles.

332   A HISTORY OF ARCHITECTURAL DEVELOPMENT.

arcade below it, and this has been the effect at Ulm. In smaller churches, such as the Lorenzkirche, Nürnberg, the treatment is not open to the same objection, as the space is so much less in height.

Faults.   One of the chief faults of many German churches is the careless manner in which the nave and choir roofs are united. In the Lorenzkirche, Nürnberg, one roof at the east end covers both choir and aisles, and rises far higher than that at the west, which is over the nave only. At S. Sebald's, in the same town, a similar mistake is made. In Vienna Cathedral the nave roof is the higher, and the considerable drop from it to the lower roof over the choir is exceedingly unpleasant. That the halves of the churches mentioned are of different date is no excuse. The want of length no doubt prevented transepts or a central tower, either of which would have concealed the differences in height, but some other means might surely have been found to prevent the ugly junctions which are often so marked between eastern and western arms.

Choirs.   The want of length referred to is owing to the shortness of the choirs. The churches were not monastic; they were built by and

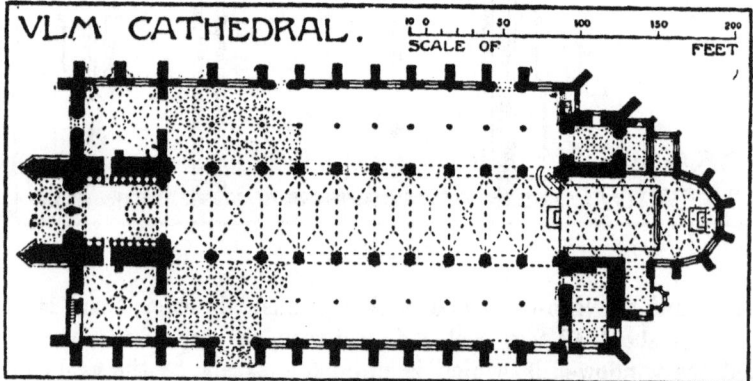

Fig. 231.

for the people; and whilst the naves are large and spacious, the choirs are short and often without aisles. The total length of Ulm Cathedral is only 416 feet, notwithstanding that its width is over 160 feet, and the height of its vault nearly 140 feet. The spirit of anti-monasticism and Protestantism was early abroad in the country; and the long choirs of England, or the many chapelled east ends of France, were unnecessary. With the exception of the churches avowedly built on French models, such as Cologne Cathedral, the fully developed chevet was rarely adopted. S. Elizabeth, Marburg, has the primitive ending of three apses. Most later choirs terminate with a semi-octagonal apse surrounded by an ambulatory, but without radiating chapels. In Ulm Cathedral the ambulatory is omitted as well. The choir of Erfurt Cathedral has no aisles, and their omission provided an opportunity for enormously tall windows, which the builders were not slow to avail themselves of. The windows are four-light traceried ones, over 50 feet high, and as the choir is raised on a lofty sub-structure their appearance is very striking. In the ruined church of S. Werner, Bacharach, on the Rhine, are others nearly as tall, and in the Cathedral of Aix-la-Chapelle, the choir windows are actually 80 feet in height.

If the masons of Germany were inferior in artistic feeling to their brethren of France, in manual dexterity they certainly surpassed them. They wrought in stone results as wonderful as those produced by the Chinese in ivory. The interpenetration of mouldings, if not their invention, was certainly practised by them to a far greater extent than it was elsewhere. The pierced spiral staircases on the outside of the towers of Ulm and Strassburg Cathedrals are marvels of technical skill. Their canopy work, for mere ornateness, has no equal. They delighted in crockets, finials, pierced parapets and buttresses; but their great *tour-de-force* was the pierced spire. Openings in spires are, to some extent, necessary for light, and when treated simply as windows, with a gable over each, as in England, produce excellent results. Most telling, also, are the simple quartrefoils and trefoils, pierced at intervals, through many of the early spires in France, as at S. Pierre, Caen, etc., but the effect of these is altogether different from that produced in many late German spires, which form simply a network of pierced tracery. Freiburg Cathedral has one of the earliest of this type (c. 1300-1350). [Manual dexterity.]

Germany stood almost alone amongst continental countries in its preference for a single tower at the west end of a cathedral, instead of the pair customary in France and England. Examples of it are at Ulm, Freiburg, Frankfurt, etc. Cologne and Strassburg Cathedrals have two western towers. In the Frauenkirche, Ingolstadt, Bavaria, the pair are placed diagonally at the end of the aisles, as was done originally at S. Ouen, Rouen. A single tower possesses this advantage, there is a probability of finishing it. The French, [Single western towers.]

334 A HISTORY OF ARCHITECTURAL DEVELOPMENT.

in the thirteenth century, discovered that a church could have too many towers; and the Germans, in the fifteenth century, showed their common sense in restricting their ambition to one. Even then most of the spires crowning towers remained unfinished for a century or more, and some have only been built in modern times. For a church to have one tower which can rank amongst the highest in the world is a distinction: to have two is an extravagance. If the Ulm plan had been adopted at Cologne, the gain to the cathedral would have been enormous. In Vienna Cathedral the towers come above the transepts, and in this example alone one feels that a pair of towers of such massive proportions are possible, because they are separated from each other by the entire width of the church. The southern one, which alone is finished, ranks amongst the finest efforts of the German builders. The

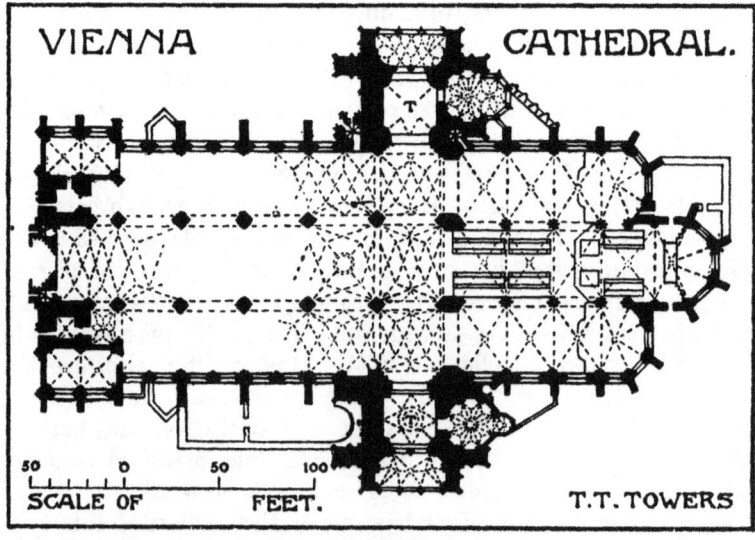

Fig. 232.

junction between tower and spire is not marked at all, and a magnificent pyramidal effect is produced, the complicated arrangement of buttresses at the angles helping the illusion that the spire springs direct from the ground.

Belgium. From the beginning of the thirteenth century to the end of the fifteenth, Belgium was one of the most flourishing countries in Europe. Bruges was chosen by the representatives of the towns composing the great Hanseatic League as their northern depôt, and Ghent, Antwerp, Ypres, etc., were also important commercial centres. With the exception of the nave and transepts of Tournai Cathedral (see Fig. 140), Belgium has no Romanesque work of especial merit, but it possesses many churches, chiefly of the fourteenth and fifteenth centuries, well worthy of attention. Most are principally of brick—even the vaults are often of that material—but several are in stone. Ypres Cathedral is one of the most important of the latter, the stone used being mainly a local blue-grey one. Interesting though the churches are, they possess no distinctive characteristics which call for detailed mention. As a rule they are fine in scale, simple in design, although some are disfigured by later rococo figures and other additions of the sixteenth century. The majority are based on French examples, whilst a few show the influence of Germany. Ypres Cathedral (c. 1225)—its west tower is later—and the church of Nôtre Dame de Pameleh, Audenarde (c. 1240), are amongst the earliest in which the Gothic feeling of Northern France is apparent. Work of the fourteenth and fifteenth centuries is well represented by the churches of Bruges, Ghent, Brussels, Antwerp, etc., the last an overgrown monster with its original plan spoilt by additions.

The secular buildings of Belgium are more interesting than the churches, but cannot be considered in this volume. Mention, however, may be made of one, the Cloth Hall at Ypres, because it is the finest example of secular Gothic in Europe. For noble simplicity it has no equal. Inside, its upper floor, which is the principal one, forms one huge chamber covered by a simple open timber roof. The outside expresses well the internal plan. It consists of a long, low, unbroken façade, 440 feet in length, perfectly simple in design, but fairly rich in detail, crowned by a steep-pitched roof. In the centre rises a grand tower without buttresses, but with battered sides, and at the corners of the top storey are the angle turrets which the Belgians and Germans delighted in. Similar turrets rise above the parapets at the two ends of the building. Altogether, this hall has the purity of a Greek temple, and no classic architect ever designed anything more absolutely symmetrical. *Secular buildings.*

The chief lesson the churches of Holland teach is that colour is not essential in Gothic art. Nearly all are whitewashed throughout inside with surprisingly fine results. Without in any way depreciating the fine colour schemes of the mediæval artist, which *Holland.*

Fig. 233.

GOTHIC ARCHITECTURE IN GERMANY, BELGIUM, ETC. 337

often included everything in a church, it is a question whether the best effects are not obtained by using colour very sparingly, and massing it in a few special places. Too little stained glass remains in Holland to enable one to judge for a certainty what the effect would be of a church whitewashed throughout, with the windows a blaze of stained glass, and no colour visible elsewhere except perhaps on the reredos over the altar; but it would probably be an exceedingly fine one. One has the glass in Chartres Cathedral, but not the whitewash; in Holland one has the whitewash, but rarely the glass. White is such a marvellous foil and frame to colour, that although the Protestants of Holland and other countries certainly did not use it for æsthetic reasons, it is a mistake to take for granted that their application of whitewash necessarily had the damaging effect which is commonly attributed to it.

CHAPTER XX.

GOTHIC ARCHITECTURE IN ITALY.

Introduction.
THAT Gothic feeling never penetrated deeply into Italy is not to be wondered at when the earlier monuments of the country are remembered. The remains of the marvellous buildings of the Romans stood in all its cities, even more numerous in the Middle Ages than they are at present. In Rome the basilican plan and ordinance had for so long been accepted as the only one for churches, that it naturally tinctured some of the subsequent work. At Pisa and the neighbouring cities, a school of building, based partly on basilican and partly on Byzantine models, had been perfected, and this survived well into the thirteenth century. In the Church of S. Caterina, Pisa (c. 1250), the façade is similar to that of the cathedral—even to the extent of the niches not centring over one another—the only difference being that the arches of the upper arcading are pointed. The crowning feature of Byzantine architecture, the dome, appears in nearly all Romanesque Italian churches, and is not entirely absent from those of later date. At Siena, the dome over the hexagonal crossing was finished about 1265; at Florence, in the fourteenth century, the east end of the cathedral was planned to be covered by a dome, although the present one was not built until the fifteenth; and at S. Petronio, Bologna (c. 1390), a dome equal in size to the Florentine one was contemplated, but never commenced. Early in the fifteenth century the Renaissance began at Florence, one hundred years before it obtained a sure footing in northern countries. The result of the early curtailment of the Gothic movement in Italy, coupled with its late introduction, is that Gothic art in that country is practically compressed into two centuries only. Even during that time it never flourished unadulterated. Classic art was not dead; it only slept. The semicircular arch was never abandoned. In the middle of the fourteenth century the nave of the Cathedral of

Lucca (S. Martino) was rebuilt with arches of that form. The Loggie del Bigallo (c. 1360), and dei Lanzi, Florence (c. 1375), have also semicircular arches; and so strongly is classic feeling manifest in the details and other features of these buildings that one hardly knows whether to regard them as evidence of lingering traditions, or as forerunners of the new movement. No country but Italy could have produced the Pisani, father and son, and Giotto. Niccolo Pisano, who lived in the middle of the thirteenth century, ignored to a great extent the work of his immediate predecessors, and took antique forms as his models; Giovanni, his son, relied more directly on nature; but there is little if any trace in the designs of either of Gothic inspiration. Of Giotto's work as a mural painter it is not necessary to speak here. That was his *métier*, and in that he excelled. As an architect he was less successful. His Campanile at Florence has beautiful detail and richness of colour, but hardly satisfactory proportions. The top-heaviness of the upper part may not be his fault, as he died before the tower was far advanced and it was finished by others.

The churches in Italy which bear the closest resemblance to the Gothic of the North were most of them built in the first half of the thirteenth century. In some, foreign masons were employed, as at S. Andrea, Vercelli (c. 1220), the designer of which is said to have been an Englishman. The clustered piers and subordinated arches are not Italian, but on the other hand, the tall octagonal cupola over the crossing shows that the designer, whoever he was, was not allowed to depart entirely from local customs. The double church of the Franciscans at Assisi also has indications of outside influence. The lower church was commenced in 1228, and the upper one is said to have been finished in 1253, but the differences in design between the two suggest a greater interval of time. The semicircular buttresses on the outside walls of the nave are reminiscent of Albi Cathedral, but if the dates given above are correct, the Italian church preceded the French one. S. Maria sopra Minerva, Rome (c. 1280), is the only Gothic church in the capital. In Venice, the church of the Frari (c. 1260), is superior to the contemporary SS. Giovanni e Paolo, but neither is really satisfactory from a Gothic standpoint. *Early Gothic examples.*

In most of the above churches the arches are of two or more orders and the piers are clustered, but the Italians never took kindly to the system of subordination which is one of the most important principles of northern art. In S. Anastasia, Verona, *Piers and arches, etc.*

(c. 1280), SS. Giovanni e Paolo, Venice (c. 1260), S. Croce, Florence, etc., and in some later churches, the columns are cylindrical, and the arches unmoulded and have flush soffits. When piers are substituted for columns, as in Florence Cathedral (c. 1300), they are generally merely squares, with flat pilasters of slight projection at the sides. The typical fourteenth-century Italian capital is perhaps the ugliest ever devised. Founded on that of the Corinthian order, it consists of three tiers of acanthus leaves

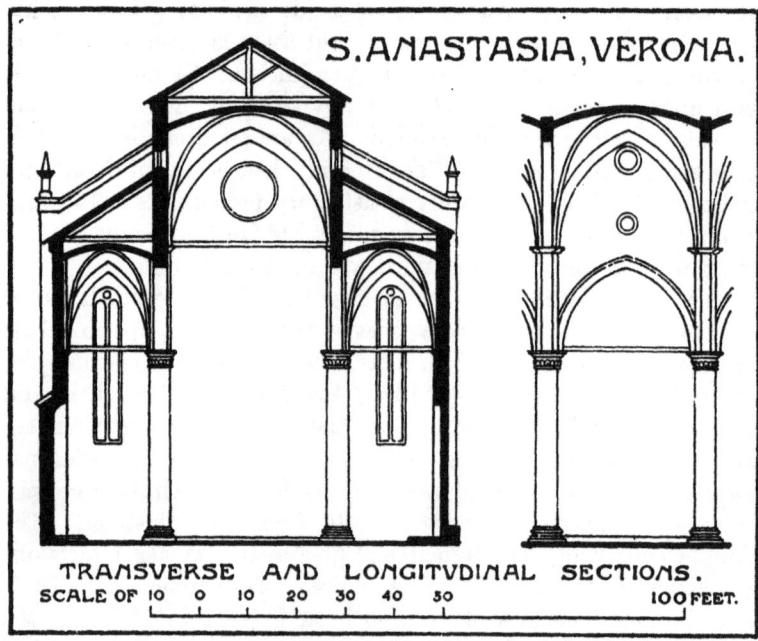

Fig. 234.

placed stiffly one above the other, surmounted by a moulded abacus which over columns is generally octagonal in plan. Unsatisfactory when there is a column below, it is particularly disagreeable when crowning a pilastered pier as at Florence. Little fault can be found with the carving itself—the Italians were always good sculptors—but the design is flat and uninteresting.

Internal ordinance. Few Italian churches have the division customary elsewhere of arcade, triforium and clerestory. The nave of S. Martino, Lucca (c. 1340), has a triforium of considerable size, with a string-course

GOTHIC ARCHITECTURE IN ITALY.

above and below it, and each bay consists of many openings as in Northern work, but this was a re-building. In S. Anastasia, Verona, there is merely a series of circular openings to mark the middle storey, and in Como Cathedral are pairs of openings which, however, together with their surrounding frames, are later in date and Renaissance in character. In the Cathedrals of Florence, Orvieto, and Siena, and in S. Croce, Florence, corbelled out galleries run round the naves immediately above the main arcades. These galleries, like the entablatures over the arches in basilican churches from which they were derived, form strong horizontal

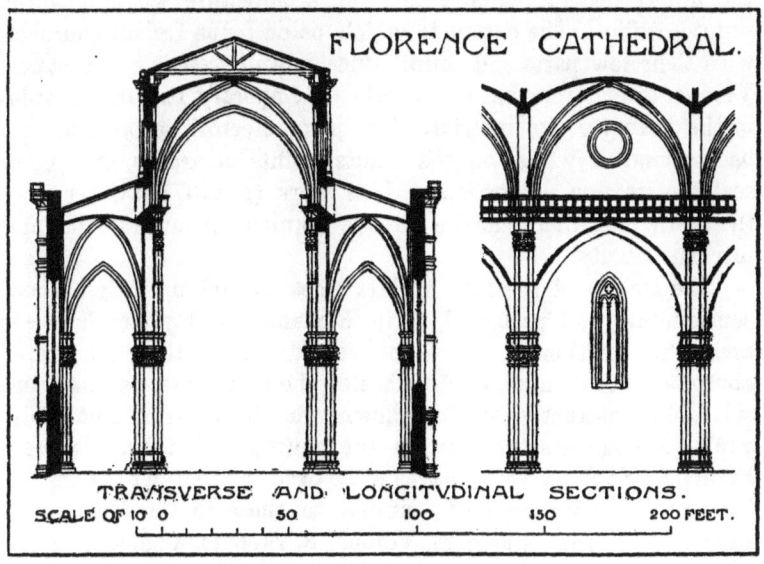

Fig. 235.

lines, which are strangely out of character in the two Florentine churches, in which the arches below are sharply pointed. At Orvieto the arches are semicircular. In this church, and also in Siena Cathedral, the walls and piers inside are faced with alternating courses of black and white marble, which in themselves form horizontal lines, so that the more strongly marked lines of the galleries are not too pronounced. Notwithstanding that triforia are either omitted altogether or are small and insignificant, little attempt was made to give prominence to the clerestory windows. Siena Cathedral is an exception. The windows there are large and have traceried heads, as in northern examples. In

Orvieto Cathedral, and in S. Croce, Florence, each bay has a lancet light which, although tall, is very narrow. The most usual opening is merely a circle, sometimes quite plain, as in Florence Cathedral, sometimes cusped, as in S. Petronio, Bologna, and S. Anastasia, Verona. It cannot be said that the result in either case is satisfactory, but in Italy the strong light rendered large windows unnecessary, and there was not the keen desire for stained glass which existed in the north. The effect inside would be better in many cases if the walls were painted (as doubtless they were originally intended to be), as then the centre of interest would be the mural decoration, and not the architecture which is often uninteresting. The extent to which paint helps Italian churches, with their few parts and simple lines, is well seen at S. Anastasia, Verona, the church that excels all contemporary Italian examples in the beauty of its interior. The painted scroll decoration, on a background of white, on the vaults, soffits of arches, etc., gives scale to its fine proportions. This work (c. 1437) is later than the fabric, but there can be no two opinions about its value and intrinsic beauty.

Scale of churches. The Italian of the late Middle Ages was often careless about construction, and preferred, as in Romanesque days, to hold his arches in position by means of tie-rods rather than by proper abutment. But in many churches of the fourteenth century considerable constructive skill is shown, and the spans of arches and vaults are far greater than in the churches of either Northern France or England. The naves of S. Croce and Orvieto Cathedral have ordinary timber roofs, similar to those in the basilicas of Rome. S. Fermo Maggiore, Verona, S. Stefano, Venice, and one or two other examples, have curious trefoil, or cinquefoil, wood panelled ceilings, like that which, in the fourteenth century, was placed over the Romanesque church of S. Zeno, Verona. With the exception of these and a few others, the large churches are vaulted throughout. The vaults are simple quadripartite ones, and the only peculiarity about them is their size. In the basilican churches of Rome the nave columns are numerous and close together. The fourteenth-century Italian architects went to the other extreme. Notwithstanding the great width of naves, the side bays are also exceedingly wide and the supports in consequence few in number. The old Roman plan of approximately square bays of vaulting was the one generally adopted; the oblong form favoured by the Gothic builders of the north being the

FIG. 236.—S. ANASTASIA, VERONA.

[*To face p.* 342.

exception and not the rule, save in the aisles.[1] (See Fig. 51.) Few supports, no doubt, possess the advantages of not interfering unduly with congregational worship, but greater reduplication gives better scale. Partly because of this, and partly owing to

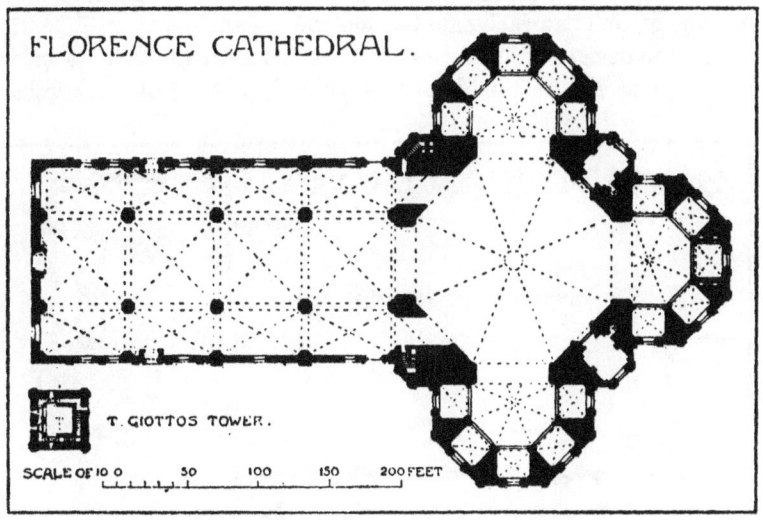

FIG. 237.

the absence of triforia and the simplicity of the upper windows, Italian churches rarely convey an impression of their real size.

In the eastern arms, the influence of the early basilican church plan is very marked. The transepts are at the extreme east end, and there is nothing beyond them save chapels. In S. Anastasia, Verona, and SS. Giovanni e Paolo, Venice, there are five chapels with apsidal ends, the centre one in each church being wider and longer than the side ones, being, in fact, the width of the nave. In S. Maria Novella, Florence, there are also five chapels similarly placed, the only difference being that all end square. S. Croce, Florence, has eleven chapels, the centre one ending with a semi-octagon, the others being rectangular. In this church the central chapel and the two flanking it are together equal to the width of the nave, thus giving an opportunity for effective grouping of a lofty chancel arch with flanking smaller side arches, over which are windows. The fully-developed French chevet is unknown in the Gothic churches of

Plan of choirs.

[1] Milan Cathedral is the most important exception.

344 *A HISTORY OF ARCHITECTURAL DEVELOPMENT.*

Italy. S. Petronio, Bologna, would have had the nearest approach to it if the choir had ever been built.[1] In Milan Cathedral the German plan of an octagonal apse surrounded by an ambulatory, but without chapels, is followed; and the transepts occupy a similar position to those in French cathedrals, and project, as they mostly do, one bay each side beyond the aisles.

Exteriors. In the designs for their west fronts, the Italians paid no more attention to the sectional outline behind in their late churches

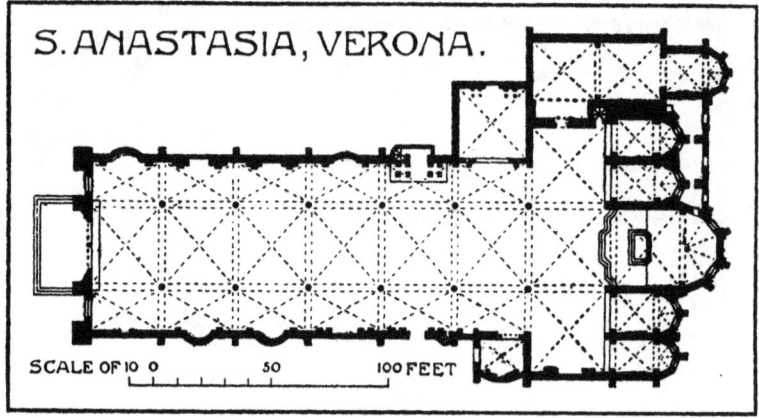

FIG. 238.

than they had done in their earlier ones. They disliked it in elevation as thoroughly as their northern brethren did, but they rarely adopted the only really satisfactory way of masking it, viz. a pair of towers. They preferred either a wide single gable, following the example set at S. Ambrogio, Milan (where, however, the roof behind is also in one span), or else three gables, the side ones being considerably lower and smaller than the central one. The latter is the design at Siena and Orvieto. These gables seldom bear any relation to the roofs behind them. At Siena, for instance, the nave roof is of flat pitch, whilst the central gable is very steep and rises far above it, and the side ones are but ornamental adjuncts. The west front is in fact simply a screen, rich in carving and sculpture, but beautiful only because of the marble with which it is faced. Other fronts are nearly as elaborate,

[1] If this church had been finished it would have been the largest in the world, with a length of nearly double that of the present nave, and with deeply-projecting aisled transepts.

FIG. 239.—SIENA CATHEDRAL: WEST FRONT.

especially in Tuscany. The sides are often plain brick, but as the churches seldom stand free, it matters little what material is used there. In northern Italy the fronts are not so rich as in the centre and south, and marble, when used at all, is banded with brick. But the churches lose little by this, and gain considerably through more attention having been paid to the design of other parts. There is never the glamour about the outside of Italian churches that there is about French ones, but there is often considerable stateliness due to their size and vast expanse of plain walling. Even in their vaulted churches the Italians were able to dispense with flying buttresses (except in Milan Cathedral), and to some

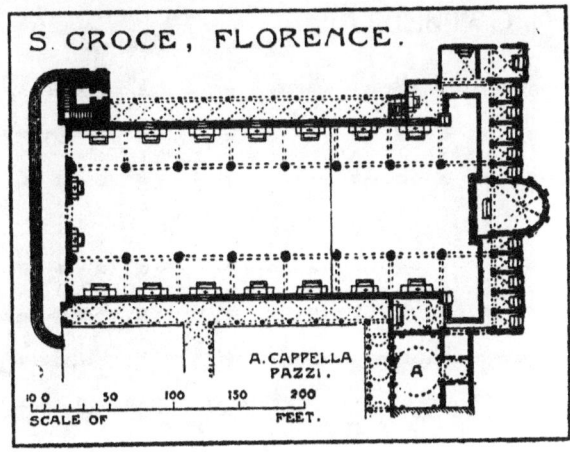

FIG. 240.

extent with ordinary buttresses, because of the smallness and paucity of the openings. The walls are nearly solid, and consequently are capable of resisting almost unaided the thrusts of the vaults, notwithstanding their great span. At the same time, few vaulted churches are entirely without external buttresses, and very effective some of these are owing to their absolute simplicity and absence of set-offs. In S. Anastasia, Verona, the brick buttresses of about 3 feet square projection rise sheer from the ground to above the eaves without a break. The conservative instincts of the northern Italian are shown in the fine tower of this church, which is only a little different from the north tower of S. Ambrogio, Milan, built two hundred years before.

Milan Cathedral (c. 1386) deserves a special word of description, because, besides being the largest of all Italian cathedrals, Milan Cathedral.

excepting St. Peter's, it is beyond doubt by far the most remarkable. A double-aisled church, it follows Bourges Cathedral in the gradation of its aisles, but is without triforia. All the roofs, which are covered with white marble tiles, are of low pitch. This accounts for the small amount of wall space inside between the tops of the arcades and the clerestories in both nave and inner aisles, which enabled its designers to dispense entirely with the middle storey. The clerestory windows themselves are small and insignificant, and although objection has already been taken to the circles which commonly constitute clerestory windows in Italy,

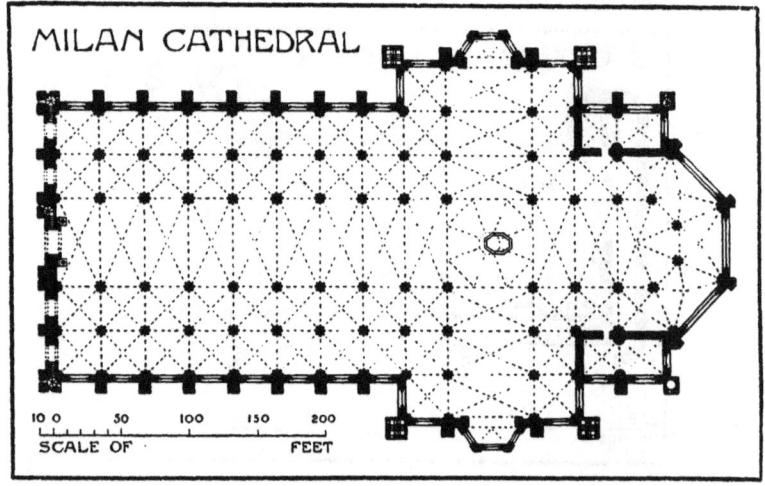

FIG. 241.

it is a question whether they are not preferable to the little traceried lights of Milan. The side windows in the aisle walls are of great size, and from these most of the light in the church is obtained. The tracery of their heads, especially in the windows at the east end, is far more fantastic than any to be found in France or England, although in S. Petronio, Bologna, the designs are equally unconstructional. One curious fact about Milan Cathedral is that the top tier of windows does not light the interior at all. The nave vaulting is very domical, and these windows are above the vault, and merely light the space between it and the tiled roof above. What the effect would have been if all the ridge-ribs of the vaulting had been level, thus allowing the clerestory windows to rise considerably higher than they do at

FIG. 242.—MILAN CATHEDRAL.

[*To face p.* 346.

present, is difficult to say, but inside the improvement would probably have been immense. The Italians, however, did not want light, and yet they had to raise the side walls above the apex of the transverse arches of the central vault, otherwise the construction of the timber roof over would have presented difficulties. A Frenchman, obliged to keep his vault domical and his windows below it small, would probably have left the upper

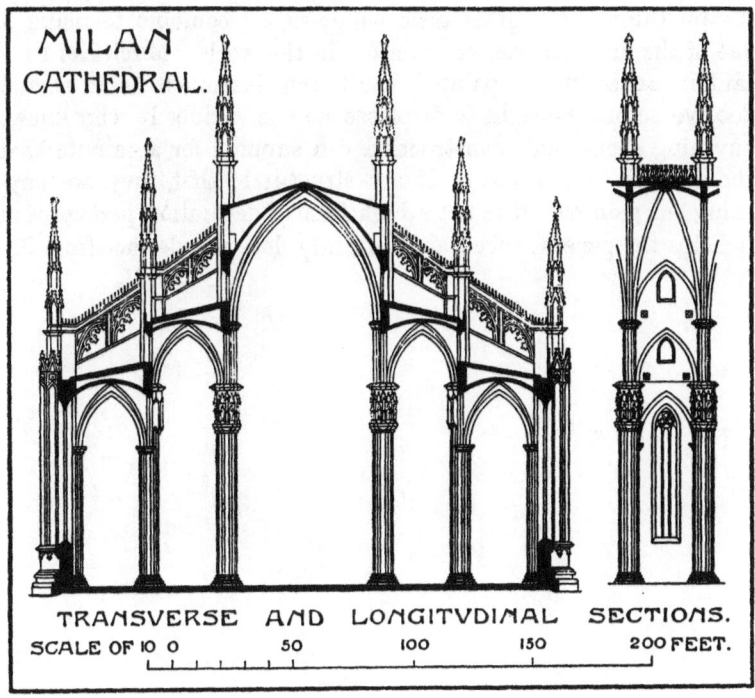

Fig. 243.

part of the wall unpierced, or have pierced it with very small openings. From the inside, of course, it makes no difference what is there, and very little from the outside, as these windows hardly show, owing to the height of the aisle walls and the crowd of pinnacles, flying buttresses, and pierced parapets in front of them.

The outside of Milan Cathedral must be seen to be understood. Full of faults, with detail coarse in the extreme, its mass, its pinnacles, and the white marble of which it is built throughout, render it most striking. A rare lesson may be learnt by a comparison of the cathedral and S. Ambrogio in the same city, the one absolutely quiet and simple, the other all shout and glitter and finery. The inside is far finer than the outside. The lofty piers, crowned by font-like shaped capitals, enriched with figures over life-size—the capitals are about twenty feet high—the great width and height of the church, the vistas across it, the dazzling rays of sunlight which, at morning and evening especially, stream through the great aisle windows, all combine to make it one of the most marvellous interiors in the world. Much has been said in abuse of the painted vault, but inasmuch as it should deceive no one, it ought to displease no one. Nobody who knows anything about vault construction can suppose for a minute that the lines he sees on the vault are structural; that they are anything but painted. It is not a high form of decoration perhaps, but it helps the general effect, and certainly does not detract from it.

CHAPTER XXI.

GOTHIC ARCHITECTURE IN SPAIN.

SPAIN exercised little influence on the early development of mediæval art, because the whole of the country, with the exception of the mountainous district near the Pyrenees and the north-west part along the Bay of Biscay, was in the hands of the Moors until the eleventh century was far advanced. The triumph of the Christians commenced with the recovery of Toledo in 1085, and this was followed by other successes, until the whole of the northern half of the country was in their possession. Seville was not recaptured until 1248, and the Moors' last stronghold, Granada, not until 1492. Street, in his "Gothic Architecture in Spain," mentions two churches in Barcelona which were probably built in the tenth century, and some eight or ten which belong to the following one, but with the exception of the great cathedral at Santiago de Compostella, the Church of S. Isidoro, Leon, and a few others, most Spanish churches are later. In one respect Spain was fortunate. It was regaining its freedom at the time when mediæval art was advancing rapidly in other countries, and although the constant fear of Moorish inroads prevented the establishment of a national school in Spain itself, the Spaniards were wise enough to turn for assistance to the builders of the many fine churches to the north of the Pyrenees, which had either just been finished or were in course of erection. Introduction.

The eleventh-century churches are mainly of two types, both of which were borrowed from Southern France. S. Pedro, Huesca (c. 1100), may be taken as typical of one. In it the internal ordinance is the same as in S. Nazaire, Carcassonne. Barrel vaults start a few feet only above the crown of the side arches, and there is no room for either triforium or clerestory. The plan of S. Pedro is very simple, and consists of an aisled nave of five bays, with three apses at the east end—the central one being a little longer than the side ones—covered by semi-domes. First type of early church.

Four of the western bays are barrel-vaulted, but over the fifth and easternmost, which is wider than the others, is a lantern. This last feature, the idea for which was doubtless taken from S. Ambrogio, Milan, or from one of the many churches in Northern Italy, Germany, or Southern France, in which similar lanterns occur, is found in nearly all early Spanish churches, and in some it is treated in a distinctly original manner, as will be shown later.

Churches of second type. Churches of the second type follow S. Sernin, Toulouse, and many churches in Auvergne, etc., in being without clerestories, and in having their barrel vaults raised well above the main arcades so as to allow space for roomy triforia. The vaults are semicircular, and are divided into bays by transverse arches as in the French examples. Some churches of this type, such as S. Isidoro, Leon, follow in plan S. Pedro, Huesca, with slight modifications, whilst others are markedly cruciform, and have fully developed ambulatories and chevets at the east end instead of three separate apses. The finest amongst the latter is the Cathedral of Santiago de Compostella (c. 1078–1128). In general ordinance and plan it is a replica of S. Sernin, Toulouse, built some twenty years before (see Fig. 157), except that the nave has only single aisles, instead of double, the transepts, however, projecting one extra bay each side by way of compensation. The examples mentioned are sufficient to show how dependent the Spaniards were at first on French models. The style on Spanish soil was an imported one, but it took root there and continued to flourish long after it had been abandoned elsewhere in favour of fully developed Gothic. The old Cathedral of Salamanca (c. 1120–1178), the Cathedral of Tarragona (c. 1131), and the church at Lerida (c. 1203–1278), differ only from earlier churches in that the principal arches are pointed, and in the substitution of ribbed vaults for barrel ones. In one respect the Spaniards improved on French work. No Romanesque church in France—or for that matter in Italy or Germany either—has so effective a central lantern as can be seen in the old Cathedral, Salamanca, in Zamora Cathedral, or in the Collegiate church at Toro. S. Sernin, Toulouse, has a taller tower; the church of Chiaravalle, near Milan, one of more peculiar shape; and many German churches have cupolas of wider span, but none is so original as the three Spanish examples mentioned. Over the crossing at Salamanca is a two-storied arcaded drum, carried on pendentives, and pierced with windows on its cardinal sides. Above is a dome, with ribs on its intrados which start from shafts between the bays of arcading of the drum. Outside, the effect is even more striking than inside. The drum forms a sixteen-sided tower, on the four principal canted sides of which are large circular turrets which help to resist the thrusts of the dome. The inner dome is covered by an outer one of steeper pitch, which has more the appearance of a strongly entasised low

Fig. 244.

stone spire than of a dome. At Toro the design is very similar, but in place of the outer dome is now a low-pitched roof.

Nearly contemporary with the church at Lerida, are the Cathedrals of Toledo (c. 1227), Burgos (c. 1221), and Leon (c. 1250), but they show a very different feeling. The fame of the cathedrals of Northern France had reached Spain, and all three were evidently designed, and doubtless partly built by French masons. Here, as in Germany, one has to regret that the people did not try and develop the style they had become accustomed to, instead of merely reproducing what had been done

Introduction of French Gothic.

in another country. To such an extent was Northern French Gothic the rage that, at Leon Cathedral, in the latter half of the thirteenth century, the west porch was built in exact imitation of the famous porches in front of the transepts at Chartres. Of this cathedral Street says, "The church from beginning to end is thoroughly French. French in its detail, in its plan, and in its general design." Toledo Cathedral, a church with double aisles, is the largest of the three, its width being as much as 178 feet, which is many feet wider than either Cologne or Bourges Cathedral, and is excelled by some 12 feet only by Milan Cathedral.

Churches without aisles. The most interesting Spanish churches of the fourteenth century are those in which the Spaniards returned to their first love—

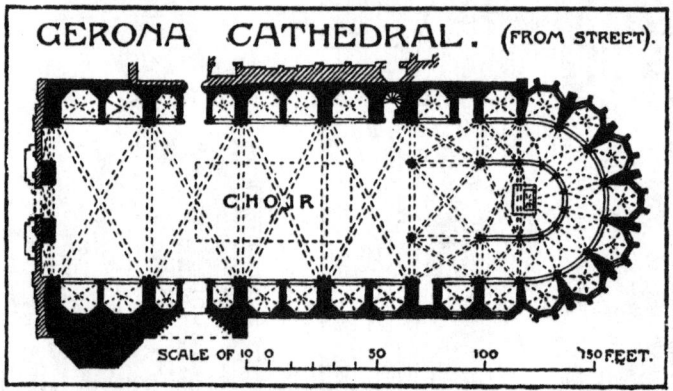

Fig. 245.

the architecture of Southern France—and took as their models the great aisleless churches of Albi and Toulouse. At Barcelona the Church of S. Maria del Pino (c. 1329) has a nave 54 feet wide, with chapels on either side, but no aisles. Although the Spaniards took the plan from France, all French churches of this type are excelled in size by the great cathedral at Gerona. The east end was built first (c. 1312–1346), and in itself presents nothing of particular interest, being divided in the ordinary way into central and side aisles with radiating chapels round a semicircular end. The great feature of the church is its aisleless nave of four bays—with side chapels as in other churches of similar plan—which was commenced in 1416. This actually has a span of 73 feet, exclusive of chapels, and a height of 117 feet. No vaulted building of such a width had been attempted since

Constantine built his basilica at Rome.[1] The side chapels follow more the Perpignan plan than the Albi one, inasmuch as they are comparatively low. Over the arches in front of them runs a small triforium with big clerestory windows above. The design is thus more commonplace than Albi Cathedral, the lofty side vaults of which, towering above the galleries, produce such splendid effects. The triple division of the earlier eastern half, however, makes a fine ending to the nave, and the piers and arches and windows over them give scale. The fault of Albi is that there is too little in the structure itself to enable one to grasp its size, and if it were not for the screen round the choir, the inside would not look even as large as it does. The idea of adding a nave without aisles to a choir with them was not a new one, as it had been done two or three centuries before at La Trinité, Angers, S. Radegonde, Poitiers, etc., but these churches, although by no means small ones, are far inferior in size to the Spaniard's masterly *tour-de-force*. The problem to be solved at Gerona was how to provide space for a large congregation, all of which could have an uninterrupted view of the high altar, and in no other example has this been more successfully accomplished. At Barcelona (besides the Church of S. Maria del Pino already mentioned) is the still larger S. Maria del Mar (c. 1328), designed with the same aim in view, but in a different manner. The church is an aisled one, and consists of a nave of four great bays, each over 40 feet square, with a narrow eastern bay and an apse beyond surrounded by an ambulatory. There are consequently only four piers each side, and these naturally offer little obstruction. In the number and size of its bays the church resembles some of the late Italian examples, such as S. Petronio, Bologna, Como Cathedral, etc., and in general ordinance it also follows these, as it is lighted mainly from the aisles, the clerestory windows being small and consisting of small traceried circles, one to each bay. Whilst the two Barcelona churches mentioned, and some others in the town, were planned for congregational worship, the cathedral, on the other hand, was especially arranged for private devotion. There are as many as twenty-seven chapels inside the church, arranged round the

---

[1] A few domed Byzantine buildings are wider, but no mediæval ones. Street gives in an appendix to his "Gothic Architecture in Spain," an extremely interesting account of the fears which this bold project raised amongst the Chapter, and of the Junta of architects it called before it would allow Guillermo Boffiy, the master of the works who proposed it, to proceed with his plan.

354 A HISTORY OF ARCHITECTURAL DEVELOPMENT.

chevet and opening out of the aisles of the nave, and, as though these were not sufficient, no less than twenty-two more are grouped round three of the sides of the cloister.

Position of choir. One peculiarity in Spanish churches deserves mention. The choir is generally placed west of the crossing in the nave, and is cut off entirely from the altar, except that a passage-way is

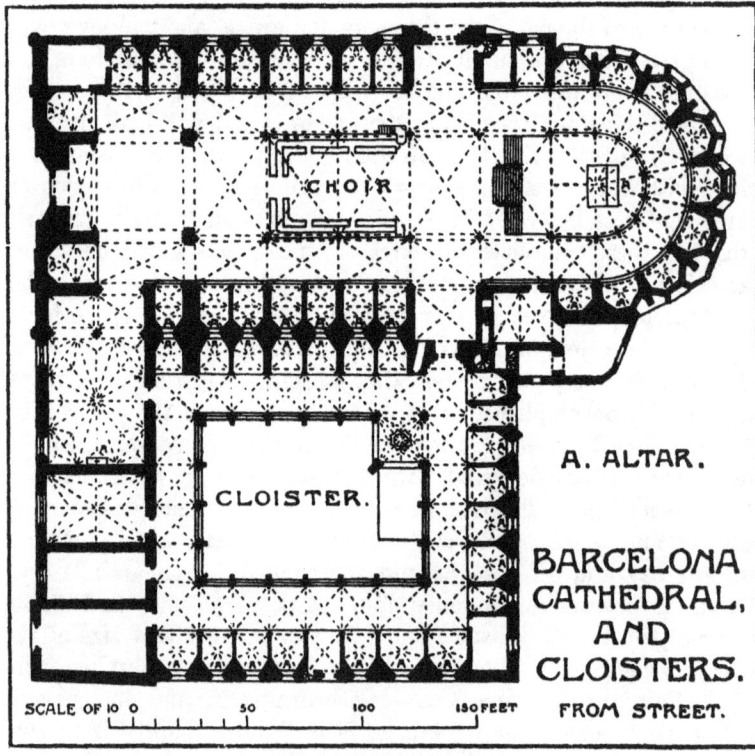

Fig. 246.

screened off for the priests to pass from one to the other. The plan doubtless originated in the short Romanesque choirs which did not allow sufficient room for the clergy after their numbers multiplied. In all countries extra provision had to be made for them, but in none, except Spain, was the altar ever divorced from the choir. The reason why it was done in that country is not clear, and Street implies that it is "a comparatively modern innovation," dating in most cases from the early days of the Renaissance. The people are admitted to the transepts in all the

GOTHIC ARCHITECTURE IN SPAIN.

large cathedrals, the nave west of the choir being, as a rule, little used. In S. Pedro, Huesca, the choir is actually placed against the west wall of the church, occupying one bay only, and is separated by four bays from the apse containing the altar.[1]

The great cathedrals of Salamanca (the new church) and Segovia, are the last words of Gothic in Spain. Salamanca Cathedral was not commenced until 1512, and considering the date it is wonderfully mediæval in feeling. Segovia Cathedral is even later. In 1522 the architect of Salamanca Cathedral was appointed to superintend the work, the greater part of which was finished some fifty years later. Both are big churches of considerable width—over 110 feet exclusive of the side chapels—but no great length, proportions that are general throughout the country, width being invariably regarded as the chief desideratum. Seville Cathedral is actually 247 feet wide, if the side chapels are included, whilst its total internal length is only about 430 feet.

Salamanca and Segovia.

What strikes one most in these late churches is the enormous height of the piers. In English cathedrals, where piers are notoriously short—often unpleasantly so—a height of 30 feet is rare, and is barely met with in Westminster Abbey, and in some of the later examples in which there is no triforium, such as Winchester. In Northern France, piers are higher, but not so high as Spanish ones. In Amiens Cathedral they are 48 feet high, being one-third of the total height. Even Milan Cathedral, with its height of 157 feet, has piers only 55 feet high. In Poitiers Cathedral, in the Hallenkirchen of Germany, and in the Church of the Jacobins, Toulouse, with its central arcade as high as its vault, the piers are exceedingly lofty, but it is hardly fair to compare these with the Spanish churches, as they have nothing above the arches, neither triforium nor clerestory. But even taking these for comparison, not many will be found to have taller piers. The most extraordinary instances of this peculiarity are at Salamanca and Segovia. These two churches are very similar in their dimensions and internal ordinances. The total height of each is about 120 feet to the apex of the vault, nearly one-half of which is pier. Sixty feet is about the full height inside of some English cathedrals, which are therefore little higher than these piers. Moreover, the greater portion of each pier is carried up to the springing of the vault, another 34 feet or so in the case of the

Height of piers.

---

[1] The arrangement in Spain is much the same as that now existing in Westminster Abbey, except that the distance from the choir to the altar is greater.

356   A HISTORY OF ARCHITECTURAL DEVELOPMENT.

Cathedral of Segovia, without any break whatsoever. At Salamanca the capitals at the springing-line of the side arcades are continued round the piers, and consequently in this church the height is broken to a small extent; at Segovia only the members

Fig. 247.

of the piers immediately under the arches at this point have capitals, the other members which form the vaulting shafts—and they are exceedingly large and numerous—having none.

Late Spanish churches, like Italian ones, rarely have more than the two divisions of arcade and clerestory. The roofs over the aisles are, as a rule, absolutely flat, and consequently no wall space inside was required. In Barcelona Cathedral there is a kind of triforium, consisting of a passage-way with a band of arcading in front, which separates the arches from the windows above, but this starts *above* the tas-de-charge of the vaults and cuts into the wall ribs. There is much to be said for a gallery in this position, both structurally and æsthetically. There is no weakening of the abutments below, no curtailment of the height of piers, and no difficulty in providing a well-lighted passage-way all round the church and easy access to the roofs at any necessary point.

CHAPTER XXII.

ENGLISH PARISH CHURCHES—TIMBER ROOFS.

OF all countries England is the most remarkable for the number, beauty, and variety of its parish churches. They cannot compare in size, as a rule, with those abroad, but they have an individual distinction of their own. The great number of country examples we possess is due to our insular position, which saved our forefathers from the ever constant fear of forays from neighbouring states that kept the continent in a continual state of unrest. The whole of England was dotted with villages, and each had its own church. In some cases the village has disappeared and only its church remains, as at Magdalen Laver, Essex. Often the villages touched one another, like Pevensey and Westham, Sussex, where two old churches are within a stone's throw of each other. In France, Germany, and other countries, villages were few and far apart. The people, for safety, were forced within walled cities. The farmers and agricultural labourers who lived outside had, in many cases, to trudge far to church; as in Brittany at the present day, where in many parts the church of a village serves a large outlying district. At S. Thégonnec, near Morlaix, and elsewhere, the peasants on Sunday mornings can be seen on the roads for miles round, walking to mass, their coats over their arms if the time be summer. Not only are there more country churches in England, but the number in towns is, or at all events was, far greater. Norwich at one time boasted sixty-one churches, and York nearly as many. The majority were small, but to this is owing much of their interest. Their construction and general ordinance differ in many respects from those of the larger churches, both English and foreign, already described. Almost all have open timber roofs. In France, the majority of town parish churches are vaulted, and there is nothing in their design to distinguish them from cathedrals; in size, even, they are often little inferior. S. Mary Redcliffe, Bristol, is one of the few

ENGLISH PARISH CHURCHES—TIMBER ROOFS.

in England of which the same may be said. Its plan, with aisled nave and choir, projecting transepts (each with east and west aisles), and Lady Chapel, its elaborate vault, and the internal divisions of its nave and choir walls, belong to a cathedral more than to a parish church. The number and smallness, as a rule, of English town churches are early evidence of that independence in religious matters which occasioned later the caustic saying of Voltaire, that England was a country with a hundred religions and one sauce. As, until a few years ago, an Englishman was disinclined to dine in public, so in the old days he preferred not to pray in public. In France, the people for private devotions betook themselves to the numerous chapels lining the naves of cathedrals. The plan had not sufficient privacy for the Englishman. He wanted a church he could call his church, which he shared with a select few; a priest he could regard as his priest. And so, almost touching one another at times, churches were crowded together in towns, hemmed in by houses, and hardly visible to the casual passer-by, each possessing its own regular congregation. Occasionally a portion of an abbey church was granted to a parish, as at Chester, where the south transept of the present cathedral is far larger than the north, and with its eastern and western aisles forms a church in itself.

English parish churches are of all shapes and sizes. Some Plans. retain their original plan, others have been altered; aisles have

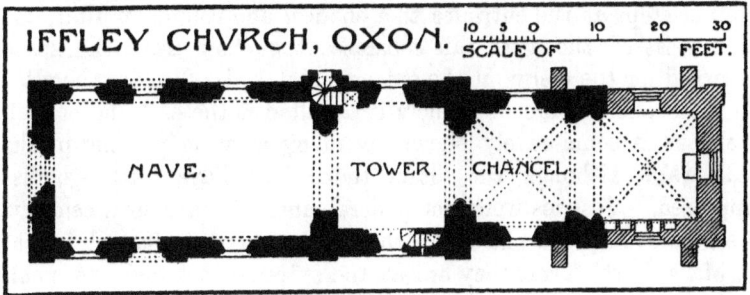

Fig. 248.

been pulled down in some, in others they have been added, and not unfrequently chapels as well built by pious founders to contain their tombs. To attempt to enumerate the many peculiarities in plan resulting from such alterations would be a tedious, lengthy task, and also an unprofitable one. The simplest form of church consists of merely a nave and chancel, with or without a tower at the west end. To this is often added a porch on the south side, and occasionally one on the north in addition. In the early centuries of mediæval architecture the entrances in parish churches were nearly always lateral; it was not until the fifteenth century that a doorway in the western wall of a tower became customary. With few exceptions the chancels end square. Warwick Church, Cumberland, however, has an apse. The Normans were able to dictate an apsidal ending for their abbey churches and cathedrals, but in the parish churches the people continued the old traditional English plan. Some Romanesque and later churches without aisles have transepts, like Old Shoreham and Alfriston, both in Sussex; but the cruciform plan is the exception and not the rule for parish churches. Before the Norman conquest churches had been built with aisles, and the aisled plan was adopted afterwards whenever the accommodation required was greater than a nave alone could contain.

Chancels. Chancels were generally built without aisles, but amongst early examples with them is S. Mary, Eastbourne, and amongst late ones, Thaxted Church, Essex, Long Melford Church, Suffolk, etc. The chancel is nearly always raised above the nave, and the altar, with very few exceptions, has one or more additional steps surrounding it. In large churches there are often as many as seven or nine steps from the nave to the level on which it stands; the number, as a rule, being an unequal one. In addition to the step or steps at the entrance to a chancel and round an altar, one step west of the altar rail separates the choir from the space reserved for the clergy at the extreme east end. Besides the altar in the chancel, there was generally an altar at the east end of each aisle, as is conclusively shown by many existing piscinæ in the side walls, although the altars themselves have long ago disappeared. Vestries were not general until the fifteenth century. As a rule, they are placed on the north side of a chancel, but at S. Mary, Eastbourne, they are at the extreme east end. A small doorway is common on the south side to enable a priest to reach his seat without walking the length of the church, and occasionally there is one to the north.

Proportion of nave to chancel. No definite rule can be stated regarding the proportion of nave to chancel in parish churches, but, roughly speaking, the later the church the smaller the chancel. In early thirteenth-century work one frequently finds the chancel two-fifths of the total length, as at Cobham Church, Kent, and sometimes chancel and nave are equal in length, as at Broadwater Church, Sussex. In churches of the fourteenth and fifteenth centuries, a common proportion was three to five, the nave frequently consisting of five bays, and the choir, when aisled, of three. In some examples built towards the end of the latter century the east end is shorter

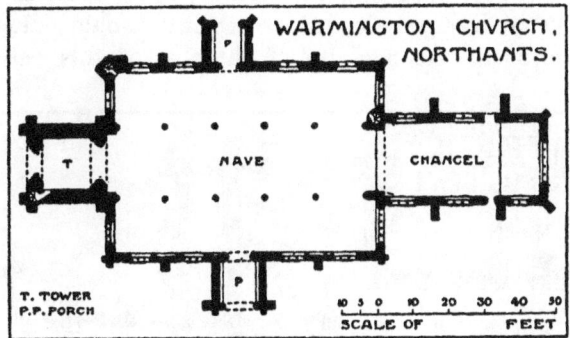

Fig. 249.

still, thus paving the way for the time when, after the advent of the Reformation, the chancel almost disappeared.

The proportionate width of aisles to nave varies considerably. In early work the former are generally narrow; in the fourteenth century they frequently approximate to the proportions customary in cathedrals, viz. width of nave double that of each aisle, as in S. Patrick, Patrington, Yorkshire. This church differs from the majority of English parish churches in having transepts of three bays, each with an aisle on both sides, and a lofty tower over the crossing crowned by a spire. In the following century the aisles are sometimes nearly as wide as the nave, as in the fine church of Walpole S. Peter, Norfolk, where the nave is 19 feet 2 inches wide, each aisle being 17 feet, and in S. Mary Magdalene, Gedney, also in Norfolk, the nave of which is 21 feet 6 inches wide, and each aisle 19 feet 6 inches. In both churches the chancels are without aisles. The aisles of Thaxted Church, Essex, are actually wider than the nave. Occasionally churches followed the plan of the Dominican order, and had but one central arcade, which divided the church in two longitudinally. Such was the plan of the old Church of S. Mary, Truro, one half of which still remains as an outer aisle to the choir of the present cathedral. The most striking characteristic of fifteenth-century churches is

Proportion of aisles to nave.

362   A HISTORY OF ARCHITECTURAL DEVELOPMENT.

their spaciousness. They were built for congregational worship, in the days when the power of the monastic orders was on the wane, and often at the sole expense of private donors who were laymen. The central idea that governed their plan was the desire to accommodate as many people as possible. With this object in view, both naves and aisles are as wide as could conveniently be spanned by timber roofs; the piers are as far apart as possible, and are, moreover, as slender as stability would allow. The western arms of the majority of churches of this period were

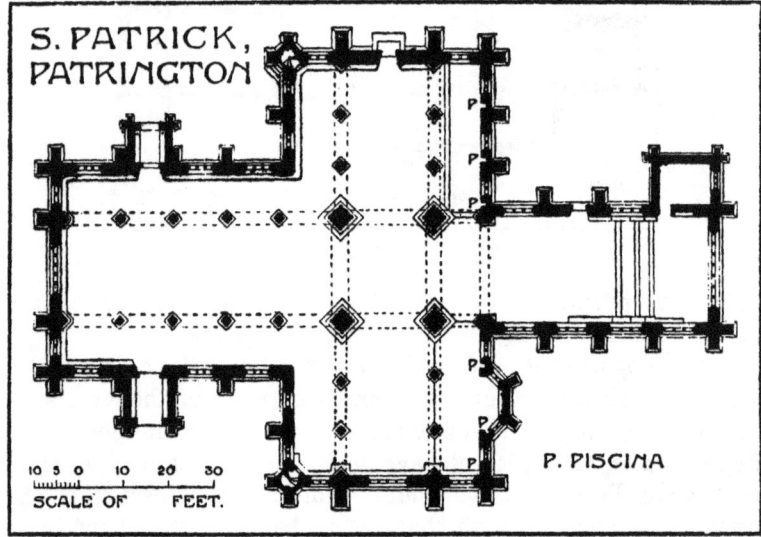

FIG. 250 (H. A. Paley).

fitted with fixed seats, with ends elaborately carved, and many of these still exist, notably in the western counties.

Sectional ordinance. The internal division of nave, triforium, and clerestory, customary in cathedrals, is rare in English parish churches. S. Mary Redcliffe, Bristol (mostly c. 1375-1440), has already been mentioned as the most conspicuous exception. This church is vaulted throughout, and although the triforium does not, strictly speaking, exist, there is a considerable space between the arches of the arcade and the windows above, which is treated with elaborate panelling similar in design to that of the choir of Wells, finished a few years previously. The majority of churches built between the middle of the eleventh century and the middle of the fourteenth have no clerestory windows. In some cases the rafters of the nave roofs are continued down to the aisle walls, so that all three divisions are covered by one roof; in others the aisle roofs are of considerably flatter pitch, and there is a small portion of walling between the eaves of the nave roof and the top of the lean-to side roofs. This occasionally in the twelfth and thirteenth centuries was pierced with quatrefoils, trefoils, etc. In churches of the first half of the century following even such small clerestories are rare. The typical aisled church of that period is lighted entirely from the sides, and from the end walls. The aisle roofs are sometimes lean-to, sometimes double-pitched like the central one so that each end shows three gables. In many country churches abroad the aisle windows rise above the eaves, and there is a series of gables along each side, as in one of

Fig. 251 (H. A. Paley).

the churches at Quimper, Brittany, but this design is rarely met with in England. The foreign examples often have an extremely picturesque appearance, but it is a question if the simpler English plan is not preferable. Owing to the absence of clerestories early fourteenth-century churches are invariably low; their lowness being most noticeable when nave and aisles are approximately equal in width and are roofed in the same way. They were made low deliberately. The builders wanted their churches to be in harmony with the countryside, and not to be blots on the landscape. When they desired a landmark they built a tower, or tower and spire. The west end of Patrington Church is only 46 feet high from the ground to the apex of the cross of the gable, whereas the spire rises to a height of 170 feet. Such disproportion—if such a term can be applied to what is really a beauty—is never found abroad. The love for length and lowness, so marked in English cathedrals, is still more characteristic of English parish churches of the period mentioned. In the latter half of the century there came a change which was continued all through the following one. Clerestory windows were reintroduced, and became almost universal. There is hardly a fifteenth-century church of any size without them. In many examples they form a continuous band from the west wall of the nave to the wall over the chancel arch, and when the chancel is aisled they are sometimes continued along it as well. Considering the added light they give it might have been thought that aisle windows would have lost their importance and become smaller. The contrary was the case; they increased in size. For this the love for stained glass was chiefly responsible. The desire for it was always existent throughout the middle ages, and in the fifteenth century it approximated to a disease. Windows reached from buttress to buttress, from plinth to parapet, and walling almost disappeared. The mason became little more than a frame-maker. Notwithstanding the large proportion of glass to frame the churches were not overlighted, because the glass was coloured. Neither was there the feeling of insufficiency of wall space which strikes one so strongly now that clear glass has taken the place of the other. Void and solid blended. The question as to which was which did not force an answer. This was especially the case in the Eastern counties, where the outside face of the walls of many of the churches was panelled. But the result was not altogether satisfactory. These churches did not look weak, but they must have looked flat, as stained glass from the outside has a very opaque appearance, and the difference between the sunk

Fig. 252.

panelling and the pierced was consequently little noticeable. Much of the charm of twelfth and thirteenth-century work in both large and small churches lies in the contrast between wall and window. This disappeared to a great extent in later churches, and the absence of it is one of the reasons for their inferiority.

Open timber roofs.

The open timber roof, treated architecturally, is almost exclusively an English feature. The basilican churches of Italy have mostly coffered ceilings, and in the few in which the timbers show, as in S. Miniato, Florence, the design is of the simplest character and the only decoration is paint. Even at Verona, where S. Zeno and S. Fermo Maggiore have more elaborate roofs, the treatment is still a panelled one. In France, a church of any size is generally vaulted, and, as mentioned before, most of the parish churches are large. Many small churches there are unvaulted, but the carpentry of their roofs shows little taste or ingenuity in design, and not unfrequently consists of timbers arranged to form a pointed barrel roof which is covered on the inside by plain boarding, with, or without, small ribs reaching from wall plate to ridge. The supremacy of the mason in France, and the square miles of oak forests which England at one time possessed, account to a great extent for the difference between the two countries.

No roofs, save a few very plain ones, exist in this country of the twelfth or thirteenth century. Most were probably of ordinary tie-beam construction, with king or queen posts, and were sometimes ceiled, as in S. Albans Cathedral, so that none of the timbers showed. Their pitch was very steep, about 60° or more, and this can often be determined in many churches, the existing roofs of which are later and flatter, by the original stone weather tabling on the east side of a western tower. Some fourteenth-century roofs remain—over a portion of Crick Abbey is a fine one with the ball flower ornament carved on the timbers—and there would be more if it were not that many were removed in the following century, when the side walls were raised to form the clerestory which the fifteenth-century builders loved. These roofs were seldom replaced, as their steepness, although not quite so great as in roofs of the previous centuries, would have made the churches too high, and their thrusts would probably have been too great for the raised walls. Many fifteenth-century roofs over fifteenth-century churches are of fair pitch; but roofs of that date over earlier churches to which clerestories have been added are invariably flat. In English roofs, with the exception of the early ceiled ones already mentioned, and a few later roofs which are panelled, all the timbers show from wall plate to ridge. These are of large scantlings, beautifully framed together and pinned—iron straps were unknown—and, except the common rafters, elaborately moulded. Sometimes the rafters are moulded as well, but they are, perhaps, most effective when they are not, as then their sturdiness is most apparent. Six inches by 4 inches is no unfrequent size for them in mediæval churches, and it must be remembered that in most instances they are laid flat, so that the width of the underside of each is the greater dimension. How different is the 4 inch by 2 inch rafter placed the other way of the builders' roof of to day! All timbers were oak. Some churches are stated to have had roofs of chestnut, but there are very few in England in which this wood was used, and possibly none.

Mediæval open timber roofs are divided into two main classes. **Types of roofs.**
(1) Single-framed roofs, in which there are no principals.
(2) Double-framed roofs, in which the rafters are supported at intervals by principals framed in different ways.

The second class can be subdivided into tie-beam roofs, hammer-beam roofs, collar-beam roofs, and roofs in which the principals consist merely of rafters stiffened by curved braces.

In single-framed roofs each pair of rafters is trussed together. **Single-framed roofs.** The foot of each rafter rests on one end of a plate laid across the wall, and the rafter is further supported by a vertical strut tenoned into it, and into the other end of the plate. A triangular truss is thus formed of considerable strength. The transverse plates are notched on to a longitudinal plate, generally in the centre of the wall, which runs the whole length of the church, or the length of the nave or chancel, as the case may be. Each pair of rafters is also united by a collar about one-half or two-thirds above the start of the roof, which is strutted from the rafters. All the different timbers are halved and pinned or tenoned together. In some examples the struts are curved like braces, and a waggon or barrel roof is formed, which is either pointed or semicircular. A moulded cornice (the only part of the roof which is not structural) usually conceals the ends of the transverse plates, and this in many examples is also carved. In several roofs of the above type, both polygonal and waggon shaped, all the timbers are concealed by boarding, which is generally divided into panels by ribs. Considerable care was exercised in the spacing of the timbers so that all the panels should be approximately square and equal in size. At Wimbotsham Church, Norfolk, is a good example of a many-sided

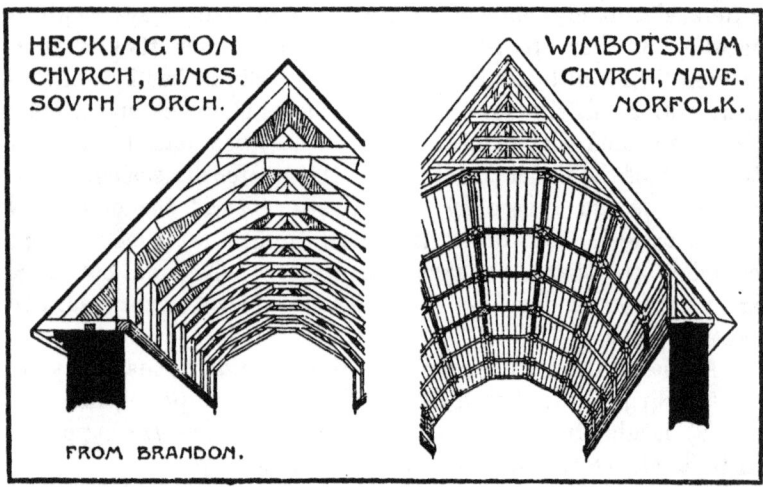

FIG. 253.

panelled roof, and in the West of England, in Cornwall especially, are several panelled waggon roofs, mainly of the fifteenth century.

Tie-beam roofs.
Roofs with tie-beams were used in all the centuries of mediæval art, but they were most common in early work and in late. In the former their high pitch allowed of either king or queen posts, which are strengthened by curved braces. The tie-beams are also supported by braces tenoned into vertical wall pieces which rest on corbels. In the numerous flat-pitched roofs with tie-beams of the fifteenth century there is little room for posts, but the spaces between the beams and principal rafters are filled with pierced or carved panelling. The tie-beams of these are seldom straight, but rise slightly towards the centre, and sometimes, in conjunction with the curved braces underneath, form a series of flat four-centred arches. In all open roofs the ridges are heavy timbers, often elaborately moulded, and frequently supported by curved braces which run longitudinally from principal to principal. In many cases the purlins are similarly strengthened.

Hammer-beam roof.
The most ingenious type of roof is the hammer-beam, or cantilever, and it is also generally the richest. It was the favourite

form in England in the fifteenth century for both wide and narrow spans. The construction of each principal is much the same as at the foot of each rafter in a single-framed roof, except that the hammer-beam, which takes the place of the transverse plate, does not rest on the wall but projects in front of it, and is supported by a wall piece and brace. The whole forms an exceedingly strong truss. In some roofs there are two or more hammer-beams to each principal, one above the other; whilst in others, instead of the upper hammer-beams, there are collars strengthened by braces. In the roof of Westminster Hall there is an unusually strong pair of braces to each principal, which start from corbels and unite all the timbers together. The suitability of the hammer-beam roof for wide spans is well illustrated in this building, which is 65 feet wide, and in the halls of

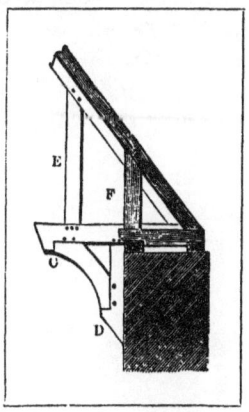

FIG. 254.—Construction of Hammer-beam.

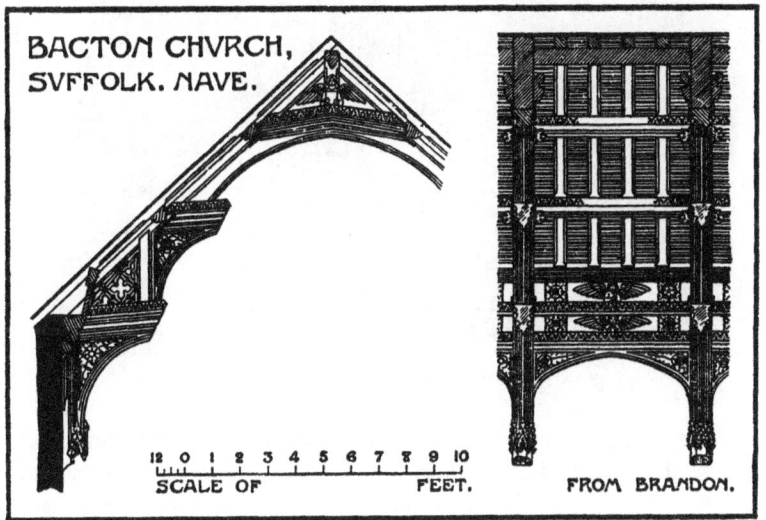

FIG. 255.

many of the Inns of Court, of the Charterhouse, Eltham Palace, and in several churches of over 30 feet span. A hammer-beam

370 A HISTORY OF ARCHITECTURAL DEVELOPMENT.

roof is preferable to a tie-beam one when the width is greater than a single beam can bridge, as scarfing is avoided, and owing to the science displayed in arranging the timbers so as to transmit all thrusts on to the wall, the absence of a horizontal tie is hardly felt.

FIG. 256.—Westminster Hall: Cross section.

Purlins, etc.

It is unnecessary to say anything about roofs with principal rafters strengthened merely by curved braces, or by collars and braces. Whatever the type of roof may be, the purlins are invariably tenoned into the principals, and do not rest upon them as in ordinary modern roofs. In roofs with timbers of light scantling this could not be done without endangering their stability, but there was no risk of this with the heavy timbers used in the Middle Ages. The method has great æsthetic advantages over the modern one, as it brings all the parts closely together, and mouldings can mitre with one another with excellent results. In many roofs, the main principals of which are constructed in any of the ways already mentioned, there are intermediate principals of lighter scantling and fewer parts. The main principals come over piers or solid walling; the others generally over windows or arches. At each end, east and west, is placed one of these half or intermediate principals, to give a finish to the roof and frame in the purlins and common rafters.

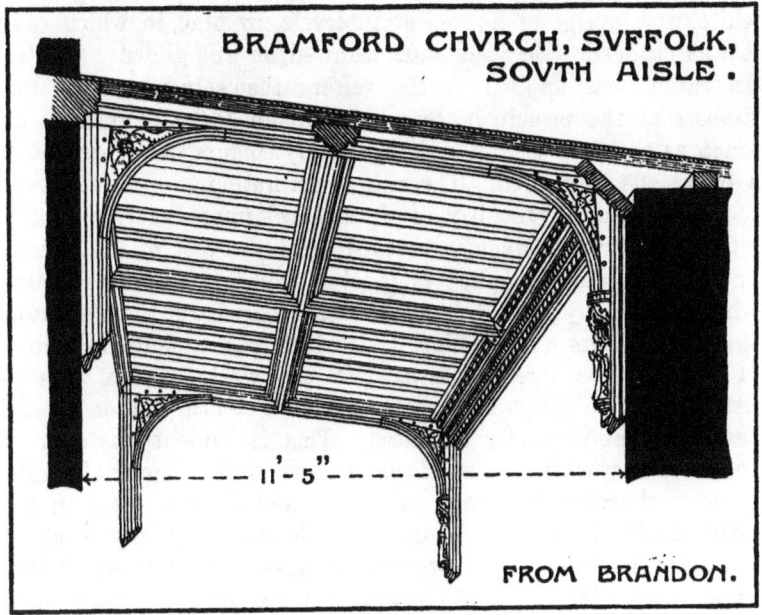

Fig. 257.

Whilst a few aisled roofs are double-pitched, the large majority are lean-to. In the hands of the mediæval carpenter this commonest form of roof acquired considerable distinction. There was no room or need for elaborate tie- or hammer-beams; but nearly all aisle roofs have braced principals, of heavier scantling than the ordinary rafters, and moulded purlins.

There are very few open English timber roofs without some carving on them, and all were originally richly painted and gilded. The cornices are crowned by battlementing or cresting, and

Aisle roofs.

Decoration of roofs.

frequently are pierced or carved; the spaces between the timbers of principals are filled with similar pierced panels or carvings, and at the ends of the beams in hammer-beam roofs are frequently carved angels with outspread wings, whilst in some cases the actual beams are carved to represent angels with their wings folded. Much of the painted decoration has disappeared, but enough remains in many churches to show how rich and effective it was. White always entered largely into the colour scheme, and "barber poling" in white and green, or red and white, was a favourite treatment for three-quarter round mouldings. The boarding between the common rafters was frequently painted white, with sprigs of flowers at intervals, or blue, in which case it was studded with lead stars screwed on and gilded. Similar decoration was applied to the rafters themselves, and to the timbers of the principals, care being taken to counterchange as much as possible, so that although many colours were introduced a broad effect resulted. The richest decoration is generally over the chancel, or in the bay of the chancel immediately over the altar. Either is frequently boarded when the rest of the church is not, and gold is applied in greater profusion there than elsewhere. In many a small parish church, otherwise of little interest, the roof imparts a distinction to it which parish churches abroad of similar size rarely possess. If the work of the masons deteriorated in England in the fifteenth century, that of the carpenters undoubtedly advanced. This is evident not only in roofs. The work in the wood screens and stalls of many fifteenth-century churches is beyond all praise, and if little mention has been made of it in this volume, it is not from any want of appreciation, but simply because to have treated these fittings at all adequately would have meant a greater space than could be spared.

APPENDIX.

TABLE OF DIMENSIONS OF TYPICAL CHURCHES.

THE following table gives the approximate *internal* dimensions of some of the principal churches in Europe. The examples chosen are grouped under heads in order to illustrate the differences in proportion in Romanesque and Gothic; in churches barrel-vaulted, rib-vaulted, and domed; in those without either triforia or clerestories, those with triforia only, and others in which the three divisions, arcade, triforium, and clerestory, are found. The dimensions are given of some large aisleless churches, and of churches which, although aisleless, have deep side recesses. The table also shows the striking differences in scale and proportion between examples in different countries, and emphasizes the characteristics of each in these respects.

Whilst no claim is made that the dimensions given are exact, considerable trouble has been taken to make them as correct as possible. The compilation of such a table is no easy matter. Plans when scaled show striking discrepancies. Dimensions given by authorities vary considerably, and it is seldom that two are found to agree. When stated in figures, as a rule there is nothing to show where they are taken from exactly. From wall to wall seems the natural measurement, but in many cases it is evident that recesses in walls have been included, or that the tape has been held to doors, or to the glass of windows, in order to gain a few extra feet of length or width.

Inaccuracies have doubtless crept in in the following table, due in some cases to the size of the plans and sections available, in others to the calculations necessary to change French feet, Prussian feet, metres, etc., into English feet; but the intention has always been to state the dimensions in the clear between walls, and to ignore casual recesses.

374 APPENDIX

TABLE OF APPROXIMATE INTERNAL DIMENSIONS IN FEET.

(a) Exclusive of chapels. (b) Inclusive of chapels. (c) Aisleless. (d) Height of aisles of crossing.
(e) Including western narthex. (f) Double bays covered by one vault. (g) Including porch. (h) Including Henry VII.'s Chapel.
(i) Height of inner aisles. (j) Height of outer aisles. (k) Including western tower.

Figs. in letterpress.	Name of example.	Width of nave between walls.	Total width of western arm.	Width of bays centre to centre of columns.	Length of nave exclusive of crossing.	Width across transepts.	Width of eastern arm.	Total length.	Height.
	Aisleless Romanesque churches, S. France (barrel-vaulted).								
	Orange Cathedral	45	65	34	140	—	—	—	65
	Abbey Church of Montmajour	43	45	21	—	97	45	—	54
	Aisleless Romanesque churches, S. France (domed).								
144–5.	Angoulême Cathedral	37	52	44	148	158	40(a), 58(b)	242	66
146.	Fontevrault Abbey Church	52	52	43	186	134	62	285	66
	Aisleless Romanesque churches, S. France (rib-vaulted).								
47, 162.	Angers Cathedral	56	56	50	155	155	56	300	80
	S. Radegonde, Poitiers	46	46	40	156	—	57(a), 71(b)	244	78
	Aisled barrel-vaulted churches, S. France, no triforium or clerestory.								
151.	S. Nazaire, Carcassonne	26	52	16	102	—	—	—	55
	Fontfroide Abbey Church	27	58	22	107	90	27 (c)	177	68

APPENDIX.

Ref.	Church								
Aisled barrel-vaulted churches, S. France, with triforium, no clerestory.									
52-3-4-5-6.	Issoire Cathedral	25	52	15	121	92	50(a), 68(b)	204	57, 71(d)
157.	S. Sernin, Toulouse	30	94	17	235	192	60(a), 85(b)	362	70
Other aisled barrel-vaulted churches, S. France.									
83, 160-1.	Autun Cathedral	31	71	18	125	106	71	264 (e)	78
150.	S. Philibert, Tournus	23	62	18	93	90	52	250 (b)	61
Aisled domed churches, S. France.									
141-2.	S. Front, Périgueux	40	72	—	—	188	70	220	92
148, 165.	Le Puy Cathedral	27	67	25	144	126	32 (c)	206	66
Aisled Romanesque churches, either timber-roofed or vaulted, Italy, Germany, Normandy.									
121.	Pisa Cathedral	43	106	17	170	246	106	308	92
125-6-7-8.	Monreale Cathedral	47	87	15	142	113	113	300 (g)	80
111-2-3.	S. Ambrogio, Milan	44	87	44	175	—	44	220	63
133-4, 137.	Worms Cathedral	39	88	36	242	111	39 (c)	356	90
135-6.	Speier Cathedral	46	113	41	235	154	51 (c)	420	108
	Mainz Cathedral	45	{ 105 (a), 183 (b) }	33	250	152	82 (c)	380	88
75, 178.	Jumièges Abbey Church	34	68	18	—	—	—	—	84
174.	S. Etienne, Caen	33	75	20	183	131	—	—	72
Romanesque and Gothic churches of England.									
99.	Norwich Cathedral	31	71	18	253	174	71	400	73
105, 178, 218-9.	Winchester Cathedral	35	86	23	270	215	88	526	78
	Gloucester Cathedral	34	87	20	187	148	84	407	68
176-7, 179, 182.	Durham Cathedral	32	80	25	198	169	76	{ 415, 472 (g) }	72
101, 213, 217.	Ely Cathedral	34	79	17	288	184	79	514 (g)	70

APPENDIX.

TABLE OF APPROXIMATE INTERNAL DIMENSIONS IN FEET—continued.

Figs. in letterpress.	Name of example.	Width of nave between walls.	Total width of western arm.	Width of bays centre to centre of columns.	Length of nave exclusive of crossing.	Width across transepts.	Width of eastern arm.	Total length.	Height.
	Romanesque and Gothic churches of England—continued.								
100, 102, 209, 210, 212.	Salisbury Cathedral	35	78	20	198	204	78	450	84
100, 214.	Lincoln Cathedral	38	82	27	205	224	84	481	74 choir, 82 nave
214.	Westminster Abbey	34	80	19	240	191	77 (*a*) / 115 (*b*)	408 originally, 505(*h*)	101
215.	Exeter Cathedral	36	74	20	—	142	74	384	70
216.	York Cathedral	47	105	27	209	225	100	486	99
94.	Canterbury Cathedral	30	73	20	182	130	88	518	80
	Gothic churches of Northern France.								
50, 61, 64, 103, 196.	Laon Cathedral	38	72 (*a*) / 100 (*b*)	30 (*f*)	180	180	100	365	81
106, 189, 197.	Nôtre Dame, Paris	46	120 (*a*) / 149 (*b*)	36 (*f*)	186	158	120 (*a*) / 149 (*b*)	409	110
194.	Chartres Cathedral	52	110	23	194	204	152	425	114
62, 187.	Reims Cathedral	45	100	24	250	162	150	455	125
193.	Bourges Cathedral	46	135 (*a*) / 165 (*b*)	45 (*f*)	—	—	135 (*a*) / 165 (*b*)	381	125, 69 (*i*), 28 (*j*)
188, 195, 208, 210.	Amiens Cathedral	46	103 (*a*) / 152 (*b*)	25	185	199	156	449	139½
97–8.	Le Mans Cathedral (choir only)	—	—	—	—	180	125 (*a*) / 178 (*b*)	—	110
	Beauvais Cathedral	—	—	—	—	184	133	—	154

APPENDIX.

Gothic churches of Southern France.									
200.	Poitiers Cathedral	{40 / 33 choir}	107	150	185	100	310	{75 choir / 85 nave}	
201-2-3.	Albi Cathedral	60	99	—	—	99	350 (k)	99	
204.	Church of Jacobins, Toulouse	63	83	—	—	83	277	93	
Gothic churches of Germany.									
226.	Cologne Cathedral	46	152	26	213	254	152 (o)	452	150
231.	Ulm Cathedral	50	160	24	310	—	51 (o)	416	138
227-8.	S. Mary, Lübeck	41	112	21	—	—	110	312	125
230.	S. Peter, Lübeck	33	78	27	—	—	78	188	67
Gothic churches of Italy.									
234, 236, 238.	S. Anastasia, Verona	35	75	33	195	110	35 (o)	284	85
	S. Maria Novella, Florence	43	90	46	250	135	43 (o)	340	86
	SS. Giovanni e Paolo, Venice	42	92	40	204	143	43 (o)	322	85
	Como Cathedral	55	125	40	180	—	—	—	95
235, 237.	Florence Cathedral	57	126	62	250	—	—	—	145
	S. Petronio, Bologna	59	{132 (a) / 188 (b)}	64	386	—	—	—	138
241-2-3.	Milan Cathedral	58	190	33	288	255	128	488	157
Gothic churches of Spain.									
245.	Gerona Cathedral	73	102	41	165	—	{85 (a) / 106 (b)}	273	117
246-7.	Barcelona Cathedral	42	{82 (a) / 118 (b)}	32	148	124	{110 (a) / 162 (b)}	284	89
	Salamanca Cathedral (new)	43	{110 (a) / 162 (b)}	33	166	162		340	118
	Segovia Cathedral	44	{114 (a) / 158 (b)}	35	169	—	153	342	125
	Seville Cathedral	46	{194 (a) / 247 (b)}	38	187	250	{194 (a) / 247 (b)}	427	110

INDEX.

Abacus—
  Octagonal, 39
  Plan of, changes in, 37-38
  Upper (pseudo-dosseret), examples of, 35
Abbeville—
  S. Ricquier, 105, 278 *note* ²
  S. Vulfran Cathedral, 33, 277, 284-285; decoration in, 121, 284
Abbotsbury (Dorset)—S. Catherine's Chapel, 71, 91, 318
Abutments, *see* Buttresses
Addison quoted, 3 *note*
Adel Church (Yorks.), 161
Aix-la-Chapelle Church, 188-139, 333
Alan of Walsingham, 315
Albi Cathedral—
  Exterior of, 289
  Fortified tower of, 106
  Gerona Cathedral compared with, 353
  Jacobins' Church (Toulouse) compared with, 292
  Plan of, 157, 289-290
  Span of, 286
Alençon Cathedral, flamboyant style in, 284
Alfriston church (Sussex), 360
Altars in Churches—
  Choir widely separated from, 354-355
  Increase in number of, 144-145
Alternation of materials or colours—
  Brick and marble, 20, 43, 109, 117, 175, 345
  Brick and stone, 117
  Bricks, glazed coloured, 109 *note*
  Marbles, coloured, 117, 175, 341
  Stone and tile, 136
Amalfi, arcading at, 52
Amiens Cathedral—
  Bourges Cathedral compared with, 274
  Chapels of, 153

Amiens Cathedral—*continued.*
  Chevet of, 149
  Cologne Cathedral modelled on, 325-327
  Commemoration of master masons connected with, 256 *note*
  Construction of, 275
  Dates of, 262, 302
  Destruction of, 262
  Double aisles of, 156
  Exterior of, 276
  Flamboyant style in, 284
  Flèche of, 276, 303-304
  Flying buttresses of, 98
  Horizontal lines in, 279
  Nave of, 152
  Piers in, 32, 355
  Plain wall space in, 272
  Plan of, 266-267
  Proportions of, 265, 272, 302-303
  Salisbury Cathedral compared with, 301-304
  Sculptured figures in, 124
  Site of, 264
  Triforium of, 271
  Vaulting in, 102
  West front of, 278, 300
Andernach Church, 190, 197 *note* ¹, 198
Angers—
  Cathedral (S. Maurice)—
    Date of, 259
    Paintings in, 123
    Plan of, 205, 226-227
    Span of, 286
    Style of, 259
    Vaulting of, 78, 86-87
  La Trinité—
    Buttresses of, 269
    Plan of, 158, 205, 226-228, 353; illustrated, 227
    Restoration of, 117 *note*, 228 *note* ¹
    Vaulting of, 79, 81
  S. Serge, 230

INDEX.

Angilbertus, Archbishop, 168
Angoulême Cathedral—
  Plan of, 207-209
  Proportions of, 210
  Towers of, 104
  West front of, 230
Animal forms supporting columns, etc., 173
Antwerp Cathedral, 156, 335
Apses in French cathedrals, piers of, 268
Apulia, churches of, 180-184
Aquileja Cathedral, 172 note
Aquitaine churches, foreign influence in, 203
Arcading of walls, 51-52, 56
Arches (see also Vaults)—
  Construction of, Roman and Mediæval, 14-16
  Cusped (foliated), 13, 14
  Elasticity of, 14
  Enrichments carved on, 127
  Extrados of, not concentric with intrados, 183 and note [2]
  Foliated (cusped), 13, 14
  Horseshoe, 13, 183, 219
  Intersecting, 10-11, 52
  Mouldings of, see Mouldings
  Ogee, 12
  Painting and gilding on, 120-121
  Parapets, of, 53
  Pointed—
    Advantages of, 10
    Early (pre-Hellenic) use of, 9
    Forms of, 11-13
    Introduction of, dates of, 10
    Vaulting, in, 77-8 and note
  Romanesque form of, 9
  Semicircular—
    Examples of, 10-12
    Popularity of, 13 note
  Sicily, in, 185-186
  Springers of, 15-16
  Squinch, carrying spires, 113
  Stilted—
    France, in, 13
    Sicily, in, 186
    Windows, of, 60
  Subordination of, 15
  Thrust of, see Thrust
  Transverse, in vaulting, 71-72 and note [1], 79

Arches—*continued*.
  Trefoil, 12-13; in Auvergne, 219
  Unmoulded, examples of, 17
  Windows, of, see *under* Windows
Arles—S. Trophime, 216, 230
Ashlar—
  Facings of, 23
  Solid piers of, 29, 45
  Walling of, 29, 45
Assisi, Franciscan church at, 339
Asti, Baptistery at, 161
Audenarde—Nôtre Dame de Pameleh, 335
Austin Canons, 243
Autun Cathedral—
  Arches in, 251 note [3]
  Cluny the model for, 223
  Doorway of, 123, 222-223
  Fluted pilasters in, 32
  Plan of, 223-225
  Porch of, 122, 222-223
  Sculpture in, 123, 124
  Vaulting in, 71
Auvergne churches—
  Arches in—
    Foliated, 14, 219
    Semicircular, 10
    Stilted, 13
    Transverse, 71
  Lighting of, 218
  Piers in, 32
  Roofs of, 218
  Similarity between, 216
  Triforia but no clerestories in, 8, 197, 216
  Upper abacus in, 35
Auxerre—
  Cathedral—
    Dates of, 264
    Vaulting in, 102
    View of, 265
    Wall thickness in, 34
  S. Eusèbe, carving in, 127
  S. Germain, tower of, 111
  S. Pierre—
    Date of, 285
    Plain wall space in, 272
Avallon, 230
Avignon Cathedral, 216

BACHARACH—S. Werner, 324, 333
Bacton Church (Suffolk), 369

INDEX.

Bâle Cathedral, 197
Bamberg Church, 324
Bangor Cathedral, 244
Baptisteries, 161-162
Barcelona—
  Cathedral—
    Chapels of, 353-354
    Interior of, 356
    Passage-way triforium of, 357
    Plan of, 353-354
  S. Maria del Mar, 353
  S. Maria del Pino, 352
Barfreston Church (Kent), 60, 161
Bari—
  Cathedral—
    East end of, 161
    East window of, 173
    Frieze of cupola of, 181
    Pierced marble window slabs in, 181
  S. Gregorio, 181
  S. Nicolo—
    East end of, 161
    Exterior of, 182 *and note*, 183
    Glass mosaic in, 181
    Plan of, 181-182
    Tower of, 108
Barisanus of Trani, 180
Barnack Church, 235, 239
Bases, development of, 40
Basilican churches—
  Middle storey of, 5
  Towers of, position of, 106
Bath Abbey, 65, 92, 317, 318
Batter—
  Buttresses, of, 50-51, 179
  Towers, of, 51, 108, 110, 179
Battlementing, 53
Bayeux Cathedral—
  Chevet in, 268
  Columns in, 32
  Date of, 301
  Destruction of original, 242
  Detached shafts in, 32, 33
Beaune Cathedral, 222, 225
Beauvais—
  Basse Œuvre, 136-137
  Cathedral—
    Chevet of, 149
    Choir of, 274
    Collapse of, 263, 275 ; cause of, 304 *note*

Beauvais—*continued*.
  Cathedral—*continued*.
    Flying buttresses of, 100
    Glazed triforium of, 271
    Gothic mixed with Renaissance in, 284-285
    Proportions of, 272
    Transept doorways of, 277
    Vaulting in, 102, 263 *note*
    Windows of, 69
  S. Etienne, 74-75 *and note*, 259
Belgium (*for towns, churches, etc., see their names*)—
  Brick buildings in, 43
  Churches of, 334-335 ; niches in, 33
  Secular buildings in, 335
Benedictine Order—
  Building activity of, 1
  Cistercian rivalry with, 158
  Decline in supremacy of, in France, 254-255
  Influence of, 203
  Mission of, to England (596), 233
  Towers to churches of, 115
Benevento Church, 183
Bergamo, Baptistery at, 161 *and note*[2]
Bernard of Clairvaux, S., 158-159, 254
Berneuil, plan of, 208
Bernières-sur-mer Church, 80, 243
Beverley—
  Minster—
    East transepts of, 278
    Plan of, 153
    Windows of, 62
  S. Mary, 129
Bilson, John, cited, 76 *and note*, 251
Bodley, G. F., quoted, 282
Boffiy, Guillermo, 353 *note*
Bologna, S. Petronio—
  Capital in, 36
  Date of, 338
  Plan of, original, 344 *and note*
  Windows of, 342 ; tracery, 346
Bonn Cathedral, 193, 199
Bordeaux Cathedral, 32
Boscherville, S. Georges de—
  Date of, 242-243
  Eastern arm of, 146, 247
  Proportions of, 248
  Vaulting of, 79
Bosses, 90-91
Boston Church (Lincs.), 62, 115

382 INDEX.

Bourges Cathedral—
　Apse of, 268
　Chevet of, 149
　Date of, 262-263
　Double aisles of, 156
　Exterior of, 274-275
　Flying buttresses of, 269
　Interior of, unique, 274
　Proportions of, 265, 272
　Section of, 274
　Shafts in, 33
　Vaulting in, 81, 102
　View of, 265
　West front of, 275, 280
　Windows of, 133
　mentioned, 328, 346
Bowtell moulding, *see under* Mouldings
Boxgrove Priory (Sussex), 91, 263, 314 *note* [1]
Bradford-on-Avon Church (S. Lawrence)—
　Dimensions of, 238
　East end of, 161, 234
　Masonry of, 236 *note*
　Plan of, 234-235
Braisne Church (S. Yved)—
　Chapels of, 325
　Lantern tower of, 104, 112
　Plan of, 326
Bramford Church (Suffolk), 371
Breamore Church, 238
Brede Church, 64
Brescia Cathedral, 139 *note*
Brick—
　Belgian churches, employment in, 335
　French churches of, in the South, 289
　German churches, employment in, 328
　Glazed, towers of, in Italy, 109 *note*
　Marble alternating with, 20, 43, 109, 117, 175, 345
　Stone alternating with, 117
Brinkburn Priory (SS. Peter and Paul), 18, 57
Brioude Cathedral, 216-218
Bristol—S. Mary Redcliffe, 91, 358-359, 362
Brittany churches, English influence in (14th century), 282-283
Brixworth Church, 238-239

Broaches, 113-114
Broadwater Church (Sussex), 361
Bronze doors, 180
Buildwas Abbey (S. Mary)—
　Date of, 10, 297
　Design of, 297-298
　Plan of, 159-160
　Windows in, 56 *note*
Burgh-by-Sands Church, 106
Burgos—
　Cathedral, 351
　Las Huelgas Church, 159
Burgundy churches—
　Barrel-vaulted, 223-225
　Carving in, 126-127
　Clerestory and triforium in, relative importance of, 225
　Monastic influence in construction of, 73, 221
　Mouldings in, 19
　Narthices in, 222-223, 230-231
　Rib-vaulted, 225-230
　Transverse arches in, 71
　Upper abacus in, 35
　Vézelay, *see that title*
　West fronts of, 280
Burial inside churches, 162-163
Burton-on-Humber Church, 235
Bury St. Edmunds Church—
　Bosses in, 180
　Date of, 244
　Plan of, 147 *note* [2], 150
Buttresses—
　Advantages of outside, 46
　Batter of, 50-51, 179
　Corner, 49-50
　Flying—
　　France, in, 51
　　Hidden, 96 *and note*
　　Piercing and panelling of, 282
　　Position of, in relation to vault thrusts, 97-98
　　Sexpartite vaults, to, 269
　　Spires, on, 114
　　Stiffeners, as, 98-99
　　Thrusts transmitted by, 97
　France, Southern, in, 46, 47 *note*
　Functions of, 46, 269
　Italy, in, 183
　Niches on, 50
　Octagonal, 50-51
　Panelled, 50

INDEX. 383

Buttresses—*continued*.
  Pilaster, 51
  Romanesque, form of, 46
  Sculptured figures on, 50, 124
  Shafts at angles of, 49
  Stages of, 47–50
  Towers, of, 110
  Weatherings of, 49
Byland Abbey, 13
Byzantine carving, 126–127
Byzantine churches, galleries of, 6
Byzantine colony of Apulia, 166
Byzantine influence on plans, etc.—
  France and Germany, in, 137–142, 203
  Italy, in, 175, 180–181
  Sicily, in, 184
Byzantine-Romanesque work, 167

CAEN—
  Abbaye-aux-Dames (La Trinité)—
    Aisles of, 146
    Apses of, 248
    Date of, 242
    Gallery lacking in, 7
    Nave of, length of, 247
    Proportions of, 249
    Triforium of, 249
    Vaulting in, 71, 80
    West front of, 230
  Abbaye-aux-Hommes (S. Etienne)—
    Apses of, 248
    Clustered piers in, 30
    Date of, 242
    Eastern arm of, 247
    Galleries of, 7
    Nave of, length of, 247
    Open space before, 264
    Proportions of, 249
    Transept altars of, 146
    Triforium of, 249
    Vaulting in, 101
    West front of, 230
  Abbaye d'Ardennes, mouldings in, 20, 301
  S. Nicolas—
    Roofing of, 243, 275
    Tower of, 111
  S. Pierre, spire of, 333
Cahors Cathedral, 207 *note*, 210
Cambridge—
  King's College Chapel—
    Dates of, 317

Cambridge—*continued*.
  King's College Chapel—*continued*.
    Dimensions and detail of, 318–319
    Elevation of, 319, 320
    Fan vaulting in, 90, 92
    Glass in, 133
    Plan of, 319
  Templar church at, 142
Campanile towers, 108, 110
Canosa Cathedral, 181, 183
Canterbury—
  Cathedral—
    Apse of, original, 247
    Chevet of, columns of, 33 *note*
    Choir of, 91, 296, 297
    Dates of, 243, 315
    Plan of, 150, 153; original plan, 146–147 *and note* ²
    Towers of, 104, 107, 110, 112
    Vaulting in, 81, 91, 101, 102
  S. Augustine's Church (on site of present cathedral), 237–238
  S. Martin's Church, 234
Capitals—
  Carving of, 126–128
  Circular, 38
  Concave, forms of, 37
  Convex, 36–37
  Functions of, 34–36
  Nature of, 36
  Octagonal, 39
  Romanesque, derivation of, 35–36
  Subordination of, 37
Carcassonne—S. Nazaire, 287; vaulting in, 10, 95, 215–216
Carileph, Bishop, 251 *and note* ²
Carlisle Cathedral—
  Date of, 244
  East window of, 62
  Vaulting in, 101
Carvings (*see also* Mouldings *and* Sculpture)—
  Advance in, during 12th century, 258
  Ball flower, 129–131 *and note*
  Byzantine workmanship in, 126–127
  Dogtooth, 129
  Italy, South, in, 180
  Paris Cathedral, on west front of, 279
  Runic crosses, 241
  Tudor rose, 131
Caserta Vecchia (Benevento), 14, 183

INDEX.

Cattaneo quoted, 75; cited, 106, 147, 168, 191 note [1], 235
Caudebec Church, 284
Cefalû Cathedral—
    Date of, 186
    Exterior of, 230
    Mosaics in, 118
    Plan of, 188
    Stucco on, 45 note [1]
Cérisy-la-forêt Church, 146, 243
Chalons-sur-Marne—Nôtre Dame de l'Epine, 284
Chamalières Church, 216–218
Chancels, raised, 163
Chantry chapels, 155 and note, 163, 311
Chapter houses, English, 315
Charlieu Church, 230
Charroux Church, 140–142, 147
Chartres—
    Cathedral—
        Apse of, 267–268
        Arcading on, stilting of, 268
        Carving in, 131
        Choir of, 268
        Crypt of, 147
        Date of, 262
        Double aisles of, 156, 266
        Nave of, 152
        Open space before, 264
        Piers in, 32
        Plain wall space in, 272
        Plan of, 276
        Porches of, transepts of, 122, 277, 280
        Proportions of, 265, 272
        Sculptured figures in, 124, 125
        Spires of, 114
        Towers of, 111, 276–277
        Triforium of, 271
        Vaulting in, 34, 102
        Wall thickness in, 34
        West front of, 278
        Windows of—
            Glass, 132
            Tracery, 58, 59, 69
            mentioned, 153
    S. Pierre, 271
Châtres, 208
Chester Cathedral—
    Date of, 244 and note
    East end of, 247
    Font in, position of, 162

Chester Cathedral—*continued*.
    Grooved shafts in, 24 and note
    Plan of, 147 note [2], 151
    South transept of, 359
    Vaulting of, 86, 91, 101, 102
Chevets, 148–150, 267
Chiaravalle Church (near Milan), 159
Chichester Cathedral—
    Alterations in, 246
    Date of, 244
    Decoration in, 118
    Eastern arm of, 247
    Foreign influence in, 297
    Nave of, 246
    Plan of, 146, 151, 154
    Shafts in, 28, 298 note
    Side chapels of, 154
    Towers of, 107
    Triforium of, 118, 249
    Vaulting of, 84 and note [2], 90, 91, 101, 102
Christ Church (Hants)—
    Chantry chapels in, 155
    Date of, 244
    Sculptured figures in, 124
    Triforium decoration in, 249
Cistercian Order, influence of, on plans, etc., 145 and note, 158–161, 295, 306
Claypole Church, 63, 64
Clerestory, functions of, 5
Clermont-Ferrand—Nôtre Dame du Port, 148, 216
Cluny Abbey—
    Narthex of, 222
    Nave of, length of, 247
    Plan of, 143, 148, 150, 153, 223
    mentioned, 220
Cobham Church (Kent), 361
Coblentz—S. Castor, 198
Coire Cathedral (Switzerland), 14
Coleshill Church, tower windows of, 111
Cologne—
    Cathedral
        Date of, 325
        Nave of, 152
        Plan of, 325–328
        Western towers of, 333
    Church of the Apostles—
        Apses of, 199–200
        Vaulting in, 195
    S. Gereon, 121

INDEX.

Cologne—*continued.*
  S. Maria in Capitolio—
    Piers and columns in, 31
    Plan of, 199–200
    Vaulting in, 195
  S. Martin—
    Apses of, 199–200
    Decoration in, 121
    Tower of, 200
Columns—
  Diminution of, 137, 179
  Doubling of, 32, 33 *note*
  Entasis of, 23, 137, 179
  Flutings of, 23
  Monolithic, 137
  "Norman," 23
  Piers—
    Alternation with, 26, 137, 175, 242, 251
    Supersession by, 24
  Rubble, of, 23
Como—
  Cathedral, 341
  S. Abbondio, 105
Compostella—S. Iago, 219, 280 *and note* [2], 350
Conques Abbey, 10, 217, 219–220
Constantinople—S. Sophia—
  Dosseret absent from, 35
  Transverse arches in, 72 *note* [1]
Corbels of parapets, 53
Corroyer, M., cited, 74 *note* [2], 77 *note*, 269
Cottingham Church, 62, 63
Coutances—
  Cathedral—
    Columns in, 32
    Date of, 301
    Detached shafts in, 32, 33
    Double aisles of, 266
    Lantern tower of, 104, 111
    Mouldings in, 20
    Ordinance of, 274
    Side chapels of, 153–154, 263
    Spire of, 114
    Towers of, 111, 276, 277
  S. Nicolas, 285
  S. Pierre, 285
Cresy and Taylor cited, 178 *note* [2]
Crick Abbey, 366
Cromer Church, 30
Croydon—Whitgift Almshouses Chapel, 319

Crypts, 163–164
Cupolas, 171 *and note*
Curves in Gothic churches, 178–180 *and note*

DALY, CÉSAR, cited, 139 *note* [2]
Daphni Church (near Athens), 188 *note* [1]
Dareth Church (Kent), 161
d'Argent, l'Abbé Marc, 282
de Cormant, Thomas and Renaut, 257, 279, 304
de Honnecourt, Villard, 256; sketch-book of, 158–159 *and note*
de Luzarches, Robert, 256 *note*, 257, 279, 304
de Noyer, 299
Decoration—
  Billet ornament, 185 *and note*
  Carving, *see that title*
  Colour schemes, 121–122
  Contrasting materials, by, 117 (*see also* Alternation of materials)
  Counterchanging, 187–188
  Diaper work, 218 *and note* [2]
  Dog-tooth ornament, 129, 269
  Egg-and-dart ornament, 37, 127
  Enrichments carved on arches, etc., 127
  Fresco painting, 119
  Inlays, 186
  Mosaics, 24, 118 *and note*, 175, 180–181
  Mouldings, of, 22
  Oil paintings, 120–121
  Paint—
    English roofs, on, 372
    General use of, in early times probable, 116–118
    Italy, in, 342, 348
  Sculpture—
    Archaic, 125
    Examples of, 123
    Framing of, 123–124
    France, in, 124–125
  Tempera paintings, 119
  Timber roofs, of, 371–372
Deerhurst—
  Church, 238
  Odda's Chapel, 45, 236 *note*, 238
Dieppe Church, 284
Dieulafoy, M., cited, 215

Dijon—
　Nôtre Dame—
　　Porch of, 222
　　Sculpture in, 123
　　Style of, 264
　　West front of, 279
　S. Benigne, 140-142, 147
　S. Michel, 225
Dimensions of principal churches in Europe, table of, 373-377
Dogtooth ornament, 129, 269
Dol Cathedral, 263-264
Domed churches, 183, 189
Domes, mosaics on, 118 *note*
Doorways of churches—
　Development of, 40
　France, in, 279-280
Dosserets, 35
Dover Castle Church, 161, 238-239
Drübeck, columns and piers in, 137
Dryburgh Abbey, 321
Durham Castle crypt, 91
Durham Cathedral—
　Apse of, original, 147 *note* [2]
　Arches in, 17
　Chapel of the Nine Altars—
　　Apse superseded by, 245
　　Circular windows in, 69
　　Date of, 161, 252
　　Marble employed in, 26-27
　　Plan and dimensions of, 306
　Clerestory windows of, 252
　Columns in—
　　Alternation of piers with, 26, 251
　　Variety of, 23
　Dates of, 76, 244, 250, 251
　Eastern arm of, length of, 150, 247
　Galilee porch of, 252
　Nave of—
　　Length of, 247
　　Vaulting of, 82, 91, 250
　Plan of, 250
　Proportions of, 248-249
　Towers of, 107, 252
　Transepts of, 248
　Vaulting of, 76-78, 82, 101, 102, 250-252

EARLS BARTON CHURCH, 235-236, 240
Early English architecture, 306-307
Eastbourne—S. Mary, 14, 360
Ebrach Church, 160
Eltham Palace, 369

Ely—
　Cathedral—
　　Date of, 243
　　East end of, 247, 305-306
　　Font in, position of, 162
　　Galilee porch of, 300
　　Galleries in, 7
　　Lady Chapel of—
　　　Crocket in, 130
　　　Sculptured figures in, 124
　　Lantern of, 152, 315
　　Nave of—
　　　Ceiling of, 91, 245
　　　Length of, 246
　　　Piers of, 250
　　Niches on buttresses of, 50
　　Piers in, 250
　　Plan of, 151-153
　　Proportions of, 248
　　Shafts in, 28
　　Towers of—
　　　Central, fall of, 245
　　　Western, 106
　　Transepts of, 248
　　Triforium of, 249
　　Vaulting in, 91, 101, 102
　Prior Crauden's Chapel, 128
England—
　Black Death (1349), effect of, 12, 64, 129, 284, 310-311
　Cathedrals of, contrasted with French, 281
　Cistercian influx into, 295
　East ends of churches in, 161, 237-238, 247
　Gothic architecture in—
　　(1200-1250), 300-307
　　(1250-1300), 307-310
　　(14th and 15th centuries), 310-321
　　Early English, 306-307
　　East ends, 305-306
　　Triforia, 309-310, 314-315
　　West fronts, 304-305
　Parish churches in—
　　Lighting of, 363, 364
　　Number and variety of, 358
　　Plan of, usual, 359
　　Proportions of, 360-361
　　Roofs of—
　　　Construction of, 367-371
　　　Decoration of, 371-372
　　　Material of, 358, 362, 366

INDEX.

England—*continued*.
  Parish churches in—*continued*.
    Roofs of—*continued*.
      Pitch of, 363, 366–367, 371
      Sectional ordinance of, 362–363
      Spaciousness of, 361–362
  Peasant Revolt (1381), 311
  Perpendicular style of 15th-century work in, 284
  Romanesque architecture in, early examples of—
    Long and short work, 236
    Pilaster treatment, 235–237
    Plan of, general, 238
    Proportions of, 238–239
    Square east ends, 237–238
    Windows, 239–240
  Romanesque cathedrals and churches of 11th and 12th centuries in—
    Alterations frequent in, 245–246
    Eastern arm, length of, 247
    Internal divisions, proportions of, 248–249
    List of, 243–244
    Naves, 250–252; length of, 246–247
    Transepts, 247–248
    Triforium design, 249–250
    West fronts, 252–253
  Severance of, from Normandy, 300
  Transitional work in (12th century), 296–298
  West, group of churches in, showing architectural progression, 322
Enlart, M., cited, 242, 255–257, 259, 264 *note*, 284
Enrichment, *see* Decoration
Entasis—
  Columns, of, 137, 179
  Spires, of, 114
Entrances of churches, English and French contrasted, 305
Erfurt—
  Cathedral, 333
  S. Severus, 330
Escomb Church (Durham), 234, 238
Eton College Chapel, 88, 317
Evreux Cathedral, 104, 259
Exeter Cathedral—
  Alterations in, 246
  Carving in, 129
  Date of, 244
  Piers in, 29

Exeter Cathedral—*continued*.
  Plan of, 146, 151, 152, 312; illustrated, 313
  Towers of, 105
  Vaulting of, 86, 91, 101, 102
  Wall thickness in, 34

FAIRFORD CHURCH (Gloucs.), 133
Figeac—S. Sauveur, 282
Fire, frequent destruction of churches by, 245–246
Flamard, Bishop, 251
Flamboyant style, 283–284
Flint—
  Towers of, 108
  Walling of, 43
Florence—
  Campanile, 107, 339
  Cathedral—
    Dome of, 338
    Piers of, 340
    Plan of, 343
    Sections of, 341
    Windows of, 342
  Loggia dei Lanzi, 339
  Loggia del Bigallo, 11, 339
  Rise of, 166
  S. Croce—
    Chapels of, 343
    Columns of, 340
    Fresco paintings in, 119
    Gallery of, 340
    Plan of, 345
    Windows and roof of, 342
  S. Maria Novella, 343
  S. Miniato—
    Ceiling of, 251
    Date of, 25 *note* [2]
    Interior of, 172
    Marble veneering in, 117, 136
    Piers of, 25
    Plan of, 173–175
    Raised chancel of, 163
    Roof of, 366
Flour Cathedral (Auvergne), 272
Fontenay Church, 159
Fontevrault Abbey, 207, 208, 210
Fortified churches, 106
Fountains Abbey—
  Addition to (13th century), 305–306
  Date of, 10, 297
  Design of, 298

Fountains Abbey—*continued*.
  East end of, 161
  Interior arrangement of, 145 *note*
  Vaulting of, 84, 91, 215
Fontfroide Abbey, 216
France (*for districts, towns, churches, etc., see their names*)
  Arches in, 78
  Buttresses in, flying, 51
  Carving in, 128
  Galleries of churches in, 7
  German early buildings under influence of, 143 *note*
  Gothic in, late survival of, 285 (*see also* France, North—Cathedrals *and* France, South—Gothic)
  East ends in, compared with English, 152
  Early churches in, 136-137
  Flamboyant style of 15th-century work in, 283-284
  Height of churches in, 46, 98, 100, 103
  Hundred Years' War, effects of, 12, 20, 262
  Mouldings in, 20-21
  Piers and columns in, examples of, 31-33
  Pinnacles in, 100
  Plain wall-space in churches of, 272
  Sculpture in, schools of, 124-125
  Side chapels in cathedrals of, 153-155
  Spires in, 114
  Vaulting shafts in, 93-94
  Vaults in, 74, 82, 83
  Windows of churches in, 58-62
France, Central—
  Arches in, 16
  Gothic architecture originating in, question as to, 259
  Priority of, in architectural art (12th to 13th century), 258
France, North—
  Architects and craftsmen in (12th to 13th century), 256-257
  Cathedrals of—
    Chevets of, 267-268
    Dates of, 262-263
    Doorways of, 279-280
    Double aisles of, 156, 265-266
    English cathedrals contrasted with, 281
    Interiors, spaciousness of, 266-267

France, North—*continued*.
  Cathedrals of—*continued*.
    Proportions of, 265
    Sites of, 264-265
    Towers of, 275-278
    Transepts of, importance of, 277
    Triforia of, 269-272
    West fronts of, 278-281
  Later Gothic work in, 281-282
  Romanesque churches in, west fronts of, 230
  Windows of churches in, 55 *note*, 56
France, South—
  Aisleless churches in, 156-158, 205, 208, 210
  Barrel vaulting in, 212-216
  Brick buildings in, 13
  Buttressing in, 47; niches, 50
  Capitals in—
    Concave, 37, 39
    Convex, 37
    Corinthian, 204
  Carving in, 126
  Classic influence in, 203-204
  Columns in, 23
  Domed churches in—
    Aisled, 211-212
    Aisleless, 205-210
  English influence on 14th-century churches in, 282-283
  Gothic churches in, Roman influence in, 286
  Transepts, omission of, 275 *note* [1]
  Vaulting in, 79, 86, 95
  Windows of churches in, 56
France, South-West, domed churches in, 9
France, West, English influence in 14th-century churches in, 282-283
Frankfurt cathedral, 333
Freiburg cathedral, 333
Fresco painting, 119
Furness abbey, 159

GABLES—
  Buttresses, on, 49
  Lucarnes, over, 114
  Towers, on, 112
Galleries, external open—
  Bari and Trani, at, 183
  Germany, in, 194
Galleries in churches, 5-7

INDEX. 389

Gedney, S. Mary Magdalene, 361
Germany (*for towns, churches, etc., see their names*)—
  Alternation of large and small supports in churches of, 26
  Apses in, 199–200; double, 191
  Arcading in, 197–198
  Arches in, pointed, date of, 11
  Backwardness of architecture in, after 12th century, 190
  Brick buildings in, 43, 328
  Capitals in, 86–87
  Carving in, 127
  Choirs of churches in, 332–333
  Colour decoration in, 121
  Columns in, 23, 137
  Cupolas and turrets of churches in, 103, 171
  Early churches in, 136, 137
  Exterior of churches in—
    Compactness of, 192
    Simplicity of, 194
    Western façades, 198
  French influence on buildings in, 143 *note*, 325–328
  Galleries—
    External, 194
    Internal, absence of, 196
  Hallenkirchen, 8, 330, 355
  Lateral entrances of churches in, 194
  Masonic dexterity exhibited in, 333
  Mouldings in, interpenetration of, 21
  Piers in, 31
  Roofs of churches in, 332
  "Round-arched Gothic" work in, 78
  Spires of churches in, 112, 114–115; pierced, 333
  Towers and turrets in, 193, 198, 200; single western towers, 333–334
  Triforia, omission of, 7, 331
  Vaulting in, 195
  Windows of churches in, 56
Germigny-les-Prés Church (Loiret), 139–140
Gernrode Church, 196
Gerona Cathedral, 352–353 *and note*
Giotto, 107, 339
Glasgow Cathedral, 323
Glass in church windows—
  Colour in, 133–134
  Early examples of, 131
  Figures in, 132

Glass mosaic, *see* Mosaic
Glastonbury Abbey, 298
Gloucester Cathedral—
  Abaci in, 34 *note*
  Capitals in, 37
  Carving in, 131
  Chantry chapels in, 155
  Columns in, 23, 25
  Date of, 243, 244 *note*
  Eastern arm of, 247
  Galleries in, 7
  Interior arrangements of, 145–147 *note* [2]
  Nave of, 246, 250
  Panelling in, 246, 315
  Proportions of, 248
  Reconstruction of, 246, 312
  Roofings of, 245
  Tower of, 107
  Transepts of, 248
  Vaulting of, 88, 91–92
  Windows of, glass in, 133
Gloucestershire, towers in, 111
Goodyear, Mr., cited, 110, 179 *and note*, 180 *and note*
Gothic, meaninglessness of term, 3 *note*
Gothic architecture—
  Curves in, theories as to, 179–180 *and note*
  England, in, *see under* England
  France, in, *see* France, North—cathedrals, *and* France, South—Gothic
  Germany, in, *see under* Germany
  Italy, in, *see under* Italy
  Renaissance style mixed with, 284–285
  Rise of, 259
  Spain, in, *see under* Spain
  Whitewashing of interiors, 335, 337
Green, J. R., quoted, 307 *note*
Greenstead Church, 233
Guingamp Church, 282
Gurgoyles, 54

HAND centers, 85
Heckington Church (Lincs.), 368
Hereford Cathedral—
  Clerestory windows of, 309
  Columns of, 23
  Date of, 243
  East end of, 247

Hereford Cathedral—*continued*.
  Nave of, 246, 250
  Tower of, 107
  Vaulting in, 91
Hexham Church—
  Crypt of, 234
  Date of, 306
  Windows of, 57
Hildesheim—S. Michael—
  Columns and piers in, 31, 137
  Turrets of, 193
Hitcham Church, 63
Hodges, C. C., quoted, 251
Holland—
  Brick buildings in, 43
  Churches in, 335, 337
Houghton-le-Dale Chapel, 43, 44, 64
Huesca—S. Pedro, 349-350, 355
Hugh, Bishop of Lincoln, 299-300
Huish Episcopi (Somerset), 111

IFFLEY CHURCH, 359
Ingolstadt—Frauenkirche, 333
Ireland, Christianity in, 232
Issoire Cathedral (Auvergne)—
  Angoulême Cathedral compared with, 209
  Arcading of, 182
  Arches in, 14, 219
  Capital in, 36
  Date of, 216
  Exterior of, 218-219
  Interior of, 219
  Plan of, 217
  Windows at crossing of, 218
Italy (*for towns, churches, etc., see their names*)—
  Alternation of large and small supports in, 26
  Arches in—
    Extrados of, not concentric with intrados, 183
    Horseshoe, 14
    Pointed, date of, 11
    Tradition influencing, 16, 78
  Buttressing in, 46
  Capitals in, 37
  Churches in, supports of, 82 *and note*
  Classic traditions dominant in, 2, 4
  Clerestories omitted in churches in, 8
  Columns in, 23
  Dosserets in, 35

Italy—*continued*.
  Gothic architecture in—
    Capitals in, 340
    Characteristics of, 338-339
    Choirs in, 343-344
    Early examples of, 339
    Internal ordinance in, 340-342
    Mural decoration in, 342
    Scale of, 342-343
    West fronts, 344-345
  Mouldings in, 20
  Piers of churches in, 24
  Porches in, 172-173
  Shafts inlaid with mosaics in, 24
  Spires in, 114
  Towers of churches in, 107
  Tuscan churches, 173-180
  Windows of churches in, 56
Italy, North—
  German influence in, 166
  Lombards, 165
Italy, South—
  Byzantine and Norman rule in Apulia, 166-167
  Byzantine-Romanesque work in, 167
  Carving in, 126
  Churches of, 180-184

JEDBURGH ABBEY—
  Interior of, 197 *note*[3]; illustrated, 322
  Piers in, 26
  Plan of, 32
Jerusalem, Church of the Holy Sepulchre at, 141-142
Jervaulx Abbey, 306
Jumièges Abbey—
  Date and style of, 242
  Towers of, 111
  Triforium of, 249

KELSO ABBEY, 244, 321-322
Kirkstall Abbey, 57

LA CHAISE DIEU (Auvergne), 288, 290
La Martorana Church, 185 *note*
Laach Abbey Church—
  Apses in, 192
  Entrances of, 194
  Western atrium of, 198

INDEX. 391

Labels, 17, 22
Lanterns, 104
Laon—
  Cathedral—
    Buttresses of, 96, 269
    Carving in, 129
    Chapels of, 154
    Columns in, 31, 81 *note*, 261 *and note*
    Date of, 262
    East end of, 269
    English features of, 269
    External arcading of, 279
    Galleries in, 7
    Horizontal lines of, 52
    Mural decoration in, 116-117 *and note*
    Plain wall space in, 272
    Plan of, 153
    Rebuilding of, funds for, 255-256
    Shafts in, 32
    Towers of, 111, 275-277; effigies of oxen on, 255
    Triforium of, 260, 269-270
    Vaulting of, 79-81, 96, 102
    West front of, 278
    Windows of, 69
  Templar church at, 142
Laud, Archbishop, 319
Lausanne Cathedral, 197
Laval—La Trinité, 227
Lavenham Church, 30, 311
Le Mans—
  Cathedral—
    Apse of, 267-268
    Chevet of, 149
    Choir of, without triforium, 271
    Dogtooth ornament in, 269
    Double aisles at east end of, 156, 266
    Exterior of, 263, 265; illustrated, 149
    Interior arrangement of, 274
    Lady Chapel of, 152
    Mouldings in, 20
    Nave of, 260-261
    Pinnacles of, 101
    Plan of, 149
    Proportions of, 272
    Sculptured figures in, 125
    Windows in, 132
  S. Pierre de la Couture, 131, 226-227 *and note*

Le Morvan, churches of, 221
Le Puy—
  Cathedral—
    Diaper work in, 218 *note* [2]
    Piers in, 32
    Plan of, 212
    West end of, 231
  S. Michel de l'Aiguille, 231 *note*
Lead, gurgoyles of, 54
Leeds, S. John Baptist Church, 319
Leominster Church, 67, 131 *and note*
Leon—
  Cathedral, 351-352
  S. Isidoro, 219 *and note*, 350
Lerida Church, 350
Lessay Abbey, 242-243
Lichfield Cathedral—
  Clerestory windows of, 309
  Choir, etc., of, 313-314
  Shafts in, 28
  Spires of, 114
  Towers of, 107
  Vaulting of, 86, 90, 91, 101, 102
Liernes, 86, 88 *and note* [2], 91
Lighting of churches, 71, 169-170
Limburg-on-the-Lahn Cathedral, 197 *note* [1], 198, 324
Lincoln—
  Cathedral—
    Angel choir of—
      Cusping in, 67
      Dimensions of, 309
      Sculpture in, 124
      Section of, 308
      Vaulting of, 82, 300
      Window screens of, 309, 314
    Arcading in, double, 300
    Buttresses in, 97
    Capital and crockets in, 130
    Chantry chapels in, 155
    Clerestory windows of, 310
    Dates of, 243, 299
    East transepts of, 278
    Eastern arm, length of, 153
    Labels, interior, in, 22
    Plan of, 151-153, 299; illustrated, 151
    Roof window of, 305
    Screen of, 178
    Shafts in, 28, 29
    Side chapels of, 154

INDEX.

Lincoln—*continued*.
  Cathedral—*continued*.
    Towers of, 104, 107
    Triforium of, 271
    Varieties of Gothic exemplified in, 300 *note*
    Vaulting in, 81, 83, 86, 88 *note*[1], 91, 93, 101, 102, 310
    West front of, 230, 304
    Western porches of, 253
    Windows of, 69; roof, 305
  S. Mary, 232
  S. Peter, 232
Lisieux—
  Cathedral (S. Pierre)—
    Chevet of, 301
    Columns in, 261
    Mouldings in, 20
    Nave of, 258–259
    Style of, 261
    Vaulting in, 80
  S. Jacques—
    Date and style of, 285
    Decoration in, 121
    Plan of, 150
Llandaff Cathedral, 244
Loches—S. Ours, 212–213
Lombardic designs—
  Influence of, on 11th-century English Romanesque, 242
  Roofs, 170
  Towers, 109, 110
Lombards, 165
London—
  Charterhouse, roofing of, 369
  Inns of Court, roofing of, 369
  Parliament, Houses of—
    Panelling of, 30 *and note*
    Victoria Tower of, 51 *note*[1]
  S. Augustine's (Kilburn), 158
  S. Mary Aldermary, 90
  S. Paul's (old)—
    Date of, 243
    Tower of, 107
  S. Saviour's (Southwark), 91
  Temple, the, 142
  Tower of—S. John's Chapel, 71, 91, 95
Long and short bonding, 236
Long Melford Church (Suffolk), 360
Louth Church (Lincs.), 114
Lucarnes, 114

Lübeck—
  Marienkirche, 328–331
  S. James, 330–331
  S. Peter, 330–331
Lucca, arcaded gallery fronts in, 171, 176
Lucca Cathedral (S. Martino), 338–339, 340–341
Lüneberg Church, 330

MAGDALEN LAVER CHURCH, 358
Mainz Cathedral—
  Arcading in, 197–198
  Columns in, 31
  Crypt of, 191–192
  Double apses of, 191–192
  Entrances of, 194
  Proportions of, 197
  Turrets of, 193
  Vaulting in, 195
Malmesbury Abbey—
  Date of, 10, 297
  Doorway of, 16
  Nave of, 298
  Parapet of, 53
  Pinnacles of, 100
  Triforium of, 249
  Vaulting of, 78
Malvern Priory, 243, 317
Manchester Cathedral, 156
Mantes Cathedral, 262
Marble—
  Alternating colours of, 117, 175, 341; roundels of green, 109
  Brick alternating with, 20, 43, 109, 117, 175, 345
  Facing with, 43
  Stone in combination with, 117
  Tesseræ, 175
  Veneer of, 43, 117, 175
Marburg—S. Elizabeth, 330, 333
Masons and masonic guilds—
  Influence of, 3, 5, 20
  Position of master masons in France (12th to 13th century), 256–257
Maulbronn Abbey, plan of, 159
Mediæval architecture—
  Origin of, 1–2
  Period of, 3–4
  Style of, 2
Melrose Abbey, 314, 321–323
Mettlach Church, 138
Metz Cathedral, 271, 328

INDEX.

Milan—
  Cathedral—
    Apse and transepts of, 344
    Exterior of, 346, 347-348
    Interior of, 346, 348
    Lighting of, 346
    Piers in, height of, 355
    Plan of, 343 *note*, 346
    S. Ambrogio contrasted with, 348
    Sections of, 347
    Window tracery in, 346
  S. Ambrogio—
    Arches of, 16, 239
    Burial crypt in, 163
    Carving in, 127
    Cathedral of Milan contrasted with, 348
    Date of, 168
    Galleries in, 7
    Lighting of, 169-170, 218
    Piers in, 30
    Pilasters on tower of, 236
    Plan of, 168-169 *and notes*
    Squinch arches of, 212
    Tower of, 109
    Vaulting of, 8, 75, 79-80
    West front of, 170, 344
  S. Lorenzo, 140, 147 *note*[1]
  S. Satiro—
    Pilaster decoration of, 235
    Plan of, 140
    Tower of, 109
  S. Vincenzo-in-Prato, 170
Moissac Abbey, 127
Molfetta Cathedral, 181, 183-184
Monastery churches, 145
Monastic Orders, *see* Benedictine *and* Cistercian
Monkwearmouth Church, 240, 241
Monreale Cathedral—
  Arcading at, 52
  Carving in, 126
  Cloisters of, 185
  Date of, 186
  Detached shafts of, 186
  Exterior of, 230
  Mosaics in, 5, 118
  Plan of, 187
  Windows of, 64
Montier-en-der Church, triforia in, 136 *note*

Montmajour—
  Abbey, 216
  S. Croix, 140
Montreal Church (Burgundy), 179, 288
Monumental slabs and brasses, 133
Moore cited, 75 *note*
Morienval Church (Oise)—
  East end of, 74 *and note*[2], 148
  Towers of, 105
Mosaic, glass, 24, 118 *and note*, 175, 180-181
Mouldings (*see also* Carving)—
  Arches, of, painting and gilding of, 120
  Bowtell—
    Pointed, 18
    Rounded, 17, 20
  Contemporary, similarity between, 21
  Different planes, on, 19-20
  Dogtooth, 129, 269
  Hood, superfluous nature of, in English cathedrals, 22, 272
  Interpenetration of, 20-21
  Material determining form of, 18, 21
  Ogee, dates of, 18-19
  Plinths, of, 52
  Roman and mediæval, contrasted, 16
  Romanesque period, of, 22
  Sections of mediæval, nature of, 17 *note*
  Timber roofs, of, 367
  Torus, *see subheading* Bowtell
  Transitional period, in, 18
  Vault ribs, of, 84-85
  Windows, of, 59
Mouthiers Church, 208
Much Wenlock Abbey—
  Bay of arcade in, 40
  Bay of triforium in, 270
  Date of, 298
  Piers in, 26
Münster Cathedral, 137
Mural decoration, *see* Decoration

Narthices or porches of churches—
  Burgundy, in, 222-223, 247
  Italy, in, 172-173
  Normandy, in, 243
Naumburg Church, 324

Naves of churches—
  Divisions of wall of, 5
  Length of, in early Romanesque in England, 246–247
Netley Church (Hants), 63
Neuss—S. Quirin, 199
Neuvy—S. Sepulchre, 140
Nevers—S. Etienne, 217, 218 note [1]
Nibs (pilasters), 24
Niches, canopied, on piers, 33
Nîmes, Baths of Diana at, 71, 138
Norman artificers, 180–181
Norman influence, 184–185
Normandy—
  Capitals in, 36–38
  Carving in, 127–129
  Clustered piers in, 26, 30
  Romanesque churches of 11th century in—
    Examples of, 242–243
      Internal divisions, proportions of, 248–249
    Transepts of, 247–248
  Severance of, from England, 300
  Towers of, 106
Northampton, Templar Church at, 142
Norwich—
  Cathedral—
    Choir of, 247
    Columns of, 28
    Date of, 244
    Eastern arm of, 247
    Interior arrangement of, 146, 147 note, 150
    Nave of, length of, 246
    Plan of, 150
    Proportions of, 248
    Roofings of, 245
    Spires of, 114
    Tower of, 106, 107
    Transepts of, 248
    Triforium of, 249
    Vaulting in, 88, 91
  S. Peter's Mancroft, section of, 365
  Churches in, number of, 358
Novara—
  Baptistery at, 161
  Cathedral, 168
Noyon Cathedral—
  Choir of, 260 note [1]
  Columns and piers in, 81 note
  Galleries in, 7

Noyon Cathedral—*continued*.
  Nave of, 258
  Plan of, 260
  Triforium of, 270
  Vaulting of, 81
Nürnberg—
  Liebfrauenkirche, 121
  Lorenzkirche, 332
  S. Sebald, 332

OAK, painting and gilding of, 121
Odda's Chapel (Gloucs.), 45, 236 *note*, 238
Orange—
  Cathedral, 216
  Theatre, 51
Orcival Church, 216
Orleans—
  Cathedral, 268, 279
  S. Aignan, 272
Orvieto Cathedral—
  Gallery and arches of, 341
  Marble in, 175
  West front of, 344
  Windows and roof of, 342
Ottmarsheim Church, 139
Ouistreham Church, 77, 243, 249
Oversailing courses, 53
Oxford—
  Christ Church Cathedral, 25, 91
  Christ Church College, 319

PAINTING, mural, *see under* Decoration
Palermo—
  Cappella Palatina, 184
  Cathedral, 185 *note*, 186–187
  La Zisa Palace, 184–186
  S. Catalda, 186, 188–189
  S. Giovanni degli Eremeti, 188
Palestine influence, 185–186
Panelling—
  14th and 15th century, 315, 317
  Buttresses, of, 50
  Exterior walls, of, 317, 364
  Flint, 43
  Marble, 188
  Piers and arches, of, 30
  Pilasters and string courses, by, 51
  Stone, 71, 111, 246
  Wood, on ceilings, 342
Parapets, 53, 114
Paray-le-Monial, 222, 225

INDEX. 395

Paris—
  Cathedral, see subheading Nôtre Dame
  La Sainte Chapelle—
    Date of, 262, 281
    Window tracery in, 59, 300
  La Trinité (Place Blanche), 158 note
  Nôtre Dame—
    Apse of, 268
    Buttresses of, flying, 97, 269
    Carvings in, 128
    Chevet of, 149
    Choir of, 268
    Columns in, 31, 81 note, 261
    Date of, 262
    Double aisles in, 156
    Galleries in, 7
    Horizontal lines of, 52
    Interior of, 268
    Open space before, 264
    Plain wall space in, 272
    Proportions of, 265, 272
    Roof of, 278-279
    Sculpture in, 123-124
    Shafts in, 32
    Side chapels of, 153
    Towers of, western, 327; transept towers omitted, 277
    Triforium of, 260, 269-270 and note
    Vaulting of, 79, 81, 85 note, 102; original, 215
    Wall thickness in, 34
    West front of, 278, 279
    Window tracery in, 59, 69
  S. Etienne du Mont, 35 note
  S. Eustache, 225
  S. Germain des Près, 31
Parma—
  Baptistery at, 161
  Cathedral, cupola towers of, 171
Patrington (Yorks.)—S. Patrick, 114, 361-364
Patrixbourne Church (Kent), windows in, 60, 62, 161
Pavia—
  S. Michele, 168
    Carving on west front of, 2
    Cupola towers of, 171
    East end of, elevation and plan of, 171
    Galleries of, internal, 7; external, 171
    Roof of, 170

Pavia—continued.
  S. Pietro in Cielo d'Oro, 168
Pendlebury—S. Augustine's, 158
Perigueux—
  S. Etienne, 205-206, 207 note
  S. Front Cathedral, 203, 205-209
Perpendicular style, 284
Perpignan Cathedral, 158, 290
Pershore Abbey—
  Date of, 243
  Tower of, 104
  Triforium omitted in, 8, 314 note [1]
Peterborough Cathedral—
  Capitals in, 25, 37
  Columns in, 25
  Date of, 244 and note
  East end of, 247
  Font in, position of, 162
  Galleries in, 7
  Nave of—
    Ceiling of, 91, 245
    Ely nave compared with, 250
    Length of, 246
  Proportions of, 248
  Towers of, 107
  Triforium of, 249
  West front of, 304
  Windows of, 55 note, 60
Piacenza Cathedral, 172
Piers—
  Alternating, of differing section, 250
  Alternation of, with columns, 26, 137, 175, 242, 251
  Apses, of, in French cathedrals, 268
  Clustered—
    Development of, 26
    Forms of, 26
    Normandy, in, 30
  Crossing, at, in cruciform churches, 103-104
  Early use of, 24
  Evolution of, 24-25
  Niches on, canopied, 33
  Oblong, 26, 29
  Rebated angles of, 26
  Shafts attached to, see Shafts
  Spanish churches, in, 355-356
  T-shaped, 25 and note [1]
  Thickness of, 2
Pilasters—
  Fluted, 32

Pilasters—*continued.*
  Panelling by, 51
  Towers, on, 235–236
  Transverse arches supported on, 24
Pinnacles, 49, 100, 114
Pisa—
  Arcaded gallery fronts in, 171, 176
  Baptistery at, 161
  Cathedral—
    Arcading in, 176
    Exterior of, 178
    Funds towards building of, 166 *note*
    Mural decoration in, 175
    Plan of, 177–179
    Upper abacus in, 35
    Windows of, 177
  Grouping of buildings in, 177
  Leaning tower of, 109–110
  S. Caterina, 338
  S. Pietro-a-Grado, 173
Pisano, Niccolo and Giovanni, 339
Pistoja churches, 176
Planning of churches—
  Aisleless plans, 156–158
  Ambulatory, eastern, 147 *and notes*
  Burial inside as affecting, 162–164
  Byzantine, 137–142
  Chancel, raised, 163
  Changes in, after 11th century, causes for, 144
  Chantry chapels, 155 *and note*
  Cistercian influence on, 158–161
  Double aisles, 155–156
  East ends, 146–153, 161
  Entrances, lateral, 193–194
  Fonts, position of, 162
  Galleries, external open, 170–171
  Porches, 172–173
  Roman, 137–138
  Side chapels, 153–155
  Transepts, 153
Plinths, 52
Poitiers—
  Cathedral—
    Curves in, 179–180
    Lighting of, 287
    Piers in, height of, 355
    Plan of, 287–288, 330
    Vaulting of, 79, 86
  S. Hilaire, 211
Polebrook Church (Northants), 120
Polignac Church, 32, 216, 217 *note*

Pont l'evêche Church, 150
Pontaubert Church (Burgundy), 222, 288
Poore, Bishop, 301
Porches of churches, *see* Narthices
Prior cited, 298

QUIMPER CHURCH (Brittany), 282, 364

RAVELLO CATHEDRAL, 180
Ravenna—
  S. Apollinare-in-Classe—
    Arcading of, 235
    Burial crypt in, 163 *and note*[2]
    Tower of, 107–108
  S. Apollinare Nuovo—
    Mosaic decoration in, 5
    Tower of, 107, 198 *note*
  S. Giovanni Evangelista, 109 *note*
  S. Vitale—
    Carving in, 127
    Plan of, 139
  Towers of churches in, 106, 107, 109 *note*, 198 *note*
Reddes—S. Pierre, 138
Reims—
  Cathedral—
    Apse of, 267
    Buttresses of, flying, 98–100
    Chevet of, 149
    Commemoration of master mason connected with, 256 *note*
    Construction of, 275
    Date of, 262
    Double aisles of, 156
    Exterior of, 279
    Horizontal lines of, 52
    Nave of, length of, 152
    North transept doorways of, 277 *and note*
    Piers in, 32
    Plan of, 266
    Proportions of, 265
    Sculpture and carving in, 124; sculpture removed for windows, 280 *note*[1]
    Section of, 99
    Side chapels, absence of, 153
    Stone seat round, 275 *note*[2]
    Towers of, 111, 276, 277
    Triforium of, 271
    Vaulting in, 34, 102
    West front of, 278

Reims—*continued*.
  Cathedral—*continued*.
    Windows of—
      Glass in, 133
      Sculpture removed for, 280 *note* [1]
      Tracery of, 58, 69
  S. Remi—
    Capital in, 86
    Galleries in, 7
    Plan of, 136
Renaissance architecture, Gothic style mixed with, 284–285
Responds, function and forms of, 30
Restoration of churches, 116–117, 122
Ridge ribs, 86, 88 *note* [1]
Ripon Cathedral, 234, 296
Rivaulx Abbey, 306
Rochester Cathedral—
  Crypt of, 71, 91
  Date of, 243
  East end of, 153, 161, 247
  Nave of, 91, 244, 246
Roman influence on plans, 137–138; few supports, 210, 286
Roman towers, 109
Romanesque, signification of term, 3
Romanesque architecture—
  Byzantine-Romanesque, 167
  England, in, *see under* England
  Normandy, in, during 11th century, *see under* Normandy
Rome—
  Basilica of Constantine—
    Proportions of, 169
    Recesses in, 157
    Vaulting of, 74 *note* [1]; abutment of vaults, 96 *note*, 157
  Caracalla's baths, 79
  S. Agnese, 6
  S. Clemente, 24, 119
  S. John, 156
  S. Lorenzo, 6
  S. Maria in Cosmedin, 24, 109
  S. Maria in Trastevere, 136
  S. Maria Sopra Minerva, 339
  S. Paolo fuori le Mura, 136, 156
  S. Peter (Basilican Church), 156
  SS. Giovanni e Paolo, 109
Romsey—
  Abbey—
    Choir bays of, 322
    East end of, 147, 161

Romsey—*continued*.
  Abbey—*continued*.
    Nun's Church, 244, 247
    Plan of, 148
    Windows of, 58
Roofing of churches—
  Germany, in, 332
  Gothic cathedrals, of, 52
  Timber, 187 (*see also under* England—Parish churches)
Roslyn Chapel, 71
Roueiha, church at, 25 *note* [1]
Rouen—
  Cathedral—
    Apse of, 267
    Date of, 262
    Proportions of, 274
    Sculpture in, 123
    Towers of, 276, 277
    Transept doorways of, 277
    West front of, 230, 280–281
  Detached shafts in churches of, 32
  S. Maclou—
    Flamboyant style of, 284
    Lantern tower of, 104
    Mouldings in, 20
    Supports in, 33
  S. Ouen—
    Apse of, 268
    Dates of, 282
    Glazed triforium of, 271
    Niches in, 33, 123
    Proportions of, 282
    Roofing of, 271
    Sculptured figures in, 124
    Shafts in, 33
    Towers of, 333
    Vaulting in, 102
    Wall thickness in, 34
    Window of, 69
Royat Church (Auvergne), 106
Rubble—
  Columns of, 23
  Regular courses of, 45
  Vault webs of, 83
  Walls of, 15, 45
Runic crosses, 241

S. Albans—
  Cathedral—
    Alterations in, 246
    Arches in, 17

INDEX.

S. Albans—*continued*.
  Cathedral—*continued*.
    Ceiling of, 91, 366
    Choir of, 247
    Date of, 243
    Eastern arm of, 151, 247
    Galleries in, 7
    Incongruities of style in, 262 *note*
    Interior arrangement of, 145, 147 *note* ²
    Nave of—
      Altars in, 144
      Length of, 246
    Paintings in, 120
    Piers in, 26
    Roman brickwork in, 43 *note*
    Shrine of S. Alban in, 121, 152
    Tower of, 106
    Vaulting of, 91
  S. Martin's Church, 34
S. Avit Senieur (South France), 77 *note*
S. Cross Abbey, 91, 161
S. David's Cathedral, 243
S. Denis (near Paris)—
  Date of, 255, 259
  Eastern transept of, 136
  Relics in, 147
  Style of, 259
  Vaulting of, 278
S. Gall Monastery Church—
  Double apses of, 191 *note* ²
  Plan of, 144
  Towers of, 193
S. Généroux, 204
S. Martin de Londres, 140
S. Nectaire Church, 216–217
S. Paul, M. Anthyme, cited, 142 *and note* ¹, 255
S. Saturnin (Auvergne), 148
Salamanca New Cathedral, 355–356
Salamanca Old Cathedral, 350–351
Salisbury Cathedral—
  Altars in, 153
  Amiens Cathedral compared with, 301–304
  Arcades of, 103
  Buttresses of, 49, 97
  Chantry chapels in, 155
  Choir of, 146, 152
  Colour effects in, 299
  Columns of, 28, 117
  Dates of, 301–302

Salisbury Cathedral—*continued*.
  East end of, 305; illustrated, 152
  East transepts of, 153, 278
  Plan of, 151, 152, 302
  Proportions of, 302–303
  Shafts in, 26–28
  Spires of, 114
  Symmetry of, 302
  Tower of, 107, 276
  Triforium of, 271
  Vaulting of, 84, 90, 91, 101–102
  View of, from north-east, 304
  Wall thickness in, 33
  West front of, 302, 304
Salonica—S. Demetrius, 24, 178 *note* ¹
Santiago de Compostella Cathedral, 219, 280 *and note* ², 350
Saracenic influence, 183–186, 219
Saulieu Church, 127
Saumur—
  Nôtre Dame de Nantilly, 216
  S. Pierre—
    Plan of, 226, 229–230
    Vaulting of, 79, 86, 199, 228
Saxon masonry, 236 *and note*
Scoinson, 68
Scotland, ruined abbeys in, 321 (*for particular churches see their names*)
Scott, Sir Gilbert, quoted, 70, 88
Sées Cathedral—
  Clerestory window screen of, 314 *note* ³
  Paintings in, 123
  Shafts, detached, in, 263
  Vaulting in, 102
Segovia Cathedral, 355–356
Selby Church, 62, 305
Semur Church, 222
Senlis, S. Frambourg, 58
Sens Cathedral—
  Columns in, 32
  Date of, 259, 264
  Flying buttresses of, 269
  Open space before, 264
  Transept doorways of, 277
Sessa Cathedral, 180
Seville Cathedral, 355
Shafts—
  Angle, 75, 76
  Attached, examples of, 26, 33
  Buttress angles, at, 49
  Counter-changing of, 32

Shafts—*continued*.
  Detached—
    Examples of, 26-28, 32
    France, in, 32
    Joints of, 27-28
    Sicily, in, 186
    Vaulting, 93-94, 101-102
    Weight on, 28-29
    Windows, of, 56
Sharpe cited, 131 *note*, 203 *note*
Sherborne Abbey—
  Alterations to (1436-1504), 317
  Date of, 244
  Panelling of piers in, 30
  Vaults of, 92 *note*
Shoreham, New, Church (Sussex), 43
Shoreham, Old, Church (Sussex)—
  East end of, 161
  Material of, 43
  Plan of, 360
Shrewsbury—S. Mary, 18
Sicily, churches of—
  Arcading on, 52
  Arches of, 185-186; date of pointed arch, 11 *and note*
  Carving in, 126
  Decoration of, by inlays, 186-187
  Domes of, 189
  Examples of, 184-189
  Mixed architecture in, 167-168
  Shafts inlaid with mosaics in, 24
  Variety of influence in, 184-185
Siena Cathedral—
  Alternating marbles in, 175, 341
  Dome of, 338
  Gallery of, 341
  West front of, 344
  Windows of, 341
Silchester Church, 232, 237
Soissons Cathedral—
  South transept of, 260
  Triforium of, 270
  Windows in, 58 *note*
Solignac Church, 208
Somersetshire, towers in, 111
Sompting Church, 237, 240, 241
Souillac, church at, 208
Southwell Minster, 129-130, 244
Spain—
  Classic traditions in, 39 *note*
  Gothic churches in—
    Choir, position of, 354-355 *and*

Spain—*continued*.
  Gothic churches in—*continued*.
    French influence on, 349-353
    Piers, weight of, 355-356
    Saracenic influence in, 219 *note*
Speier Cathedral—
  Arcading in, 197-198
  Columns in, 31
  Entrance of, west, 194
  Galleries of, external, 194
  Plan and section of, 196
  Proportions of, 197
  Turrets of, 198
  Vaulting in, 195
  Western apse, absence of, 191
Spiers, R. Phené, cited, 208 *note*
Spires of churches—
  Angle of, 114
  Base of, 113; broaches at base, 113-114
  Entasis of, 114
  Flying buttresses on, 114
  French examples of, 111
  Germany, in, 333
  Lucarnes of, 114
  Octagonal, 112, 115
  Roofings of, 113 *note*
  Sixteen-sided, 115
  Stone, 111, 113; construction of, 114
  Timber, 111-113; construction of, 112-114
Stanton Harcourt Church, 51
Stone—
  Brick alternating with, 117
  Marble in combination with, 117
  Pierced panelling of, 246
  Pierced slabs of, for windows, 239
  Spires of, *see under* Spires
  Tiles alternating with, 136
  Walls of, 43
Stone Church (Kent), 60, 61
Strassburg Cathedral, 328, 333
String-courses, 51-53
Street cited, 219 *note*, 275, 349, 353 *note*; quoted, 352, 354
Stucco, 237; tempera painting on, 119
Suger, Abbé, 255
Supports, Roman method as to, contrasted with Gothic, 210, 286
Switzerland, churches in—
  Arcading of, 197
  Entrances of, 194

Switzerland, churches in—*continued.*
　Windows of, 56
Symbolism, semi-barbaric, in carving, 2, 127

TAG EÏVAN, 215
Tarragona Cathedral, 350
Tas-de-charge, 93 *and note*, 94
Taunton—S. Mary Magdalene, 111
Templar churches, 142 *and note* [2]
Tewkesbury Abbey—
　Abaci in, 34 *note*
　Capitals in, 37
　Chantry chapels in, 155
　Chevet of, 150
　Columns of, 23, 25
　Date of, 243
　Nave of, 246, 250
　Proportions of, 248
　Roofings of, 245
　Tower of, 104, 106
　Vaulting of, 84 *note* [1], 88, 91
　West front of, 252-253
　West window of, 253 *note*
Thaxted Church (Essex), 360
Thrusts—
　Arches, of, 47
　Buttresses' transmission of, 97
　Concentration of, 71, 72, 95
　Counterpoise of, summary regarding, 101
　Timber roofs, of, 99
　Vaults, of, compared, 88, 98
　Wall ribs, of, 95
Tiercerons, 86, 88, 91
Tiles alternating with stone, 136
Timber—
　Churches of, 233
　Roofs of, 187 (*see also under* England—Parish churches)
　Spires of, *see under* Spires
　Vaults of, 314 *note* [2], 315
Tintern Abbey, 28
Tiverton Church, 111
Toledo Cathedral, 351-352
Torcello Cathedral—
　Burial crypt in, 163
　Mosaics in, 118
　Upper abacus in, 35
Toro, Collegiate Church at, 350-351
Torregiano, 318
Toscanella—S. Maria and S. Pietro, 173

Toulouse—
　Augustines, Church of the, 292
　Cordeliers, Church of the, 292
　Jacobins' Church at, 157, 290-292, 355
　S. Sernin—
　　Apsidal chapels of, 148
　　Eastern arm of, length of, 247
　　Nave of, length of, 247
　　Plan of, 217, 219, 220
　　Relics in, 147
　　Vaults of, 10
　　mentioned, 292
Tournai—
　Cathedral—
　　Apses of, 200-202
　　Spire of, 112
　　Towers of, 105, 276-277
　　Transepts of, 260, 335
　　View of, from the south, 201
　Churches, towers of, 202
Tournus, Burgundy—S. Philibert—
　Arcading of, 133
　Arches in, 298
　Date of, 223
　Dome of, 212 *note*
　Exterior of, 194
　Narthex of, 222
　Plans and sections of, 214
　Vaulting of, 95, 213-215
Tours—
　Cathedral—
　　Capitals in, 38
　　Date of, 263
　　Gable of, 279
　　Piers in, 32
　　Shafts in, 33
　　Tower of, western, 277
　　Vaulting in, 102
　S. Martin, 147
Towers of churches—
　Batter of, 51, 105, 179
　Beacon or watch towers, as, 108
　Belfries, as, 107, 108
　Buttressing of, 110
　Campanile, 108, 110
　Central, 103-104
　France, in, 275-278
　Gables on, 112, 243
　Italy, in, three schools of, 108-109
　Louvres of, 111 *note*
　Octagonal, 115; square with octagonal top, 111

INDEX. 401

Towers of churches—*continued*.
  Pilaster treatment of, 235-236
  Positions of, 103
  Refuges, as, 106, 108
  Round, 108
  Saddle-back, 111-112
  Transepts, over, 104-105, 334
  West end, at, 104, 106
Tracery of windows, *see under* Windows
Trani—
  Cathedral—
    Bronze doors of, 180
    Columns of, 181 *note*
    Crypt of, 168
    East end of, 161
    Exterior of, 182 *and note*, 183
    Tower of, 107
  S. Maria Immaculata, 183-184
  Churches in, pierced marble window slabs of, 181
Transepts of churches, 277-278
Transoms, 64-65
Tréguier Cathedral, 104-105, 282
Trier—
  Cathedral—
    Entrances of, 194
    Galleries in wall of, 194
    Plan of, 198-199
    Vaulting in, 228 *note*²
  Liebfrauenkirche, 325-326
Triforium—
  English cathedrals, in, varieties of, 249-250
  Nature and function of, 5
  Omission of, 8, 196
Troja Cathedral, 175-176, 180-181
Troyes Cathedral, 156, 262, 266
Truro Cathedral, 162 *note*, 361
Tudor rose, 131
Tuscan churches—
  Examples of, 173-180
  Galleries, outside, 175-176
Tynemouth Priory, 57

ULM CATHEDRAL, 331-333

VALPOLICELLA district (near Verona), double apse of church in, 191
Vaults (*see also* Arches)—
  Barrel, 70-71
  Bays in, marking of, 71 *and note*
  Dates of, 74

Vaults—*continued*.
  Fan, 88-90
  Flying buttresses' position in relation to, 97-98
  Intersecting (groined), 71
  List of English examples, 91
  Oblong spaces, over, 79, 82
  Painted, 348
  Plastered, 83, 86
  Pointed arches of, 77-78 *and note*
  Ribbed, 72-77; Roman, 73-74 *and note*¹
  Ribs of—
    Extra, 86
    Sections of, 84
    Setting out of, 92-95
    Windows in relation to, 90
  Sexpartite, 80-81; flying buttresses to, 269
  Shafts of, 93-94, 101-102
  Tas-de-charge, 93 *and note*
  Thrusts of, 95, 97 (*see also* Thrusts)
  Tie-beams' position in relation to, 99-100 *and note*
  Timber, 314 *note*², 315
  Transverse arches of, 71-72 *and note*¹, 79
  Web of, 83-86
Vendôme Abbey, 278 *note*², 284
Venice—
  Frari, Church of the, 339
  S. Mark's, 166—
    Carving in, 127
    Mosaics in, 118
    S. Front compared with, 206-208
    Tower of, 108 *and note*
  S. Stefano, ceiling of, 172 *note*, 342
  SS. Giovanni e Paolo—
    Arches in, 20, 340
    Chapels of, 343
  Towers of Venetian school, 108-109
Vercelli—S. Andrea, 339
Vermenton Church (Burgundy), 125
Verona—
  Cathedral, porch of, 172
  S. Anastasia—
    Arches in, 20, 340
    Chapels of, 343
    Decoration in, 121, 342
    Internal ordinance of, 341
    Plan of, 344

Verona—*continued*.
  S. Anastasia—*continued*.
    Sections of, 340
    Tower and buttresses of, 345
  S. Fermo Maggiore—
    Ceiling of, 172 *note*, 342, 366
    Pilasters of, external, 179
  S. Stefano, plan of, 147
  S. Zeno—
    Arches of, 16, 172
    Bronze doors of, 180
    Capitals in, 1, 36
    Plan of, 172
    Porch of, 172
    Raised chancel of, 163
    Roof of, 172, 366
    Supports in, large and small, 172, 251
    Tower of, 105, 109, 112
Vézelay Abbey—
  Choir of, 264; columns in, 23
  Date of, 221-222, 264
  Narthex of, 222, 259
  Nave of, length of, 247
  Piers in, 32
  Plan of, 221-222
  Sculpture in, 124
  Simplicity of, 158
  Vaulting of, 79
Vienna Cathedral—
  Plan of, 334
  Proportions of, 330
  Roofing of, 332
  Towers of, 105, 334
Vignory Church (Haute-Marne), 148
Villefranche-de-Rouergue Church, 47 *note*
Viollet-le-Duc cited, 83, 85 *and note*, 86, 124-125
Vitré, gurgoyle at, 54
Von Steinbach, Irwin, 257

WALLS—
  Arcading of, see *under* Arcading
  Decoration of, see Decoration
  Materials of, 43-45
  Plastered, 45
  Thickness of, 72 *note*²; above supports, 33-34, 45, 213-214 *and note*
Walpole S. Peter (Norfolk), 361
Waltham Abbey—
  Columns of, 23

Waltham Abbey—*continued*.
  Date of, 244
  Triforium of, 249
Warmington Church (Northants), 361
Warwick Church (Cumberland), 360
Waverley (near Farnham), Cistercian settlement at, 295
Wells—
  Bishop's palace at, banqueting hall in, 65
  Cathedral—
    Buttresses of, sculptured figures on, 50, 124
    Chantry chapels in, 155
    Construction of, 299
    Date of, 298-299
    East end of, 146, 151
    Piers and shafts of, 298-299
    Presbytery and Lady Chapel of, 313-314
    Screen of, 178
    Towers of, 107
    Triforium storey of, 299
    Vaulting in, 91, 101-102; vaulting shafts, 299
    West front of, 304-305
Westminster Abbey—
  Chapter-house of, 59
  Chevet of, 150
  Choir—
    Position of, 146, 247, 355 *note*
    Section of, 308
    Vaulting of, 91
  Cloisters of, vault over, 83-84
  Columns of, 28, 117
  Cusping in, 67
  Doorway, north, of, 305
  Flying buttresses of, 307
  French influence in plan and proportions of, 300, 307
  Galleries in, 7
  Henry VII.'s Chapel—
    Carvings in, 131
    Fan vaulting in, 88-90, 92
    Panelling in, 30 *and note*
    Side chapels of, 318
    Tomb in, 317
  Labels, interior, in, 22
  Nave of—
    Comparison of, with eastern arm, 312
    Piers in, 29

Westminster Abbey—*continued*.
  Nave of—*continued*.
    Vaulting of, 86, 91
    Width of, 239
  Piers in, 29, 355
  Proportions of, 272, 309
  Shafts in, 26-28
  Tas-de-charge in, 93
  Tomb of Edward the Confessor, 24 *note*
  Triforium of, 309
  Wall thickness in, 34
  Windows of, clerestory, 307-310
Westminster Cathedral, mosaics in, 118
Westminster Hall, roofing of, 369, 370
Whitby Abbey, 306
Whitewashing of churches, 119-120
William of Edington, Bishop, 311
William of Malmesbury, quoted, 45
William of Sens, 38 *note*, 81, 260, 296
William of Wykeham, Bishop, 246, 311, 317
Wimbotsham Church (Norfolk), 368
Winchester Cathedral—
  Alterations in, by William of Wykeham, 246, 317
  Ceiling of transepts of, 245
  Chantry chapels in, 92, 155
  Choir of, position of, 146
  Crypt of, 76
  Dates of, 243, 315
  Font in, position of, 162
  Length of, 223
  Nave of—
    Date of, 315
    Length of, 246
    Remodelling of, 317
    Vaulting of, 91
  Piers in, 355
  Proportions of, 248
  Sculptured figures in, 124
  Shafts in, 101 *and note*; angle shafts, 75-76
  Tas-de-charge in, 93
  Transept aisles of, 220, 248, 250
  Triforium of, 249
  West front of, 315
  Windows of, 65
Windows of churches—
  Arches of, 67-68; stilted, 60, 62 *note*
  Cuspings of, 66-67
  Decoration of jambs, etc., 59, 66

Windows of churches—*continued*.
  Development of, 55; (1200-1350), 261
  Early Romanesque in England, 239
  German Gothic churches, in, 333
  Grouping of, 55-56, 59
  Increase in size of (15th century), 364
  Mouldings of, 59, 66
  Mullions of, 55 *note*, 59, 65-66
  Pierced slabs in, 55, 136, 239
  Romanesque, 55
  Rose, 68, 278
  Tracery of—
    Bar, 59
    English and French periods of advancement in, compared, 300
    Lincoln Cathedral, at, 309, 314
    Origin of, 60
    Plate, 59
    Screen arrangement of, 314
  Transoms of, 65
  Wall ribs in relation to 90
  Wheel, 60, 68
Windsor—St. George's Chapel, 88, 317, 318
Wing Church, 238
Wittering Church, 238
Wood, *see* Timber
Worcester Cathedral—
  Buttresses in, 97
  Columns in, 28
  Date of, 243
  East end of, 247
  Marble work in, 117
  Nave of, 312
  Piers in, 29
  Presbytery of, shafts in, 28
  Retro-choir of, 299
  Shafts in, detached, 28, 298
  Tower of, 107
  Triforium of, 310
  Vaulting in, 91
Worms Cathedral—
  Arcading in, 197-198
  Columns in, 81
  Exterior of, 194-195
  Plan of, 193
  Turrets of, 193
  Vaulting in, 195-196
Worth Church, 238-240
Wren, Sir Christopher, 90
Wulfstan, Bishop of Worcester, 295
Wykham Church, 239

XANTEN CHURCH, 325

YATTON KEYNELL CHURCH, 110
York—
  Cathedral—
    Chapter-house of, 315
    Choir of—
      Date of, 315
      Height of, 151
      Length of, 153
      Position of, 146
      Triforium of, 314 *note* [2]
      Vaulting of, 91
    Flying buttresses of, 314 *note* [2]
    Nave of, date of, 313
    South transept of, 306
    Towers of, 104, 107
    Vaulting of—
      Material of vault, 314 *note* [2]

York—*continued*.
  Cathedral—*continued*.
    Vaulting of—*continued*.
      Vaulting shafts, 101
      Wall ribs, 90 *and note*, 95
    Windows of—
      East, 65 *note* [1], 314
      Glass in, 132–133
      North transept—" Five Sisters " window, 58, 132, 306
      South transept, 60
      West, 62
  Cathedral (old—destroyed), date of, 243
  Churches in, number of, 358

YPRES—
  Cathedral, 335
  Cloth Hall, 335–336

ZURICH CATHEDRAL, 194, 197

THE END

www.ingramcontent.com/pod-product-compliance
Lightning Source LLC
Chambersburg PA
CBHW032027150426
43194CB00006B/180